# European
# Prehistory

This is a volume in

*Studies in Archeology*

*A complete list of titles in this series appears at the end of this volume.*

# European Prehistory

SARUNAS MILISAUSKAS

*Department of Anthropology*
*State University of New York at Buffalo*
*Buffalo, New York*

Academic Press

New York   San Francisco   London

*A Subsidiary of Harcourt Brace Jovanovich, Publishers*

ACADEMIC PRESS, INC.
111 Fifth Avenue, New York, New York 10003

*United Kingdom Edition published by*
ACADEMIC PRESS, INC. (LONDON) LTD.
24/28 Oval Road, London NW1 7DX

Library of Congress Cataloging in Publication Data

Milisauskas, Sarunas.
    European prehistory.

    (Studies in archeology)
    Bibliography: p.
    1.   Man, Prehistoric--Europe.   I.   Title.
GN803.M49      936            78-212
ISBN 0-12-497950-5

*To my wife Vita
and my daughter Aida*

# Contents

# Acknowledgments

I am grateful to the Czechoslovakian, Dutch, German and, especially, the Polish archaeologists who have contributed to my knowledge of European prehistory. Professor Witold Hensel of the Polish Academy of Sciences was extremely helpful. His continuous support and guidance made it possible for me to conduct archaeological research in Poland. During my stays in Poland, Dr. Janusz Kruk and Doc. Zenon Woźniak in Kraków, Doc. Jan Kowalczyk in Warsaw, and Mrs. Anna Kulczycka-Leciejewiczowa in Wrocław were of great assistance. In Łódź, the late Dr. Lidia Gabałówna and Professor Konrad Jażdżewski did not hesitate to devote many hours that were to my benefit. My family and I will always remember the gracious hospitality of Dr. Stefania Dąbrowska and her daughter Doc. Elżbieta Dąbrowska in Kraków.

I thank Dr. Gregory Johnson (Hunter College, City University of New York), Dr. Peter Reid (University of Windsor), Dr. John Speth (University of Michigan), and Dr. H. Martin Wobst (University of Massachusetts) for reading the manuscript and making a number of helpful comments and suggestions. Dr. Wobst and I worked together on Chapters 1, 2, and 10 and I am grateful for his stimulating help. Dr. Richard I. Ford (University of Michigan) made helpful suggestions in interpreting the data pertaining to subsistence strategies. Dr. Homer Thomas (University of Missouri) was kind enough to comment regarding my Neolithic chronological chart.

I am indebted to Mr. Robert Fitzpatrick, vice president for research, and Ms. Shirley Stout, assistant to vice president for research at the State University of New York at Buffalo for help with my grant proposals. Ms. Marilyn

Haas of the State University of New York at Buffalo Library has been most helpful in ordering books dealing with European prehistory.

In particular, I thank Ms. Nancy Schmid, Ms. Dorothy Stiles, Ms. Jean Grela, and especially Ms. Marlene Bauer of the Anthropology Department of the State University of New York at Buffalo for typing my manuscript. Also, Ms. Marion Dickson, Ms. Lee Ecker, Ms. Katherine Ellis, Ms. Diane Jaskier, and Ms. Winnifred Seubert made my work in the Anthropology Department much easier with their assistance. I also thank Mr. Gordon Schmahl for devoting long hours to the drawings appearing in the Neolithic, Bronze Age, and Iron Age chapters. The figures appearing in Chapter 3 were done by Mr. Ozzievelt Owens. Mr. Donald Griffiths helped me with computer programs and Mr. Hal Foss helped to compile data on the estimated animal weights used in the tables of this book.

My wife Vita and daughter Aida aided me throughout my archaeological work. I am grateful to them for their support, encouragement, and help.

My special thanks are due to Dr. James E. Griffin, professor emeritus and former director of the Museum of Anthropology, University of Michigan, who helped me to get started in the field in Europe and who is always a source of support in my archaeological career.

I also express my thanks to the editorial staff of Academic Press for their assistance in producing this book.

Finally, my thanks go to a number of granting agencies and institutions for supporting my field work in Poland and subsequent data analysis: the Smithsonian Institution (grants SFG-1-1064, SF3-00109, and FR4-60106); the National Science Foundation (grant (S) 36415-001); the State University of New York system (faculty research fellowships and grant-in-aid in 1971 and 1972); SUNY at Buffalo (institutional funds grants in 1972 and 1975), and the American Council of Learned Societies (fellowship in 1976).

Suffice it to say that all errors and shortcomings of this book are my own.

# European
# Prehistory

*Chapter 1*

---

# Introduction

The purpose of this book is three-fold: (*a*) to introduce English-speaking students and scholars to some of the outstanding archaeological research that has been carried out in Europe, (*b*) to integrate this research within an anthropological frame of reference, and (*c*) to evaluate key questions of culture change and culture process in the light of the European archaeological record.

The reader might suppose that sufficient archaeological information is available in all parts of Europe for an extensive and balanced discussion of these subjects. However, that is not the case. Large-scale, problem-oriented excavations or systematic regional surface surveys are necessary to produce the kind of data archaeologists need for process analyses. Such work has been done only recently, and mainly in central and eastern Europe. That research is my focal point. Furthermore, because the author is familiar with these areas through his own research and fieldwork, a large emphasis in this book is placed on central and eastern Europe.

Europe and its archaeological resources are foreign to most English-speaking readers because much of the literature is dissembled in numerous publications, many of which reach only a small number of North American libraries. Since archaeological specialization is more advanced in Europe than in many other areas of the world, it is difficult for the newcomer to sort out what is significant and to keep up with scientific advances in the discipline. Although large-scale efforts to integrate this archaeological mosaic for an English-speaking reader have been occurring for 50 years or more, the data have been expanding rapidly, and the questions archaeologists ask have multiplied even faster. Therefore, an up-to-date treatment is urgently needed, not so much for the details of culture history, but to investigate general questions to which European prehistory may contribute answers.

I will rely on ethnographic models or analogies to interpret the ways of life of prehistoric European societies. Most interpretations of archaeologically derived materials come from works of ethnologists who as a group have spanned the globe in their studies of a wide range of societies at different levels of sociopolitical development during the nineteenth and twentieth centuries. Some archaeologists may doubt that a model derived from a nineteenth-century society is applicable to prehistoric Europe. However, it is assumed here that cultural processes operated in the past in ways similar to those of the present. Of course, the ethnographically derived models must be evaluated against archaeological data.

The weak development of scientific method in archaeology limits discussion of certain topics such as ethnic and linguistic groups in Europe during the Neolithic and the Bronze Age. For this reason, such topics will not be examined, but this does not mean that they are not significant or worth pursuing.

Frequently, data from the Mediterranean region are used by archaeologists to evaluate hypotheses about culture change and culture process. Given the general nature of publications in English on Mediterranean and Near Eastern archaeology, one wonders if we have not received an oversimplified picture of European prehistory, and possibly even of general evolution, because of this Mediterranean bias. The models that have been developed on this relatively narrow geographic base and the hypotheses that have been evaluated against it may not be adequate to accommodate slightly different situations. Little is gained, scientifically, by repeating the evaluation in those same regions in which the hypotheses were developed and originally tested. For this reason, I will try to weigh and evaluate previously constructed interpretations and hypotheses against archaeological data from other parts of Europe. Furthermore, I wish to introduce English-speaking readers to the prehistory of other regions of Europe and to the immense quantity of information emanating from the scholars of eastern and central Europe. Hopefully, this work will increase the shared knowledge of our discipline.

This volume is structured around a selected number of general topics that should contribute to a new understanding of culture change, stimulate discussion among archaeologists, and also make it easier for the newcomer to gain an overview of European prehistory.

Throughout this book, various Paleolithic, Neolithic, Bronze Age, and Iron Age cultures will be described, analyzed, and discussed. It should be noted that when archaeologists talk about "cultures" they are usually referring to excavated "archaeological manifestations," that is, collections of stone, clay, bone, metal, and other artifacts, and sometimes patterns of graves, structures, etc. The relationship between such manifestations and real human communities, populations, ethnic groups, and societies (i.e., what ethnologists would call a culture) is, to say the least, problematic. Strictly speaking, archaeologists should not use the term *culture* at all; however, they do by the convention of the discipline. Usually European archaeologists use the term in the sense of Childe's (1950:2) definition:

> A culture is defined as an assemblage of artifacts that recur repeatedly associated together in dwellings of the same kind and with burials by the same rite. The arbitrary peculiarities of implements, weapons, ornaments, houses, burial rites and ritual objects are assumed to be concrete expressions of the common social tradition that bind together a people.

This definition is reflected in the names of the various prehistoric cultures appearing in this book. It is evident that "archaeological cultures" usually are not defined as information or adaptive systems.

Before beginning, let me say that as an archaeologist I have always found prehistory to be a dynamic field because it reflects in simplified form some of the processes of human development that are at work, but in a greatly amplified manner. The body of data that comprises European prehistory represents a rich record of fossilized culture change as well as a laboratory in which to develop and evaluate our knowledge of cultural behavior, past and present. It is my hope that the following pages will contribute to that effort.

*Chapter 2*
___

# The Present Environment— A Geographic Summary

This chapter describes the present environment of Europe: its topography, its climate, and its characteristic associations of plants, animals, and soils. It introduces the reader to the geography of the continent, develops the environmental background for the societies of the last 8000 years, and provides a point of departure against which we can compare the environments of the more distant past.

## Topography

Of all aspects of the human environment, the topography, that is, the configuration of surface and relief, changes most slowly. Nevertheless, it is important for human societies. It structures space; it interacts with the climate upon which plants, animals, and soils depend; and it impinges upon human behavior by creating barriers to movement and trade, transport, and communication. In this sense, the topography can be viewed as the stage for human societies, past and present.

On maps of the Old World, Europe appears as a large peninsula; it is approximately four times smaller than Asia, to which it is contiguous. The boundary between the two continents is traditionally drawn at the Ural Mountains in the USSR and across the lowlands that extend between these mountains and the Caspian Sea to the south. This boundary is rather arbitrary, however, since human groups, particularly nomadic ones, have moved freely across it during various periods. In the southeast, the Caucasus Mountains define the boundary between Europe and Asia. This alpine chain extends between the Caspian and the Black seas and reaches elevations of more

5

than 5000 m in places. Thus, it forms a rather effective barrier to travel and communication. Elsewhere, Europe is bordered by water. In the south, we find the Caspian Sea, the Black Sea (with its appendages, the Bosporus, the Sea of Marmara, and the Dardanelles, which separate the European and Asiatic parts of Turkey), and the Mediterranean Sea (with the Strait of Gibraltar). The Atlantic Ocean adjoins Europe in the west, and the North Sea, the Norwegian Sea, and the Barents Sea border the continent in the north (M. Shackleton 1965).

As Figures 2.1 and 2.2 indicate, Europe could be viewed as a funnel, lying on its side with its mouth to the east. At its eastern border with Asia (the Ural Mountains), the funnel reaches a width of more than 3000 km in a north–south direction. More than 4500 km further west, where the Pyrenees Mountains separate France from Spain, the width of the funnel has decreased to less than 400 km north–south. A number of peninsulas and islands are appended to the body of the continent: the Scandinavian peninsula and the British Isles in the north; the Iberian peninsula (Spain and Portugal) in the west; and the Apennine (Italy and Sicily) and Balkan peninsulas (south of the Danube, bordered by the Adriatic, Ionian, Aegean, and Black seas) in the south.

The major geographic units of Europe are large expanses of level lowlands (the North European Plain, the Carpathian Basin, and the lowlands west and north of the Black Sea), mountainous zones of intermediate elevation (the German mountains adjoining the North European Plain, the French Massif Central, the Serbian uplands in Yugoslavia, and the Transylvanian mountains in Romania), level uplands (the Alpine Foreland, the Bohemian Basin, the Central Russian Uplands), and high mountain chains (the Pyrenees, the Alps, the Carpathians, the Dinaric Alps, and the Balkan Mountains). The level lowlands and the high mountain chains are particularly important because they help to structure interregional travel and communication and because they exert an influence on the climate and thus affect the distribution of plants, animals, and soils.

Aside from the large peninsulas, the largest contiguous geographic units are the level lowlands of approximate east–west orientation. For example, the North European Plain extends, without major interruption, from the Ural Mountains in the east to the Pyrenees in the west. At longitudes east of Leningrad, USSR, one can travel 2500 km from the Black Sea to the Barents Sea without encountering elevations above 300 m. Further west, in the Federal Republic of Germany or in France, the plain has narrowed to less than 200 km. A similar wedge of lowlands, also oriented east–west and gradually decreasing in width along the way, stretches from the plains north of the Caspian Sea to the Ukrainian steppes north of the Black Sea, and to the Walachian Plains of Romania.

Like the lowlands, the high mountain chains are arranged in an east–west direction. They form an almost uninterrupted wall from the Atlantic coast of Spain in the west (Cantabrian Mountains, Pyrenees) to the Black Sea coast of Bulgaria in the east (Balkan Mountains, Rhodope Mountains). This wall

**Figure 2.1.** Political map of Europe.

reaches its greatest width in the center of the continent. Here, the parallel ridges of the Alps, from 2000 to more than 4000 m high, broaden into a zone more than 200 km wide. Further east, the Alps proper branch into a number of separate chains: the Dinaric Alps and the high mountain chains of the Balkan peninsula to the southeast (Pindus Mountains of Greece, Rhodope and Balkan mountains of Bulgaria), and the arch of the Carpathian Mountains to the northeast. Another offshoot of the Alps, the Apennines, extends the high mountain zone into the Apennine peninsula of Italy in the south.

Much of the remainder of the continent is taken up by hilly or mountainous zones of intermediate elevation. For example, south of the North European

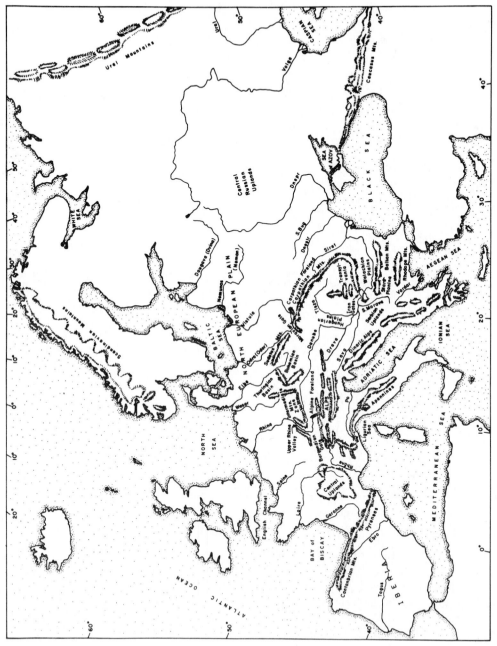

Figure 2.2.  Geographic map of Europe.

Plain, there is a nearly continuous belt of minor mountain ranges. These make up a mountain barrier where the alpine chains are interrupted (Massif Central, Serbian uplands), or they constitute a broad belt of hills and mountains between the lowlands in the north and the high mountains farther south. This zone reaches its greatest extent in the Federal Republic of Germany (some 500 km north–south). Its width decreases from here toward the west (with the Vosges and Jura Mountains of France and Switzerland) and toward the east (Bohemian Forest, Ore Mountains, Sudetes, and Carpathian Foreland). In this sense, the mountains of intermediate elevation also form a geographic belt on an east–west axis and contribute to the latitudinal arrangement of the European relief.

It is illustrative of the surface configuration of Europe that its geographic center, the Carpathian Basin, can be reached only through a number of well-defined corridors. This complex of interconnected lowlands in and around Hungary is approximately 400 km in diameter. Traversed by the Danube River and its tributaries Drava, Sava, and Tisza, it is surrounded on all sides by mountains (Bohemian Mountains, Moravian Heights, Carpathians, Serbian uplands, Dinaric Alps, and Alps). The Vardar (Greece, Yugoslavia) and Marica valleys (Bulgaria) link these plains with the Aegean Sea. The Danube connects the Carpathian Basin with the Alpine Foreland and the Rhine drainage in the west, and with the Black Sea in the east (through the Iron Gates between Yugoslavia and Romania, a 3-km-long gorge cut by the river through the Carpathians). And the Moravian Gate, a low saddle between the Sudetes and the Carpathians in Czechoslovakia, opens the Basin to the North European Plain. Elsewhere, high mountain passes have to be overcome.

Aside from these larger topographic units, the surface is structured by the valleys of the larger rivers. In the north, these rivers generally follow a northwestern direction. They empty into the Bay of Biscay (Garonne, Loire), the English Channel (Seine, Rhine), the North Sea (Weser, Elbe), and the Baltic Sea (Odra [Oder], Vistula, Nemunas [Neman], Daugava [Dvina]). Only a low divide separates these rivers from the ones draining southeastward into the Black Sea (Dnestr, Southern Bug, Dnepr) and the Caspian Sea (Volga and Ural). All these rivers link the plains with the mountains and hills, but only the Rhine and the Odra and their tributaries penetrate deeply into the continent. The most "European" of the European rivers is the Danube whose course traverses or touches upon nine different countries. It ties together the center of the continent with the Black Sea shore, the Balkan peninsula, and the Alpine Foreland (and thus the Rhine drainage and the Atlantic coast). Its tributaries generally run in a north–south direction and provide entry points into the high mountain chains (Alps, Carpathians, Dinaric Alps). Almost of equal importance is the French Rhône River. Its tributaries connect the Mediterranean coast with the western Alps and central France. In addition, through the low saddle of the Burgundian Gate, the Rhône communicates with the Alpine Foreland, and thus with the Rhine and Danube drainage.

Outside of the lowland plains, large stretches of level land are rare. The largest among them tend to be river basins, such as the French Rhône Basin or the Italian Po valley, and intramountain uplands—the upper Rhine valley and the Alpine Foreland of southern Germany, the Bohemian Basin in Czechoslovakia, and Transylvania in Romania. The remainder of the continent, if not hilly or mountainous, is taken up by discontinuous valley corridors and narrow valley segments. The size of these smaller subunits tends to be related to the age of the mountains in which they are found: They tend to be larger where the mountains are older (like most of the mountain ranges of intermediate elevation). The Alps proper and the younger mountain ranges farther east are more sharply compartmentalized, and the compartments tend to be poorly interconnected. This is most extreme in the limestone mountains of southeastern Europe where small intramontane basins are frequently surrounded on *all* sides by mountains.

## Climates

The topography of Europe is important to its climate for several reasons. First, whereas Europe is relatively small itself, it is a part of the world's largest land mass, the Eurasian continent. Large bodies of land tend to be associated with *continental* climates, that is, with hot summers, cold winters, and rapid transitions between seasons. Second, Europe is bordered on three sides by oceans and seas, their branches penetrating deeply into the land. Large bodies of water tend to give adjacent land areas an *oceanic* climate, that is, relatively cooler summers, milder winters, and more gradual transitions between seasons. Third, there is an almost continuous mountain wall that acts as a climatic divide between the north and south of the continent. Fourth, there are virtually no geographic obstacles with a north–south axis. Combined with the latitudinal arrangement of relief, this implies gradual transitions in climate from west to east. Finally, Europe is located mainly within the temperate zone, from about 65° to 40° north latitude. This zone has a moderate climate compared with the polar climates farther north and the subtropical and tropical climates in the south.

The continent shares in three essentially different climates. The northern and northwestern margins (the Atlantic coast of western and central Europe and Scandinavia) are under the influence of a strongly oceanic climate. Here, temperatures are relatively mild year-round, precipitation is evenly distributed throughout the year, and seasonal changes are comparatively small and very gradual. A continental climate reigns along the eastern margins of the continent (the area north and east of the Black and Caspian seas), with large annual temperature ranges, pronounced and rapid temperature changes between seasons, and a strong peak in precipitation in spring or summer. The southern margins (the Mediterranean coastline south of the high mountain barrier) show a climate of subtropical type with hot summers and mild winters with much of the precipitation concentrated in the winter.

The bulk of Europe is transitional between the continental and oceanic extremes. Annual temperature range, seasonality, and average winter cold increase toward the northeast, whereas summer temperatures increase latitudinally toward the south. Annual precipitation tends to rise with elevation, reaching its peak along the north slopes of the Alps. Since most of the precipitation is brought by the prevailing northwesterly winds, annual totals decline with distance from the Atlantic Ocean to low points in the Carpathian Basin and beyond. The seasonality of precipitation increases along the same axis. It is particularly marked along the shores of the Adriatic and Aegean seas where most of the annual rainfall is concentrated in winter. Superimposed upon these regional trends are the effects of local topography, particularly altitude, which can produce sharp differences in local climates over relatively short distances.

## Biogeography

The topographic and climatic patterns are closely mirrored in the regional associations of plants, animals, and soils. At present, Europe has six major vegetation belts: Mediterranean forests in the south, a broad belt of mixed forest at middle latitudes, boreal forest and tundra in the north, and steppe and semidesert in the east (Figure 2.3). The mixed forest, dominated by deciduous trees such as oak, elm, lime, elder, or beech, is the largest in area. Its distribution is controlled by cold winter temperatures in the north and along mountain ranges—the northern boundary is at approximately 60° north latitude—and by excessive summer drought in the south (Mediterranean climate). This forest accommodates a most diverse fauna, particularly if animals are counted that only recently have become rare or extinct such as aurochs, elk, brown bear, wolf, lynx, otter, and beaver. Today, red and roe deer, wild pig, hare, rabbit, fox, duck, and partridge are its most important prey species. The soils of the mixed forest zone (the so-called podzolized soils of brown-earth type) tend to be rich in nutrients and organic matter. If they are well drained, they are quite attractive to agriculturalists. Particularly fertile and easy to work are the soils developed on loess. This yellowish fine-grained sediment occurs in a broad, discontinuous belt from the Atlantic coast of France to the Carpathian Basin and beyond.

In the Mediterranean Basin, the deciduous forest is replaced by open woodland and parkland. Here, evergreen hardwoods, such as live oak and cork oak, are the dominant trees. Their small, leathery leaves are coated with waxlike substances allowing them to withstand the pronounced summer droughts. Much the same types of animals are associated with the Mediterranean forest as with the mixed forest farther north, although the more demanding forest species such as elk, bison, otter, or beaver are rarer, whereas the

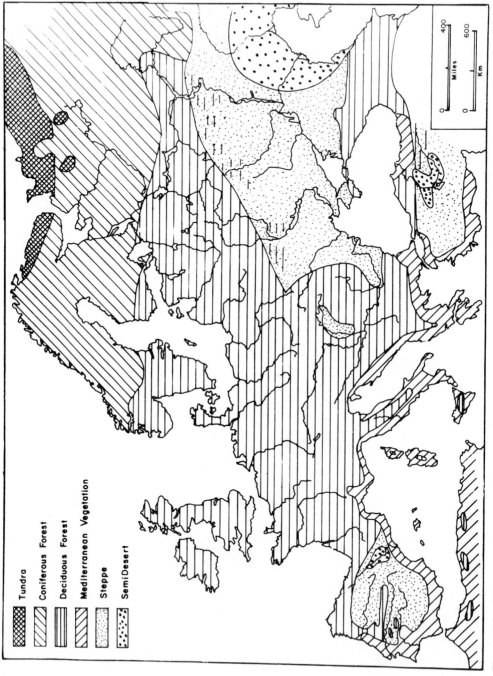

Tundra

Coniferous Forest

Deciduous Forest

Mediterranean Vegetation

Steppe

Semi Desert

400

600

Miles

Km

Figure 2.3. Main vegetation zones of Europe. (After Schlette 1958.)

12

number of smaller kinds of animals (reptiles, molluscs, and the like) is greater. Few areas remain as forests today, and few of the larger mammals have been able to survive the impact of state societies. While the soils of the Mediterranean Basin can be very productive, they have suffered a great deal from erosion in hilly and mountainous areas because of many millennia of intensive agricultural exploitation. They are deepest and most fertile in the occasional lowlands and basins (Rhône Valley, Po Valley).

To the north, in Scandinavia and in the northern parts of the USSR, the mixed deciduous forest gives way to the so-called taiga or boreal forest, a tree association that closely resembles the coniferous forest at the higher elevations of the central European mountain ranges. Only a few species account for practically all of its trees, including, in order of their abundance, these conifers: spruce, pine, larch, and fir. Although the fauna is not as rich and diverse as in the mixed forest, the two vegetation belts share many of the same animals. Today, elk, bear, and deer in the south, and reindeer in the north are its largest prey species. In addition, there are a large number of smaller fur bearers: badger, beaver, fox, hare, lynx, marmot, muskrat, etc. Podsols, or "ashy" soils due to their grayish color, are dominant in this region; strongly leached and frequently underlain by a bed of hardpan, they are only marginally productive for agricultural purposes.

Tundra vegetation is at present confined to a narrow belt north of the boreal forest, beyond the Arctic Circle (65°north latitude). A similar plant community is also found above the tree line in the mountain ranges farther south. The true tundra is an association of lichens, mosses, and sedges that lacks trees except for occasional dwarfed birches, willows, and other cold-tolerant species. Only a few animals are natives of the tundra. Important prey include reindeer, arctic hare, and migratory birds. What it lacks in number of species, the tundra makes up in the number of individuals per species. Reindeer form seasonally large herds, and the periodic migration of the lemmings (the area's dominant rodent) has become proverbial. Crop agriculture cannot be practiced at all: The growing season is too short, the ground in many areas is permanently frozen and often waterlogged, and little soil development takes place.

A gradient of declining precipitation (from northwest to southeast) governs the zoning of plant communities north of the Black Sea, Caucasus, and Caspian Sea: The mixed forest is gradually replaced by forest steppe (in the Ukraine, USSR); a belt of true steppes, that is, tall grasslands, follows in the southern and eastern Ukraine; finally, semidesert forms the southeastern edge of the steppes around the Caspian Sea. In this progression, forests become more and more open until, in the true steppe, they are confined to a few sheltered refuges along the major rivers. In the semidesert even the steppe grasses no longer cover the ground completely. The fauna becomes more rarefied along the same gradient, even though, in the absence of agriculture, a number of large, gregarious animal species would roam the steppe pastures, including saiga antelope, wild ass, aurochs, and wild horse. The soils of the virgin grassland—the *chernozems*, or black earths—have deep profiles, are rich in organic matter and nutrients, and are generally well drained and aerated, making them very attractive for agricultural uses.

## Some Implications for Human Occupants

Several geographic characteristics of Europe are relevant to its history of culture change and cultural evolution. First, many of its major vegetation belts extend well beyond, and reach their largest extent outside of, the continent. They include the steppe and semidesert in the east that attain their maximum size in Central Asia, and the boreal forest and tundra of the north that broaden considerably in Asia east of the Ural Mountains. Similarly, Mediterranean vegetation also covers the coastal areas of the Near East and North Africa. Thus, access to the margins of the continent is not impeded by major environmental (or topographic) boundaries. The relative ease of travel and communication on the Mediterranean Sea, or on the plains of eastern Europe, suggests that these regions are relatively open to, and can share in, the cultural developments of Central Asia, the Near East, or North Africa. Nomadic peoples from Central Asia, such as the Bolgars and Hungarians in historic times, frequently moved westward across the steppes to settle in Europe, and the empires of Greeks, Romans, and Ottomans repeatedly tied together areas of Mediterranean Europe with the Near East and North Africa.

Second, the mixed forest is the only environment that reaches its greatest extent in Europe. Interposed between the Atlantic Ocean and the environments of Central Asia, separated from the Mediterranean Basin by a mountain wall, the exploitation of this environment requires adaptations that are specifically European—in terms of hunting strategies, prey, and settlement patterns for prehistoric hunter–gatherer populations, and in terms of domestic animals, crop species, and agricultural technology for early agriculturalists.

Third, while access to the margins of the continent is relatively without geographic obstacles, its hilly and mountainous heartland can be reached only through a limited number of well-defined corridors. These corridors are either narrow gateways, such as the Burgundian Gate of France or the Iron Gates along the Danube, or long linear channels like that of the upper Rhine or Rhône rivers. Communication is similarly constrained within the heartland and forced into a number of strategic gateways, passes, straits, and narrows. This tends to concentrate cultural interchange between regions in a small number of focal points.

Finally, the main body of the continent is compartmentalized into a relatively large number of subunits of differing size, with differential access to routes of communication, and with other characteristics distinct from their neighbors. Compartmentalization and variability both facilitate and impede the integration of the subunits into larger entities and contribute directly to the rich history of culture change of the European continent.

*Chapter 3*

# Preagricultural Background

The prehistoric hunter and gatherer societies during the Paleolithic (Old Stone Age) and the Mesolithic (Middle Stone Age) periods in Europe are examined in this chapter. The majority of English-speaking archaeologists are probably quite familiar with these periods. One reason for this is the great interest in the human fossil record of the time. Furthermore, these periods were studied extensively by a number of American and British archaeologists: L. and S. Binford (1966), L. Binford (1973), Bricker (1976), Burkitt (1933), J.G.D. Clark (1936, 1954, 1972, 1975), Coles and Higgs (1969), Collins (1970), Freeman (1973), Garrod (1926), Howell (1966), Jelinek (1977), Jochim (1976), Klein (1966, 1969, 1973), Mellars (1969, 1973), Montet-White (1973), Movius (1960, 1966), Price *et al.* (1974), Whallon (1974), Roe (1968), Sackett (1966), Tringham (1973), Wobst (1974, 1975), etc. Also a number of continental archaeologists, Bordes (1961b, 1972, 1973), Klima (1962), de Lumley (1969, 1975), Schild (1976), Valoch (1968), etc., published in English about the Paleolithic and the Mesolithic. A number of international congresses, such as in Nice in 1976, produced in international languages numerous publications containing valuable information about the European Paleolithic (Combier 1976, Freeman 1976, Klima 1976, J. Kozłowski 1976, S. Kozłowski 1976, Leroi-Gourhan 1976, Valoch 1976). The reader is referred to the works of these archaeologists to gain a more extensive perspective about these two periods.

## Pleistocene

The Paleolithic and Mesolithic fall into the geological period called Quaternary. This geological period is subdivided into the Pleistocene and Holocene

15

or Recent epoch. The Pleistocene began approximately 2.4 million years ago (Table 3.1) and ended around 10,000 years ago. The Holocene began 10,000 years ago and continues at present.

Traditionally the Pleistocene was defined by the appearance of modern fauna such as *Elaphas* (elephant) and *Equus* (horse). These mammalian remains were found in northern Italy, and from that locality they were called Villefranchian fauna. Now it is evident that the Villefranchian stage extends into the Pliocene, the period before the Pleistocene.

The Pleistocene is characterized by fluctuations of temperature. A cycle of cold climatic periods is associated with mountain glaciations such as Alpine and Continental, or Scandinavian, in the northern latitudes. The periods between glaciations that reflect warmer temperatures are called interglacials (Table 3.1). However, there were lesser climatic fluctuations within glacial periods called stadials and within interglacial called interstadials. Table 3.1 presents in a simplified form the various glaciations and interglacials in Europe. It should be emphasized that there is no agreement regarding how many glaciations occurred during the Pleistocene in Europe. This is especially difficult to determine before the Günz glaciation. Furthermore, the various sequences worked out in different regions are not easy to correlate or are not even comparable. Also, it should be noted that the maximum cold and warm periods are not characteristic for the Pleistocene. Intermediate climate, that is, between the two extremes, was much more prevalent.

The Pleistocene is divided into three periods: Lower, Middle, and Upper Pleistocene. The boundaries between these periods are defined by the beginning or the end of the different glaciations or interglacials (Table 3.1). Different geologists and archaeologists frequently do not agree on the dividing line between the Lower and the Middle Pleistocene (see de Lumley 1975).

During the glaciations some of the ocean water and seawater was locked up as ice. Thus, as the glaciers increased in size, the sea level fell. The lowlands adjoining the continent, which were previously covered by water, became dry land and available for human exploitation. For example, England was only separated by a river from the Continent. When periodically the glaciers melted, the sea level rose again and extended into dry land. It seems that most of the interglacials were not of long duration.

The climatic changes during the Pleistocene affected the distribution of fauna and flora. The vetation during glaciations consisted of arctic steppe, tundra, and forest-steppe. For example, the tundra were covered by mosses, lichens, shrubs, and dwarfed trees. The less cold areas as exemplified by the forest-steppe had grasses, herbs, and coniferous trees such as pines. During the interglacial periods many of the same areas were covered by deciduous forests.

The animal species associated with the arctic steppe, tundra, and forest-steppe were reindeer, mammoth, musk-ox, horse, saiga antelope, bison, and wooly rhinoceros. Herds of reindeer, mammoths, etc., migrated seasonally between winter and summer grazing on feeding grounds. It is evident that

**TABLE 3.1**  Glaciations, Interglacials, and Subdivision of Pleistocene and Paleolithic in Europe[a]

| Approximate dates (B.P.) | Alpine glaciations and interglaciations | Scandinavian or continental glaciations and interglaciations in western and central Europe | Subdivision of Pleistocene | Subdivision of Paleolithic |
|---|---|---|---|---|
| | Würm | Weichsel (Vistulan) | | Upper Paleolithic from 40,000–35,000 B.P. to 10,000 B.P. |
| 75,000 | | | Upper Pleistocene | |
| | Riss–Würm interglacial | Eem | | Middle Paleolithic |
| | Riss | Warthe-Saale | | |
| 300,000 | | | | |
| | Mindel–Riss interglacial | Holstein | Middle Pleistocene | |
| | Mindel | Elster | | |
| | Günz–Mindel interglacial | Cromerian | | |
| 700,000 | | | | Lower Paleolithic |
| | Günz | Menapian | | |
| | Donau–Günz interglacial | Waalian | | |
| | Donau | Eburonian | Lower Pleistocene | |
| | Biber–Donau interglacial | Tiglian | | |
| | Biber | Praetiglian | | |
| 2,400,000 | | | | |

[a]Data are from Butzer 1971; Chmielewski 1975; de Lumley 1975.

the treeless environment was able to support a large variety of grazing animals. Butzer (1971) noted that the Pleistocene low-latitude tundras probably had a greater *biomass*, that is, kilograms of meat available per km², than modern tundras in the high altitudes. During the warm periods, when deciduous forests covered parts of Europe, solitary animals such as deer, wild pig, and elk predominated.

### Human Evolution

The earliest human biological evolution occurred during the Lower Pleistocene and probably the latest part of the Pliocene in Africa. In an article,

absent from the European part of the USSR. There are local or regional names for various assemblages during the Paleolithic, and my intention is to keep reference to these names at a minimum. Also the reader should not think that the diagnostic artifacts, such as hand axes, were predominant in an entire assemblage at a site. Various other tools occurred, such as retouched flakes, sidescrapers, endscrapers, and burins. Flakes and chips were usually the most numerous finds.

Traditionally the Middle Paleolithic is characterized by a great frequency of tools made on flakes. However, Middle Paleolithic assemblages contain blades, usually less than 10% of the total assemblage, but a few have frequencies between 15% and 30% (Mellars 1973). The blades were produced from specially prepared cores. Sometimes the Middle Paleolithic is called the Mousterian period or culture in Europe, the Near East, and North Africa. This term usually implies that the cultural remains are associated with the Neanderthals. There is no sharp break or boundary between the Late Acheulean and Early Mousterian periods. Almost every Mousterian stone tool had its antecedent in the Late Acheulean.

Bordes (1961a, 1961b) has defined four different types of Mousterian assemblages: (*a*) Mousterian of Acheulean Tradition A and B; (*b*) Typical Mousterian; (*c*) Denticulate Mousterian; and (*d*) Charentian Mousterian, which is further subdivided into Quina and Ferrassie types. The differences among these assemblages are based on the frequency of occurrence of artifact types such as hand axes, sidescrapers, points, and denticulates. Bordes concluded that each of these assemblages represents a different ethnic unit or *tribe*.

This interpretation concerning Mousterian assemblages was challenged by L. and S. Binford (1966), and in various later publications by L. Binford (1973). Studies of Mousterian assemblages in various caves and rock shelters, such as Combe-Grenal, indicate that the assemblages did not occur in a regular stratigraphic sequence, but that various assemblages alternated through time. Thus we may have Typical, Denticulate, Typical, Ferrassie, Typical, Ferrassie, etc. assemblages alternating in the same cave. L. and S. Binford (1966: 240) observed that this implies, using Bordes's explanation, "a perceptual movement of culturally distinct peoples, never reacting to or coping with their neighbors. Nor do they exhibit the typically human characteristics of mutual influence and borrowing. Such a situation is totally foreign, in terms of our knowledge of *sapiens* behavior."

L. and S. Binford (1966) assumed that the Mousterian settlement system consisted of different types of sites reflecting various hunter and gatherer activities throughout the year. The different sites within the settlement system were associated with specific activities or functionally specific tool kits. They concluded that the variability in the Mousterian assemblages reflected the different functions of the specific assemblages.

The Upper Paleolithic usually has been characterized as having more tools made on blades than the Middle Paleolithic. However, the main characteristic for the Upper Paleolithic is the advancement of stone tool technology. New types of stone tools, such as strangulated blades, Gravette points, truncated pieces, and pressure-flake leaf-shaped points, appeared during this period (Mellars 1973). Also we find a variety of tools made of bone, antler, and ivory. Mellars observed that the Mousterian populations utilized fragments of bone and antler but rarely made an attempt to shape them into appreciable form.

Frequently, the presence of cave art is greatly emphasized in characterizing the Upper Paleolithic. In addition, various decorated bone pieces, as well as figurines of humans and animals made of bone, ivory, and fired clay are found. Mellars (1973) noted that in southwestern France grooved and perforated animal teeth, perforated marine shells, and bone beads and pendants were used for the first time for personal adornment in the Upper Paleolithic. With Mousterian populations, perhaps the evidence for body painting is found, since fragments of coloring material of red ocher and black manganese oxide occur in Mousterian sites.

During the Upper Paleolithic we have more numerous "cultures" based on stone tools in Europe such as Aurignacian, Gravettian, and Magdalenian. Frequently the differences among them are based on the presence or absence of certain tools, variability in the artifact frequencies at archaeological sites, or stylistic differences. This does not imply that some of them do not reflect chronological differences, for example, Magdalenian occurs later in time than Aurignacian. Only modern humans, *Homo sapiens sapiens*, are found with the Upper Paleolithic cultures.

L. Binford (1973: 235) noted that no "patterned 'stylistic' variability has been demonstrated in the archaeological record prior to the upper paleolithic." He observed that the typology of stone tools during the Middle Paleolithic is useful in monitoring activity variation but not stylistic differences. Thus he assumed that there was no ethnic composition of groups before the Upper Paleolithic, since this phenomenon if it had existed would have been reflected in stylistic variants of analogous stone tools. However, perhaps there was no need for stylistic variables to show the presence of ethnic groups.

It is very hard to define style. Wobst (1977: 321) "equates styles with that part of the formal variability in material culture that can be related to the participation of artifacts in processes of information exchange." Wobst notes that styles serve a number of functions in cultural integration and differentiation, boundary maintenance, compliance with norms, and enforcement of conformity.

There is a possibility that there was no need for stylistic differentiation in stone tools during the Middle Paleolithic, for the population density was low. Perhaps the Mousterian social groups were quite mobile, were fluid in their organization, and had little territoriality. During the Upper Paleolithic there was an increase in population, which will be discussed later in this chapter. This probably led to more restricted territoriality, mating system closure, and use of style in group identification and boundary maintenance. Furthermore, the presence of more style groups or cultures suggests decreased interaction rates between groups. Thus the presence of style in one period and its absence in another perhaps only reflects different demography.

## Subsistence Strategies

Judging from the recovered archaeological evidence, it would appear that a hunting economy was dominant during the Pleistocene, for the data for fishing and especially gathering are very poor. Near the end of the Pleistocene, we have much more data on exploitation of water resources. While studies of contemporary hunting and gathering cultures indicate that exploitation of plant foods in temperate and tropical climates is more important in the subsistence strategy than hunting, Eskimo and other groups living in northern climates depend heavily on meat.

Studies in ethnoarchaeology of hunters and gatherers have contributed greatly in understanding their various behavior patterns (Binford 1976, Campbell 1968, Yellen 1977). For example, Campbell (1968) studied the Tuluaqmiut band of the Nunamiut Eskimo group mainly inhabiting the tundra environment of Alaska. They rely heavily on caribou herds for subsistence as the following estimates of importance of various food procuring activities indicate: (*a*) gathering of plant food—considerably less than 5%; (*b*) fishing, in most years—less than 15%; (*c*) fowling—less than 5%; and (*d*) hunting—around 80–85%. Perhaps this analogy was also applicable for colder periods during the Pleistocene.

The first good evidence on subsistence comes from Acheulean sites such as Torralba and Ambrona in Old Castile, Spain. These sites probably belong to the late Mindel or early Mindel–Riss interglacial. The sites are located along a seasonal migration route of animals that moved to the north in the spring and to the south in the late summer. The majority of the animals found at those sites reflect adaptation to grasslands (Table 3.2).

TABLE 3.2   Frequency of Animals from 1961–1963 Excavations at Torralba[a][b]

| | Number of animals | Percentage |
|---|---|---|
| Elephant | 30[c] | 29.7 |
| Horse | 26 | 25.7 |
| Deer (red, fallow, and roe) | 25 | 24.7 |
| Aurochs | 10 | 9.9 |
| Steppe rhinoceros | 6 | 5.9 |
| Unidentified carnivores | 4 | 4.0 |
| Totals | 101 | 99.9% |

[a]Data are from Butzer 1971.

[b]Since the weight estimates for many extinct Pleistocene mammals are hypothetical, I will not estimate the amount of available meat in this chapter.

[c]The number for elephants is the lowest estimate, for it may be as high as 55 elephants.

The faunal remains from Ambrona reflect a greater variety of species, and some of the animals are woodland types. In addition to large grazing animals such as horse and elephant, wolf, weasel, hare, cercopithecoid monkey, two species of duck, grouse, and falcon are represented at Ambrona. The large grazing animals provided substantial quantities of meat; the average estimated weight of the extinct rhinoceros is 3663 kg and this provides 2179 kg of edible meat.

The data from Middle and Upper Paleolithic sites reflect subsistence strategies also based on hunting large herbivores. However, we can observe differences in frequencies of various animals at two sites in the USSR and one in the Federal Republic of Germany (Table 3.3). One of these sites, Kiik-Koba, is a cave in the Crimea, and the other two are open-air sites: Il'skaya in the steppe region north of the Caucasus, and Salzgitter-Lebenstedt, near Braunschweig in the Federal Republic of Germany. These observed differences in animal frequencies can be explained by different environmental zones, topography, seasonal variation in hunting strategies, etc.

The regional differences in faunal remains are clearly reflected in the Upper Paleolithic sites. Klein (1969) observed this in the USSR. For example, in the Upper Paleolithic sites located on the Don River, in the eastern part of European USSR, large herbivores, especially mammoth and horse, predominate. However, in the southern part of European USSR, bison remains are

**TABLE 3.3  Frequency of Animals at Kiik-Koba, Il'skaya, and Salzgitter-Lebenstedt[a]**

| | Number of individuals | | |
|---|---|---|---|
| | Kiik-Koba (Horizon IV) | Il'skaya | Salzgitter-Lebenstedt[b] |
| Wooly mammoth | 3 | 3 | 16 |
| Wooly rhinoceros | 1 | — | 2 |
| Horse | 6 | 3 | 4 or 6 |
| Ass | 2 | 2 | — |
| Cattle | 1 | 30 | 6 or 7 |
| Sheep | 1 | — | — |
| Saiga antelope | 5 | — | — |
| Giant deer | 8 | 1 | — |
| Red deer | 1 | 3 | — |
| Reindeer | 1 | — | 80 |
| Wild boar | 1 | 1 | — |
| Wolf | 1 | 2 | 1 |
| Red fox | 2 | — | — |
| Arctic fox | 3 | — | — |
| Steppe fox | 5 | — | — |
| Bear | 1 | 1 | — |
| Cave hyena | 1 | 4 | — |

[a]Data are from Butzer 1971, Klein 1969.
[b] Single specimens of muskrat, duck, crane or swan, vulture, perch, pike, unidentified fish, and mollusca were found here also.

most abundant, and in the most western part of the country, reindeer and horse predominate. Mellars (1973) noted that reindeer, horse, bovids, and red deer were most frequently hunted in southwestern France, although reindeer remains are usually most numerous at various sites. In addition, the sites in southwestern France yielded remains of chamois, ibex, fallow deer, roe deer, wild pig, common fox, arctic fox, wooly rhinoceros, and mammoth.

At some sites very large numbers of herbivores were found. For example, at Předmost in Czechoslovakia, remains of over 900 mammoth were found. These remains clearly predominated at this site, but also bones of bison, horse, musk-ox, wolf, and arctic fox were found. Probably Předmost was a seasonal camp, from which the Upper Paleolithic people exploited various herd animals, especially mammoth.

Near the end of the Upper Paleolithic we find more evidence of fowling and fishing. In southwestern France grouse remains are most frequently found, and the fish remains mostly belong to salmon (Mellars 1973). Also, remains of trout, carp, bream, pike, dace, and chub were recovered. Engravings and sculptures of fish suggest their greater importance in subsistence strategy.

Between 13,000 and 11,000 years ago, mammoth, rhinoceros, giant elk, and musk-ox disappeared from Europe. It is evident that near the end of Würm glaciation, as the ice began to retreat, a number of changes in climate and topography occurred throughout Europe. This also affected the fauna and flora. For example, some areas that were open country around 11,000 years ago were covered by coniferous forests 4000–5000 years later, and by deciduous forests somewhat later than that. The herbivores that were adapted to the grasslands, such as mammoth, were no longer able to survive in the new environment, for their former ecological niches were eliminated.

Thus, around 13,000–11,000 years ago we find the last Upper Paleolithic hunters in central Europe. For example, at the Meiendorf and Stellmoor sites near Hamburg in the Federal Republic of Germany, the subsistence strategy still reflects heavy reliance on hunting of herd animals (Rust 1937, 1943). Out of 668 mammals found at Stellmoor, 650 were reindeer. These animals were adapted to the tundra environment. At Stellmoor we have concrete archaeological evidence for utilization of bow and arrow by the late Upper Paleolithic hunters. Plain wooden arrows and pine arrow shafts that could have been used with flint arrowheads have been found. Perhaps flint arrowheads were used to kill larger animals, but one plain wooden arrow was found in the vertebra of a wolf.

### Settlement Organization

It is very difficult to reconstruct the settlement organization of Paleolithic societies from archaeological data. There are a number of reasons for the poor settlement data that are available for us. Most of the land surface in Europe before the Upper Paleolithic was either destroyed by continental glaciations or was deeply covered by sediments of later periods. Thus the settlement data are not well preserved for most parts of the Paleolithic. Some of the blame should be placed on archaeologists. Continuous excavation of individual sites is not very useful for reconstructing the settlement system of prehistoric hunters and gatherers. Even if we studied all the sites in one valley, it would not mean that we would find all ranges of sites. We may find only one type of site in a valley. Thus a reasonable research approach to the Paleolithic settlement systems must be on a regional level, and it should take into consideration paleo-environment, topography, spatial and temporal organization of the animal and plant species, size of the territory occupied by the hunting and gathering group, etc. This implies that a systematic survey should be conducted in the region before any excavations are undertaken. The definition of the settlement system depends very much on the ability of archaeologists to infer the different human activities at the various sites. This is a very difficult task for Paleolithic archaeologists.

Paleolithic archaeologists assume that the spatial distribution of artifacts and features will reflect the specific activities that were carried out at a site. As Whallon (1973: 115) expressed this, "artifacts classified into separate tool types, should be differentially distributed on prehistoric occupation floors as a result of their differential utilization in the various separate activities carried out by human groups at each location used or inhabited." It is also assumed that the artifacts were discarded in the same general area in which the activities occurred. This last assumption was questioned by L. Binford (1973, 1976) on the basis of his study of Nunamiut Eskimos in Alaska. His study led him to call the technology of the Nunamiut *curated,* as opposed to poorly organized or more expedient technologies. L. Binford (1976: 342) observed that "in curated assemblages, where tools are transported and returned to a residential location for repair (as in the case of the Nunamiut), we can expect there to be no necessary regular relationship between the by-products of activities in which tools were used and the numbers of tools themselves." This has great implications for archaeologists. We would not find butchering tools at butchering locations or wood-working tools at wood-collecting locations, for "such items are curated, transported and, if broken in the context of use, frequently transported to residential locations where they may be recycled or repaired for future use [L. Binford 1976: 342]." However, the presence of specific activities still can be determined, for "the differences in the sites are clearly reflected and very marked in the differential remains of consumption and of processing of animals in the context of logistics of getting the animal from its location of kill to its location of consumption [L. Binford 1973: 242]." Thus in studying archaeological assemblages, archaeologists should anticipate differences deriving from curated technologies as opposed to those exhibiting expedient manufacture, use, and abandonment of the artifacts in the place of use.

Our evidence about the Paleolithic settlement organization comes from caves, rock shelters, and open-air sites. The evidence for the presence of any

**Figure 3.1.** Reconstructed hut at Terra Amata. (From "A Paleolithic Camp at Nice," by H. de Lumley. Copyright © 1969 by Scientific American, Inc. All rights reserved.)

open-air structures is very poor during the Middle Pleistocene. De Lumley (1969) excavated a series of huts built one over another in successive layers at Terra Amata, southern France. He dated them near the end of the Mindel glaciation. The huts were oval in shape, 8 to 16 m in length and 4 to 6.5 m in width (Figure 3.1). The presence of huts is indicated by postmolds (the stains left by the decay of the original posts) 8 cm in diameter and stones parallel to the postmolds, probably for bracing the walls of the shelters. Various concentrations of flint artifacts, ash, and organic matter were found inside the huts. There were also empty spaces surrounded by flint debris in the huts. Probably the empty spaces were occupied by people as they carried out various activities inside the hut. Probably the same human group visited Terra Amata every year. This would also give evidence for the presence of territoriality among human groups at that time, which, in turn, may suggest the presence of a resource that was "worth defending" by the group.

The evidence for the Middle Paleolithic is not much better. We know that numerous caves and rock shelters were occupied, but open-air shelters very rarely are found. One example comes from Molodova Ia site on the Dnestr River in the Soviet Union (Figure 3.2). It is dated near the end of the Middle Paleolithic. The structure at Molodova Ia was delimited by mammoth bones, and it was of oval shape, 10 × 7 m. Flint tools, animal bones, and charcoal accumulations were found inside the house. The charcoal perhaps represents the remains of hearths.

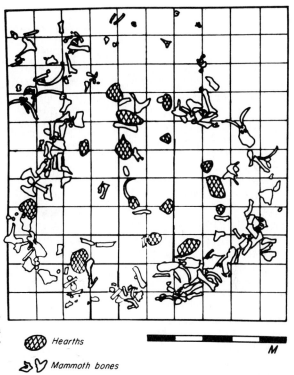

**Figure 3.2.** Remains of a Mousterian hut at Molodova Ia. (From R. G. Klein, *Ice-Age Hunters of the Ukraine,* © 1973 by The University of Chicago Press.)

Hearths

Mammoth bones

M

Mellars (1973) studied Mousterian sites in one area of southwestern France. He noted that most sites are rock shelters and small caves, rarely exceeding 20–25 m in any dimension. By the Upper Paleolithic period, the dimensions of sites usually had increased (Table 3.4) in France. Probably larger groups were occupying the sites. Furthermore, using Peyrony's (1949) data in one area of southwestern France, Mellars noted the great increase in number of sites during the Upper Paleolithic, as compared with the Middle Paleolithic. This increase would also indicate a rise in population. Only rock shelters and caves were available for this comparison. There were 32 Mousterian and 168 Upper Paleolithic sites. In that region, the Mousterian and Upper Paleolithic occupation periods were roughly of similar duration, 25,000–30,000 years. It should be noted that open-air sites existed, but the sparse data for them were not considered in the study.

We find the largest number of open-air sites during the Upper Paleolithic in central and eastern Europe. There are spectacular sites with structures built of mammoth bones in Czechoslovakia, Poland, and the USSR such as at Pushkari I in the Ukrainian S.S.R. (Figure 3.3). Probably the nonmountainous terrain and the absence of caves in some parts of the USSR accounted for the presence of so many open-air structures.

**TABLE 3.4  Dimensions of Some Upper Paleolithic Sites in Southwestern France[a]**

| Period | Type of site | Dimensions (in meters) |
|---|---|---|
| Aurignacian | | |
|   La Quina | Rock shelter | 52 × 10 |
|   Laussel | Rock shelter | 50 × 12 |
|   Abri Pataud | Rock shelter | 50 × 10 (?) |
| Upper Perigordian | | |
|   Laussel | Rock shelter | 72 × 10 |
|   Abri Pataud | Rock shelter | 50 × 10 (?) |
|   Les Vachons | Rock shelter | 50 × 5 |
|   Laugerie Haute | Rock shelter | 180 × 35 |
| Solutrean | | |
|   Laugerie Haute (Lower Sol.) | Rock shelter | 180 × 35 |
|   Laugerie Haute (Middle Sol.) | Rock shelter | 180 × 35 |
|   Badegoule | Rock shelter/open site | 45 × 25 |
| Magdalenian | | |
|   Laugerie Haute | Rock shelter | 180 × 35 |
|   La Madeleine | Rock shelter | 5,000 m² |
|   Solvieux | Open site | 10,000 m² |

[a]From Mellars 1973: 265.

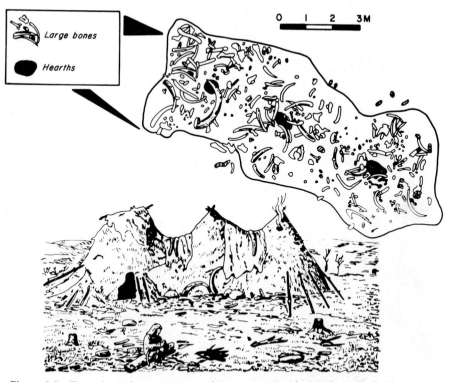

**Figure 3.3**  Floor plan and reconstruction of the house at Pushkari I. (From R. G. Klein, *Ice-Age Hunters of the Ukraine*, © 1973 by The University of Chicago Press.)

Numerous large-scale excavations of open-air settlements were conducted in the USSR that are described in a great number of articles and books (Borikovskij 1958; Chernysh 1953, 1961; Efimenko 1953, 1958; Gerasimov 1969; Pidoplichko 1969, 1976; Rogachev 1970). The Kostenki–Borshevo region along the Don River in the USSR has numerous sites with houses built of large mammoth bones. There was little wood for construction during the glaciations, therefore, mammoth bones were used in building the frames of shelters. Here we find small and large houses. For example, we find small houses 5 × 4 m and 8 × 6.5 m, and longhouses 34 × 5.5 m and 23 × 5.5 m. The small houses have an oval shape, and the longhouses are narrow, elongated, and have oval ends. Concentrations of ashes, probably hearth ashes, were found in the houses. The 23-m longhouse contained nine small pits with ash contents, approximately 1.5 m in size. Also, the floor of the house was dug 20 to 35 cm below the ground. If the nine pits with ashes are hearths and if they are contemporaneous, then we can speculate that a very large group occupied this structure. Perhaps individual families did their own cooking. It is not clear if the variability in house size reflects functional differences, implying that in some houses different human activities occurred. Most likely the differences reflect seasonal variability in the size of the social unit occupying each house. Perhaps the longhouses are associated with multifamily social groups.

Most settlements during the Upper Paleolithic do not reflect continuous occupations because the people were hunters and gatherers. Probably the settlements were occupied seasonally, as for example, when animal herds were present in the area. These sites of longer occupation are usually called base camps by archaeologists. The various smaller sites that represent activities of short duration, such as kill sites, are rarely found.

Campbell's (1968) study of the Tuluaqmiut band of Eskimos shows the complexity of their settlement system. He recorded the following six types of sites:

1. Base camp or central base; usually occupied by all or nearly all members of the Tuluaqmiut band of approximately 50 people during at least the months of April, May, and August through October. Also base camp was often used during other months. Campbell (1968: 16) notes that "when all members were present, it contained 10 or 12 surface dwellings, built of willow sticks and covered with moss and caribou hides." The concentration of the entire band in one area during the previously mentioned months depended on the caribou herds' presence in the area.
2. Camps of two or more families from November to January or from November to March. This resulted from seasonal breakup of the central base.
3. Hunting and fishing camps of males (one to five), usually of 2 to 5 days in duration. They occurred throughout the entire year.

4.  Single shelter for nonfood-collecting activities, such as chalcedony, spruce wood, and gyrfalcon feathers. These sites were found at nearly all times of the year.
5.  Camps that were located outside Tuluaqmiut territory for the purpose of courting, visiting, and trading. They were found at any time of the year.
6.  Overnight camps; they were used for traveling between sites of the other five types.

Campbell observed that it is easiest to recognize a type 1 site, that is, the base camp or central base. Also he observed that it is difficult to find sites of types 3, 4, and 5 after 5 years of abandonment. Using this ethnographic analogy, archaeologists usually find base camps, which are type 1 sites, seldom type 2 sites, and probably very rarely sites of types 3, 4, 5, and 6. It should be noted that there are many more sites of types 2, 3, 4, 5, and 6 than of type 1 throughout the year.

The settlement system of the Upper Paleolithic people varied seasonally depending on the distribution, location, type, and seasonality of resources. Since the subsistence reflected in the archaeological record shows mainly the exploitation of large mammals, we assume that it required cooperation among several adult males to kill a large mammal such as a mammoth or an elephant.

The evidence for groups splitting up into small units such as families is hypothetical, since the data for exploitation of plant or water resources are minimal. It should be noted that near the end of the Paleolithic we find greater exploitation of water resources. How large a territory was exploited by one hunting and gathering group also remains hypothetical.

### Social and Ritual Organization

During the Paleolithic, the hunters and gatherers were organized in the so-called band societies. This observation is based on ethnographic analogy, since modern hunters and gatherers usually exhibit the band level of sociopolitical organization. Previously only cultural anthropologists such as Service made theoretical contributions in studies about band society. However, a number of Paleolithic archaeologists, such as Wobst, have since contributed greatly to our understanding of organization of Paleolithic societies.

"A band is only an association, more or less residential, of nuclear families, ordinarily numbering 30–100 people, with affinal ties allying it with one or a few other bands [Service 1971: 111]." Also Service (1966: 7–8) states

> The loose integration of families in a band society is achieved only by conceptions of kinship extended by marriage. [Furthermore, the] band society is simple in that there are no specialized or formalized institutions or groups that can be differentiated as economic, political, religious, and so on. The family itself is the organization that undertakes all roles. The important economic division of labor is by age and sex statuses; even the most prominent ceremonies are typically concerned only with an individual's life-crisis rites of birth, puberty, marriage, and death. This fact exemplifies why the band level of society is a familistic order in terms of both social and cultural organization.

Wobst (1974) noted that Steward (1969) introduced two useful terms for analysis of hunters and gatherers: the *minimum* and the *maximum social aggregate* or *band*. The minimum band consists of several families tied by consanguineous and/or affinal ties. They share a common settlement and engage in a number of activities during some part of a year. "Its size is large enough so that it will survive prolonged periods of isolation through the cultural practices of cooperation among its members, division of labor according to age and sex, and mutual food-sharing. On the other hand it is sufficiently small to not place an undue strain on the local food resources [Wobst 1974: 152]." The size and stability of the minimum bands varied with the social and natural environments of Paleolithic societies.

The maximum band is a loosely interacting unit composed of minimum bands. This is accomplished by rituals, communication, and exchange. Steward (1969: 290) defined the maximum band as "little more than a group with which its members somewhat vaguely identify." Wobst (1974: 152) observed, "It essentially constitutes a marriage network which guarantees the biological survival of its members, since the members of a minimum band have to rely on a larger number of persons than their own membership in order to provide a member with a mate upon reaching maturity."

Wobst (1974: 173), using a demographic simulation model, concluded that the maximum Paleolithic band probably ranged in size from 175 to 475 people, whereas the minimum band had approximately 25 people. This implies that a Paleolithic society was comprised of between 7 and 19 minimum bands. The specific task-oriented groups such as hunting parties, groups organized to obtain raw materials, and aggregates for rituals varied in size, membership, and composition depending on the specific society.

Using Wobst's demographic simulation model (1974, 1976), we can estimate the population for various areas of Europe. He noted that ethnographic studies indicate that inland hunters and gatherers in Alaska, Canada, and Siberia had population densities from .5 to .005 persons/km². If we use density of .005 persons/km², the territory occupied by a maximum band would be 95,000 km². A territory of this size would include all of southwestern France, and would stretch from the Mediterranean Sea to the Atlantic Ocean. At .05 persons/km² density, the territory's size would be 9500 km². This would encompass all sites found in the Périgord region.

The population estimates for any European country will be low using Wobst's model. For example, he estimates that a minimum band exploits a territory of 1250 km² at a population density of .02 persons/km². Thus, Hungary, with an area of 93,030 km², would be occupied by 74 minimum bands with the total population of 1850. If we use 7 minimum bands to form a maximum band, Hungary would be occupied by 10 maximum bands.

The archaeological evidence for various rituals is poor for the Lower Paleolithic period. By the Middle Paleolithic we find evidence that might be related to ritual behavior. For example, at Monte Circeo, Italy, a Neanderthal skull was found lying upside down with stones surrounding it in the middle of the cave. An incision had been made around the foramen magnum, which would allow easy extraction of the brain. This does not necessarily imply cannibalism. In central European caves such as Drachenloch in Switzerland and Petershöhle in the Federal Republic of Germany, we find numerous bear skulls. At Petershöhle, Mousterian artifacts associated with Neanderthals were found in addition to 10 bear skulls in a niche inside the cave. Archaeologists sometimes consider these finds of bear skulls as reflecting "cave bear cult."

From ethnographic analogy we know of the bear ceremonials of Ainu in Japan. They captured young bears, filed their teeth, and kept them in cages. Later they killed the bears during ceremonials and treated their remains with respect. It is doubtful that bears would be hunted frequently for food during the Middle Paleolithic. It is more likely that a bear would kill the hunter carrying a spear or a club before the hunter got the bear. Probably extensive hunting of bears would affect social organization, especially sex ratios, since many men would be killed.

Upper Paleolithic art is most frequently cited as an example of ritual behavior during that period. There are two types of Paleolithic art: (*a*) engraved or sculptured objects (portable art) such as figurines made of stone, bone, clay, and engraved pieces of bone; and (*b*) engravings and paintings on the walls and ceilings of the caves. Animals were the most frequently painted subjects in the caves. The sculptured objects have a wide geographical distribution, whereas cave paintings are found only in western Europe and in the Ural Mountains, such as Kapova cave in the USSR. Various interpretations have been presented for the existence of cave paintings: hunting magic, fertility magic, male and female symbolism (Ucko and Rosenfeld 1967). It is possible that rituals were conducted by the band society in such caves.

Figurines of mammoth, cave bear, and other animals have been found. However, the most frequently found figurines represent females, the so-called Venuses. They have large breasts, stomachs, and buttocks. Traditionally they were interpreted as "mother goddesses." However, all these interpretations are only speculations.

At present, the incisions on bones are being interpreted by some scholars as lunar calendars. This interpretation is based on shaky scientific ground and convincing only to its believers.

Near the end of the Paleolithic, we find archaeological data at Stellmoor that reflect seasonal rituals or reindeer hunters. It seems that these hunters made annual sacrifices of the first killed reindeer. The reindeer were filled with rocks and taken out in the lake and dropped in the water. Over 30 reindeer skeletons containing stones have been found at Stellmoor. Also at Stelmoor a pole, approximately 2 m high, was found; it was pointed at one end and on the other end a reindeer skull was mounted. It is possible that this was a totem pole.

# Holocene

The Holocene or Postglacial period began around 10,000 years ago. As previously mentioned, the Holocene began in many areas when pioneer species such as birch, willow, and pine moved into the formerly treeless environments as the ice mass retreated north. Thus, during this period, forests slowly covered most parts of Europe.

In addition, the retreating ice mass near the end of Würm affected the actual physical makeup of the land. One effect of this was the sea level's rising from the melting of the glacial ice. Also the land underneath the glaciers began to rise, especially in the Scandinavian area. The isotastic rise of the land in Scandinavia affected the shore lines because as the land mass rose there were periodic dammings and openings of areas to the sea. At different periods, as the retreating ice mass reached Scandinavia, the present Baltic Sea was sometimes a lake and sometimes a sea. Table 3.5 illustrates changes in climate, dominant vegetation, and sea level stages of the Baltic Sea during the Late Pleistocene and throughout the Holocene.

## Introduction to the Mesolithic

The Mesolithic period consists of that part of the Holocene before the appearance of agriculture in the different parts of Europe. In southeastern Europe, the term *Mesolithic* is not used frequently, and the Epipaleolithic period represents the latest Paleolithic before the occurrence of farming cultures.

Technological changes are reflected in the Mesolithic. The Mesolithic is characterized by microlithic tools, that is, very small flint tools. Although such tools were already present in the Upper Paleolithic, it should be emphasized that microlithic tools predominate during the Mesolithic. Since forests covered most of Europe at that time, we find axes and adzes, or woodworking tools, to combat the forest environment. Also we find more equipment associated with exploitation of water resources such as paddles, canoes, barbed-bone points, and fishhooks. As during the Paleolithic, there were various regional cultures during the Mesolithic, such as Tardenoisian and Maglemose. The reader is referred to a symposium held in Warsaw, Poland in 1973 (S. Kozłowski 1973) to get a more extensive perspective on regional cultures during the Mesolithic.

## Subsistence Strategies

The Paleolithic subsistence strategy based on hunting of large herd animals was replaced during the Mesolithic mostly by exploitation of solitary animals such as roe deer, wild pig, and elk. They were typical forest animals, and they did not migrate in large herds. They could not be exploited the same way that

**TABLE 3.5  Late Pleistocene and Holocene Climatic and Vegetational Periods and Sea-Level Stages of the Baltic Sea in Northern Europe[a]**

| Name of period | Dates (B.C.) | Dominant vegetation | Climate | Sea level stages of the Baltic Sea | |
|---|---|---|---|---|---|
| Subatlantic | After 300 | Beech | Maritime | Present Baltic Sea | |
| | | | | | 2000 B.C. |
| Subboreal | 3000–300 | Oak, beech | More Continental | Littorina Sea | |
| | | | | | 5500 B.C. |
| Atlantic | 6200–3000 | Oak, elm | Warmer and Maritime | Ancylus Lake | |
| Boreal | 7500–6200 | Hazel, pine, oak | Warmer and Continental | | |
| Preboreal | 8300–7500 | Birch, pine | Warm Continental | | |
| | | | | | 7800 B.C. |
| | | | | Yoldia Sea | |
| | | | | | 8300 B.C. |
| Younger Dryas | 8900–8300 | Forest tundra | Arctic | Baltic Ice Lake | |
| Alleröd | 9800–8900 | Birch, pine | Temperate Continental | | |
| Older Dryas | 10,100–9800 | Tundra | Arctic | | |
| Bölling | 10,800–10,100 | Birch parkland | Subarctic | | |
| Oldest Dryas | Before 10,800 | Tundra | Arctic | | |

[a]Data are from Clark 1952, Butzer 1971, Schild 1975, Więckowska 1975.

herds of mammoth or reindeer were exploited during the Paleolithic. Only the red deer congregated into larger groups during certain seasons, as shown at the famous Mesolithic site Star Carr in England. Remains of a camp of the so-called Maglemosian hunters at Star Carr, dated around 7600 B.C., were found at the edge of an extinct lake (Clark 1954, 1972).

The site was occupied for approximately 5 or 6 months, October through April, and this was related to the movement of red deer. During those winter months the herbivorous animals sought shelter on low-lying ground. Most of the animals killed at Star Carr were adult males (stags). The adult stags separate from the females and immature young animals during their occupation of winter quarters. Perhaps there was a deliberate selection of mainly adult males for killing. The preservation of females for reproduction and the young for the future seasons is a sensible approach. However, since males are separated from the females, their killing may not be intentional if they are the nearest group to the hunters. Only the stags have antlers, which were needed for making barbed points. At Star Carr, 188 of 191 barbed points were cut from stag antler splinters. Remains of other animals in addition to red deer were also found (Table 3.6). No remains of fish or fishhooks were recovered at Star Carr. The red deer clearly was the most important animal during the seasonal occupation of Star Carr. Clark (1972) estimated the amount of meat that was available daily for a band consisting of three or four families at Star Carr. He assumes that each family consisted of two adults and three children. Clark constructed a model on the red deer using modern studies by Darling (1969) of these animals in the Scottish Highlands. It is evident that there is a wide variation in the carrying capacity of different territories. Darling noted that some areas carried one deer per 40.5 hectares (ha), whereas other areas had one deer per 12.1–16.2 ha. For Clark's model the lowest density was adopted, that is, one red deer per 40.5 ha. Also Clark made various hypothetical estimates for site territory, population of red deer, killing percentage of red deer, etc. (Table 3.7). It should be noted that analysis of the bone material from Star Carr yields the estimated average weight of an adult male (stag) to be 190.5 kg, which is greater than that of the modern red deer in Great Britain.

Clark estimated that at Star Carr 60% of the animal protein was obtained from red deer. Using the model based on red deer, Clark arrived at the conclusion that there would have been sufficient meat alone for a three-family group and perhaps even for a four-family unit. However, we should not forget the other animals and flora, such as marsh plants. These would make it possible to support a four-family group or about 20 individuals. This comes close to Wobst's estimated number for the size of a minimum band.

The Mesolithic sites in Denmark yielded much more varied information about the subsistence strategy. The data come from three cultures, Maglemose, Kongemose, and Ertebølle. The Maglemosian is the earliest culture and the Ertebølle the latest. With the Late Ertebølle we find ceramics; thus

TABLE 3.6   Frequency of Animals Found at Star Carr[a]

| | |
|---|---|
| Red deer | 160 |
| Aurochs | 18 |
| Elk | 22 |
| Roe deer | 66 |
| Pig | 10 |

[a]From Clark 1972.

there are disagreements among archaeologists as to whether the late phase belongs to the Mesolithic. Petersen (1973) presents a list of fauna, flora, and fish that were found at Maglemose, Kongemose, and Ertebølle sites (Table 3.8). All Maglemose data come from inland sites, whereas all Kongemose evidence comes from coastal sites. The Ertebølle data come from inland and coastal sites. Perhaps this accounts for the variability in the number of animal species exploited: Maglemose 58, Kongemose 33, and Ertebølle 86. The Ertebølle culture shows the most extensive evidence of marine fishing, fowling, hunting, and intensive gathering of marine molluscs.

## Settlement Organization

As during the Paleolithic, the settlement system depended mainly on seasonal availability of resources, such as fauna, flora, and fish. Also the size of the group varied seasonally. In Denmark, most Mesolithic sites are located close to water, reflecting the greater exploitation of water resources as com-

TABLE 3.7   Yields of Meat from Four Alternative Site Territories at Star Carr and Two Rates of Killing Red Deer[a]

| Site territory in km² | Population numbers of Red deer | Killing numbers of Red deer | Deadweight in kilograms | Available amount of meat; 60% of deadweight |
|---|---|---|---|---|
| 29 | 117.45 | $\frac{1}{6}$ : 19.56 | 3,726 | 2,236 |
| | | $\frac{1}{5}$ : 23.49 | 4,475 | 2,685 |
| 44.8 | 181.44 | $\frac{1}{6}$ : 30.24 | 5,761 | 3,457 |
| | | $\frac{1}{5}$ : 36.28 | 6,911 | 4,147 |
| 65.2 | 264.06 | $\frac{1}{6}$ : 44.0 | 8,382 | 5,029 |
| | | $\frac{1}{5}$ : 52.8 | 10,058 | 6,035 |
| 107.5 | 435.37 | $\frac{1}{6}$ : 72.5 | 13,811 | 8,287 |
| | | $\frac{1}{5}$ : 87.0 | 16,574 | 9,944 |

[a]From Clark 1972.

TABLE 3.8  Faunal and Floral Species Recovered from Maglemose, Kongemose, and Ertebølle Culture Sites in Denmark[a]

| | Maglemose | Kongemose | Ertebølle |
|---|---|---|---|
| Floral | | | |
| Hazelnut | X | X | X |
| Seeds of yellow water lily | X | | |
| Molluscan | | | |
| Native oyster | | X | X |
| Common cockle | | | X |
| Common mussel | | | X |
| Common periwinkle | | | X |
| Flat periwinkle | | | X |
| Netted dog whelk | | | X |
| Cross-cut carpet shell | | | X |
| Pullet carpet shell | | | X |
| Golden carpet shell | | | X |
| Fish | | | |
| Spur dog | | X | X |
| Salmon | | | X |
| Pike | X | X | X |
| Tench | X | | |
| Roach | X | | X |
| Bream | X | | |
| Wels | X | X | X |
| Eel | X | | X |
| Garfish | | | X |
| Cod | | X | X |
| Haddock | | | X |
| Coalfish | | X | X |
| Perch | X | | X |
| Mackerel | | | X |
| Sea scorpion | | | X |
| Three-spined stickleback | | | |
| Flounder | | X | X |
| Reptiles | | | |
| European tortoise | X | X | X |
| Birds | | | |
| Red-throated diver | | | X |
| Black-throated diver | X | | X |
| Little grebe | | | X |
| Great-crested grebe | | | X |
| Red-necked grebe | | | X |
| Dalmatian pelican | | X | X |
| Gannet | | X | X |
| Cormorant | X | | X |
| Heron | X | | |
| Bittern | X | | |
| Black stork | X | X | X |

*(continued)*

[a] From Petersen 1973.

TABLE 3.8  (*Continued*)

|  | Maglemose | Kongemose | Ertebølle |
|---|---|---|---|
| Whooper swan | X |  | X |
| Bewicks swan |  |  | X |
| Mute swan | X | X | X |
| Grey lag goose | X |  | X |
| Brent goose |  |  | X |
| Mallard | X |  | X |
| Teal |  |  | X |
| Pintail | X |  |  |
| Wigeon | X |  | X |
| Shoveler | X |  | X |
| Pochard |  | X |  |
| Tufted duck | X |  | X |
| Golden-eye |  |  | X |
| Long-tailed duck | X |  | X |
| Eider duck |  |  | X |
| Common scoter |  |  | X |
| Velvet scoter |  |  | X |
| Smew |  |  | X |
| Goosander | X |  |  |
| Red-breasted merganser | X |  | X |
| Osprey | X | X | X |
| Kite | X | X |  |
| Buzzard | X |  | X |
| Golden eagle |  |  | X |
| White-tailed eagle | X | X | X |
| Marsh-harrier | X |  |  |
| Capercaillie | X |  | X |
| Black grouse | X |  |  |
| Crane | X | X |  |
| Coot | X |  |  |
| Redshank | X |  |  |
| Dunlin | X |  |  |
| Common gull |  |  | X |
| Herring gull |  | X |  |
| Greater black-backed gull | X |  |  |
| Black-headed gull | X |  | X |
| Great auk |  | X | X |
| Razorbill |  |  | X |
| Guillemot |  |  | X |
| Tawny owl |  |  | X |
| Greater-spotted woodpecker |  |  | X |
| Raven |  |  | X |
| Crow |  | X |  |
| Jay | X |  | X |
| Mammals |  |  |  |
| Hedgehog | X |  | X |
| Brown hare | X |  |  |
| Red squirrel | X |  | X |

(*continued*)

**TABLE 3.8**  *(Continued)*

| | Maglemose | Kongemose | Ertebølle |
|---|---|---|---|
| Beaver | X | X | X |
| Water vole | X | | X |
| Short-tailed vole | | | X |
| Wolf | X | X | X |
| Dog | X | X | X |
| Red fox | X | X | X |
| Brown bear | X | X | X |
| Pine marten | X | | X |
| Polecat | X | | X |
| Badger | X | | X |
| Wolverine | | | |
| Otter | X | | X |
| Wild cat | X | X | X |
| Lynx | | | X |
| Common seal | | | X |
| Ringed seal | | X | X |
| Harp seal | | | X |
| Grey seal | X | X | X |
| Wild pig | X | X | X |
| Roe deer | X | X | X |
| Red deer | X | X | X |
| Elk | X | X | X |
| Reindeer | | | |
| Aurochs | X | X | X |
| Wild horse | | | |
| Blue whale | | | X |
| Bottle-nosed dolphin | | | X |
| Common dolphin | | | X |
| Killer whale | | | X |
| Common porpoise | | X | X |

pared with their exploitation in the Paleolithic. Also the hunting of solitary animals implies that the human groups were smaller than those during the Paleolithic. The large herd animals during the Paleolithic made possible larger aggregations of human groups, at least during certain seasons.

Since very few Mesolithic structures have been found, the discussion of the settlement system is quite speculative. Some structures associated with Maglemose culture were found in Denmark (Becker 1945; K. Andersen 1951). The huts had preserved floor layers from 18 to 25 m² (Petersen 1973). Inside the huts, fireplaces were found. These huts were always found near the lake shore. Except for one hut at Holmegaard V, all the discovered huts probably represent summer occupation. The summer sites contain numerous remains of fish, while at Holmegaard V no barbed-points or fish remains were found. Some specific activity sites were found, such as Skottemarke. At this site, the remains of six butchered elks were found, and at least one of them was killed during the winter. Also, sites were found along the coast, which implies exploitation of sea resources. Petersen (1973: 95–96) concludes, "The Maglemose settlement pattern . . . does not only show seasonal variation within the inland sites but also within some coastal sites as reflected in the site catchment and the typological differentiation."

The size of the Maglemose site is small. The Star Carr site is 16.5 × 14.5 m or 239.25 m². It is evident that the Mesolithic people exploited various ecological zones, and we can observe a seasonal variation within the settlement system. Any estimate on the size of the group during the different seasons is quite hypothetical. As previously mentioned, the size of the group at the Star Carr during the winter months was approximately 20 individuals.

## Social and Ritual Organization

As during the Paleolithic, the Mesolithic sociopolitical organization was based on band society. The main characteristics of a band's social organization were presented in the Paleolithic section.

The evidence for ritual activities is very scanty for the Mesolithic. The cave art disappeared with the Paleolithic; only decorated bone objects and figurines of animals are found for the Mesolithic. The animal figurines may be related to rituals. The rare Mesolithic burials supply us with some information about the presence of rituals. For example, the Janisławice burial in Poland contained a skeleton of a man, 30 years old, buried in an oblong pit (Chmielewska 1954). The grave goods consisted of 21 elongated triangles and trapezoids, 4 cores, 11 blades, 1 hammerstone, 2 points made from shoulder blade of auroch, 1 antler point, 4 knifelike tools of boars' tusks, 2 chisels of boars' tusks, 1 deer antler, 1 double-pointed bone gorge for fishing, 5 stag tines, 1 necklace made of over 20 stag incisors and canines, and bones of beaver, wild feline, and mussels. Most of the flint artifacts were made of nonlocal flint. The Janisławice burial reflects death ritual activities.

In conclusion, it can be said that the data are too poor to speculate extensively about the Mesolithic ritual activities.

# Chapter 4

# Neolithic

The Neolithic in Europe is defined as the time segment starting with the first appearance of agricultural communities and lasting until the appearance of bronze metallurgy, which marks the beginning of the Bronze Age. Many archaeologists, however, do not extend the Neolithic to the Bronze Age, but terminate it with the appearance of copper-using societies. They employ the terms *Aeneolithic*, *Copper Age*, or *Chalcolithic* to describe the period of copper tool use before the onset of the Bronze Age in Europe. In this survey, however, the so-called Aeneolithic period is included in the Neolithic.

The use of the term *Neolithic* does not imply that uniform sociopolitical developments took place among the various societies in Europe. In some areas, hunters and gatherers persisted throughout the period, while other regions witnessed the development of the earliest societies with "hereditary inequality" in so-called ranked societies or chiefdoms.

I will divide the European Neolithic into three phases: Early, Middle, and Late. The beginning and end of these time periods vary in different parts of Europe. For example, by the time earliest farming, which characterizes Early Neolithic societies, was established in central Europe, the Middle Neolithic had already begun in southeastern Europe. Or, perhaps, I may be discussing Early Neolithic trade or settlement systems among farmers in central Europe at a time when hunting and gathering societies were still flourishing in Scandinavia. It should be emphasized that this further subdivision of the Neolithic and other periods in European prehistory is for analytical purposes only. These different periods are not separated from one another by any sharp boundaries or breaks, for the changes occurring in various aspects of culture are generally gradual.

Just as traditional archaeological usage distinguished the various Paleolithic cultures on the basis of their stone tools and other lithic remains, so Neolithic cultures are usually classified by their ceramic styles, that is, the shape and decoration of their pots.

## Neolithic Tribal Society

Many archaeologists and ethnologists have associated the Early Neolithic with the first tribal societies in Europe. I will consider the tribal level as a particular phase in the sociopolitical development of human cultures, preceded in this general scheme by the band level of society, represented in Europe by Paleolithic and Mesolithic societies.

Service (1971: 101) has contrasted these two levels of sociopolitical development as follows:

> A tribe is an association of a much larger number of kinship segments which are each composed of families. They are tied more firmly together than are the bands, which use mostly marriage ties alone. A tribe is of the order of a large collection of bands, but it is not simply a collection of bands.

Although the ethnographic record shows great variability among tribal societies, it is possible to construct a general model for them. Archaeologists should not shrink from making speculative statements, though they should be prepared to evaluate these propositions through archaeological data. We should especially note the organizational differences that distinguish tribal societies from band societies. Lewis (1968) observed that tribes are distinguished from bands by their greater population density, increased opportunity to meet with others, and more types of coordinated activity. The Neolithic agriculturalists may have had, in comparison with Paleolithic and Mesolithic hunting and gathering societies, greater population densities, more complex sociopolitical organization, cooperate agricultural enterprises, the herding of domesticated animals (raiding for livestock), different emphasis in organized rituals, and more types of associations or sodalities that cut across residential units.

Sahlins (1968: 15) described clearly in abstraction the general organization of a tribe:

> the tribe is divided into concentric circles of kith and kin: the household in central position, a circle of lineage kinsmen surrounding it, a wider circle of village relations, on out to the tribal and inter-tribal spheres.
>
> The constituent units of a tribal society on the ground make up a progressively inclusive series of groups, from the closely-knit household to the encompassing tribal whole. Smaller groups are combined into larger ones through several levels of incorporation. The particular arrangements vary, of course, but the scheme might read something like this: families are joined in local lineages, lineages in village communities, villages in regional confederacies, the latter making up the tribe or "people"—itself set in a wider, inter-tribal field. The smaller groups are usually

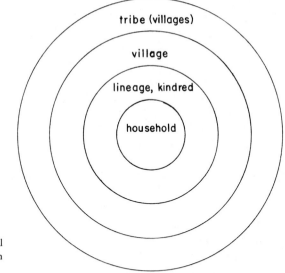

tribe (villages)

village

lineage, kindred

household

**Figure** 4.1. Generalized tribal design. (After Sahlins 1968, with modifications.)

cohesive kinship groups. The larger appear as social compacts of the smaller, integrated perhaps by personal kinship, clanship, or intermarriage. [See Figure 4.1.]

This organization affects social relations. Individuals with close kinship ties have more social obligations and exhibit greater generosity and sociability toward one another. As social relations expand, the sociability and generosity usually decline. In tribal societies, moral sanctions such as those against theft or murder are only applicable in certain contexts. Stealing from a stranger or even killing him or her may be considered morally acceptable, whereas such behavior toward one's kin would be totally unacceptable.

This discussion of tribe proceeds from the viewpoint of an individual participating in the system. The archaeologist is not situated to perceive the system as a nest of ever-widening social relations arranged in a concentric pattern. For an archaeologist, a tribe would appear as an array of settlements, cemeteries, camps, and industrial sites, with varying time depths, the integration of which would, eventually, resolve itself into a rather impersonal interconnected system of groups and communities.

Tribes do not have centralized political or economic organization, nor are the individual members ranked in a permanent hierarchy of social stratification. We are still dealing with a decentralized and nonstratified sociopolitical structure. The village communities that constitute a tribe are small, rarely exceeding more than 250 people, and, generally, are politically and economically autonomous. The inhabitants of the different villages in a tribe are linked socially by kin relations, or by common membership in sodalities, that is, nonkinship, nonresidential institutions such as warrior societies or age groups. Tribal society is quite egalitarian. Status is based on age, sex, and personal talents, achievements, and charisma. For example, a man may attain the role of war leader or ritual practitioner through his own abilities in these fields; however, he cannot significantly coerce his fellows by force nor invest his position with the permanent authority of an office. It is clear that this type of leadership is not inherited. However, some temporary tribal leaders such as Sahlins' (1963) "Big Man" in Melanesia can greatly affect the decision making especially in household production within the villages even if they do not have institutionalized political authority. But, generally, in a tribal society all the economic, political, and religious functions can be performed by the same people, without any specialized economic, political, or religious institutions; usually any person can fill the appropriate roles as the occasion demands.

Various corporate groups such as lineages, clans, and kindreds, are important in tribal societies, for they not only play a role in social relations but also frequently function as landholding units. Land is usually controlled by a clan or lineage, even if individual families work their own small plots. Voluntary or task-oriented association brings people together to carry out a variety of economic, social, military, and ritual activities.

In tribal society, rituals play an important role in governing life. A variety of rituals are performed in the different segments of tribal organization. At the household level, the family may conduct rituals for personal well-being. Planting and harvesting, diseases, or lack of rain may involve an entire village, and various communal rituals may be performed. Reliance on domesticated plants and animals differentiates rituals of agriculturalists from those of hunters and gatherers. Hunting and gathering groups meet during the year to perform various rituals, but among agriculturalists, who are involved in planting and harvesting at predictable times of the year, time-dependent rituals are performed (Yengoyan 1972).

## Appearance of Domesticates in Europe

There are three possible explanations usually given for the appearance of domesticated plants and animals in Europe: a diffusion of the plant and animal species in question, along with the idea of domestication; a gradual expansion of the agriculturalists themselves from Anatolia and the independent domestication of certain species in Europe. The controversy over whether certain plants and animals were first domesticated in Europe or diffused from elsewhere is not very important in terms of cultural process. There is little evidence that any plants were domesticated for the first time during the Early Neolithic period in Europe. Wild einkorn wheat is found in southeastern Europe, but it was domesticated earlier in the Near East. In the light of the present evidence, it is possible that some animals were domesticated first in

Europe, since the earliest remains of domesticated cattle and pig occur around the same time in the Balkans and the Near East (Higgs and Jarman 1972). It is also possible that some fruit trees such as vines were domesticated first in the Aegean area during the Late Neolithic (Zohary and Spiegel-Roy 1975).

A gradual expansion by agricultural populations would seem to be the most likely explanation for the spread of agriculture, although there have been many differences observed in the archaeological record between southeastern Europe and the Near East that are not entirely consistent with such a conclusion. Early Neolithic villages in Greece or Yugoslavian Macedonia differed from those in the Near East. Villages in Europe consisted of freestanding houses, not blocks of contiguous houses or series of houses grouped around a courtyard as in the Near East. This basic village pattern was repeated in most European Neolithic societies, although the size of the houses, their internal spacing within a community, and their distribution within the settlement varied. Also, in Europe most houses were constructed of wood and the walls were plastered over with mud or clay, whereas in the Near East they were built of sun-dried mud. To some extent this variation can be accounted for by different environmental conditions between Europe and the Near East.

It is doubtful, however, that southeastern European hunters and gatherers would have readily changed their mode of adaptation, for the advantages of agriculture would not have been self-evident (Tringham 1973). Hunting and gathering groups that adapted successfully to their environment probably would not have attempted to change their mode of life if there were no disturbances in the environment or in the demographic structure of a region (L. Binford 1968). But if this balance were upset by farmers, hunters and gatherers may have been under pressure to change their subsistence strategy.

Assuming that agriculture spread by means of population expansion, we must look for its causes. Population increase or pressure is frequently suggested as the cause for expansion by agriculturalists into new territories. This does not necessarily mean that a group splits off from its parent community because the population has actually reached the limit imposed by the carrying capacity of the local environment. There is no simple one-to-one relationship between population density and carrying capacity. Ethnographic data indicate that horticultural communities exploit their environment at levels varying between 7 and 75% of the carrying capacity (Sahlins 1972: 44–45). They could produce more, but there is no need to increase the production beyond providing sufficient means of livelihood. However, the actual population densities of tribal communities do not depend on the theoretical carrying capacity, but on the limits imposed by periodically recurring "bad years." Thus, human population in an ecosystem is adapted not to the "average" conditions, but to the predictable "bad years," that is, those periods when food resources are scarce. It should be noted that the adaptation of human populations is also affected by social and technological factors, such as the presence of storage facilities. This would also affect population densities.

Too often archaeologists tend to maximize variables like population: "Population pressure" is not a single factor but includes various social, political, and economic factors. A group may split off from a parent group because of internal friction. At this level of sociocultural development an internal friction may be settled by one faction moving away and establishing a new community. Hostilities between communities may drive one group to seek refuge in a new area. Thus, in addition to increase of population, various other factors can affect the establishment of new communities in an area.

Assuming that Neolithic populations did expand throughout Europe, they encountered resident hunting and gathering groups and not just an uninhabited environment rich in wood, salt, minerals, flora, and fauna. The spread of agriculturalists did not mean an abrupt end to hunting and gathering groups, for at first farmers occupied only areas with good soils, such as loess, chernozem, and fertile alluvial soils. In the northernmost areas of Europe, those covered by tundra or boreal forest, the hunting, gathering, and fishing way of life continued until historic and even recent times.

The expansion of agricultural societies probably precipitated conflicts with hunters and gatherers. The competitive advantage was with the agriculturalists, whose communities usually had larger populations. By the end of the Neolithic, hunters and gatherers were found only in areas marginal to agriculture. The spread of farming also modified the European landscape. For the first time, large areas of forests were cleared and nonlocal plants were introduced by farmers.

## The Spread of Farming Societies in Europe

The earliest agricultural communities with domesticated plants and animals appeared in Greece around 6000 B.C., and by 3500 B.C. (based on uncalibrated radiocarbon dates) agriculturalists were established in Denmark (Figures 4.2 and 4.3). These dates are set appreciably earlier when the correction factors derived from calibrating radiocarbon dates to tree-ring dates are applied: 7000 and 4190 B.C., respectively. Where possible, both the uncorrected and corrected radiocarbon dates will be given, for example, 1900–1800 B.C. (2180–2140 B.C.). The calibration method established at the Applied Science Center for Archaeology, the University Museum, University of Pennsylvania, is followed in this book (Ralph *et al.* 1973). As previously mentioned, the occurrence of the earliest use of bronze marks the end of the Neolithic period in Europe. This occurred approximately 2700–2600 B.C. (3340–3180 B.C.) in Greece and around 1900–1800 B.C. (2180–2140 B.C.) in central Europe—Austria, Czechoslovakia, Germany, Hungary, and Poland.

From Crete and Greece, where the earliest Neolithic villages occurred in Europe, we can trace the expansion of village farmers along two or three major routes. In the Mediterranean zone of Europe, from Greece to Spain, the

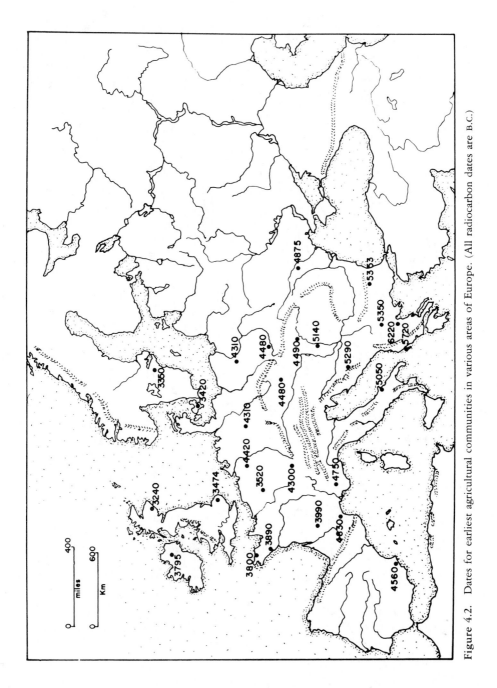

Figure 4.2. Dates for earliest agricultural communities in various areas of Europe. (All radiocarbon dates are B.C.)

Chronological chart

| | 6500 B.C. calibrated / 5500 B.C. radiocarbon | 5240 / 4500 | 4180 / 3500 | 3110 / 2500 | 1710 / 1500 |
|---|---|---|---|---|---|

**Greece:** Proto–Sesklo — Sesklo — Dhimini — Larissa — Rachmani

**Yugoslavia:** Impresso — Starčevo–Körös — Danilo — Hvar — Brijun — Jadran–Ljubljana; Sopot–Lengyel — Lasinja — Vučedol; Vinča–Tordos — Vinča–Pločnik — Baden–Kostolac

**Bulgaria:** Karanovo I–II — Veselinovo — Karanovo IV — Maritsa — Gumelnitsa — Ezero

**Romania:** Starčevo–Körös — Linear — Boian — Salcutsa — Ocher Grave — Corded Ware; Vadastra — Gumelnitsa — Tripolye

**Moldavia, Ukraine:** Dnestr–Bug — Linear — Tripolye — Gumelnitsa — Dnepr–Donets — Ocher Grave — Globular Amphora

**Hungary:** Starčevo–Körös — Linear — Tisza — Lengyel — Bodrogkeresztur — Baden — Bell Beaker; Bükk — Tiszapolgár

**Italy:** Impresso — Matera — Square Mouthed Pottery — Lagozza — Rinaldone; Serra D'Alto — Diana — Remedello

**France:** Impresso — Linear — Breton Primary Neolithic — Seine–Oise–Marne; Chassey — LesMatignons–Pou Richard — Bell Beaker

**Iberia:** Impresso — Linear — Almerian — Los Millares — Bell Beaker

**Czechoslovakia:** Linear — Stroke Ornamented — Lengyel — Bodrogkeresztur — Baden — Corded Ware — Bell Beaker; Bükk — Tiszapolgár — Boleraz — Funnel Beaker

**Poland:** Linear — Stroke Ornamented — Lengyel — Funnel Beaker — Globular Amphora — Baden — Bell Beaker; Corded Ware

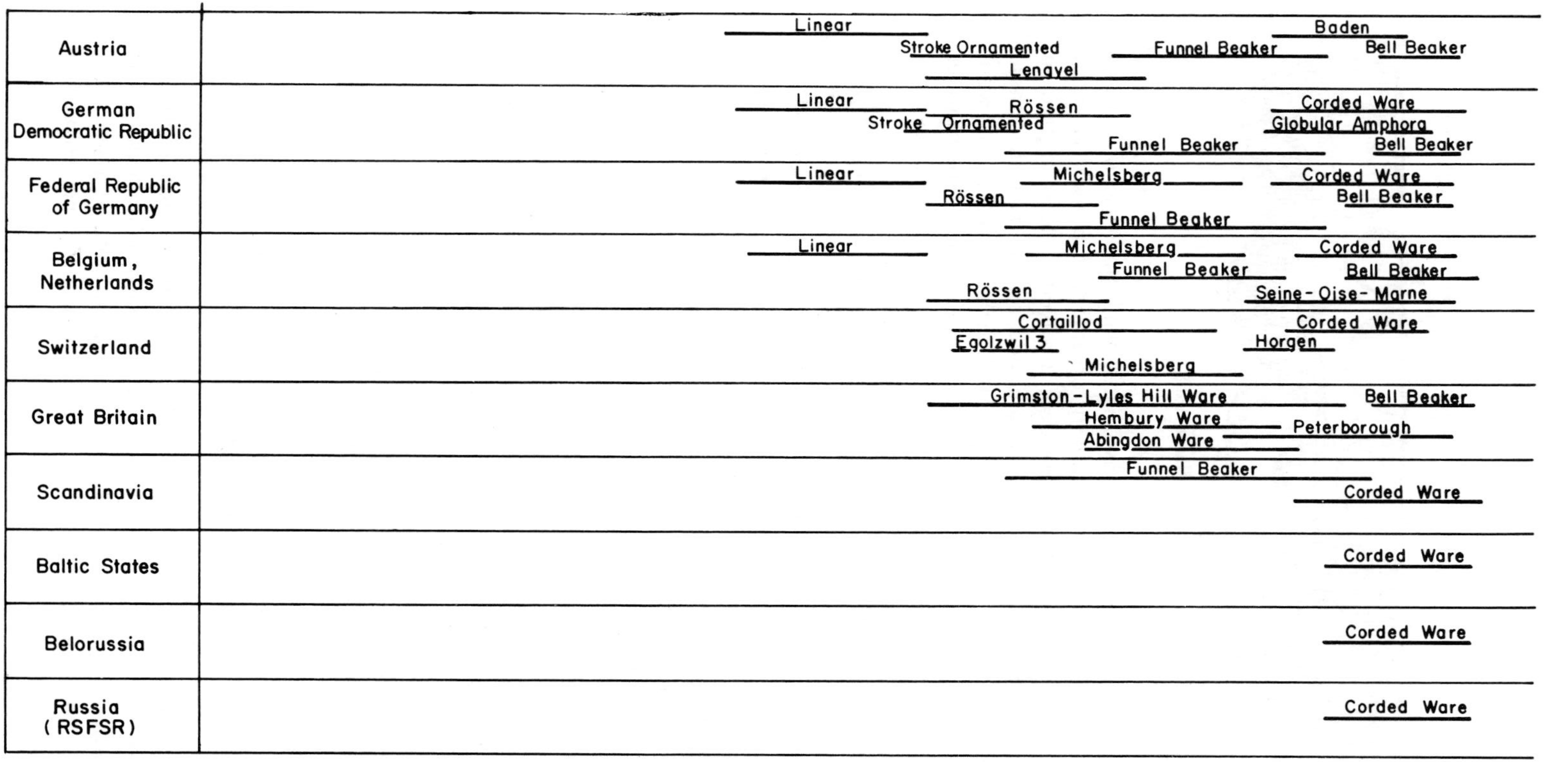

| Region | | | | | | |
|---|---|---|---|---|---|---|
| Austria | Linear | Stroke Ornamented | Lengyel | Funnel Beaker | Baden | Bell Beaker |
| German Democratic Republic | Linear | Stroke Ornamented | Rössen | Funnel Beaker | Corded Ware / Globular Amphora | Bell Beaker |
| Federal Republic of Germany | Linear | Rössen | Michelsberg | Funnel Beaker | Corded Ware | Bell Beaker |
| Belgium, Netherlands | Linear | Rössen | Michelsberg | Funnel Beaker | Seine–Oise–Marne / Corded Ware | Bell Beaker |
| Switzerland | Egolzwil 3 | Cortaillod | Michelsberg | Horgen | Corded Ware | |
| Great Britain | Grimston–Lyles Hill Ware | Hembury Ware / Abingdon Ware | Peterborough | Bell Beaker | | |
| Scandinavia | Funnel Beaker | Corded Ware | | | | |
| Baltic States | Corded Ware | | | | | |
| Belorussia | Corded Ware | | | | | |
| Russia (RSFSR) | Corded Ware | | | | | |

Figure 4.3. Chronological table for selected Neolithic cultures in Europe. All dates are approximate. For the U.S.S.R. I included only those cultures or their phases in the Neolithic that had domesticated plants and animals. Soviet archaeologists usually defined the Neolithic on the basis of the presence of pottery. (Data are from Ehrich 1965; Neustrupný 1968; C. Renfrew 1974; Thomas 1967).

or some areas within a site, reflects, more probably, such functional differences, rather than social or cultural ones. Pottery can occur among hunters and gatherers, and it is not exclusively associated with Neolithic villages. Likewise, not all farming communities need possess pottery. Vessels made of wood, leather, bark, bone, or stone can be used for storage, drinking, serving, and cooking. Such vessels indicate levels of complexity of material culture similar to those indicated by the presence of pottery.

## Central Europe

To the north of the Early Neolithic farmers in southeastern Europe, the earliest agricultural communities are characterized by Linear ceramics. This so-called Linear culture is one of the most intensively investigated aspects of the European Neolithic. Various other names are applied to this complex: Danubian Ia, *Bandkeramik* or Linear Pottery culture. Childe (1929) used the term *Danubian* to describe the entire sequence of Neolithic cultures in central Europe, and the Linear culture he called Danubian Ia. However, since the term *Danubian* is not limited to any one specific culture, I will not use it here. Childe objected to the various clumsy, alternative names including the Linear Pottery culture (Childe 1957: 106), but for brevity's sake, I will use the term *Linear culture*. The most characteristic descriptive attributes of the Linear culture are the ornamentation style of its finely made ceramics (Figure 4.6), which consists of straight or curved incised lines and which gives the culture its name; a particular type of polished adze–axe stone tool; and a settlement type consisting of villages made up of longhouses (Figure 5.8).

Except for parts of Hungary and Romania where the Linear culture was preceded by the Körös culture, Linear sites represent the earliest Neolithic or agricultural occupation in central Europe. The earliest phase of the Linear culture is found in the middle Danube area (Quitta 1967:264). There is speculation that Linear culture groups expanded from this area north into central Europe following the major water routes such as Danube, Vltava, Neckar, and Vistula. Radiocarbon dates for the earliest Linear sites range between 4600–4500 B.C. (5290–5240 B.C.).

Linear culture material is found over a vast territory in Europe from the Maas (Meuse) River valley in the Low Countries to the Dnestr River in the USSR (Figure 4.7). Some Linear culture ceramics are even found as far as the Southern Bug River (Passek and Chernysh 1963). Linear material extends from the Drava (Drau) River in the south and up to the mouth of the Odra (Oder) River in the north.

The productivity of the simple agriculture practiced by the Linear people was probably sufficient to permit the population to increase. However, the fact that productivity may have allowed an increase does not explain why the population increase occurred. The initial agricultural settlement of central

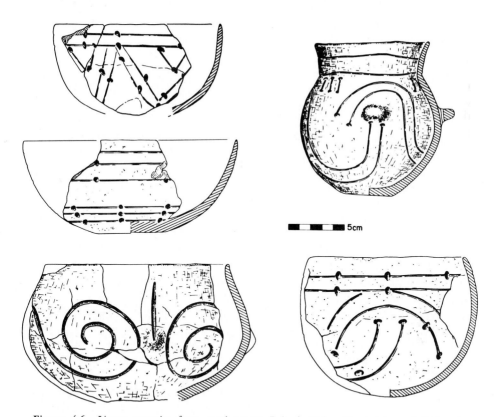

**Figure 4.6.** Linear ceramics from southeastern Poland. (After Kamieńska and Kulczycka Leciejewiczowa 1970; Kulczycka-Leciejewiczowa 1970a; Milisauskas 1976b.)

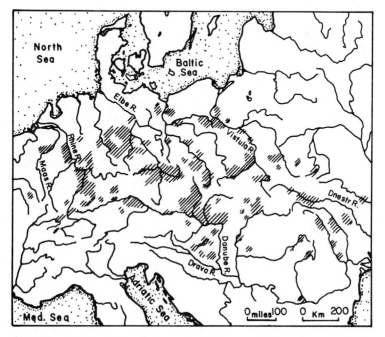

**Figure 4.7.** Distribution of Linear culture sites in Europe. (After Kulczycka-Leciejewiczowa 1970a.)

Europe may have been labor intensive, since heavy labor was needed for clearing forests, initial village construction, etc. Therefore, a high birthrate, that is, large families, would be advantageous for a large supply of labor. This increase in population and other processes associated with it, such as internal conflicts in communities, may have led to a segmenting process whereby daughter communities budded off from established ones and set up their villages elsewhere. In this splitting up of settlements, it is not likely that a daughter community would have been an exact replication of the parent village. Thus, in the long run, physical variation in the population (due to genetic drift) and stylistic differences in their artifacts (due to communication discontinuity) would result. For example, some differences in pottery ornamentation could have occurred in the daughter community because it did not include a representative sample of the pottery styles present in the parent village. If a person made certain stylistic variants of ceramics in a village, this style could have become dominant when his or her family moved to establish a new community. Also, when a village split into two parts there was less communication or interaction between people inhabiting different communities than when they lived in a single community. This may have led to greater stylistic differences among the artifacts produced in the two communities.

However, I am not implying that population, pressing on the absolute carrying capacity of the environment, forced Linear communities to expand. They were expanding into regions unexploited by farmers and could be very selective about how long they would exploit an area. When yields fell due to soil exhaustion, they could move into new territory. To some archaeologists this model of gradual expansion is too slow to account for the rapid spread of the Linear culture throughout central Europe. The earliest radiocarbon dates for the Hungarian, Moravian, and Bohemian sites are not much earlier than those of the first Linear sites in Holland, Germany, and Poland. For this reason some archaeologists postulate a migration of Linear people over central Europe. However, they offer no explanation as to the sociocultural processes that could have stimulated such a migration. It is doubtful that people possessing domesticated animals, such as pigs and cattle, would undertake long migrations into an unknown territory. We can estimate how many hypothetical generations it would take the Linear people to cover the straight-line distance of 1000 km (620 mi.), from Budapest, Hungary, to Elsloo, Netherlands. It would have taken only six to nine generations to expand over that distance at approximately 111–167 km per generation.

Ammerman and Cavalli-Sforza (1972) used radiocarbon dates to measure the rates at which farming spread in Europe. The rate for the Linear culture was the fastest, 5.59 km per year. In the Mediterranean area, the rate was 1.52 km per year, and for all of Europe, the average was 1.08 km per year. It is evident that the Linear people expanded very rapidly over central Europe.

The spread of the Linear culture into areas that were occupied by hunting and gathering people occurred during the Atlantic climatic period. At that time, mixed deciduous forests covered most of central Europe, except in areas with low precipitation, in which open woodland vegetation prevailed. Most of the currently known sites of the hunting and gathering people are found in areas with sandy soil, but it would be presumptuous to assume that they avoided loess lands. The expanding agriculturalists probably displaced the hunters and gatherers from these lands. A society organized into sedentary village communities possesses great competitive advantages over small migratory bands. However, the appearance of the Linear culture did not mean the end of the hunting and gathering groups. In central Europe the Linear settlements had an island-like character, and very likely the hunting and gathering way of life continued in areas unoccupied by the Linear people.

The early Linear culture exhibits little stylistic differentiation in pottery ornamentation throughout central Europe. This probably can be accounted for by the small size of the original Linear population, its rapid expansion into central Europe, and the probable practice of intercommunity marriage. Numerous studies such as the one by Meier-Arendt (1966) in the Main area of Germany reflect regional stylistic differences in the later phases. During the Late phase of the Linear culture, the Želiezovce style is found in the eastern flank of the Linear culture area and the Šarka style in the western part. The breakup into stylistic zones probably reflects more intense communication and trade between Linear communities within individual style areas and an increased frequency of regional endogamy as population density increased. The greater density of Linear settlements in any particular region offered an opportunity to find a mate closer to home.

Furthermore, during the Middle and Late phases of the Linear culture, ceramics of the so-called Bükk culture appear in Slovakia and northeastern Hungary, like a wedge in the territory of the Linear style. The Bükk pottery is better made and is ornamented with incised spirals, lines, meanders, and geometric forms. The incised lines frequently are much more closely spaced than those on the Linear ceramics (Figure 4.8).

Around 3900–3800 B.C. (4540–4470 B.C.), the Linear ceramics disappeared in central Europe and the Stroke Ornamented, Lengyel, and Rössen styles of ceramics begin to dominate at archaeological sites (Figure 4.9) (Quitta 1967:264). This stylistic change signifies, in traditional nomenclature, the beginnings of the Middle Neolithic. Indeed, the Lengyel style began to develop in Czechoslovakia and Hungary around 4000 B.C. (4600 B.C.). It should be noted that archaeologists frequently put the beginning of the Middle Neolithic around 3600–3500 (4350–4190) B.C. based on the radiocarbon dates in central Europe. For our purposes, it is the disappearance of the Linear ceramics that marks the end of the Early Neolithic in central Europe. There are many changes in pottery form and ornamentation throughout the entire Neolithic period, but frequently we do not know what these changes imply. It is often unclear how these changes are associated with sociopolitical, economic, ritual, or any other changes.

Around 3800 B.C. (4470 B.C.), the earliest Neolithic cultures appeared in

**Figure 4.8.** Bükk ceramics. (From Lichardus 1974.)

the Alpine zone—cultures such as the Cortaillod culture in Switzerland. The first farming societies in England also date from this time. The earliest Neolithic cultures in Switzerland, northern and central France, and England are probably related to those in central Europe.

By the end of the Linear ceramic phase, farming groups were undoubtedly penetrating into western Europe, into regions still occupied by hunters and

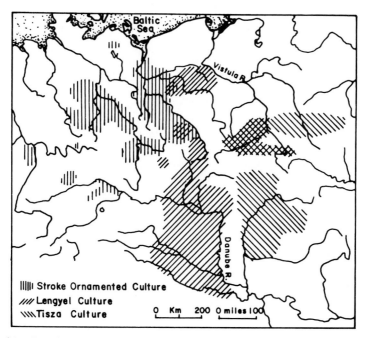

**Figure 4.9.** Distribution of Stroked Ornamented pottery, Lengyel and Tisza sites. (After Kamieńska and Kozlowski 1970.)

gatherers (Case 1976). These latter populations may have been eliminated or absorbed by the Neolithic peoples, or they may themselves have adopted farming. Any of these processes, or others, could account for the appearance of these new archaeological manifestations. Unfortunately, archaeologists have devoted little attention to the problem of the interaction between farmers and hunters and gatherers so that little can be said, as yet, about the processes that actually occurred at this time.

The latest farming societies to appear in Europe were in the northern regions such as Scandinavia, the Baltic states, and Byelorussia. For example, the first farmers in Denmark date to around 3500 B.C. (4190 B.C.). As previously mentioned, in the most northerly regions of Europe, that is, in the tundra zone, hunters and gatherers persisted until recent times.

*Chapter 5*
_____

# Early Neolithic

## Economic Organization: Subsistence Strategies

This chapter deals with the different food resources exploited by the Early Neolithic farmers in Europe: cultivated plants and domesticated animals, and wild game, fish, and plant foods. Land-use patterns in the Early Neolithic are also discussed, as well as the patterns of interregional exchange that existed at that time.

However, we should treat with caution claims of various archaeologists concerning differences in the roles played by plants and animals in the Early Neolithic sites of Europe. Usually they attempt to explain that these differences are caused by ecological and cultural factors. But these differences may be artificially caused by differential preservation of bone and plant material, chronological factors, different archaeological excavation techniques, or sampling errors.

### Greece

The economy of Early Neolithic villages in Greece and adjacent areas of Bulgaria and Yugoslavia was based on domesticated animals and plants supplemented by wild animals and plant foods. Fishing can be inferred from the presence at some sites of fish bones, shells, and bone fishhooks. However, when dealing with the subsistence of the Neolithic people in Greece or any other regions in Europe, we must consider the potential productivity of the various subsistence activities, agriculture, gardening, and animal husbandry, plus hunting, fishing, and gathering. The productivity from these different resources varied among Neolithic societies, just as the availability of potential resources probably fluctuated from year to year. We should also note that the potential yield of a food resource is largely determined by the techniques by which it is exploited. For example, during the Early Neolithic at least, farming was done using hoes and digging sticks, not plows, for which no evidence has been found. We would expect that such horticulture would not be as productive as plow agriculture.

We should not overlook the fact that the collecting of wild plants and the hunting of animals played an important role in the subsistence strategies of the Neolithic people. The role of such activities has traditionally been underestimated by archaeologists, who rather simplistically equated the Neolithic with an exclusively farming adaptation, in contrast to the exclusively collecting subsistence strategies of the Mesolithic.

The appearance of agricultural villages in Europe does not imply neglect of nondomestic food resources. The simple agriculture of Neolithic people probably had fluctuating results, good and bad years, and in lean years hunting and gathering could have made a great difference. Thus, agriculture can be considered as just one subsystem of a larger mixed subsistence strategy.

Our picture of Neolithic subsistence activities is far from complete. The poor preservation of organic remains, the lack of careful recovery of such materials, and the general lack of interest in subsistence strategies by many archaeologists have all combined to give us little data on which to base an analysis of Neolithic subsistence.

Judging from the bone remains recovered at Argissa (Greece), Nea Nikomedeia (Greece), and Anza I (Yugoslav Macedonia), sheep–goats were numerically predominant in faunal assemblage. Perhaps these animals played a role in rituals, as is suggested by clay figurines of the animals found at these sites. However, cattle supplied the largest amount of meat (Table 5.1). The particular emphasis on sheep–goats that is apparent in Greece and adjacent areas is appropriate to the Mediterranean environment. As in many other Neolithic villages, more than half of the domestic animals at Nea Nikomedeia were killed in their immature stage. This suggests that young animals were slaughtered for meat. The killing of young males especially would be an efficient method of herd cropping or culling, since only a few males would be required to maintain the herd size. It would be inefficient to keep many young males during the winter when fodder is limited. Some of the wild animals that are represented by one or two bones at a site might be accounted for by natural death.

The role played by various animals in the subsistence strategies of the Neolithic people is not easy to establish because there are various ways of interpreting the archaeological data. One problem is whether archaeologists use the actual count of the bones of a given species or attempt to estimate the minimum number of individual animals. Also, the identification of specific species from bone remains is not a simple matter. For example, it is not easy to differentiate domestic pig or cattle from the wild variety. Some scholars, such

TABLE 5.1  Frequency of Animals and Amount of Usable Meat at Anza I[a]

|  | Kilograms of usable meat[d] | Number of animals | Percentage of total number of animals | Total estimated weight | Percentage of estimated weight | Kilograms of usable meat from total estimated weight |
|---|---|---|---|---|---|---|
| Cattle (700)[b,c] | 350 | 12 | 10.9 | 8,400 | 60.0 | 4,200 |
| Sheep–goat (25) | 12.5 | 80 | 72.7 | 2,000 | 14.3 | 1,000 |
| Pig (30) | 15 | 8 | 7.2 | 240 | 1.7 | 120 |
| Dog (10) | 5 | 2 | 1.8 | 20 | 0.2 | 10 |
| Aurochs (900) | 450 | 3 | 2.7 | 2,700 | 19.3 | 1,350 |
| Red deer (190) | 95 | 2 | 1.8 | 380 | 2.7 | 190 |
| Wild pig (107.5) | 53.75 | 2 | 1.8 | 215 | 1.5 | 107.5 |
| Hare (4.5) | 2.25 | 1 | 0.9 | 4.5 | — | 2.25 |
| Totals |  | 110 | 99.8 | 13,979.5 | 99.7 | 6,989.75 |

[a] Data are from Gimbutas 1974.
[b] Numbers in parentheses indicate estimated adult weight in kilograms.
[c] Weights except for dog are based on Clason 1973.
[d] Kilograms of usable meat represent 50% of estimated weight.

as Tsalkin, combined the domestic cattle with aurochs in one group because the ranges of variation in various morphological features of these species overlap to a considerable degree. It is also frequently impossible to differentiate goats from sheep.

In analyzing the subsistence role played by domesticated and wild animals, I use, whenever possible, the minimum number of individuals of different species present at a site and not the number of bones. This will show not only the proportion of the various animals in the economy, but also the quantity of available meat. The same number of cattle and sheep may occur at a site, but from cattle the quantity of available meat may be 10 times greater. In estimating the weight of animals, I ignore the differences due to sex and age, that is, that juveniles weigh less than adults and that females usually weigh less than males. Thus, I estimate the weight based on adult animals. It should be pointed out that palaeozoologists use varied methods in estimating the minimum number of individuals, and frequently it remains unclear how they arrive at their estimates in the various publications. Archaeologists should always be aware of the problems when using the estimates of the minimum number of individuals made by various palaeozoologists.

The difference in the number of calories obtained from the various sources of meat is equally impressive. A kilogram of sheep or goat meat supplies roughly 1500 calories, cattle 2000 calories, and pig 3700 calories (Flannery 1969).

A considerable controversy exists about whether to estimate the number of animals present at a site by calculating the minimum number of individuals or by simply counting the number of bones. The use of the minimum number of individuals in estimating the importance of different animal species can alter our views about Neolithic subsistence. For example, Soudský states that 80% of the animals present at Bylany, Czechoslovakia, were cattle (Soudský and Pavlů 1972:323). However, this is based on the number of cattle bones found at the site. But by using the minimum number of individuals, the proportion of cattle decreases to 25%. However, the weight of edible meat from cattle makes up 60% of the total weight of edible meat represented at the site when using the minimum number of individuals. Furthermore, in terms of the different amounts of calories per kilogram available from different kinds of meat, 80% of the food energy derived from meat at this site was supplied by cattle. Thus we have come full circle back to Soudský's original figure. These different approaches to interpreting animal remains can be used in various ways to support one's favorite hypothesis.

The plants cultivated by the Early Neolithic farmers of Greece (Table 5.2) differed in yield, vitamin content, resistance to disease, and climate and soil needs, and therefore in their usage. The variability in plant cultigens thus reflects the ecological variability with which the early farmers were faced or a very mixed subsistence strategy. Failure of one type of crop in a mixed strategy is not necessarily associated with failure of other crop types. This gives farmers insurance against failure of one crop.

Wheat was the most important plant in the economy. Emmer wheat is present at most of the sites, and it is represented by the greatest percentage of specimens at Ghediki (Murray 1970). Throughout the Neolithic and later periods different varieties of wheat, but particularly emmer, were extensively cultivated in the temperate zones of Europe. Wheat grows best on well-drained brown clay soils. It needs comparatively high winter temperatures and annual rainfall of about 50.8–76.2 cm (J. Renfrew 1973:65). Although new varieties of wheat came into use throughout European prehistory, the older types persisted. In addition, variations among wheat species in their tolerance of cold weather, resistance to diseases, and yield and usage ensured that a variety of wheat types would be cultivated in different areas in temperate Europe. For example, the occurrence of bread wheat in greater quantities during the Bronze Age and Iron Age did not mean elimination of other types such as spelt wheat. Although bread wheat is more prolific and more easily harvested and threshed than the spelt wheat (Jarman 1972:19), the latter species has greater winter hardiness and resistance to smut and rust fungi. In areas where there is a greater possibility of frost damage for the sown wheat, spelt wheat would have been a good choice for planting.

Barley is a hardier cereal than wheat, and it can be cultivated on poorer soils. Furthermore, barley exhausts the soil less than wheat. Barley prefers loam soils, but it also tolerates alkaline conditions. It can be grown on soils derived from chalk or limestone.

**TABLE 5.2  Domesticated and Wild Plants Found in Early Neolithic Sites in Southeastern Europe, 6000–4500 B.C. (7000–5240 B.C.)[a]**

| Sites | Wheat, unspecified | Einkorn wheat | Emmer wheat | Bread wheat | Club wheat | Barley, unspecified | Barley, hulled, two-row | Barley, naked, two-row | Barley, hulled, six-row | Oats | Millet | Peas | Lentils | Vetch | Acorns | Pistachio nuts | Cornelian cherry | Apples | Blackberry | Grape | Flax |
|---|---|---|---|---|---|---|---|---|---|---|---|---|---|---|---|---|---|---|---|---|---|
| Nea Nikomedeia, Greece | X | | | | | | | | | | | | | | | | | | | | |
| Knossos, Crete | | | X | X | | | X | | | | | | X | | | | | | | | |
| Ghediki, Greece | | | | | | X | | | | | | | | | | | | | | | |
| Aceramic layer | | X | X | | | | X | | | | | | | | | | | | | | |
| Sesklo, Greece | | | | | | | | | | | | | | | | | | | | | |
| Aceramic layer | | | X | | | | | X | | | | X | X | X | | X | | | | | |
| Argissa, Greece | | | | | | | | | | | | | | | | | | | | | |
| Aceramic layer | | X | X | | | | | | | | | X | | | X | X | | | | | |
| Achilleion, Greece | | | | | | | | | X | | X | | X | | | | | | | | |
| Aceramic layer | | | X | | | | | | | | | | | | | | | | | | |
| Soufli, Greece | | | | | | | | | | | | | | | | | | | | | |
| Aceramic layer | | | X | | | | | | | X | | | | | X | X | | | | | |
| Karanovo I, Bulgaria | | X | X | | | | | | | | | | X | | | | | | | X | |
| Azmak, Bulgaria | | X | X | X | | | | | X | | | | X | | | | | X | X | X | |
| Obre I, Yugoslavia | | X | X | | X | | | | | | | X | | | | | X | X | X | X | |
| Chevdar, Bulgaria | | X | X | X | | X | | | | | X | X | | | | | X | X | X | X | X |

[a] Data are from J. M. Renfrew 1969, 1973; Murray 1970; Gimbutas 1970; Hopf 1975.

## *Mediterranean*

The farmers of the so-called Cardial or Impresso culture of the Early Neolithic in Dalmatia, Italy, Provence, Spain, and the Mediterranean islands possessed domestic cattle, sheep–goats, barley, and einkorn, emmer, and bread wheat. Barley, in particular, apparently was cultivated extensively by these people. The percentage of barley in some sites is very high in comparison to other cereals. For example, at Cova de l'Or cave in Spain, einkorn wheat amounts to .89%, emmer wheat 13.4%, bread wheat 20.2%, whereas six-row barley is 65.44% (Hopf 1971a). A subsistence strategy based on barley and sheep–goats is particularly suitable to the hot, dry Mediterranean environment. However, at Alcoy, Valencia, the percentage of barley drops to 14% (Hopf 1971b).

## *Southeastern Europe*

The Early Neolithic villagers in southeastern Europe cultivated emmer wheat, einkorn wheat, club wheat, barley, millet, lentils, and legumes. The lentils may have been wild as is suggested by the small size of seeds recovered from Azmak, Bulgaria (J. Renfrew 1969:154). Remains of bread wheat were also found, but it is unclear if it was separately cultivated from emmer wheat. However, Hopf's (1975) analysis of plant remains from the Azmak mound in Bulgaria, shows that in some occupation layers bread wheat predominated (Table 5.3). Around 6000 B.C. bread wheat was already found at Knossos, Crete.

Emmer wheat was also the most extensively cultivated plant in southeastern Europe (Table 5.3). As previously mentioned, it is quite sensitive to environmental variation, having only a very limited tolerance of changes in soil conditions, temperature, and rainfall. It would have been risky to rely exclusively on growing emmer, for a bad harvest could threaten the existence of the entire community. Insurance was provided by other domesticated and wild

TABLE 5.3  Frequencies of Plant Remains Found at the Azmak Mound (Karanovo I Culture, Occupation Layers I, II, III)[a]

| | Occupation layer I C[14] date Bln 292 4928 ± 100 B.C. Number of grains | Occupation layer II Number of grains | Occupation layer III C[14] date Bln 297 4725 ± 100 B.C. Number of grains |
|---|---|---|---|
| Emmer wheat | 218 | 204 | 50 |
| Einkorn wheat | | 22 | |
| Bread wheat | | 527 | |
| Bread-club wheat | | | 10 |
| Six-row barley | 9 | 2 | 1 |

[a] Data are from Hopf 1975.

plants or animals. Thus, the cultivation of barley, the hunting of wild animals, and the collecting of wild plants were very important in the subsistence strategy. As previously mentioned, barley is a hardier cereal than emmer wheat, and it could be very important in years of poor wheat harvest. The utilization of wild animals and plants served a similar function.

Until recent years, the remains of wild plants were seldom recovered by archaeologists, but now we have data from several Early Neolithic sites in southeastern Europe. At the site of Chevdar in Bulgaria, blackberry, grape, flax, and Cornelian cherry were found (Dennel 1972, 1974). Dennel (1974) thinks that flax grew in wheat fields as a segetal plant. It could have been used for making fibers or oil. In addition, apples were found at the Obre I site in Yugoslavia (J. Renfrew 1973: 203–204).

Dennel's (1972) work on plant remains from Early Neolithic sites in Bulgaria is very interesting. He demonstrates very clearly how different archaeological contexts can produce different frequencies of plant remains (Table 5.4). Cereal remains occur in different frequencies on the house floors and in the pits, ovens, or middens. For example, at the Chevdar site, emmer wheat recovered from ovens varied in frequencies from 7.2 to 94.3%, whereas the frequencies of emmer found on the floor of the houses ranged from 18.8

TABLE 5.4  Plant Remains from Chevdar and Kazanluk[a]

| | Percentage of total sample | | | | | | | Total number of seeds in sample |
|---|---|---|---|---|---|---|---|---|
| | | Bread | | | | | | |
| | Einkorn | Emmer wheat | Barley | (Cereals) | Legumes | Fruit | Others | |
| Chevdar: Contents of samples from floors, ovens, and burnt clay | | | | | | | | |
| Floors | 4.4 | 30.9 | — | 13.2 | (48.5) | 38.5 | 0.8 | 12.5 | 136 |
| | 5.9 | 29.9 | 2.6 | 34.2 | (72.5) | 12.8 | 0.9 | 13.7 | 117 |
| | 1.3 | 33.9 | 0.4 | 40.6 | (76.3) | 11.6 | — | 12.1 | 224 |
| | 0.9 | 18.8 | — | 25.2 | (44.9) | 15.6 | 29.4 | 10.1 | 218 |
| Ovens | 1.2 | 94.3 | 3.1 | 0.4 | (99.0) | 0.4 | — | 0.8 | 1,000 |
| | 2.1 | 90.7 | 2.9 | 2.6 | (98.3) | — | — | 1.7 | 1,000 |
| | 1.4 | 84.6 | 1.8 | 6.6 | (94.4) | 0.7 | 1.4 | 3.5 | 147 |
| | 0.7 | 7.2 | 0.8 | 88.6 | (97.3) | 0.2 | 0.6 | 1.9 | 1,109 |
| Burnt clay | | Rare | | Very common | | | | | |
| Kazanluk: Contents of samples from floors and middens | | | | | | | | |
| Floors | 8.9 | 55.1 | 1.2 | 14.4 | (79.4) | 10.1 | — | 9.6 | 167 |
| | 11.3 | 60.4 | 3.3 | 4.2 | (79.2) | 7.3 | 2.3 | 11.3 | 576 |
| Middens | 3.3 | 25.0 | 6.5 | 14.1 | (48.9) | 32.6 | — | 18.5 | 92 |
| | — | 26.0 | 1.0 | 6.3 | (33.3) | 43.8 | 2.1 | 20.8 | 96 |
| | 3.6 | 40.1 | 1.0 | 18.5 | (63.2) | 25.0 | 2.4 | 9.5 | 168 |
| | 3.9 | 23.5 | 3.9 | 5.9 | (37.2) | 50.9 | 2.0 | 9.9 | 102 |

[a] From R. W. Dennel, The interpretation of plant remains: Bulgaria. In *Papers in economic prehistory*, edited by E. S. Higgs. New York: Cambridge University Press, 1972.

to 33.9%. It is evident that some of the suggested differences in the subsistence strategies of the Neolithic communities may be accounted for by sampling errors in the excavations of individual sites.

Cattle, sheep–goat, pig, and dog were domesticated animals kept by the villagers in southeastern Europe. At this time cattle started to play a more important role in the economy, as is shown by the increase in cattle bone in relation to sheep–goat at Starčevo sites. However, sheep–goat still predominates at some Körös sites in Hungary and Yugoslavia (Table 5.5).

A great variety of wild animals were hunted by Early Neolithic farmers in southeastern Europe, but most were wild ungulates, that is, hoofed animals such as wild pigs and aurochs. The percentages of wild ungulates appear smaller at some sites because of various small animals such as hare. However, the contribution of wild ungulates to the diet in terms of the total weight of meat was much greater than that shown by bone percentages. Most of them were forest animals, such as red deer. At Lepenski Vir, this animal was the most important one in the diet (Table 5.6). The location of this site would have necessitated a subsistence strategy based on hunting and fishing. Lepenski Vir is located along the Danube River in the Iron Gates area of Yugoslavia; in this location we would not expect to find a community relying mainly on domesticates. The nonforest animals are represented by the wild ass that inhabits parklands. The presence of chamois at Lepenski Vir in a Starčevo culture layer indicates hunting in the mountains was practiced. Wild animals not only supplied meat for food, but also raw materials. Bone and antler were utilized for making tools such as awls, points, "shovels," and sickle handles. Skins could be utilized for clothing. Bökönyi's (1974) analysis of bone remains from Körös sites shows a great variety of wild birds and some fish (Table 5.5), even though most species are represented by very small numbers.

### Central Europe

In central Europe, we have good data on the subsistence strategy of the first farmers. Over two decades ago when Childe (1957) presented his brilliant synthesis of European prehistory, only a limited quantity of data was available for the subsistence activities of the Linear people. This consisted mainly of domestic plant remains: wheat, barley, oats, flax, lentils, and peas.

Further studies have allowed us to broaden our concept of the economy of Linear people. For example, at Langweiler, Germany (2, 3, and 6C sites), a variety of domestic and wild plants were recovered (Table 5.7). At two Polish Linear sites, Strzelce (Klichowska 1959) and Olszanica (J. Kozłowski and Kulczycka 1961), as well as at Wien-Vöseldorf in Austria (Brandtner 1949), rye was found, although probably it was occurring as a weed together with other cereal remains. Wheat was the most important cereal in the Linear culture economy and probably the main source of carbohydrates. Emmer wheat was the most extensively cultivated. For example, at Bylany in Czecho-

**TABLE 5.5  Frequency of Animals and Estimated Amount of Usable Meat at Körös Sites**[a]

| | Kilograms of usable meat | Number of animals | Percentage of total number of animals | Total estimated weight in kilograms | Percentage of estimated weight | Kilograms of usable meat from total estimated weight |
|---|---|---|---|---|---|---|
| **Köszke-Ludvar, Hungary** | | | | | | |
| Cattle (700)[b] | 350 | 15 | 9 | 10,500 | 34 | 5,250 |
| Sheep–goat (25) | 12.5 | 64 | 39 | 1,600 | 5 | 800 |
| Pig (30) | 15 | 4 | 2 | 120 | — | 60 |
| Dog (10) | 5 | 5 | 3 | 50 | — | 25 |
| Aurochs (900) | 450 | 12 | 7 | 10,800 | 35 | 5,400 |
| Wild horse (600) | 300 | — | — | — | — | — |
| Red deer (190) | 95 | 24 | 15 | 4,560 | 15 | 2,280 |
| Roe deer (21) | 10.5 | 10 | 6 | 210 | 1 | 105 |
| Wild pig (107.5) | 53.75 | 14 | 9 | 1,505 | 5 | 752.5 |
| Wild ass (350) | 175 | 5 | 3 | 1,750 | 6 | 875 |
| Other wild animals[c,d] | — | 12 | 7 | — | — | — |
| Totals | | 165 | | 31,095 | | |
| **Ludas-Budzsák, Yugoslavia** | | | | | | |
| Cattle (700)[b] | | 25 | 12 | 17,500 | 46 | 8,750 |
| Sheep–goat (25) | 12.5 | 124 | 58.5 | 3,100 | 8 | 1,550 |
| Pig (30) | 15 | 3 | 1.5 | 90 | — | 45 |
| Dog (10) | 5 | 3 | 1.5 | 30 | — | 15 |
| Aurochs (900) | 450 | 8 | 4 | 7,200 | 19 | 3,600 |
| Wild horse (600) | 300 | — | — | — | — | — |
| Red deer (190) | 95 | 8 | 4 | 1,520 | 4 | 760 |
| Roe deer (21) | 10.5 | 7 | 3 | 147 | — | 73.5 |
| Wild pig (107.5) | 53.75 | 3 | 1.5 | 3,225 | 8 | 1,612.5 |
| Wild ass (350) | 175 | 16 | 7.5 | 5,600 | 14.5 | 2,800 |
| Other wild animals[c,d] | — | 15 | 7 | — | — | — |
| Totals | | 212 | | 38,412 | | |

[a] Data are from Bökönyi 1974.

[b] Numbers in parentheses indicate estimated adult weight in kilograms.

[c] In addition, the following wild birds and fish were found at Köszke-Ludvar: catfish 1, pike 1, fish 26, European pond tortoise 11, cormorant 1, grey heron 2, grey leg goose 2, wild goose 1, mallard 1, tufted duck 2, short-toed eagle 1, black grouse 1, demoiselle crane 1, great bustard 1, curlew 1, wood pigeon 1, birds 4.

[d] In addition, the following wild birds and fish were found at Ludas-Budzsák: unidentified fish 6, catfish 1, carp 1, pike 1, European pond tortoise 5, birds 29.

slovakia, 80% of the recovered wheat is emmer, 15% is einkorn, and 5% is bread or club wheat. Tempir (1971: 1326) analyzed the wheat remains from 14 pits at Opava-Katerinky in Czechoslovakia, and in 12 of the pits the percentages for emmer wheat ranged between 62.2 and 78.1%, while those for einkorn ranged between 21.9 and 36.8%. However, at Langweiler in Germany einkorn remains predominant.

**TABLE 5.6** Frequency of Animal Bones at Lepenski Vir[a]

| | Phase I | | Phase II | | Phase III | |
|---|---|---|---|---|---|---|
| | Number of bones | Percentage of total number of bones | Number of bones | Percentage of total number of bones | Number of bones | Percentage of total number of bones |
| Cattle | | | | | 375 | 15.8 |
| Sheep–goat | | | | | 81 | 3.4 |
| Pig | | | | | 8 | 0.3 |
| Dog | 21 | 4.9 | 23 | 11.2 | 140 | 5.9 |
| Aurochs | 14 | 3.3 | 7 | 3.4 | 174 | 7.3 |
| Chamois | | | | | 2 | 0.1 |
| Red deer | 115 | 27.1 | 111 | 53.9 | 862 | 36.4 |
| Roe deer | 4 | 0.9 | 1 | 0.5 | 36 | 1.5 |
| Wild swine | 10 | 2.4 | 6 | 2.9 | 211 | 8.9 |
| Wild ass | | | | | 7 | 0.3 |
| Wild cat | | | | | 1 | |
| Lynx | | | | | 6 | 0.2 |
| Marten | 6 | 1.4 | 3 | 1.4 | 3 | 0.1 |
| Badger | 3 | 0.7 | | | 7 | 0.3 |
| Brown bear | | | 1 | 0.5 | 27 | 1.1 |
| Wolf | | | | | 7 | 0.3 |
| Fox | | | | | 1 | |
| Beaver | 2 | 0.5 | | | 4 | 0.2 |
| Brown hare | | | | | 7 | 0.3 |
| Birds | 6 | 1.4 | 1 | 0.5 | 10 | 0.4 |
| Cyprinids | 86 | 20.3 | 1 | 0.5 | 14 | 0.6 |
| Catfish | 3 | 0.7 | 5 | 2.4 | 22 | 0.9 |
| Other fishes | 154 | 36.3 | 47 | 22.8 | 364 | 15.4 |
| Totals | 424 | | 206 | | 2369 | |

[a] From S. Bökönyi, Animal remains from Lepenski Vir. *Science* 167:1702–1704. Copyright 1970 by the American Association for the Advancement of Science.

TABLE 5.7  Domesticated and Wild Plants Found at Langweiler 2, 3, and 6C Sites in Germany[a]

| | Langweiler 6C<br>Sample size: 21.4dm³[b]<br>Number of samples: 5 | Langweiler 3<br>Sample size: 11.9dm³<br>Number of samples: 5 | Langweiler 2<br>Sample size: 48.9dm³<br>Number of samples: 84 |
|---|---|---|---|
| Einkorn wheat<br>(*Triticum monococcum*) | | | |
| Grain | 15 | 8 | 38 |
| Spikelet | 19 | 289 | 156 |
| Glume | 68 | 3,147 | 620 |
| Emmer wheat<br>(*Triticum dicoccum*) | | | |
| Grain | 24 | 3 | 38 |
| Spikelet | 9 | 113 | 63 |
| Glume | 27 | 299 | 129 |
| Einkorn–Emmer | | | |
| Grain | 149 | 66 | 546 |
| Spikelet | 54 | 460 | 75 |
| Glume | 4 | 141 | — |
| Rye brome (*Bromus secalinus*) | 154 | 27 | 380 |
| Peas (*Pisum sativum*) | 6 | 2 | — |
| Horsebean (*Vicia cf. birsuta*) | — | — | 4 |
| Lentil (*Lens culinaris*) | — | — | 1 |
| Flax (*Linum usitatissimum*) | — | — | 8 |
| Broomcorn millet (*Panicum sp.*) | — | 1 | — |

*(continued)*

[a] Data are from Knörzer 1972, 1973.
[b] dm = decimeter; 10 dm = 1 m.

TABLE 5.7 (Continued)

| | Langweiler 6C Sample size:21.4dm³ᵇ Number of samples:5 | Langweiler 3 Sample size:11.9dm³ Number of samples:5 | Langweiler 2 Sample size:48.9dm³ Number of samples:84 |
|---|---|---|---|
| Cockspur grass (Panicum crus-galli) | — | — | 2 |
| Opium poppy (Papaver setigerum) | 2 | — | 4 |
| Hazelnut (Corylus avellana) | 1 | 1 | 7 |
| Mallow (Malva sp.) | — | — | 2 |
| Wild apple (Pyrus malus) | — | — | 8 |
| Sloe (Prunus spinosa) | — | — | 3 |
| Goosefoot (Chenopodium album) | 489 | 317 | 1,749 |
| Oak-leaved goosefoot (Chenopodium cf. glaucum) | — | — | 4 |
| Goosefoot (Chenopodium sp.) | 47 | — | — |
| Black bindweed (Polygonum convolvulus) | 49 | 13 | 87 |
| Timothy grass (cf. Phleum sp.) | 17 | — | 111 |
| Barren brome (Bromus sterilis) | 4 | 3 | 19 |
| Pink weed or persicaria (Polygonum persicaria) | 3 | — | 3 |
| Sorrel (Rumex tenuifolius) | 1 | — | 1 |
| Dock (Rumex sp.) | — | — | 14 |
| Nipplewort (Lapsana communis) | 1 | — | 6 |
| Cleavers (Galium spurium) | — | 1 | 5 |
| Blue grass (Poa sp.) | — | — | 3 |
| Red fescue grass (Fastuca cf. rubra) | — | — | 1 |
| (Silene Nutans) | — | — | 1 |

Müller (1964) has analyzed bone remains from Linear culture sites in the German Democratic Republic and found that a wide range of domesticated and wild animals were exploited. Thus it is evident that the subsistence of Linear people was based on agriculture, the keeping of livestock, gardening, hunting, fishing, and gathering. Hunting probably played a greater role in the economy than has been emphasized by archaeologists who have relied primarily on Müller's analysis. Müller's analysis shows only 10% or less of wild animals among the bones at various sites. However, the analysis of faunal material from other areas in Europe, utilizing the minimum number of individuals derived from the bones found, raises this estimate of the percentage of wild animals to 20%, 30%, or even higher (Table 5.8). This estimate probably comes closer to reality. The discrepancy between using percentage of bones or the minimum number of individuals derived from the bones found was discussed earlier. Fishing and exploitation of water fowl is indicated by finds of carp, sturgeon, wild goose, and wild duck remains (Müller 1964).

Domesticated cattle usually played the most important role in the economy in terms of the quantity of meat available for human consumption. Wild ungulates such as aurochs, red deer, wild pigs, and horses contributed the greatest percentage of meat among wild animals. It appears that castration of bulls was already practiced (Müller 1964). They may have been used as draft animals, but no ard (primitive plow) marks in the fields or wheels are found at this time in central Europe. Males can be disruptive in a herd of animals; one way of eliminating this problem is to kill them when young or castrate them. As the Early Neolithic populations expanded from southeastern Europe, the importance of pigs relative to sheep–goats increased in the economy. Deciduous-forest environments are ideal for pig breeding. Keeping pigs would have been very efficient in such an environment, since they have a very high reproduction rate. One female pig produces several offspring per litter.

Among contemporary tribal societies, pig breeding is very important in Melanesia. Pigs are important in Melanesia not merely as a food source, but as the currency of social relations: Pork is consumed on ceremonial occasions, and debts can be paid off with the meat or the animals. However, as their numbers increase, pigs create social problems, such as wandering into a neighbor's garden and eating the neighbor's crops (Rappaport 1967). I assume that pigs may likewise have caused some disruption in the Linear culture villages.

In discussing or trying to explain the observable range of variation exhibited by the faunal and floral remains found at different Linear sites, we should always ask whether our data are representative for the period, region, or even the particular sites. In some cases, even this is not true. In order to make valid generalizations, we need to assume that in most cases the data are representative. However, we should be skeptical about unique or nonrepresentative sites. For example, an examination of the relative frequencies of various species of animals at 12 Linear sites reveals that the Hungarian site of Györ

**TABLE 5.8** Frequency of Animals and Estimated Amount of Usable Meat at Linear Sites

| | Kilograms of usable meat | Number of animals | Percentage of total number of animals | Total estimated weight in kilograms | Percentage of estimated weight | Kilograms of usable meat from total estimated weight |
|---|---|---|---|---|---|---|
| Müddersheim, Germany[a] | | | | | | |
| Cattle (700)[b] | 350 | 7 | 27 | 4,900 | 47 | 2,450 |
| Sheep–goat (25) | 12.5 | 4 | 15 | 100 | .01 | 50 |
| Pig (30) | 15 | 3 | 12 | 90 | .01 | 45 |
| Dog (10) | 5 | 1 | 4 | 10 | — | 5 |
| Aurochs (900) | 450 | 4 | 15 | 3,600 | 35 | 1,800 |
| Wild horse (600) | 300 | 2 | 8 | 1,200 | 12 | 600 |
| Red deer (190) | 95 | 1 | 4 | 190 | .02 | 95 |
| Roe deer (21) | 10.5 | 1 | 4 | 21 | — | 10.5 |
| Wild pig (107.5) | 53.75 | 2 | 8 | 215 | .02 | 107.5 |
| Other wild animals[c] | — | 1 | 4 | — | — | — |
| Totals | | 26 | | 10,326 | | |
| Bylany, Czechoslovakia[d] | | | | | | |
| Cattle (700)[b] | 350 | 7 | 25 | 4,900 | 76 | 2,450 |
| Sheep–goat (25) | 12.5 | 3 | 11 | 75 | 1 | 37.5 |
| Pig (30) | 15 | 8 | 29 | 240 | 4 | 120 |
| Dog (10) | 5 | 1 | 4 | 10 | — | 5 |
| Aurochs (900) | 450 | 1 | 4 | 900 | 14 | 450 |
| Wild horse (600) | 300 | — | — | — | — | — |
| Red deer (190) | 95 | 1 | 4 | 190 | 3 | 95 |
| Roe deer (21) | 10.5 | 1 | 4 | 21 | — | 10.5 |
| Wild pig (107.5) | 53.75 | 1 | 4 | 107.5 | 2 | 53.75 |
| Other wild animals[a] | — | 5 | 18 | — | — | — |
| Totals | | 28 | | 6,443.5 | | |
| Jeleni Louka, Czechoslovakia[e] | | | | | | |
| Cattle (700)[b] | 350 | 8 | 26 | 5,600 | 72 | 2,800 |
| Sheep–goat (25) | 12.5 | 11 | 36 | 275 | .035 | 137.5 |
| Pig (30) | 15 | 4 | 13 | 120 | .015 | 60 |
| Dog (10) | 5 | 1 | 3 | 10 | — | 5 |
| Aurochs (900) | 450 | 1 | 3 | 900 | .115 | 450 |
| Wild horse (600) | 300 | 1 | 3 | 600 | 8 | 300 |
| Red deer (190) | 95 | 1 | 3 | 190 | 2 | 95 |
| Roe deer (21) | 10.5 | 1 | 3 | 21 | — | 10.5 |
| Wild pig (107.5) | 53.75 | 1 | 3 | 107.5 | 1 | 53.75 |
| Other wild animals[c] | — | 2 | 6 | — | — | — |
| Totals | | 31 | | 7,823.5 | | |

[a] Data are from Stampfli 1965.
[b] Numbers in parentheses represent estimated adult weight in kilograms.
[c] In estimating the weight of animals, the category "other wild animals" was not included.
[d] Data are from Clason 1967.
[e] Data are from Kratochvil 1972.

(*continued*)

# TABLE 5.8 (Continued)

| | Kilograms of usable meat | Number of animals | Percentage of total number of animals | Total estimated weight in kilograms | Percentage of estimated weight | Kilograms of usable meat from total estimated weights |
|---|---|---|---|---|---|---|
| **Samborzec, Poland**[f] | | | | | | |
| Cattle (700)[b] | 350 | 36 | 36 | 25,200 | 75 | 12,600 |
| Sheep–goat (25) | 12.5 | 13 | 13 | 325 | 1 | 162.5 |
| Pig (30) | 15 | 24 | 24 | 720 | 2 | 360 |
| Dog (10) | 5 | — | — | — | — | — |
| Aurochs (900) | 450 | — | — | — | — | — |
| Wild horse (600) | 300 | 9 | 9 | 5,400 | 16 | 2,700 |
| Red deer (190) | 95 | 7 | 7 | 1,330 | 4 | 665 |
| Roe deer (21) | 10.5 | 5 | 5 | 105 | — | 52.5 |
| Wild pig (107.5) | 53.75 | 3 | 3 | 322.5 | 1 | 161.25 |
| Other wild animals[c] | — | 2 | 1 | — | — | — |
| Totals | | 99 | | 33,402.5 | | |
| **Györ Papai, Hungary**[g] | | | | | | |
| Cattle (700)[b] | 350 | 354 | 60 | 247,800 | 83 | 123,900 |
| Sheep–goat (25) | 12.5 | 100 | 17 | 2,500 | 1 | 1,250 |
| Pig (30) | 15 | 64 | 11 | 1,920 | 1 | 960 |
| Dog (10) | 5 | 5 | 0.8 | 50 | — | 25 |
| Aurochs (900) | 450 | 51 | 7 | 45,900 | 15 | 22,950 |
| Wild horse (600) | 300 | — | — | — | — | — |
| Red deer (190) | 95 | 2 | — | 380 | — | 190 |
| Roe deer (21) | 10.5 | 5 | 0.8 | 105 | — | 52.5 |
| Wild pig (107.5) | 53.75 | 8 | 1.2 | 860 | — | 430 |
| Other wild animals[c] | — | 1 | — | — | — | — |
| Totals | | 590 | | 299,515 | | |
| **Bekásmegyer-Vörös Csilag, Hungary**[h] | | | | | | |
| Cattle (700)[b] | 350 | 17 | 40 | 11,900 | 64 | 5,950 |
| Sheep–goat (25) | 12.5 | 8 | 19 | 200 | 1 | 100 |
| Pig (30) | 15 | 4 | 9 | 120 | 1 | 60 |
| Dog (10) | 5 | 1 | 2 | 10 | — | 5 |
| Aurochs (900) | 450 | 6 | 14 | 5,400 | 29 | 2,700 |
| Wild horse (600) | 300 | — | — | — | — | — |
| Red deer (190) | 95 | 3 | 7 | 570 | 3 | 285 |
| Roe deer (21) | 10.5 | — | — | — | — | — |
| Wild pig (107.5) | 53.75 | 3 | 7 | 322.5 | 2 | 161.25 |
| Other wild animals[c] | — | 1 | 2 | — | — | — |
| Totals | | 43 | | 18,522.5 | | |

(continued)

[f] Data are from Kulczycka-Leciejewiczowa 1970b.
[g] Data are from Bökönyi 1959.
[h] Data are from Bökönyi 1974.

TABLE 5.8 *(Continued)*

| | Kilograms of usable meat | Number of animals | Percentage of total number of animals | Total estimated weight in kilograms | Percentage of estimated weight | Kilograms of usable meat from total estimated weight |
|---|---|---|---|---|---|---|
| Pilismarót-Szobi Rév, Hungary[i] | | | | | | |
| Cattle (700)[b] | 350 | 7 | 35 | 4,900 | 68 | 2,450 |
| Sheep–goat (25) | 12.5 | 4 | 20 | 100 | 1 | 50 |
| Pig (30) | 15 | 3 | 15 | 90 | 1 | 45 |
| Dog (10) | 5 | 1 | 5 | 10 | — | 5 |
| Aurochs (900) | 450 | 2 | 10 | 1,800 | 25 | 900 |
| Wild horse (600) | 300 | — | — | — | — | — |
| Red deer (190) | 95 | 1 | 5 | 190 | 3 | 95 |
| Roe deer (21) | 10.5 | — | — | — | — | — |
| Wild pig (107.5) | 53.75 | 1 | 5 | 107.5 | 1.5 | 53.75 |
| Other wild animals[c] | — | 1 | 5 | — | — | — |
| Totals | | 20 | | 7,197.5 | | |
| Neszmély-Tekeres Patak, Hungary[j] | | | | | | |
| Cattle (700)[b] | 350 | 70 | 48 | 49,000 | 78 | 24,500 |
| Sheep–goat (25) | 12.5 | 32 | 22 | 253 | 0.5 | 126.5 |
| Pig (30) | 15 | 18 | 12.5 | 540 | 1 | 270 |
| Dog (10) | 5 | — | — | — | — | — |
| Aurochs (900) | 450 | 13 | 9 | 11,700 | 19 | 5,850 |
| Wild horse (600) | 300 | — | — | — | — | — |
| Red deer (190) | 95 | 5 | 3.5 | 950 | 1.5 | 475 |
| Roe deer (21) | 10.5 | 1 | 1 | 21 | — | 10.5 |
| Wild pig (107.5) | 53.75 | 3 | 2 | 322.5 | 0.5 | 161.25 |
| Other wild animals[c] | — | 3 | 2 | — | — | — |
| Totals | | 145 | | 62,786.5 | | |
| Pomaz-Zdravlyak, Hungary[k] | | | | | | |
| Cattle (700)[b] | 350 | 30 | 38 | 21,000 | 80 | 10,500 |
| Sheep–goat (25) | 12.5 | 17 | 22 | 425 | .016 | 212.5 |
| Pig (30) | 15 | 16 | 20 | 480 | .018 | 240 |
| Dog (10) | 5 | 3 | 4 | 30 | — | 15 |
| Aurochs (900) | 450 | 4 | 5 | 3,600 | 14 | 1,800 |
| Wild horse (600) | 300 | — | — | — | — | — |
| Red deer (190) | 95 | 2 | 2.5 | 380 | 1 | 190 |
| Roe deer (21) | 10.5 | 1 | 1 | 21 | — | 10.5 |
| Wild pig (107.5) | 53.75 | 4 | 5 | 430 | .016 | 215 |
| Other wild animals[c] | — | 2 | 1 | — | — | — |
| Totals | | 79 | | 26,366 | | |

*(continued)*

[i] Data are from Bökönyi 1974.
[j] Data are from Bökönyi 1974.
[k] Data are from Bökönyi 1959.

74

TABLE 5.8 *(Continued)*

| | Kilograms of usable meat | Number of animals | Percentage of total number of animals | Total estimated weight in kilograms | Percentage of estimated weight | Kilograms of usable meat from total estimated weight |
|---|---|---|---|---|---|---|
| **Floreshti, USSR[l,m]** | | | | | | |
| Cattle (700)[b] | 350 | 20 | 28 | 14,000 | .565 | 7,000 |
| Sheep–goat (25) | 12.5 | 6 | 8 | 150 | .006 | 75 |
| Pig (30) | 15 | 12 | 17 | 360 | 1 | 155 |
| Dog (10) | 5 | 4 | 5 | 40 | — | 20 |
| Aurochs (900) | 450 | 8 | 10 | 7,200 | 29 | 3,600 |
| Wild horse (600) | 300 | — | — | — | — | — |
| Red deer (190) | 95 | 10 | 13 | 1,900 | 8 | 950 |
| Roe deer (21) | 10.5 | 2 | 3 | 42 | — | 21 |
| Wild pig (107.5) | 53.75 | 10 | 13 | 1,075 | 4 | — |
| Other wild animals[c] | — | 4 | 5 | — | — | — |
| Totals | | 76 | | 24,767 | | |
| **Noviye Ruseshti, USSR[n,o]** | | | | | | |
| Cattle (700)[a] | 350 | 56 | 22 | 39,200 | 55 | 19,600 |
| Sheep–goat (25) | 12.5 | 36 | 14 | 900 | 1 | 450 |
| Pig (30) | 15 | 36 | 14 | 1,080 | .015 | 540 |
| Dog (10) | 5 | 5 | 2 | 50 | — | 25 |
| Aurochs (900) | 450 | 18 | 7 | 16,200 | 23 | 8,100 |
| Wild horse (600) | 300 | 17 | 6.5 | 10,200 | 14 | 5,100 |
| Red deer (190) | 95 | 12 | 5 | 2,280 | 3 | 1,140 |
| Roe deer (21) | 10.5 | 14 | 5 | 294 | — | 147 |
| Wild pig (107.5) | 53.75 | 10 | 4 | 1,075 | .015 | 537.5 |
| Other wild animals[c] | — | 56 | 21.5 | — | — | — |
| Totals | | 260 | | 71,279 | | |
| **Traian, Romania[p]** | | | | | | |
| Cattle (700)[b] | 350 | 9 | 29 | 6,300 | 73 | 3,150 |
| Sheep–goat (25) | 12.5 | 3 | 10 | 75 | 1 | 37.5 |
| Pig (30) | 15 | 5 | 16 | 150 | 2 | 75 |
| Dog (10) | 5 | — | — | — | — | — |
| Aurochs (900) | 450 | — | — | — | — | — |
| Wild horse (600) | 300 | 1 | 3 | 600 | 7 | 300 |
| Red deer (190) | 95 | 6 | 19 | 1,140 | 13 | 570 |
| Roe deer (21) | 10.5 | 3 | 10 | 63 | 1 | 31.5 |
| Wild pig (107.5) | 53.75 | 3 | 10 | 322.5 | 4 | 161.25 |
| Other wild animals[c] | — | 1 | 3 | — | — | — |
| Totals | | 31 | | 8,650.5 | | |

[l] Data are from Passek and Chernysh 1963.

[m] Tsalkin (1970) presents more complete analysis of the faunal remains from Floreshti, but he groups cattle and aurochs together.

[n] Data are from David and Markevich 1967.

[o] Not included: five bears, three elks, six wild dogs, eight foxes, two beavers, one marten, three lynx, four bison bonasus, six badgers, one wild cat.

[p] Data are from Necrasov and Haimovici 1962.

Papai has a very low frequency of wild animals and twice as many cattle as 10 other sites. It is highly unlikely that one site would have 100% more cattle; the statistical probability is .01. Furthermore, it is reasonable to assume that there is no association between frequencies of particular animals and specific sites within the grouping of Linear faunal assemblages. Using the chi-square test, we find this assumption to be supported if Györ-Papai and Neszmély-Tekeres Patak sites are excluded from the sample. Therefore, we may assume that a sampling error had resulted in a high frequency of cattle. Thus, I consider the Györ-Papai site as nonrepresentative. Often in archaeological reports, different frequencies of various artifact or faunal remains are explained by referring to sociocultural or ecological changes. In many cases, we should take a closer look at sampling problems and other factors that permit archaeologists to hypothesize about various changes.

Many archaeologists assume that the Linear people practiced slash-and-burn (swidden) agriculture and thus were forced to shift their villages periodically because of soil exhaustion. Before discussing further the practice of slash-and-burn agriculture by Linear communities, a look at the ethnographic data on this subsistence pattern is necessary. Harris (1972) has presented a number of general observations about contemporary slash-and-burn cultivators:

1. It is a small-scale form of agriculture. The plots cleared for cultivation are usually only .4 hectare (ha) or less in size. Rarely do they exceed 1 ha in area.

2. It is a *land extensive* and *labor-intensive subsistence system*: "Because plots are only cultivated for short periods of time—perhaps one to three years on the average—before being abandoned for longer periods, there is normally a considerable excess of fallow over cultivated land within the effective agricultural area of a given population. At the same time the processes of clearance, cultivation and harvesting involve intensive human effort in the use of hand tools such as axes, knives, hoes, and digging sticks [Harris 1972: 246]."

3. It is highly productive. "It is an unproductive system per unit of land cultivated, but in terms of yields per unit of labour expended its productivity can equal or even exceed that of some types of permanent, fixed-field agriculture [Harris 1972: 247]."

4. It is associated with low densities of population and dispersed settlements. "Because fallow must substantially exceed cultivated land if there is to be adequate time before re-cultivation for soil fertility to be restored under a regenerating cover of vegetation, there is always need for a large amount of land per head of the population [Harris 1972: 24]." The amount of land needed for cultivation varies with the time interval necessary to allow a plot to recover its former fertility.

5. The population of villages seldom exceeds 250 people.

6.  "The spatial distribution of settlements normally relates to their average size in such a way that the larger the village units the greater the cultivable area that separates one village from another; conversely, the smaller the units the more closely spaced they tend to be [Harris 1972: 248]."

7.  Shifting of settlements is associated with pioneer cultivators, for example, the Iban of Sarawak who consider forest resources as unlimited or expendable.

8.  Slash-and-burn agriculture is best adapted to forest ecosystems. "Because the living vegetation cover of a plot represents a major potential source of nutrients for food production, which clearance and burning makes available to the crops chiefly in the form of ash, it follows that clearance of forest vegetation tends to provide a larger and richer supply of nutrients than clearance of shrubs or herbaceous vegetation [Harris 1972: 252–253]." Thus the production potential of slash-and-burn cultivation is greater in forested than in nonforested areas.

9.  The length of time during which a plot can be profitably cultivated is related to the nature of the crop itself. Protein-rich seed crops, such as wheat or barley, demand a greater supply of nutrients in the ash and soil than root crops. The seed crop systems are less stable. Thus shifting cultivation involving cereals requires a more rapid rotation of plots and a larger total area of land per community.

10. Permanent settlements depending on slash-and-burn agriculture are possible in tropical-forest environments where low nutrient-demanding crops such as yams or sweet potato are cultivated.

*[margin note: not applicable to Europe.]*

At the end of his article, Harris makes some observations about the European Neolithic. According to him, cultivation of wheat or barley in the absence of any fertilizer other than the ash derived from burning of trees and the haphazard droppings of livestock, must have made heavy demands on the fertility of the soil. Regeneration of forest may have been slower because of free-ranging domestic animals browsing in them. "Animals browse the protein-rich buds and young growth of woody plants in preference to grazing herbaceous vegetation [Harris 1972:255]," thus retarding the regeneration of woody plants and accelerating the conversion of forest into grasslands. As previously mentioned, grasslands would not be ideal for slash-and-burn agriculture. It is evident from the Harris article that the Linear people as pioneer cultivators would have been forced by their subsistence system to expand rapidly into central Europe.

*[margin note: not possible?]*

In recent years, Soudský (1962, 1966; Soudský and Pavlů 1972) has argued strongly for slash-and-burn cultivation and for the cyclical movements of Linear culture villages. He estimated the length of one occupation phase to have been 14 or 15 years by counting the number of linings or layers in storage pits. Soudský assumes that these storage pits were "annually daubed inside to provide a new basal lining and burned for disinfection [Soudský 1962: 198]." After shifting their settlement, the Linear people would not occupy the same general area for 30 years to allow the soil and the forest to recover (Soudský and Pavlů 1972). However, this contradicts other statements made by Soudský. He has defined over 20 phases of the Linear culture based on ceramic styles at Bylany. If each of these phases involved 15 years of occupation of the village, followed by 30 years of abandonment, then the Bylany sequence would have lasted some 9 centuries. However, the estimated period of the duration of the Linear culture in Europe is only 700–600 years based on radiocarbon dates.

This author has excavated a Linear site of Olszanica in which pits were uncovered with alternate layers of pit fill and loess; but there was no evidence here to indicate that the pits had been daubed or lined annually. Also, it is doubtful that the pits located outside the longhouses were used for storing grain, especially if it was necessary to preserve some of the cereal for the next year's seed. Pits located outside of houses probably could serve well for tuber plants; however, there is no evidence of cultivation of such plants at that time in central Europe. Humidity and temperature are the two most important factors that affect the length of time that stored grain, such as rye, can preserve its ability to germinate. Grain stored in outside pits would be exposed to cold and rain. It would also be exposed to the scavengings of animals, both domestic and wild. Rodents, cattle, bears, and feral and domestic pigs would have found such hoards of grain impossible to resist. Since no evidence has been found of pigpens or enclosures, it is difficult to see how our hypothetical grain storage pits could have been protected from them.

Using Harris's article as an analogy, it would seem that the Linear people practiced slash-and-burn agriculture. This is also supported by analysis of charcoal remains at the Langweiler 2 site in Rheinland, Germany (Table 5.9). Many trees such as wild apple, wild pear, and hawthorn represent secondary growth flora. They appeared after the primary forest trees—elm, ash, oak, and hazelnuts—were cleared for cultivation of plants. However, this need not imply the shifting of villages. We should note that we have a mixed-grain and livestock farming tradition in Europe and not just dependence on domestic plants as in some other areas of the world.

It can be argued against the need for shifting the Linear culture villages every 10 to 15 years by considering a number of variables: soil fertility, availability of land that can be cultivated, production techniques, and size of population. Probably a digging stick was used for working the cultivated fields. The crops were harvested with flint sickles inserted in wooden handles. The soil exploited by the Linear people was fertile and probably did not get exhausted in 1 or 2 years, even with cereal cultivation. The population estimates for the Linear culture villages vary from 60 to 150, depending on the assumptions and methods used in making the estimates. For example, we can

TABLE 5.9    Types of Wood Found at Langweiler 2 Site[a]

| | Number of charcoal pieces | Number of pits in which found[b] | Percentage of total number of charcoal pieces |
|---|---|---|---|
| Elm (*Ulmus* sp.) | 430 | 15 | 46 |
| Ash (*Fraxinus excelsior*) | 123 | 17 | 52 |
| Oak (*Quercus* sp.) | 267 | 17 | 52 |
| Hazelnut (*Corylus avellana*) | 169 | 13 | 39 |
| Wild apple, hawthorn (*Pyrus, Malus, Crataegus*) | 197 | 18 | 55 |
| Pear, apple, hawthorn (*Pyrus pyraster, Malus silvestris, Crataegus* sp.) | 176 | 19 | 58 |
| Rowan (*Sorbus aucuparis, Sorbus aria*) | 3 | 3 | 9 |
| Blackthorn (*Prunus spinosa*) | 43 | 8 | 24 |
| Sloe (*Prunus* sp.) | 3 | 2 | 6 |
| Maple, spruce (*Acer* sp. *Picea*) | 4 | 3 | 9 |

[a] Data are from Schweingruber 1973.

[b] Total number of pits: 33.

ask, What size area would a village of 100 people need per year? Using slash-and-burn agriculture, a nineteenth-century Russian peasant produced 1000 to 1200 kg of wheat from 1 ha of land (Soudský and Pavlů 1972). However, the comparison between the economics of Neolithic horticulturalists and historic peasant agriculturalists from Russia should be made with caution. A significant portion of the peasant effort and crop yield was devoted to rent payment, the surplus being more or less forcefully extracted from the peasants by the politically dominant landlord class of a state society. No such factor of political economy operates in the case of tribal farmers. A poor Russian peasant of the nineteenth century needed 210 kg of potatoes and 280 kg of rye annually for subsistence. In terms of calories, this is roughly equivalent to 270 kg of wheat (Soudský and Pavlů 1972). Assuming that adult males utilized 2500 calories daily, females and children 2000 and 1500 respectively, a family of four would need to cultivate approximately 1 ha of land to obtain 1000 to 1200 kg of wheat from 1 ha of land (Soudský and Pavlů 1972). Even now, half of the world's population has an average daily intake of less than 2250 calories (Fourastié 1960). Some of the grain would have been set aside for seed and probably for feeding animals. Archaeologists usually overlook the possibility that even Neolithic or Bronze Age societies might have needed to feed some grain to the animals if they were to survive during the winter. However, Linear people did not depend only on wheat for food; meat from domesticated and wild animals and food from other plants were also utilized. A population of 100 people in a Linear culture village would need roughly 100 ha of land for cultivation if they totally depended on wheat for food. There is much more land than this available for cultivation around Linear villages. For example, at Olszanica, there is several times more land suitable for cultivation available within a walking distance of 2–4 km from the site. Thus, the people could have shifted fields without moving their villages. This would tend to support Modderman (1971), who has argued for longer occupation of the Linear culture villages—up to 25 years. Furthermore, the existence of cemeteries containing individuals from at least one generation suggests a greater stability of the Linear culture settlements than Soudský postulated. I am assuming that the Linear people only used a village cemetery when they actually were living in that village. This excludes the possibility that a particular plot was used for burials even after the people had moved elsewhere.

It is unclear what methods and weapons were used for hunting or fighting by the Linear people. Very few projectile points have been found in the Linear sites of Czechoslovakia or Poland. It is possible that bows and arrows were not utilized in hunting and fighting by the Linear people in parts of Germany, Czechoslovakia, and Poland. This may indicate that traps were used in hunting animals. Such hunting methods tend to increase the size of the exploited territory. The small quantity of projectile points may indicate relatively peaceful interaction among Linear communities. On the western flank of the Linear culture, more projectile points are found, which may indicate the utilization of bows and arrows. The greater number of projectile points does not indicate increased wild animal utilization. There is also more evidence for warfare in the western flank of the Linear culture. (When I use the term *warfare* during the Neolithic, it may refer to a low level of hostility such as raiding.) The Late Linear culture settlements at Köln-Lindenthal (Buttler and Haberey 1936) and Langweiler (Kuper *et al.* 1974) in Germany were enclosed by a ditch. This may indicate an increase in competition near the end of the Early Neolithic in some areas of central Europe, perhaps over land or other resources.

### Bükk Culture

We have little information about the subsistence activities of Bükk communities in Slovakia and northeast Hungary. The faunal and floral remains recovered from Bükk sites indicate a subsistence strategy based on domestic and wild resources. Remains of emmer, einkorn, club wheat, six-row barley, broomcorn, millet, lentils, peas, wild green millet, and pale persicaria have been found (Lichardus 1974). The faunal remains consist of cattle, sheep–goat, pig, dog, hare, roe deer, red deer, wild pig, auroch, bear, fox, and badger; fish bones have also been found.

### Alpine Region

The remains of wood, plants, berries, and fruits used and eaten by the early farmers have been remarkably well preserved in the Early Neolithic sites of the Alpine region. Remarkable evidence is available in the Alpine region for a subsistence strategy based on agriculture, livestock, gardening, hunting, collection, and fishing. The role of hunting was particularly important (Table 5.10). The most frequently hunted animals were red deer, roe deer, aurochs, and wild pigs. The hunters chose their prey such as red deer selectively, apparently concentrating on young males as at the Burgäschisee–Süd site (Jarman 1972), realizing, perhaps, that females are more important for maintaining a stable herd size. The excellent preservation also gives a clearer picture of the utilization and feeding of some domestic animals in the economy. For example, sheep were not used for wool, since most recovered fabrics were made from flax. Roughly 40 to 60% of the livestock was slaughtered for meat at an early age (Table 5.11).

From the Cortaillod site of Egolzwil 4 in Switzerland, we have evidence that the cattle were kept in the village during the winter. At the village entrance, one building contained layers of vegetable matter and masses of pupae of the common housefly. This suggests that cattle were stalled for the winter in that building, and the flies were laying their eggs in the dung. That plants were collected near the village for winter fodder is suggested by the stacks of leaves, twigs of mistletoe, and hay found at this site.

We know that the Cortaillod people had the following domesticated plants: einkorn wheat, emmer wheat, club wheat, bread wheat, barley, millet, peas, flax, and poppy. A variety of wild berries, such as raspberries, strawberries, bilberries, blackberries, and elderberries, and hazelnuts, acorns, crab apples, wild pears, and wild plums or sloe, as well as other nuts, fruits, and mushrooms were exploited. It has been suggested that apples were domesticated. However, Villaret-von Rochow's (1969) analysis indicated that they were probably wild. She observed that the mere presence of quantities of apples does not by itself demonstrate that fruit was cultivated. We also find dried apples. Archaeologists have compared 100 gm of fresh and dried apples and have noted that the dried apples contain a greater amount of vitamins (Guyan 1954, Wiślański 1969). We should note that a fruit, upon drying, will retain its vitamin content and loses only the weight represented by its liquid content. Thus a dried apple that weighs considerably less than a fresh apple will have the same vitamin content.

It is very important for subsistence analysis to determine when the earliest milking of cows and production of cheese occurred in Europe. Cheese would be a significant addition to the food supply, since it can be preserved for many months. Most of our evidence for these activities is indirect. We find clay strainers in some Neolithic sites, and although these finds are not numerous, they may indicate milking of cows and making of cheese. In Swiss Neolithic sites, wooden pots and tools were preserved that may have been used in milk processing. Some of the collected plants, such as goose grass (*Galium palustre*), could have been utilized for the curdling of milk (Tschumi 1949).

TABLE 5.10   Frequency of Animals and Estimated Amount of Usable Meat at Cortaillod Sites[a]

| | Kilograms of usable meat | Number of animals | Percentage of total number of animals | Total estimated weight in kilograms | Percentage of estimated weight | Kilograms of usable meat from total estimated weight |
|---|---|---|---|---|---|---|
| **Burgäschisee Süd** | | | | | | |
| Cattle (700)[b,c] | 350 | 8 | 2 | 5,600 | 9 | 2,800 |
| Sheep–goat (25) | 12.5 | 20 | 5 | 500 | 1 | 250 |
| Pig (30) | 15 | 23 | 5 | 690 | 1 | 345 |
| Dog (10) | 5 | 13 | 3 | 130 | — | 65 |
| Aurochs (900) | 450 | 18 | 4 | 16,200 | 27 | 8,100 |
| Red deer (190) | 95 | 119 | 28 | 22,610 | 38 | 11,305 |
| Roe deer (21) | 10.5 | 39 | 9 | 819 | 1 | 409.5 |
| Bison (575) | 287.5 | 5 | 1 | 2,875 | 5 | 1,437.5 |
| Wild pig (107.5) | 53.75 | 72 | 17 | 7,740 | 13 | 3,870 |
| Bear (170) | 85 | 7 | 1 | 1,190 | 2 | 595 |
| Badger (8) | 4 | 21 | 5 | 168 | — | 84 |
| Beaver (16) | 8 | 29 | 7 | 464 | 1 | 232 |
| Elk (355) | 177.5 | — | — | — | — | — |
| Horse (600) | 300 | | | — | — | — |
| Other wild animals | | 55 | 13 | | | |
| Totals | | 429 | | 58,968 | | |
| **Burgäschisee Süd-West** | | | | | | |
| Cattle (700)[b,c] | 350 | 49 | 23 | 34,300 | 57 | 17,150 |
| Sheep–goat (25) | 12.5 | 23 | 11 | 575 | 1 | 287.50 |
| Pig (30) | 15 | 34 | 16 | 1,020 | 2 | 510 |
| Dog (10) | 5 | 9 | 4 | 90 | — | 45 |
| Aurochs (900) | 450 | 14 | 7 | 12,600 | 21 | 6,300 |
| Red deer (190) | 95 | 34 | 16 | 6,460 | 11 | 3,230 |
| Roe deer (21) | 10.5 | 15 | 7 | 315 | — | 157.50 |
| Bison (575) | 287.5 | — | — | — | — | — |
| Wild pig (107.5) | 53.75 | 16 | 7 | 1,720 | 3 | 860 |
| Bear (170) | 85 | 5 | 2 | 850 | 1 | 425 |
| Badger (8) | 4 | 4 | 2 | 32 | — | 16 |
| Beaver (16) | 8 | 5 | 2 | 80 | — | 40 |
| Elk (355) | 177.5 | 3 | 1 | 1,065 | 2 | 532.50 |
| Horse (600) | 300 | 1 | — | 600 | 1 | 300 |
| Other wild animals | | 3 | 1 | | | |
| Totals | | 215 | | 59,707 | | |

(continued)

[a] Data are from Murray 1970.
[b] Numbers in parentheses indicate estimated adult weight in kilograms.
[c] In estimating weight, the category "other wild animals" was excluded.

TABLE 5.10  (*Continued*)

| | Kilograms of usable meat | Number of animals | Percentage of total number of animals | Total estimated weight in kilograms | Percentage of estimated weight | Kilograms of usable meat from total estimated weight |
|---|---|---|---|---|---|---|
| **Egolzwil II** | | | | | | |
| Cattle (700)[b,c] | 350 | 122 | 13 | 85,400 | 38 | 42,700 |
| Sheep–goat (25) | 12.5 | 76 | 8 | 1,900 | 1 | 950 |
| Pig (30) | 15 | 79 | 9 | 2,370 | 1 | 1,185 |
| Dog (10) | 5 | 27 | 3 | 270 | — | 135 |
| Aurochs (900) | 450 | 58 | 6 | 52,200 | 23 | 26,100 |
| Red deer (190) | 95 | 250 | 27 | 47,500 | 21 | 23,750 |
| Roe deer (21) | 10.5 | 73 | 8 | 1,533 | 1 | 766.50 |
| Bison (575) | 287.5 | 13 | 1 | 7,475 | 3 | 3,737.50 |
| Wild pig (107.5) | 53.75 | 60 | 7 | 6,450 | 3 | 3,225 |
| Bear (170) | 85 | 23 | 3 | 3,910 | 2 | 1,955 |
| Badger (8) | 4 | 26 | 3 | 224 | — | 112 |
| Beaver (16) | 8 | 34 | 4 | 544 | — | 272 |
| Elk (355) | 177.5 | 40 | 4 | 14,200 | 6 | 7,100 |
| Horse (600) | 300 | — | — | — | — | — |
| Other wild animals | | 29 | 3 | | | |
| Totals | | 910 | | 223,976 | | |
| **St. Aubin** | | | | | | |
| Cattle (700)[b,c] | 350 | 137 | 26 | 95,900 | 81 | 47,950 |
| Sheep–goat (25) | 12.5 | 108 | 20 | 2,700 | 2 | 1,350 |
| Pig (30) | 15 | 80 | 15 | 2,400 | 2 | 1,200 |
| Dog (10) | 5 | 66 | 12 | 660 | 1 | 330 |
| Aurochs (900) | 450 | 5 | 1 | 4,500 | 4 | 2,250 |
| Red deer (190) | 95 | 35 | 7 | 6,650 | 6 | 3,325 |
| Roe deer (21) | 10.5 | 16 | 3 | 336 | — | 168 |
| Bison (575) | 287.5 | — | — | — | — | — |
| Wild pig (107.5) | 53.75 | 10 | 2 | 1,075 | 1 | 537.50 |
| Bear (170) | 85 | 5 | 1 | 850 | 1 | 425 |
| Badger (8) | 4 | 5 | 1 | 40 | — | 20 |
| Beaver (16) | 8 | 14 | 3 | 224 | — | 112 |
| Elk (355) | 177.5 | 7 | 1 | 2,485 | 2 | 1242.50 |
| Horse (600) | 300 | — | — | — | — | — |
| Other wild animals | | 49 | 9 | | | |
| Totals | | 537 | | 117,820 | | |

**TABLE 5.11**  Age at Which Livestock Was Slaughtered at Four Cortaillod Culture Sites, in Percentages[a]

|  | Egolzwil 2 | Egolzwil 4 | St. Aubin IV | Seematte-Gelfingen |
|---|---|---|---|---|
| Cattle mortality | $N=161$ | $N=45$ | $N=122$ | $N=50$ |
| (in months of age) |  |  |  |  |
| 1–13 | 30.5 | 52.0 | 37.0 | 41.2 |
| 14–24 | 11.8 | 12.0 | 16.4 | 25.9 |
| 24–36 | 10.4 | 7.0 | 12.1 | 3.5 |
| Over 36 | 48.4 | 30.0 | 36.1 | 29.4 |
| Pig mortality | $N=71$ | $N=54$ |  | $N=62$ |
| (in months of age) |  |  |  |  |
| 0–12 | 31.0 | 36.0 |  | 45.2 |
| 13–25 | 38.0 | 33.4 |  | 38.7 |
| Over 25 | 30.9 | 29.7 |  | 16.1 |
| Sheep–goat mortality | $N=90$ | $N=35$ | $N=147$ | $N=27$ |
| (in months of age) |  |  |  |  |
| 0–12 | 40.2 | 42.2 | 61.2 | 33.3 |
| 13–24 | 18.9 | 11.1 | 15.7 | 22.2 |
| Over 25 | 39.8 | 46.6 | 23.1 | 46.4 |

[a] Data are from Higham 1968.

Bökönyi (1974: 109) has discussed the earliest evidence for the milking of cows. In the Near East, pictures of cows with large udders appear in the fourth millennium B.C. He has argued that we can infer from large udders that the animals were milked. The earliest representation of milking of cows occurs in Ur, Mesopotamia, after 2400 B.C. Bökönyi noted that some cattle figurines from Middle Tripolye (Middle Neolithic) sites in the Ukraine have well-developed udders that may imply milking. Zeuner (1963) has shown a Late Minoan representation from Knossos, Crete, illustrating the milking of cows. The cow is milked from the rear, as is usually done with goats.

Good evidence for the milking of cows is available much later in areas north of the Alps. Grüss (1933) found remains of carbonized milk in a Hallstatt period vessel at the Mühlbach-Bischofshofen site.

## Trade

When considering trade during the Early Neolithic, it is necessary to view it in its proper sociopolitical context. As previously mentioned, the Early Neolithic European societies were probably at the tribal level of cultural development. The networks of exchange or trade involved hundreds of small independent but interconnected sociopolitical units, and trade between such societies is not a simple matter. Sahlins (1972: 302) has pointed out that "trade between primitive communities or tribes is a most delicate, potentially a most explosive, undertaking." Exchange among relatives usually is carried out by means of generalized or balanced reciprocity; but with nonkin, the prevailing mode may be negative reciprocity: Shortchanging, chicanery, even robbery with violence are all ethically possible when dealing with strangers. However, primitive trade functions as a mechanism for extending social relationships, friendships, and peaceful ties among communities, tribes, or individuals. To avoid conflict, "the most tactful strategy is economic good measure, a generous return relative to what has been received of which there can be no complaints [Sahlins 1972: 303]."

Most of our evidence for Early Neolithic exchange networks comes from nonperishable materials such as stone, flint, shells, obsidian, and ceramics. Trade in foodstuffs rarely leaves evidence at archaeological sites and can only be inferred from the distribution of the preserved artifacts. Trade in perishable goods usually occurs over short distances; it is a local trade involving only neighboring villages or tribes. The exchange of certain kinds of nonperishable goods may involve long-distance as well as local trading. In long-distance trading, goods may move through many intermediaries. The value of a traded item depends on several factors: weight, place of origin, distance from any given community, rarity in the neighborhood of any given community, status of the individuals involved in the exchange, etc. Thus, it can be seen that an item has no fixed and absolute value; rather its value will vary considerably over its range of distribution.

## Southeastern Europe

Intercommunity trade in the Early Neolithic is indicated by the presence of nonlocal raw materials or products such as stone, obsidian, and *Spondylus* shells at sites in southeastern Europe. This does not mean that all these products were exchanged over the entire territory. At present, no estimates are available for the quantity of such goods at the different sites. Without quantitative studies of the distribution of trade goods, it is not possible to establish with any certainty what the mechanisms of exchange were.

## Central Europe

We have much more data for central European Early Neolithic trade than for that of southeastern Europe. The presence at many sites of nonlocal raw materials or finished products without evidence of local manufacture indicates an exchange system existed linking Linear as well as non-Linear communities. Material goods were exchanged for a variety of reasons. Lack of access to desired raw materials is an obvious reason. However, the Linear villages were self-sufficient in the raw materials and goods needed for domestic purposes. The basic raw materials needed for tool manufacture—bone, stone, flint, and wood—were available locally.

Since the Linear villages probably lacked political centralization, such sociopolitical integration as may have been necessary within and among villages may have been accomplished through rituals and ceremonies. It is quite likely that the products made of nonlocal raw materials were obtained for these purposes. Another purpose for nonlocal goods may have been to express differences in social status. Some goods may have been obtained from other villages that specialized in the production of certain items. Such specialization would involve communities in extensive trade. However, no evidence exists at this time for specialization by particular villages in production of craft objects. Furthermore, we should look at trade not only as means of acquiring material products, but also as a means of social communication. Exchange extends social ties and reduces conflicts among communities (Wilmsen 1972).

The evidence usually cited for the practice of trade in the central European Early Neolithic is the presence of *Spondylus* shells in some Linear sites. These items are rare and usually occur in burials that may be associated with higher-status individuals. The habitat of shellfish of the genus *Spondylus* includes the coastal waters of the Black and Mediterranean seas. To obtain the shells, the Linear communities would have been involved in exchange with communities of the Vinča A culture, and others of southeastern Europe (Figure 5.1). Recently, oxygen isotype analyses carried out on *Spondylus* shells from the Balkans indicate that they came from the Aegean (N. Shackleton and C. Renfrew 1970).

To explain the trade in *Spondylus* shells during the Balkan Neolithic, N.

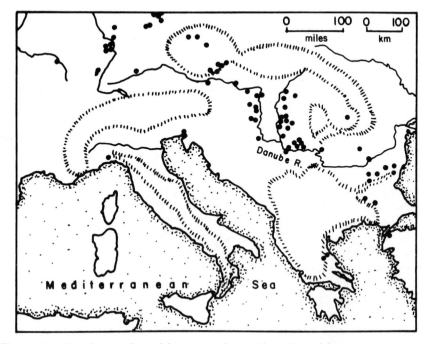

**Figure 5.1.** Distribution of *Spondylus* shell artifacts. (After Tabaczyński 1970.)

Shackleton and C. Renfrew (1970) have proposed a prestige-chain exchange model. This model has four characteristics:

1.  Exchange of goods takes place between high-status individuals on a basis of balanced reciprocity.
2.  The prestige goods are passed on in subsequent exchanges.
3.  These goods are not utilized in daily activities.
4.  These goods are usually found in burials or in other contexts through accidental breakage or loss.

They compare the exchange in *Spondylus* shells to the *kula* trade of the Trobriand Islanders. In the *kula* trade some of the exchanged goods had a social and ideological significance far transcending their utilitarian value.

It should be noted that the *kula* goods were not buried with the dead. B. Malinowski (1922/1961:152) states, "A dying man is surrounded and overlaid with valuables which all his relatives and relatives-in-law bring in loan for the occasion, to take it back when all is over while the man's own *vaygu'a* are left on the corpse for some time after death." The *vaygu'a* are *kula* valuables (Malinowski 1922/1961: 90). Plate LXV in the book *Argonauts of the Western Pacific* shows that all the valuables, including personal possessions, will be removed from the corpse immediately before the internment (Malinowski 1922/1961). It is evident that it would be difficult for archaeologists to demonstrate from the burial data in the Trobriand Islands this type of exchange system. This contradicts Shackleton and Renfrew's assumption that they are usually found in burials.

However, in the *kula*-ring type of exchange model, not only prestige goods are being passed on between individuals, but also many subsistence goods are exchanged at the same time. This type of exchange probably did not occur among the Linear people. The Linear communities were self-sufficient in subsistence needs. They occupied good land, and the population was small; thus there would be little pressure to exchange foodstuffs for subsistence needs. This does not imply that some foodstuffs were not exchanged, for sometimes the idea of giving a gift was more important than the value of the gift. The goods exchanged, such as *Spondylus* shells, among the Linear people probably were to reinforce status differences. ?

The preserved evidence shows that, in addition to *Spondylus* shells, obsidian, stone, flint, and pottery were exchanged. The distribution of these materials is not uniform in all parts of central Europe. For example, Slovakian and Hungarian obsidian is found mostly in northeast Hungary, Slovakia, eastern Moravia, southeastern Poland, and adjacent areas of Soviet Union and Romania. It is not clear what products were exchanged by Linear communities in return for obsidian. Cores found at the sites indicate that obsidian was traded in lumps and used for making tools such as blades, flakes, and sickle blades. We should not think that huge quantities of goods moved across the Carpathians. At Olszanica B1, in an excavated area of 3400 m², approximately 130 pieces were found. The cultural layer at Olszanica B1 contained 40 pieces of obsidian, thus one piece per 85 m² in area. The obsidian tools could have been utilized for special needs or occasions, such as the first harvest, or for castrating bulls, since the obsidian blades are sharper than flint ones.

It is very interesting that many more burins have been found at Olszanica than in Linear culture sites in western Europe. Newell (1970) has found only 27 burins among the flint material from the extensively excavated Linear sites of Elsloo, Sittard, and Stein in the Netherlands. At Olszanica, approximately 50 burins were found in just one part of the village. They were made of local flint. This may indicate differences in socioeconomic activities or trade zones between eastern and western Linear sites. It is possible that burins at Olszanica were utilized to produce some bone, antler, or other products for exchange with Early Neolithic communities in Slovakia and Hungary. Also artifacts made of flint from Poland, which could have been used in exchange for obsidian, occur in Slovakian and Hungarian Linear communities. The distribution of exotic items in Linear settlements and cemeteries indicates that not all families or individuals participated equally in exchange. For example, the distribution of obsidian at Olszanica shows that it clusters only around some of the longhouses, whereas other contemporary longhouses have very little obsidian. Probably the obsidian exchange occurred between more prominent families or individuals. Most of the polished stone tools made of nonlocal material in Linear cemeteries, such as Nitra in Slovakia, are associated with adult males.

The polished stone tools are frequently made of nonlocal material such as amphibolite from the Wrocław area in Silesia, Poland, approximately 200 km (124 miles) from Olszanica. Finished amphibolite tools occur in Poland, Czechoslovakia, Germany, and the Netherlands. For example, some polished stone tools at Olszanica and at Müddersheim in Rheinland were made from the Silesian amphibolite (Figure 5.2). It is possible that stone tools were exchanged only among males, since they usually occur in male burials. Probably there were regional exchange zones in central Europe that may be indicated by other differences within the Linear culture area, such as style zones. For example, the Želiezovce style of pottery ornamentation occurring in the eastern area of Linear culture generally corresponds with the distribution of obsidian from Slovakia and Hungary.

### Relationship of Farmers to Hunters and Gatherers

One of the more interesting problems of the Early Neolithic is the relationship of farmers to hunters and gatherers. Since actual archaeological evidence for any type of interaction is almost nonexistent at the present time, most of my comments are speculative. Hopefully, some of the hypotheses presented here about the relationship of farmers to hunters and gatherers will be tested with archaeological data in the future.

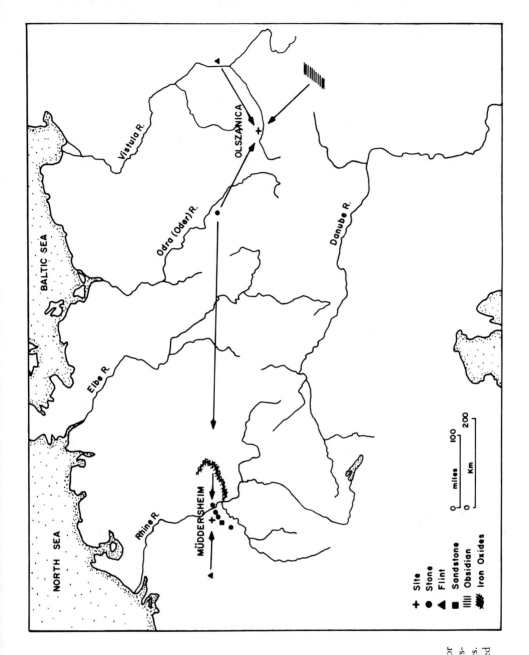

**Figure 5.2.** The evidence for trade networks at the Müddersheim and Olszanica sites. (Müddersheim data adapted from Schietzel 1965).

One of the major problems in establishing this relationship is the inability of archaeologists to date more precisely the sites of the so-called Mesolithic hunters and gatherers. Most of the recovered archaeological material from Mesolithic sites consists of flint artifacts that are impossible to date precisely by present techniques. The dating problem is well illustrated in southern Poland. There are many Mesolithic sites in southeastern Poland in the post-Pleistocene period (after the ninth millennium B.C.), but using the typology of flint artifacts, only very general chronological observations can be made (Figure 5.3). Sites containing flint artifacts without ceramics are always classified as being Mesolithic. However, it is possible that some of the Mesolithic sites belong to farmers; that is, they were hunting camps of agriculturalists or other activity sites where no pottery was utilized. The hunting and gathering sites are located both in the uplands and lowlands. Access to streams and rivers was important for hunters and farmers, for they both utilized water for drinking, fishing, and transportation.

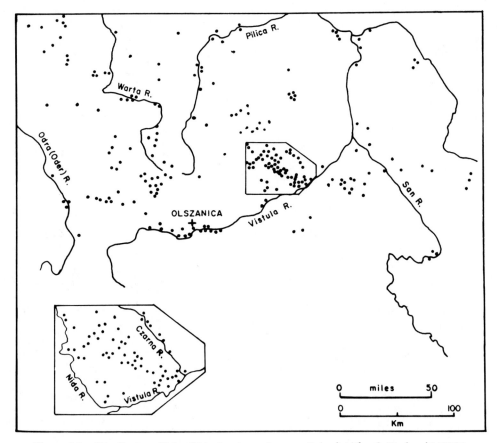

**Figure 5.3.** Distribution of Mesolithic sites in southeastern Poland. (After S. Kozłowski 1972.)

A simple model of interaction would have the hunters and gatherers supplying most of the wild animals to the farmers and the farmers supplying grain to
the hunters and gatherers. Perhaps the scarcity of projectile points at Linear
sites can be explained by this type of interaction. Middle and Late Neolithic
sites have more projectile points; also at that time the number of hunters and
gatherers was declining in Europe as farmers expanded into areas occupied by
hunting and gathering societies. Alternatively, the increase in projectile
points during the Middle Neolithic may point to an increase in internal warfare
or the appearance of new hunting methods. Furthermore, it may be due simply
to a more stationary economy, in which more activities were originating in the
same settlement.

## Settlement Organization

In presenting the Early Neolithic settlement organization, I consider both
the internal arrangement of structures of individual settlements and the distribution of settlements within a region. The functional interrelationships
among sites within the settlement system are analyzed. When dealing with
individual structures or single settlements, I consider the types of activities
carried out in them and their function in the larger units or systems. Population estimates at these three levels of settlement studies also are presented.

### Greece

The earliest Neolithic villages in Europe are found in the northeastern part
of continental Greece. The settlement sites in Greece and adjacent parts of
southeastern Europe take the form of *tells,* or mounds made up of the debris of
long occupations. The houses in such villages had mud walls, which eventually
collapsed and were replaced by new mud-walled houses. The accumulation
of debris from such structures, as well as the general refuse of the settlements,
resulted in tell sites. No such tells occur in other parts of Europe. Perhaps the
area of the mounds was occupied continuously, without shifting the location of
the village. Probably the extremely rich alluvial soils made possible this settlement stability.

The Early Neolithic villages in Greece and adjacent parts of Yugoslavia or
Bulgaria were located by rivers or lakes. This provided easy access to water
and made it possible to exploit rich alluvial soils. For example, the site of Nea
Nikomedeia in northern Greece was located near a shallow lake, or possibly
the Aegean Sea itself, which may have, at that time, intruded that far inland,
although the evidence for this is unclear (Rodden 1962, 1965). However,
Bintliff (1976) reinterpreted the data and the results differ from previous
studies of the Plain of Macedon development. Bintliff considers Nea
Nikomedeia as an inland site surrounded by well-drained lacustrine silts.

Another Early Neolithic site, Anza I in Yugoslavian Macedonia, was situated on a low terrace of a small river. At the time of occupation, a moderately Mediterranean climate prevailed in the region. This is indicated by analysis of charcoal remains, which show that local vegetation consisted of junipers, oaks, and elms.

Judging from contemporary Near Eastern sites and from later ones in southeastern Europe, an Early Neolithic village such as Nea Nikomedeia in northern Greece occupied an area of at least .5 ha. At Nea Nikomedeia, dated 6220 ± 270 B.C. (probably the radiocarbon date is 500–600 years too early), six houses were excavated in an area of approximately .2 ha. It is possible that these houses were all occupied at the same time. Only a part of the village was excavated; therefore, we can only assume that it was larger. The houses at Nea Nikomedeia are square or rectangular, a form of house that recurs repeatedly throughout Europe during the Neolithic. Only in the Mediterranean region and in western Europe are round houses to be found (Piggott 1972). Early Neolithic houses in Greece were small, probably occupied by only one family; for example, at Nea Nikomedeia two houses were 8 × 8 m (64 m$^2$). The interior of the houses did not represent only living space, for features such as hearths and storage basins are found. The occurrence of hearths and storage basins inside the houses suggests that individual families may have done their own cooking and had individual storage of food supplies. There is little evidence for communal activities in relation to food preparation.

The population of Nea Nikomedeia can be estimated using Naroll's method (1962). Using ethnographic data from 18 societies, he estimated population size by equating it to one-tenth of the floor space of a structure measured in square meters:

$$\text{Number of persons} = \frac{\text{Total floor space of all houses in m}^2}{10}.$$

Substituting the Nea Nikomedeia data into the formula, we get:

$$\text{Number of persons} = \frac{15\ (8 \times 8)}{10} = 96.$$

This is assuming, of course, that 15 houses have comprised the Nea Nikomedeia village of at least .5 ha and the houses were occupied at the same time.

In villages such as Nea Nikomedeia, a variety of economic and social activities were carried out, some of which were localized in particular areas of the site. Such areas are manifested archaeologically by concentrations of the particular artifacts appropriate to a certain activity. Woodworking is indicated by axes, adzes, and chisels of stone; hunting and fighting, by flint projectile points. The harvesting of cereals was done by sickles with wooden or bone handles, into which flint blades or flakes were inserted. Such sickle blades can be distinguished by the sheen or gloss that they acquire through use. Flint scrapers were utilized for working on hides or skins. Various flint blades and flakes could have been used for the cutting, scraping, incising, or sawing of the different raw materials used in making a variety of objects or tools. The presence of fishing is indicated by bone fishhooks. Bone needles were utilized for sewing clothing. Pottery was used for storage, drinking, serving, and cooking. It is usually assumed that only monochrome (pottery painted only in one color) vessels were used in the first Neolithic villages in Greece. However, both monochrome and polychrome pottery might have appeared in Greece around the same time (Nandris 1970). The villagers wore ornaments made of stone, bone, and shell, possibly including labrets, or lip plugs; stone objects that may have been such jewelry have been found on several Greek Early Neolithic sites. There is even evidence for musical instruments; bone flutes were found at Anza I (Gimbutas 1972). Perhaps they were utilized as herders' pipes.

Clay stamps have been found in the Early Neolithic villages in Greece and southeastern Europe. In the Near East, similar artifacts usually were used to impress signs into clay plugs, which were used to seal pottery vessels and other containers. They were probably signs of ownership. In the tribal societies of the European Early Neolithic, such stamps may have been used to indicate the proprietorship of corporate kin (or other) groups over certain goods and not necessarily private ownership. As an alternative interpretation, clay stamps could have been used for body decoration. *or anything else!*

### Southeastern Europe

The Early Neolithic farming villages of southeastern Europe were frequently located on the terraces in river valleys and only rarely in the uplands. However, this does not mean that their occupants did not exploit the plant and animal resources of the uplands. By locating their villages along rivers, these farmers were able to exploit fertile alluvial soils. For example, the Kazanluk site in Bulgaria is located in a fertile valley, 20 km wide (Dennel 1972).

Each settlement had its own farming territory. In the area around Nova Zagora in Bulgaria, Dennel and Webley (1975) noted that the average distance between settlements is about 5.2 km. They also noted that larger tells (presumably the site of larger settlements) were located in the most productive territories. The Early Neolithic farmers must have practiced some sort of rotation system of crops, since growing cereals on the same plot would have led to soil exhaustion if the land was not flooded every year. Perhaps they rotated cereals and legumes (Dennel and Webley 1975).

Permanent villages were not the only types of settlements used by the Early Neolithic farmers in southeastern Europe. Cultural material belonging to these farmers is also found in caves, which may indicate a seasonally shifting subsistence pattern, such as transhumant herding. Upland resource exploitation is suggested by the location of some alluvial sites. In Bulgaria, the

Chevdar site is located on the Topolnitsa River, but hills up to 1500 m high rise on both sides of the river. The inhabitants of the site had easy access to higher mountain slopes (Dennel 1972) to which some of the villagers may have driven the village animals for summer pasture.

These villages contained small, rectangular houses, the traces of which are often obliterated. For example, the occupation layer at some Yugoslavian Starčevo sites was destroyed by natural causes or the activities of later prehistoric cultures. Since no remains of houses are found at some sites, large pits are usually classified as pithouses. However, the identification of these features as pithouses should be treated with skepticism. Pithouses may have existed during the Neolithic in Europe, but too often archaeologists have classified any large pit, especially one containing a hearth, as a pithouse. McPherron has found areas with scattered pieces of fired mud and chaff, probably from Starčevo houses, at Divostin, Grivac, and Banaj near Kragujevac in Yugoslavia. He suggests that burned or abandoned houses were destroyed by weather if they were not covered by soil wash (McPherron and Srejović 1971: 9).

We can take a closer look at two Early Neolithic villages in southeastern Europe, Obre I in Yugoslavia and Karanovo I in Bulgaria. Obre I is located on a terrace of the Bosna River, the rich alluvial soils of which are well suited to the cultivation of cereal and other crops. The approximate area of the site is 12,500–17,500 m² (250 × 50–70 m) or 1.25–1.75 ha (Gimbutas 1970). At Obre I, the Starčevo village consisted of rectangular houses that appear to have been arranged in rows. The houses were built by erecting a wooden framework and then daubing it with clay.

Inside the houses, there were round ovens and hearths. One of the houses differed from the others in that it was larger and built with stone foundations. If it were contemporary with the other houses, it may indicate functional or social differences within this settlement. It may have served as a place for communal rituals, or it may have been the residence of a villager with a higher social status than the others.

The Karanovo I village near Nova Zagora in Bulgaria is one of the more extensively excavated Early Neolithic sites in southeastern Europe. Karanovo, like some other sites in this part of Europe, is a mound or a tell, the diameter of which varies from 180 to 250 m at base (Mikov 1959). An area of about 1700 m² has been excavated in this mound, or approximately 5% of its total area (assuming a basal area of 36,286.6 m² [3.6 ha] from an average basal diameter of 215 m). Since the Karanovo mound has other Neolithic and Bronze Age occupations, it is doubtful that the diameter of the mound can be used for estimating the size of the Early Neolithic village. Bulgarian archaeologists have claimed that up to 60 houses were present in the bottom layer at Karanovo (Mikov 1959). It is highly unlikely that such a large village existed in one time period. Data from other archaeological sites and ethnographic analogy suggest that the population in this type of village seldom

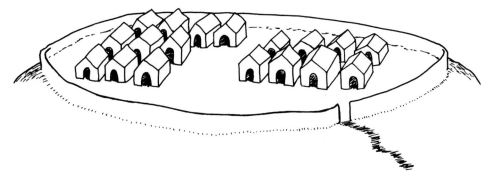

**Figure 5.4.** Karanovo I village as reconstructed in the National Archaeological Museum, Sofia. (After Tringham 1971.)

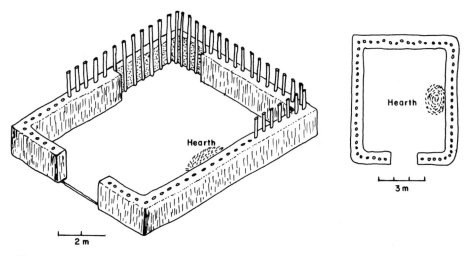

**Figure 5.5.** Karanovo I house. (After Tringham 1971.)

exceeded 200. It is more likely that the settlement contained between 15 and 30 single-room houses at any one time. The reconstructed village model at the National Archaeological Museum in Sofia has 18 houses (Tringham 1971: 72) (Figure 5.4). Assuming that these small square houses, 6 × 7 m, were occupied by single family units, the village population probably consisted of 75 to 150 people depending on how many persons are assigned to one family. Using Naroll's method, a population of 76 persons may be estimated for a single occupation of the site.

The houses were constructed by erecting a framework of upright wooden posts, on which thick walls of clay or mud were daubed (Figure 5.5). At Karanovo I, the floors of the houses were covered with wooden planks. The houses were situated close to one another and were arranged in parallel rows. Inside the houses, there were hearths, grinding stones, pots, and flint, stone, and bone artifacts. Again, cooking was probably done by individual families.

Some archaeologists have claimed that as agriculture spread over southeastern Europe, some hunters, gatherers, and fishermen began to live in semisedentary or even permanent settlements (Srejović 1972). Certain sites in the vicinity of the Iron Gates, on the Danube in Yugoslavia and Romania, are cited as examples of this process.

At Lepenski Vir in Yugoslavia, a village consisting of small trapezoidal houses on stone-built foundations was found (Figure 5.6). Inside the houses, there were hearths, bones, and artifacts, and also, inside or in front of them, large stone sculptures. There are three main occupational phases at Lepenski Vir, and Srejović, the excavator, believes that the first two were not those of farmers, but of hunters, gatherers, and fishermen.

The bones of domesticated dogs were found in the first two occupation phases. Faunal remains indicate that various animals were extensively hunted at Lepenski Vir during all occupational phases, especially red deer. Fishing played an important role in the economy.

However, the early occupations at Lepenski Vir may not represent the permanent settlements of hunters and gatherers. Probably the trapezoidal houses at Lepenski Vir were built by farmers, as is the case at similar sites in the Iron Gates area, for example, Padina (Jovanović 1973). The foundations of the houses were dug into earlier layers representing the seasonal occupations of the hunters and gatherers, and the materials were mixed.

### Impresso (Mediterranean)

We do not have adequate data on the settlement organization of the Impresso farmers in the Mediterranean regions. Since much of our evidence about the Impresso culture comes from caves, there is a suspicion that we are dealing just with the camps of herders involving sites where seasonal exploitation of local resources by one segment of the population, perhaps adolescent males acting as sheep herders and goat herders occurred. Thus, the settlement system of Impresso people was probably more complex, constituting permanent villages and seasonal camps.

In summary, it is evident that the Early Neolithic villages in southeastern Europe and probably the Mediterranean region were small, probably with populations of less than 150. The villages most likely consisted of 10 to 20 houses and the individual structures rarely exceeded 10 m in length or 60–70 $m^2$ in area. The area occupied by a village probably ranged from .5 to 1.5 ha.

### Central Europe

The early Neolithic settlement system in central Europe can be reconstructed on the basis of data from Linear culture sites. The Linear culture settlements were not distributed evenly or continuously throughout central Europe (Childe 1958: 49), but were mainly limited to the loess lands or other

**Figure 5.6.** Plan of Lepenski Vir. (From Srejović 1967.)

regions of good soils. Studies carried out in various areas of the Federal Republic of Germany and the German Democratic Republic indicate that from 68 to 97% of the Linear sites were located on loess soils (Sielmann 1971, 1972). The loess soils themselves exhibit various degrees of fertility. Usually the Linear people selected well-drained soils. The sites are frequently located near or on low-lying terraces of rivers or major streams. Along such rivers or major streams, the Linear culture sites occur in clusters and are not evenly distributed in an area. They vary in size, and the differences may to some extent be functional (Kruk 1973a). However, it is possible that at one time period the size of the Linear settlements was quite homogeneous. The differences in the size of the settlements may reflect differences in occupational phases. Sites having numerous occupational phases usually cover a larger area than the ones with a single occupation. The density of Linear culture sites is low if it is expressed in terms of sites per square kilometers; however, the density appears greater if we consider it in terms of distances along the rivers or streams. For example, Kruk (1973a) has listed 72 Linear sites in an area of over 2300 km² northeast of Kraków, Poland (Figure 5.7). The actual number of sites in this area may, in fact, be greater, since Kruk was unable to survey all of it. The average density of sites per unit of area is 1 per 32 km². However,

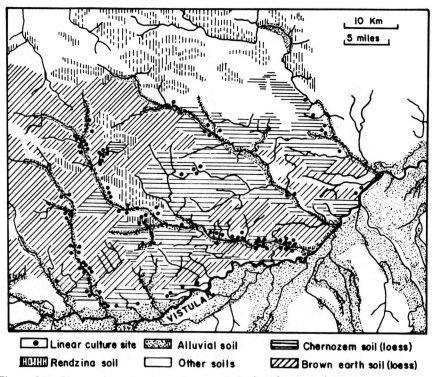

Figure 5.7. Linear culture sites in southeastern Poland. (After J. Kruk 1973a.)

along the Dłubnia River, the site density per linear unit is 20 per 25 km or 1 per 1.25 km.

We do not know how many of these sites were occupied in any one time period; thus the estimate of regional population is little more than an educated guess. Assuming that all 72 sites were occupied at one time and that each village consisted of 100 people, the total regional population could be estimated as over 7000. However, it is doubtful that the first assumption is valid, and, therefore, the population of the region was probably less.

The density of Linear sites in central Europe varied through time. For example, the initial expansion of Linear communities in the Middle Neckar area (7200 km²) of Germany was carried out by a very small population, whose settlement density was only one community or village per 1028.5 km². The following estimates, derived from Sielmann's (1972) article, demonstrate a "filling in" process by farmers of that area:

| Phase | Number of sites | One site per km² |
|---|---|---|
| Phase 1 | 7 | 1028.5 km² |
| Phase 2 | 62 | 116.1 km² |
| Phase 3 | 122 | 59.0 km² |
| Phase 4 | 59 | 122.0 km² |

However, population density in central Europe was much higher in areas occupied by Linear communities than those inhabited by hunters and gatherers.

A Linear village consisting of longhouses and various other features such as pits occupied an area of 2–3 ha (5–7 acres). Frequently there is more than one Linear culture occupation at a site, thus cultural material and features may occur over a much larger area than was occupied by any one village. Sites with multiple occupations may be 10, 20, or even 50 ha in size. For example, Bylany in Czechoslovakia occupies 22 ha, and Olszanica in Poland, 50 ha. The longhouses usually are spaced 15 to 20 m apart, and 7 to 12 of them comprised a village at one time period (Figure 5.8). At Bylany, there were 7 to 10 houses during each occupational phase (Soudský and Pavlů 1972). At least 8 longhouses formed a village during the so-called music note phase at Olszanica in Poland (Milisauskas 1972, 1976a, 1976b). Linear longhouses range from 7 to 45 m in length and from 5 to over 6 m in width. The extreme length of the longhouses is overemphasized by archaeologists in some sites (Figure 5.9), such as at Bylany, where 24 of the 48 houses described were less than 14 m in length.

The frames of the rectangular houses were built of five rows of wooden posts, two exterior rows and three interior rows (Figure 5.10). The interior postmolds are usually larger than the exterior. In the earlier phases, posts belonging to the two exterior walls were sometimes inserted in wall slots or

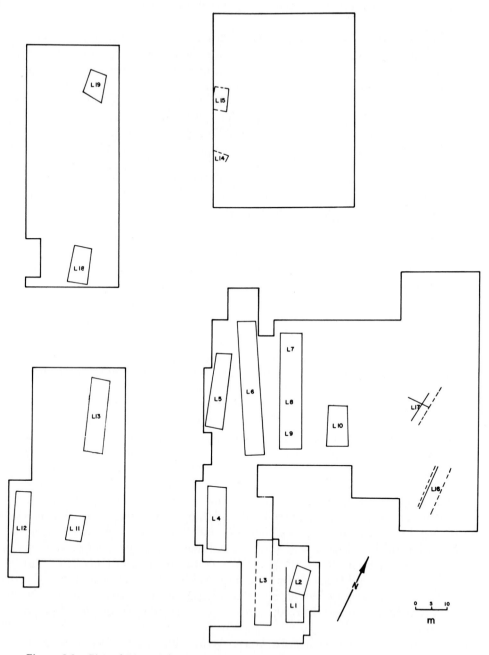

**Figure 5.8.** Plan of Olszanica. (L represents longhouse.)

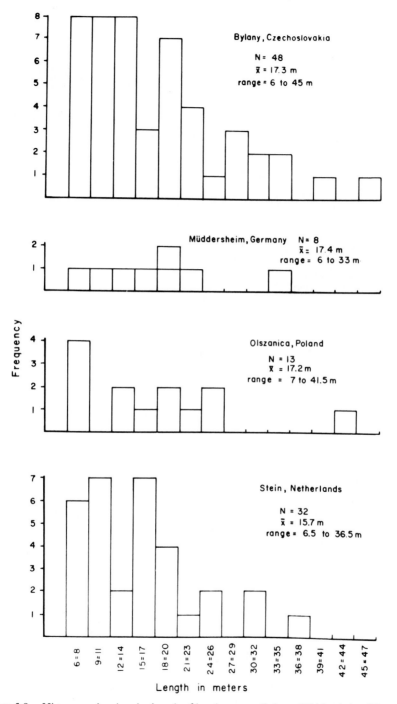

**Figure 5.9.** Histogram showing the length of longhouses at Bylany, Müddersheim, Olszanica, and Stein. (Data are from Soudský and Pavlů 1972; Schietzel 1965; Milisauskas 1976b; Modderman 1970.)

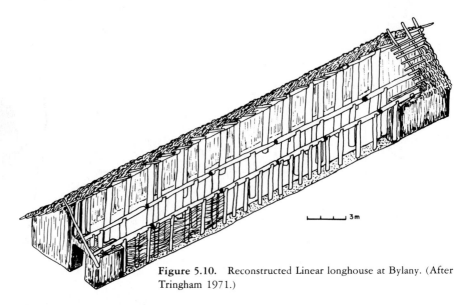

**Figure 5.10.** Reconstructed Linear longhouse at Bylany. (After Tringham 1971.)

trenches, rather than postholes. The earth from pits along the side of long-houses was used for daubing the walls. The longhouses were usually built of deciduous trees such as oak at Bylany; elm, ash, or oak at Langweiler 2 (Table 5.9), but at some sites, for example, Olszanica in Poland, they were con-structed of coniferous trees. At Bylany, usually 10 to 11-year-old oak trees were used for building houses (Soudský and Pavlů 1972). That the roofs of these houses were gabled, to better shed rain and snow, is suggested by clay house models from Middle Neolithic sites in central Europe. Sangmeister (1951) has postulated that the gabled roofs of Linear houses had a 45° inclina-tion; thus if walls were 2 m high, the entire house would have been 4 to 5 m high. The extremely long longhouses, 35 or 40 m in length, show structural differences from the ordinary types—larger postmolds and postmold pits—and may have been functionally different from others. They may have served for some kind of communal activities, for if their size depended only on the size of the social unit inhabiting them, we would expect to find no structural differences. Also, around these longhouses certain kinds of artifacts such as polished stone tools occur in greater quantities. An example of such a com-munal house is longhouse No. 6 at Olszanica (Figure 5.11) (Milisauskas 1972, 1976a, 1976b).

In the past, archaeologists probably overestimated the population of Linear culture longhouses. In estimating the population, it was assumed that the size of the social group inhabiting a longhouse was reflected by the structure's length. Soudský (1964, 1966), for example, concluded that 5 to 6 m of house length was occupied by one family, based on analogy with Lengyel or Tripolyean houses of the Middle and Late Neolithic period.

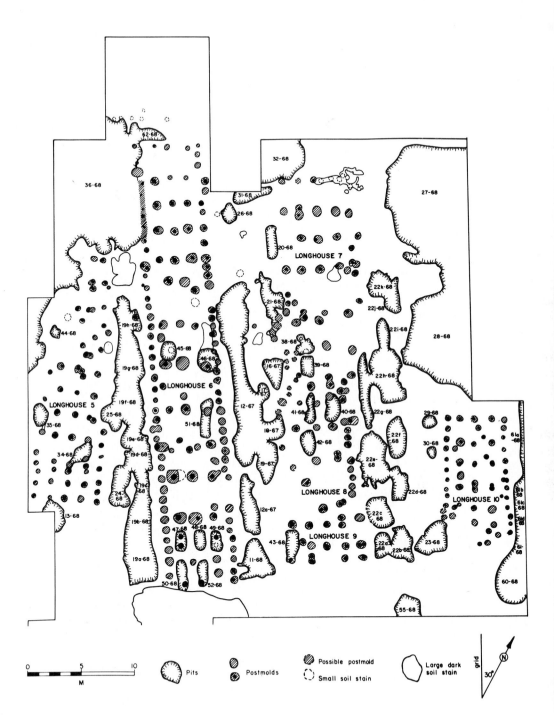

**Figure 5.11.** Plan of the northern area of Olszanica B1.

In using this method to estimate population, first we have to make a number of assumptions:

1. In the Tripolyean or Lengyel houses, each oven or hearth was used by one family.
2. The ovens or hearths in Tripolyean or Lengyel houses were contemporaneous.
3. The number of ovens or hearths and the number of families were functionally related to the length of the house.
4. Processes producing the same relationship between the ovens or hearths and the families as in the Tripolyean and Lengyel cultures were also operating in other Neolithic cultures.

The validity of all these assumptions can be questioned. This does not mean, however, that there is no relationship between the increase in length or area of Tripolyean houses and the greater number of ovens. I ran a product moment correlation test to check the relationship between the number of ovens and the area, length, and width of houses from Kolomiischchina I, a Tripolyean site in the Ukraine. The following results were obtained for the correlation of the ovens with:

$$\text{Area } r = .78; \text{ Length } r = .71; \text{ Width } r = .72$$

These results are statistically significant at the .001 level, and the best correlation is with area. It should be noted that the correlations are not too strong; thus in a straight statistical sense, 50% of the variability can be explained by this factor. No hearths or ovens have been found in Linear culture houses, although during the winter, hearths would probably have been needed inside the longhouses. Also, there are no internal divisions inside longhouses that could be associated with individual families. Perhaps extended families inhabited Linear houses, and their variability in size is reflected in the lengths of longhouses.

Using Soudský's method, and estimating 6 persons per family, and 24 families per occupation phase, an estimate of 125–150 people is obtained as the population of a Linear village for a single occupation. This figure, however, is probably excessive, since the quantity of archaeological material, such as pottery in Linear sites, is small and hardly compatible with the estimated population. This would indicate a small population or may be accounted for by a postulated short duration of the settlements on account of slash-and-burn agriculture. It is also possible that parts of the houses were occupied by animals. Linear people kept domesticated animals such as cattle, goats, sheep, and pigs in their villages; during the winter these animals would have needed to be put in stalls, but no special structures for animals have been identified.

To test the hypothesis that animals and humans occupied the longhouses together, this author carried out an experiment at Olszanica in Poland. If, indeed, parts of the longhouses were used as barns, we would expect that the soil in these areas would have a higher nitrogen content, as a result of the accumulation of the dung of animals located there three or four winters in succession. Such an accumulation would not result from contemporary or recent grazing of animals. Chemical tests were carried out in 1973 to test this hypothesis on one longhouse. The result was that the nitrogen content was found to be higher inside the longhouse than in the areas outside; however, no variability occurred within the house. It is therefore possible that animals as well as people occupied these longhouses. However, occupation solely by people has not been ruled out. A successful test on one longhouse is not a positive proof for the hypothesis.

There are a number of differences that can be seen between the Early Neolithic sites in central Europe and those in southeastern Europe. The total area occupied by a Linear village at one time was greater than that of the Early Neolithic community in southeastern Europe (Table 5.12). The houses were usually larger, and the spacing between individual houses was greater. As previously mentioned, judging from the reconstruction of Karanovo I village in the National Archaeological Museum in Sofia, Bulgaria, 18 small houses closely clustered together comprised the village. The basic plan of Linear villages consists of staggered rows of houses. We do not know what the greater variability in the size of individual Linear houses indicates in terms of socioeconomic organization. It may simply reflect demographic fluctuations, although the overall population of the Early Neolithic villages in central Europe probably was not greater than that in southeastern Europe. An Early Neolithic village in Bulgaria had smaller houses than the Linear culture, but it had a greater number of them.

There is more evidence for communal activities in the central European Early Neolithic sites than in those of southeastern Europe. In Linear culture villages we find so-called domestic areas that contain pits with ovens. These features probably served to dry grain for the entire community. Some Linear culture houses appear to have been used for communal activities. The evidence for southeastern European sites suggests that storing, cooking, or drying of the grain was done in individual houses because they contain ovens and hearths. Except for Nea Nikomedeia and Obre I, there is little differentiation in the size or artifactual content of houses in southeastern Europe.

### Bükk Culture

The settlement organization of the Bükk culture is very interesting. Bükk sites are found in the karst area of northeastern Hungary and southeastern Slovakia, a region dissected by many canyons and valleys. They are found in an area of 700 km² (Figure 5.12). The northern part of this region is 700–800 m above sea level (a.s.l.) and the southern part 300–400 m a.s.l. Its soils are not very fertile. The obsidian sources at the Slovakian–Hungarian border region lie within the zone occupied by the Bükk culture.

TABLE 5.12 Summary Data on the Early Neolithic Villages in Southeastern and Central Europe

| | Estimated size of a village (in ha) | Estimated number of houses | Estimated number of houses per 1 ha | Estimated population per average house[a] | Estimated population of a village |
|---|---|---|---|---|---|
| Nea Nikomedeia (Greece) | .5 | 15 | 30 | House = 8 × 8 m<br>= 64m²/10 m²<br>= 6.4 people/house[a] | 96 |
| Karanovo I (Bulgaria) | ? | 18 | ? | House = 6 × 7 m<br>= 42 m²/10 m²<br>= 4.2 people/house | 76 |
| Bylany (Czechoslovakia) | 2.5 | 7–10 | 3–4 | House = 17 × 5 m<br>= 85 m²/10 m²<br>= 8.5 people/house | 60–85 |
| Olszanica (Poland) | 2.5 | 8–9 | 3–4 | House = 17 × 5 m<br>= 85 m²/10 m²<br>= 8.5 people/house | 68–77 |

[a] Estimated using Naroll's (1962) formula.

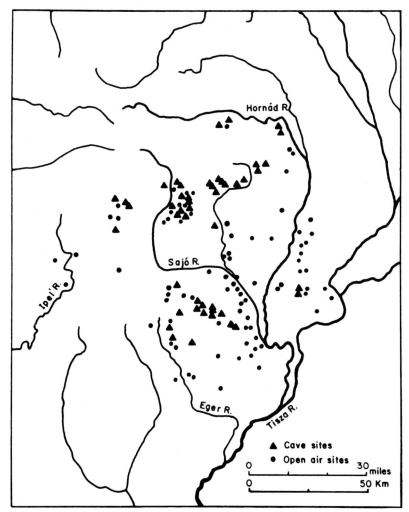

**Figure 5.12.**   Distribution of Bükk culture sites. (After Lichardus 1974.)

The Bükk culture is represented by both open-air and cave sites, and most of our information about the culture comes from the latter (Lichardus 1974). This would imply that a transhumant population existed in this area of the Carpathians: The open sites were the main settlements, and the caves were seasonally occupied shepherd's camps. However, the material in cave sites reflects a variety of activities and does not seem to differ greatly in function from open-air sites.

Observations about the open-air sites must be treated with caution, since no extensive excavations have been carried out on these. The open-air sites differ from one another in size: Large ones, probably the villages, are located along the rivers and streams in the valleys. Small open-air sites are frequently found near the top of low elevations and often are situated not far from the cave sites. It is evident that the Bükk culture settlement system is not simple, but more excavations are needed to define the relationship among the various sites.

## Alpine

In the Alpine zone of Europe, mainly in Switzerland, the Early Neolithic Cortaillod sites are found along rivers and lakes. The Cortaillod villages consisted of small square or rectangular wooden houses. For example, the Swiss settlement of Egolzwil 4 had 10 houses that were located close to each other, so that the area occupied by a village was smaller than that of the Linear culture villages. The small size of the houses, which I assume were occupied by individual families, would likewise indicate a smaller population. If a single family consisted of 4 or 5 persons, the population of the village was probably 40 to 50 people at any one time. No longhouses are found in the Alpine zone.

Perishable materials such as wood, bone, textiles, and crop remains, which are not usually recovered from archaeological sites, are exceptionally well preserved in some of the Swiss sites. These finds reflect a sophisticated Neolithic technology as it pertains to woodworking, fishing, hunting, and clothing (Figures 5.13, 5.14, and 5.15). They were preserved because the settlements were covered by water or marsh after their abandonment, due to the rise in the levels of the lakes to which they were adjacent. These lake sediments sealed the sites in an airless environment that greatly inhibited the action of the bacteria, etc., which normally cause decay. Incidentally, earlier European archaeologists believed, because of the situation in which these sites were found, that they had actually been built out over the water, on stilts. We know now, however, that these so-called Lake Dweller sites were on dry land when they were occupied. The excellent preservation gives us information about the type and age of wood utilized in construction. At Egolzwil 3, a site belonging to the Cortaillod culture, ash trees were most commonly used in building (Table 5.13). The next two most frequently utilized wood types are oak and alder. The great majority of trees used in construction range from 10 to 50 years in age (Table 5.14). Furthermore, the Swiss Neolithic sites show a great variability and excellence in woodworking techniques for making various domestic utensils. This is well illustrated by Wyss's (1969) synthesis on the Neolithic economy and technology in Switzerland (Figure 5.13). We can assume that similar wooden tools were made by Neolithic farmers in the other regions of Europe; however, they have not been preserved.

## Social Organization

It is difficult to discuss the social, political, and ritual aspects of Early Neolithic European societies, since little archaeological work has been directed specifically and systematically at these problems. However, even ar-

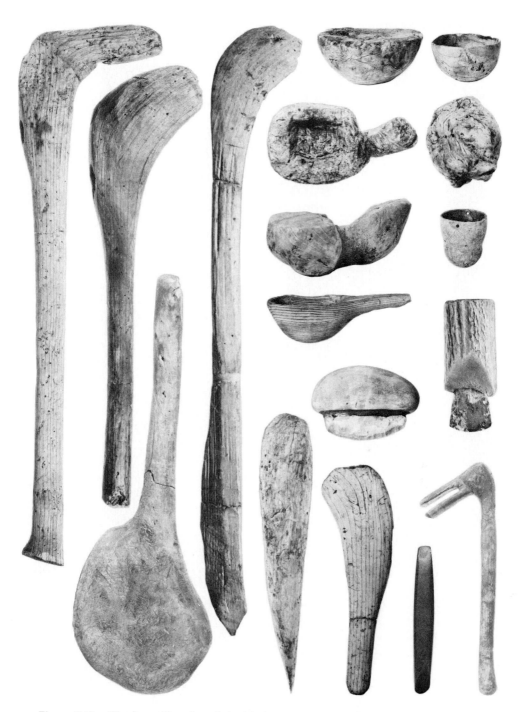

**Figure 5.13.** Wooden artifacts from Swiss Neolithic sites. (From Wyss 1969.)

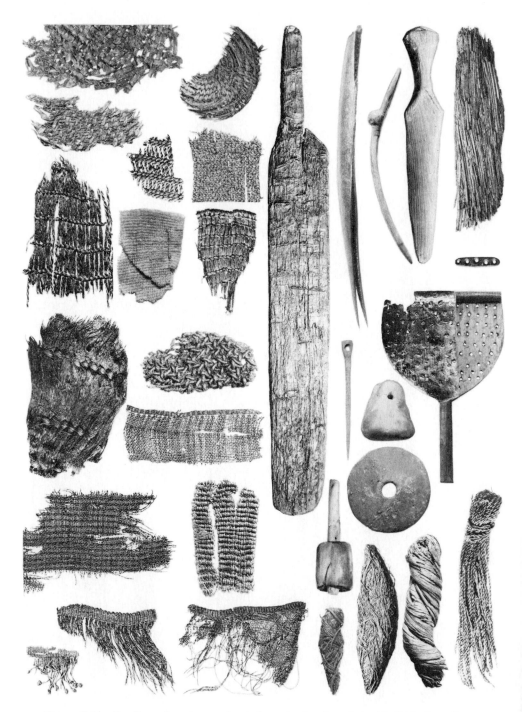

**Figure 5.14.** Textiles and equipment for their production from Swiss Neolithic sites. (From Wyss 1969.)

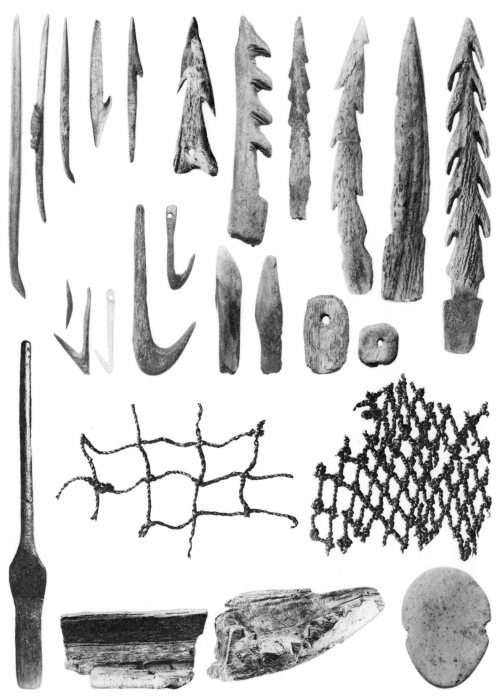

**Figure 5.15.** Fishing equipment from Swiss Neolithic sites. (From Wyss 1969.)

**TABLE 5.13   Types of Wood Utilized at the Egolzwil 3 Site, Switzerland (N = 335 Posts)**[a]

|              | Number | Percentage |
|--------------|--------|------------|
| Ash          | 171    | 52         |
| Oak          | 71     | 21         |
| Alder        | 30     | 9          |
| Maple        | 17     | 5          |
| Hazel        | 14     | 4          |
| Elm          | 14     | 4          |
| Poplar       | 6      | 1.8        |
| Willow       | 4      | 1.2        |
| Birch        | 2      | 0.6        |
| Mountain ash | 2      | 0.6        |
| Beech        | 1      | 0.3        |

[a] From Vogt 1954.

**TABLE 5.14   Age of Wooden Posts at Egolzwil 3 Site, Switzerland**[a]

|              | 1–9 years | 10–19 years | 20–29 years | 30–39 years | 40–49 years | 50–59 years | 60–69 years | 70–79 years | Totals |
|--------------|-----------|-------------|-------------|-------------|-------------|-------------|-------------|-------------|--------|
| Ash          |           | 19          | 57          | 31          | 48          | 14          | 4           | 1           | 174    |
| Oak          |           | 3           | 47          | 19          | 2           |             |             |             | 71     |
| Alder        | 1         | 2           | 22          | 5           |             |             |             |             | 30     |
| Maple        |           | 1           | 3           | 8           | 1           | 1           | 1           | 1           | 16     |
| Hazel        |           |             | 9           | 4           | 1           |             |             |             | 14     |
| Elm          |           | 6           | 7           | 1           |             |             |             |             | 14     |
| Poplar       |           | 1           | 5           |             |             |             |             |             | 6      |
| Willow       |           |             | 3           |             |             |             |             |             | 3      |
| Birch        |           |             | 1           | 1           |             |             |             |             | 2      |
| Mountain ash |           |             | 2           |             |             |             |             |             | 2      |
| Beech        |           |             |             |             | 1           |             |             |             | 1      |
| Totals       | 1         | 32          | 156         | 69          | 53          | 15          | 5           | 2           | 333    |

[a] From Vogt 1954.

chaeological projects aimed mainly at reconstructing culture histories have provided data from settlements and cemeteries that can be used for our purposes. Especially helpful are burial data indicating the different statuses of individuals.

## Status Differences

The archaeological data recovered from cemeteries suggest that, in some parts of Europe, status differences did exist in Early Neolithic communities. This observation is further supported by some of the settlement data. In analyzing the cemetery material, I am following Saxe (1971:39) in assuming that:

> an individual's treatment at death is a reflection of the position occupied in a status system in life, and that differences between individual interments reflect the type of status system participated in (e.g., egalitarian versus ranked), the outlines of extinct status systems should be ascertainable.

Various artifacts found in burials may reflect the social roles and status of the individual with whom they are buried. We can postulate that different segments of a population—males, females, and different age groups—will be associated with different activities. House building, fighting, hunting, and cutting trees for clearing of agricultural land are probably male activities; thus it is to be expected that male burials would contain artifacts appropriate to such tasks. Nonlocal raw materials and their products may express wealth and status differences. Their presence in burials may indicate that certain males or females had higher status than others and participated in interregional exchange.

We know very little about the burial customs of the Early Neolithic farmers of Greece or of the other countries in southeastern Europe. At Nea Nikomedeia in Greece, the dead were buried in pits outside the houses. Few or no grave goods have been found with these burials. At Anza I in Yugoslavian Macedonia, 28 skeletons were found within the settlement (Gimbutas 1972). It seems that people were buried in settlements and no special areas were assigned for cemeteries.

At present, much more information is available from Early Neolithic cemeteries in central Europe than in the southeastern part of that continent. Thirty years ago, we had little data from Linear culture cemeteries, but now we are beginning to get good excavations and analyses of burials: Sondershausen (Kahlke 1954), Elsloo (Modderman 1970), Rixheim (Gallay and Schweitzer 1971), Nitra (Pavúk 1972) and Sengkofen (Osterhaus and Pleyer 1973). It is very unfortunate that at Elsloo the skeletal material was not preserved. Usually the Linear cemeteries are located 100 to 500 m from the settlement (Figure 5.16).

In considering the central European Early Neolithic cemeteries, we can examine the Nitra cemetery in Slovakia as a good example. At Nitra, the artifacts associated with burials indicate that status differences were based primarily on age and sex. *Spondylus* shells and other artifacts made of nonlocal raw material are strongly associated with old males (Figure 5.17). This may indicate that the older males were more important in the community and participated in an interregional exchange system. At the Sondershausen cemetery in the German Democratic Republic, females as well as males were buried with *Spondylus* products. At this cemetery, burials that contained *Spon-*

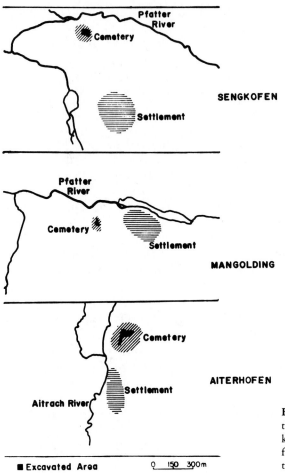

Figure 5.16. Linear culture settlements and cemeteries at Sengkofen, Mangolding, and Aiterhofen in eastern Bavaria. (After Osterhaus 1975.)

*dylus* had more burial goods than burials that did not. The tendency toward male "gerontocracy" at Nitra is further supported by the association of polished stone tools and chipped stone artifacts with adult or old males. Incidentally, pottery, usually assumed to be the artifact appropriate to female tasks, is not associated with women at the Nitra cemetery.

Polished stone tools were probably valued as prestige items and functioned in the social and ideological systems of the culture, rather than being mainly utilitarian woodworking tools. There are relatively few of these, and some are made from nonlocal materials. For example, 39 polished stone tools, including several small chips, were found at Olszanica B1 in Poland. Ten longhouses from two or three Linear occupations were found in the 3400 m² area. This gives an average of 3.9 polished stone tools per house or probably not more than 2 per adult male at one time period. It is possible, however, that this quantity represents only a portion of all the polished stone tools that existed in

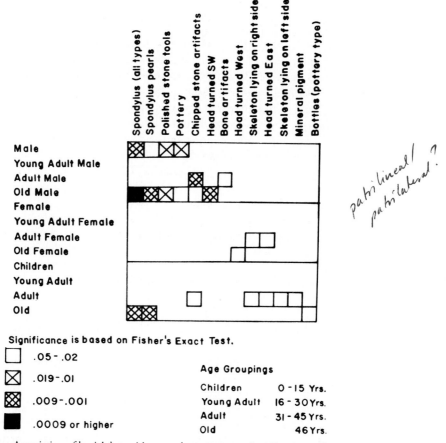

**Figure 5.17.** Association of burial data with sex and age groups at the Nitra cemetery. (Data are from Pavúk 1972.)

this community. Some may have been lost or discarded when broken away from the village, perhaps in the forests where they were used to fell trees or shape logs. On the other hand, over 16,000 flint artifacts were found at Olszanica B1, and only approximately 6% were retouched tools. The total contained approximately 300 endscrapers, 35 were macro-endscrapers, and 160 sidescrapers. Probably some of these scrapers were used for woodworking. At Elsloo, Modderman (1970) found only one endscraper in 113 burials. It appears that artifacts used mainly for utilitarian purposes were rarely deposited in burials. The polished stone tools that were deposited in graves required more time to manufacture than endscrapers or other chipped-stone artifacts. Furthermore, since many of the polished stone tools are made of nonlocal stone material, it is clear that objects of value were being deposited in the graves. Archaeologists usually assume that imported goods found in graves reflect a higher status.

## Mortality, Longevity, Sex Ratios, and Population Composition

For the Early Neolithic populations in Greece, we have Angel's (1973) analysis of the human skeletal material at Nea Nikomedeia. In regular burials, 13 adults, 13 children, and 9 infants were found. Thirty-one adults, 21 children, and no infants were represented by single bones or by very incomplete skeletons. Thus, altogether, the remains of 87 humans were found. However, Angel increases the total population number to 105. Since no infants were represented by single bones, he suggests that the probable infant population was three times higher than was found. The longevity of 20 adult males was 31.0 years, and 29.9 years for 23 females. The male stature was 168 cm. He also estimated the fecundity rate from seven female pelvises studied. The estimate was five births per female.

Pavúk's (1972) excellent work at the Nitra cemetery gives us some information about the population composition, mortality, and sex ratios in central Europe during the Early Neolithic. He excavated 74 skeletons; one of them, belonging to a child, is probably of the Late Neolithic Baden culture. Out of the 73 Linear human skeletons represented here, 9 reached the age of 50 (Table 5.15). Thus, if this sample is representative, one would have only a 12% chance at birth to reach the age of 50. Twenty-two skeletons were those of children aged 15 years or younger, 10 (45%) of which had no burial goods. This is comparable to adult females, 10 out of 23 (45%) of which had no burial goods. The adult males received differential or preferential treatment. Only 6 out of 27 (25%) were without burial goods. Usually there are more adult males found in Linear culture cemeteries than females. This is the case in many Neolithic sites (Häusler 1966) (Table 5.16). Frequently, the number of children buried in Neolithic cemeteries is not great.

Data from modern populations indicate that male and female births occur in approximately equal proportions. However, this parity is not always reflected in archaeological data. Various cultural practices may account for the unequal sex ratios. If there existed the practice of female infanticide or differential treatment of children by parents, such as a better diet for males, more females than males would have died at a younger age. In the event that female

TABLE 5.15 Proportions of Each Sex by Age Group at Nitra[a]

| | Young adult 16–30 years | | Adult 31–45 years | | Old 46 years | | Totals | |
|---|---|---|---|---|---|---|---|---|
| | N | % | N | % | N | % | N | % |
| Female | 11 | 23 | 7 | 15 | 4 | 8 | 22 | 46 |
| Male | 5 | 10 | 16 | 33 | 5 | 10 | 26 | 53 |
| Age group totals | 16 | 33 | 23 | 48 | 9 | 18 | 48 | 99 |

[a] Data are from Pavúk 1972.

TABLE 5.16 Neolithic Cemeteries

| Cemetery | Culture | Total number of burials found | Number of adults identified | Number of children identified | Number of adult males identified[a] | Number of adult females identified[b] | Source |
|---|---|---|---|---|---|---|---|
| Sondershausen, Germany | Linear | 28 | 22 | 5 | 12 (55%) | 10 (45%) | Kahlke 1954 |
| Nitra, Czechoslovakia | Linear | 73 | 50 | 22 | 27 (54%) | 23 (46%) | Pavúk 1972 |
| Rixheim, France | Linear | 16 | 13 | 3 | 8 (62%) | 5 (39%) | Galley and Schweitzer 1971 |
| Brześć Kujawski, Poland | Lengyel | 36 | 30 | 6 | 19 (63%) | 11 (37%) | Gabałówna 1966 |
| Zengövárkony, Hungary | Lengyel | 368 | | 70 | 80 (63%) | 47 (37%) | Dombay 1960 |
| Tiszapolgár-Basatanya I, Hungary | Tiszapolgár | 57 | 38 | 19 | 25 (69%) | 11 (29%) | Bognár-Kutzián 1963 |
| Tiszapolgár-Basatanya II, Hungary | Bodrogkeresztúr | 87 | 78 | 9 | 38 (51%) | 36 (49%) | Bognár-Kutzián 1963 |
| Budakalacz, Hungary | Baden | 305 | | 53 | 44 (61%) | 28 (39%) | Banner 1956 |
| Vikletice, Czechoslovakia | Corded Ware | 130 | 86 | 32[c] | 18 (69%) | 8 (31%) | Buchvaldek and Koutecký 1970 |
| Vychvatintsi, Soviet Union | Late Tripolye | 59 | 19 | 33 | 12 (63%) | 7 (37%) | Passek 1961 |

[a] In each cemetery, there were one or two skeletons that were questionably identified as male or female. I included them by the sex identified.
[b] Percentages refer to the ratio of adult males to adult females.
[c] Juveniles (12–18 years) were included with adults; 12 juveniles were found.

infanticide was practiced, we would not expect to find the victims buried in the cemeteries.

The disproportion between sexes is not so evident in Linear culture cemeteries (Table 5.16). There are only a few more males than females. It is possible that, as a culture expanding into an unused agricultural territory, the Linear people did not need to practice cultural methods such as female infanticide to limit population.

Linear culture females had less of a chance to reach old age, as is shown by the Nitra cemetery data. Seventeen out of 21 females died between the ages of 16 and 40, whereas only 11 males out of 26 died in the same age group. Warfare could have accounted for many of the young males' deaths, while death in childbirth would have ended the lives of many young women. However, both sexes would probably have suffered equally from warfare, since, at this level of sociopolitical development, war consisted more of sudden raids on villages than of pitched battles between male warriors. On the other hand, death in childbirth might have been regarded, as it is in some ethnographically known societies, as a punishment for some breach of the moral code. Such women may have been denied burial in the community cemetery; hence, they would be absent from our calculations. But some young males, killed in war or in hunting accidents away from home, would also be absent from our calculations. The age of the children at death is revealing. The majority of them died before they reached 6 years of age. This correlates well with the observation that children's mortality at such a level of socioeconomic development is greatest during the first few years of life (Cook 1972).

At Niedermerz, a Linear culture cemetery in Germany, two of the eight skeletons possessed the Carabelli trait on their molars (A. and H. Czarnetzki 1971:658). The size of the population is very small at Niedermerz, but still we should note that this frequency of Carabelli's cusp is comparatively similar to modern European populations. For example, it occurs in roughly 19.9% of the population in Germany (Kallay quoted by Krauss 1959:119). This trait has a low frequency of occurrence among populations in Asia (Moorrees 1957:40).

### Postmarital Residence Patterns

Most archaeological studies of postmarital residence patterns have been done by American archaeologists (Deetz 1965, Hill 1970, Longacre 1970). However, some Europeans are interested in these problems (Soudský 1962). It is the Linear culture that has been most intensively studied in this regard.

Many archaeologists have speculated that the Linear society was matrilocal and perhaps even matrilineal. This is frequently based on very general ethnographic analogy. For example, when subsistence derives mainly from female activities, when there is no intensive warfare, and when the political integration is at a low level, the matrilocal rule of residence would be the one most likely to be present (Murdock 1949:205). Ethnographic data indicate that longhouses are frequently associated with matrilocal (e.g., Iroquois) and bilocal societies (e.g., Iban of Borneo). Ember's cross-cultural study (1973) indicates that societies possessing houses with an area of more than 70 m² are usually matrilocal. He assumes that two or more married women would more likely live together in a house in matrilocal societies than in patrilocal ones. Thus, matrilocal societies usually would have larger houses than patrilocal societies. Many Linear culture houses are over 70 m² in area, but there are also many small houses (Figure 5.9). We should be aware of the great variability in the length of the Linear culture houses especially when trying to demonstrate by ethnographic analogy the presence of matrilocality or matrilineality within that culture. Furthermore, it should be remembered that in utilizing ethnographic data from the Old and the New World for comparative purposes, we should be aware that New World societies had very few, if any, domesticated animals. In the Old World, part of the house could have been occupied by animals; therefore, a meter-to-meter comparison is not necessarily valid.

Divale (1974) has shown that in a cross-cultural perspective, matrilocal residence is frequently associated with a population migrating into a new territory. This may be applicable to the Linear culture, since it was expanding over central Europe. In matrilocal societies, man's agnatic (male) kin are dispersed among neighboring villages; therefore, any fight with these communities would involve one in a struggle with one's kin. As a result, there is less internal warfare. The warfare of matrilocal societies is externally oriented, that is, directed toward other cultural groups. This gives such societies an advantage in warfare with nonmatrilocal societies that are frequently involved in internal warfare. However, if matrilocal societies did possess such a tactical advantage, we would expect them to be much more frequent in the ethnographic record.

During his career, Soudský, the excavator of the large Linear culture site of Bylany in Czechoslovakia, has made important contributions to the study of European Neolithic. On the basis of distribution of different pottery decorative motifs in Linear sites, Soudský (1962, 1964, 1966) argues that a matrilocal postmarital residence rule was prescribed and that the Linear society was matrilineal:

> I should like to point out, . . . that a correlation of this type of evidence with the anthropological data from cemeteries of the Linear pottery culture, with analyses of fingerprints on the vessels (consistently female), and with the determination of the individual and local traditions in pottery production, suggests that the kin relations were matrilinear [Soudský 1962:198].

It is questionable that sex can be determined from fingerprints on Neolithic pottery. Also, it is very difficult to demonstrate postmarital residence rules without even mentioning descent rules—whether an individual traces descent through the female or male line (Deetz 1968; Allen and Richardson 1971). As yet, no one has been able to demonstrate matrilocality in Linear communities.

*patrilocal*

*bilateral*

Even if we assume that the Linear culture was matrilocal or even matrilineal, the burial data suggest that males held domestic authority and political power within the group.

The Linear people may have possessed a very flexible social organization that was, perhaps, a kindred, which is simply a group made up of an individual's relatives. Corporate groups such as clans or lineages usually function as landholding groups. However, since the Linear people were not restricted in their choice of land, there may be no need to postulate the presence of corporate landholding groups.

## Sociopolitical Organization

The available information on Early Neolithic settlement systems suggests their sociopolitical organization possessed only one administrative level. That is, the communities were politically independent from one another and approximately equivalent in their structure and functioning. The only observed differences among settlements relate to subsistence activities, such as permanent villages and herding and hunting camps in a single group's settlement system. Societies with one level of administration have been classified as tribal societies (Johnson 1973). For example, the Linear people in central Europe represented the tribal level of sociocultural development. Their settlement system indicates no integration above the level of the individual community. We can assume that the individual villages were politically and economically autonomous. Villages located close together may have been linked by kin relationships or by common membership in nonkinship sodalities or associations such as warrior or ceremonial societies or by the charismatic qualities of some individual.

The data from cemeteries have indicated that older males probably had higher statuses. Some males may have been leaders in a village, and perhaps some of them achieved so-called Big-Man status (Sahlins 1963). This type of leadership depends on the person's charisma and personal skills. As long as he can impress the other members of the community with his deeds or achievements, he is a leader. For a variety of reasons, his followers may reject or abandon him at any time. It is evident that this type of leadership cannot be inherited. Furthermore, some of these Big Men may even have had political influence on neighboring villages during their lifetimes. Such a leader can greatly influence decision making, especially in the household production of a village. In attempting to extend his fame to neighboring villages, he might make too many demands, e.g., pushing for increased production of agricultural products for gifts to nonkin. Excessive demands or attempts to exploit kinsmen may bring about his downfall.

The extremely long longhouses found at some Linear sites may be associated with the village leadership. As previously mentioned, these longhouses may have been used for communal activities or for the activities of tribal associations or sodalities. However, it is also possible that the most important man, such as the Big Man in the village, inhabited the longest longhouse. This does not imply that there was inherited ranking of individuals in Linear society, but only that a man or woman could achieve greater status on the basis of personal skills or personality traits, and would therefore have the responsibility of acting as host to visitors and villagers alike.

In general, there is little evidence of warfare during the European Early Neolithic. Few Linear settlements were fortified, except those at the Late Linear villages of Köln-Lindenthal and Langweiler in the Federal Republic of Germany. Possible weapons are not numerous: Only small quantities of projectile points have been found, and the relatively few stone axes could well have served other purposes.

## Ritual Organization

I assume that the Early Neolithic people performed a variety of religious activities or rituals. However, there is a major problem in determining what structures or artifacts were used for ritual purposes during the Early Neolithic. Unusual kinds of structures or buildings containing nonutilitarian artifacts may indicate their "sacred" purpose. Various figurines, especially of females, are considered to have been used in rituals. However, the only evidence that these figurines are of ritual significance is their formal characteristics and sometimes the context of their discovery. *isn't this sufficient?*

Some evidence exists for possible communal ritual activities in southeastern Europe. At Nea Nikomedeia, the largest structure, approximately 13 × 15 m, was located in the center of the excavated area, and inside it were found five female figurines. This house could have been used for communal rituals. If we are dealing with a tribal society, the various rituals probably played an important role in holding the community together.

No special ceremonial structures have been identified at the Karanovo I site in Bulgaria, although anthropomorphic clay figurines found at this site could have played a role in rituals. Most such figurines depict females. They have small breasts and large buttocks, as if they had steatopygia, that is, unusually fatty or large buttocks.

Animals may have been important in rituals at some settlements. The Starčevo layer at Lepenski Vir in Yugoslavia contained the remains of many dogs: This is the only site where these animals were numerous. Most of the animals were adults, and the majority of the skeletons were articulated, indi-

ritual? or just doing?

cating that the animals had not been dismembered or butchered for meat prior to their burial. The burials appear to be deliberate and suggest that dogs played some role in the rituals of the people.

In central Europe, the Linear people probably placed different emphasis on rituals than the Early Neolithic people in southeastern Europe. Some differences may be reflected by the rare occurrence of the so-called mother-goddess figurines, which were common throughout the entire area of southeastern Europe. Indeed, figurines of any type are much rarer in central and northern Europe throughout the Neolithic, than in southeastern Europe. Figurines not only can reflect some types of ritual but also can supply information about dress and body treatment. Some of the Linear culture figurines are ornamented with small pits or impressions that might indicate that the people practiced body decoration or tattooing.

# Chapter 6

# Middle Neolithic

We have seen that there was considerable cultural homogeneity among the Early Neolithic farming societies of Europe, especially in central Europe. In contrast, the Middle Neolithic reflects a period in Europe of increasing cultural diversity and complexity. We can observe changes in the economy, society, politics, and rituals. The following suggested variables probably were among those involved in these changes: (*a*) technological advances, (*b*) demographic variations, (*c*) competition for resources, (*d*) increase in warfare, and (*e*) change in subsistence strategies and exchange networks. These suggested sources of change are interrelated, and there is no single causal factor responsible for the greater socioeconomic complexity in Europe during the Middle Neolithic.

The Middle Neolithic witnessed a further expansion of farming societies into parts of Europe previously inhabited only by hunters and gatherers: Switzerland, Scandinavia, and England. Some of these societies such as Cortaillod were discussed in Chapter 5. The apparent expansion of farming societies into areas of central Europe previously exploited by hunters and gatherers may suggest population increase. As discussed in Chapter 5, the appearance of farmers in areas such as Scandinavia that were previously occupied by hunters and gatherers is a very labor-intensive process. The opening of new agricultural areas may be related to population increase. Furthermore, the Middle Neolithic saw the first major expansion of cultivation in nonloess soil areas in central Europe. This too may be a labor-intensive enterprise. Thus, as we move from the Early Neolithic to the Middle Neolithic, increasing amounts of land were under cultivation by agriculturalists.

An increase in Europe's population during the Middle Neolithic is reflected in data from settlements and cemeteries. For example, Kruk has found 72 Linear (Early Neolithic) sites in an area of over 2300 km² in southeastern

Poland (Figure 5.7). The same area contained 99 Funnel Beaker sites (Kruk 1973a). The time spans for these two cultures are roughly similar in this region.

Population increases are also suggested by data from cemeteries in central Europe. For example, the Middle Neolithic cemetery of Zengövarkony in Hungary had 368 burials. This contrasts with the Early Neolithic Linear culture cemeteries, which were small. The largest Linear cemeteries at Flomborn in Germany and Elsloo in the Netherlands contained 85 and 113 burials, respectively. However, this data may also indicate that Middle Neolithic settlements were occupied for longer periods than Early Neolithic ones.

The changes occurring at the end of the Middle Neolithic are also reflected in the greater variability of artifact types and changes in stone technology, which can be demonstrated for flint, stone, and clay tools. For example, in addition to polished stone axes, we find numerous polished flint axes and adzes. A greater variability is also reflected in the size of flint tools. Most of the flint tools made in central Europe during the Early Neolithic were not very long, having been made from short cores: The majority of Linear culture blades, for example, range in length from 2 to 6 cm. In contrast, some of the blades of the Middle Neolithic Funnel Beaker culture are 25 cm long (Balcer 1971). Such artifacts can be produced only from long cores, and long cores only are locally available. The greater variability in the size of flint tools probably is associated to some extent with flint mining, which itself suggests regional or occupational specialization, and, therefore, increasing sociocultural complexity. More intensive exploitation of flint sources is related to increased demand associated with warfare, trade, and various domestic uses.

Similar changes can be observed in pottery. Linear pottery consists of two main types, finely and coarsely made. Most vessels are bowls, whereas only a small proportion are bottles or other types. The largest of the coarsely made vessels, some of which have a volume of 18 l, were probably used for storage. During the Middle Neolithic, not only were a greater variety of vessels manufactured, but some of them were very large. Large Funnel Beaker vessels may have four or five times the capacity of those of the Linear culture. Large amounts of grain could have been stored in such vessels.

The Middle Neolithic began around 4500–4400 B.C. (5240–5100 B.C.) in Southeastern Europe. Veselinovo (Karanovo III), Vădastra, Dudesti, and Vinča-Tordos are some of the characteristic Middle Neolithic cultures in this region. The Veselinovo culture was located in southern Bulgaria, Vădastra and Dudesti in southern and central Romania. Vinča-Tordos material is found in western Bulgaria, southwest Romania, and Yugoslavia.

The Tripolye culture characterizes the Middle Neolithic developments in parts of the Ukraine, Moldavia, and Romania (Figure 6.1). However, the late phases of this culture fall within the Late Neolithic. This culture is sometimes referred to as the Cucuteni–Tripolye culture after the two sites in the Ukraine and Romania, respectively, at which it was first defined. However, for the sake of simplicity, the term *Tripolye* will be used throughout this text.

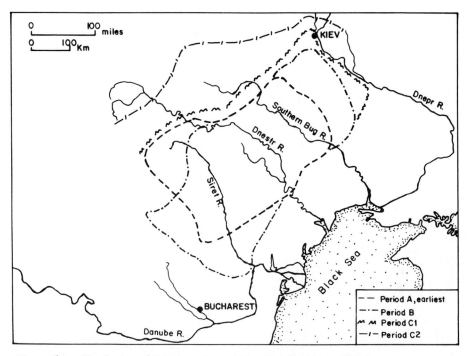

**Figure 6.1.** Distribution of Tripolye culture. (After Passek 1961, modified.)

Archaeologists divide Tripolye culture into phases A, B, and C, and a number of subphases, on the basis of differences in pottery styles. It covers a long period of time, roughly from 3800 (4470 B.C.) to 2200–2100 B.C. (2670–2550 B.C.), spanning the Middle and Late Neolithic. The early phase of this culture has a limited distribution; it is found only along the middle Dnestr and Southern Bug rivers. Later, the Tripolye culture expanded further east, west, and north, until it extended roughly from the Siret River in Romania to the Dnepr River in the Ukraine. The territory covered by the Tripolye culture, whose people inhabited the forest–steppe zone of south-western Ukraine and Romania, is noted for its fertile *chernozem* or black-earth soils.

Much of our information about the Tripolye culture comes from the excellent work of Passek (1949, 1961), who was one of the pioneers of this time period in the technique of uncovering large contiguous areas of a site at one time. This was a great contribution by Soviet archaeologists not only to Paleolithic studies, but also to the Neolithic in the 1930s. Nevertheless, the data on the Tripolye settlement system are very general, and more detailed analyses of the variability within the Tripolye settlement system are needed. Furthermore, impressive large-scale excavations of Neolithic sites were carried out by Buttler (Buttler and Haberey 1936) at Köln-Lindenthal in Germany and Jażdżewski (1938) at Brześć Kujawski in Poland.

The major Middle Neolithic archaeological manifestations in central Europe
are Funnel Beaker, Lengyel, Tisza, Stroke Ornamented, Rössen, and
Michelsberg. The Funnel Beaker culture, sometimes called TRB, Trichter-
becher, or First Northern, is named for the shape of a particular ceramic type
distinctive to it (Figure 6.2). It occurred in northern and central Germany, the
Netherlands, Denmark, southern Sweden, lower Austria, Moravia, Bohemia,
Poland, and areas of the Ukraine adjacent to Poland (Figure 6.3). The earliest
Funnel Beaker culture material dates to ca. 3600 B.C. (4350 B.C.) and the latest
to ca. 2300–2200 B.C. (2870–2670 B.C.). In Scandinavia it constitutes the
earliest Neolithic or farming culture. Some archaeologists claim that the
earliest Funnel Beaker ceramic material is limited to Denmark, northern
Germany, and northern Poland. However, recent excavations indicate that the
early ceramic material of the Funnel Beaker culture has a much wider distribu-

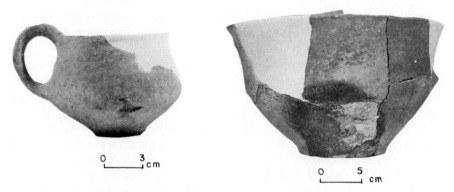

**Figure 6.2.** Funnel Beaker vessels from Bronocice, Poland. (From J. Kruk and S. Milisauskas
excavations; W. Hensel, project director.)

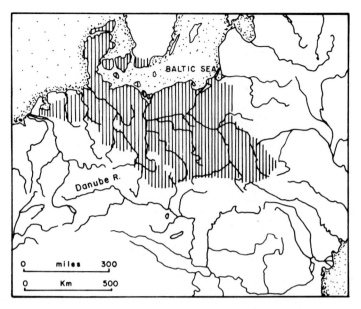

**Figure 6.3.** Distribution of Funnel Beaker sites. (After Jażdżewski 1936; Bakker, Vogel, and Wiślański 1969.)

tion. In central Europe the Funnel Beaker culture occurred during the Middle and Late Neolithic periods.

The Michelsberg culture, which some archaeologists consider just an extension of the Funnel Beaker culture, occurred in Switzerland, southern Germany, northeastern France, and Belgium.

The Lengyel culture, named for its type site in Hungary, is found in lower Austria, Czechoslovakia, Poland, Hungary, and parts of Yugoslavia. Ceramics of the Lengyel culture have a variety of forms, most of which are not ornamented (Figure 6.4). In some areas, the distribution of Lengyel and Funnel Beaker artifacts overlap. The earliest phase is dated around 4000–3900 B.C. (4600–4540 B.C.), and the latest, around 2800–2700 B.C. (3440–3340 B.C.). Thus in some regions of Poland and Czechoslovakia, Lengyel and Funnel Beaker sites may be contemporaneous. This is based on a number of radiocarbon dates. It is evident in some regions that the homogeneous and self-contained stylistic zones that are associated with the territories of the Early Neolithic societies are not duplicated during the Middle Neolithic. Perhaps the increase in stylistic heterogeneity is related to control of prime agricultural land. Ceramic styles may be used for group identification, and during the Middle Neolithic this is more important because the access to increasingly rare prime agricultural land could be achieved only through group membership. This might imply the appearance of corporate kin groups. We should emphasize that the large Funnel Beaker culture sites in Poland and Czechoslovakia date between 3200–2300 B.C. (3650–2870 B.C.) when the Lengyel culture appears to have been declining. It should be pointed out that I present

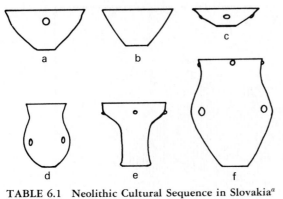

Figure 6.4. Lengyel ceramics from Czechoslovakia. Scale in a–b is 2:9; in c–f it is 1:9. (After Koštuřík 1972.)

**TABLE 6.1  Neolithic Cultural Sequence in Slovakia[a]**

|  | Western Slovakia |  |  | Eastern Slovakia |  |
|---|---|---|---|---|---|
| 4600–4500 B.C. |  |  |  |  |  |
|  | Early Linear |  | Barca III | Early Linear |  |
|  | Late Linear |  |  | Late Linear |  |
|  | Železovce Phase of the Linear Culture |  |  | Bükk |  |
| **Lengyel group** | Lužianky |  |  | Potiská |  |
|  | Nitriansky Hrádok |  |  |  | Herpály ? |
|  | Svodin Pečeňady |  | **Polgár group** | Tiszapolgár-Csöszhalom-Oborin |  |
|  | Brodzany-Nitra Ludanice Bajč-Retz |  |  | Tiszapolgár Bodrogkeresztúr I Bodrogkeresztúr II Lažňany |  |
|  | Boleráz Group |  |  | (Barca) |  |
|  |  | Classic Baden |  |  |  |
|  | Bošáca group  Kostolac group  Kosihy-Čaka group |  |  | Nyirség-Zatin group | Eastern Slovakian Mound group |
| 1900–1800 B.C. |  |  |  |  |  |

[a] After Pavúk and Šiška 1971, with modifications.

a very simplified picture of archaeological cultures in the different regions during all the periods. For example, one chronological and cultural chart for western and eastern Slovakia can illustrate how complex the picture can be (Table 6.1).

The contemporary occurrence of different archaeological manifestations in the same region in various parts of Europe during the Middle Neolithic raises a number of questions. If they differed only in their pottery, we would not be justified in inferring great differences in ways of life among them. Ceramic differences may reflect ethnic differences, but we are unable to demonstrate this scientifically at the present time. However, there are more differences between the Lengyel and the Funnel Beaker than just those in ceramics.

Human figurines are present in Lengyel sites but are absent in those of Funnel Beaker. During the later phases of the Funnel Beaker culture, burial mounds and dolmens appeared in some areas. The houses of the Funnel Beaker culture show great variability in construction, but they are, in general, different from Lengyel houses.

Most likely there were ethnic differences during the Middle Neolithic, but at present we cannot demonstrate this with archaeological data. Since we are unable to investigate these differences from an ethnic point of view, the most productive research approach is to commence with an examination of subsistence strategies, that is, the way in which the people obtained a living from their environment. Barth's (1958) ethnographic studies indicate that different cultural groups can live in the same area if they exploit different ecological niches or practice different subsistence strategies. Thus in Swat, in northern Pakistan, live the Pathans who are sedentary agriculturalists and the Gujars who are mainly nomadic herders. However, archaeological research has not yet revealed any significant differences in the subsistence of the Lengyel and Funnel Beaker cultures. Furthermore, they are not exploiting different ecological niches. Also we know from ethnographic data that different ethnic groups can live and coexist in the same region or even the same settlement and even practice the same subsistence strategy. But, at present, no explanation is possible for their coexistence in one area at the same time period.

## The Problem of Writing

While the Linear culture dominated central Europe, the Balkan Middle Neolithic cultures such as Vinča flourished in southeastern Europe. Probably these societies possessed more complex social and political organizations than Linear or Bükk cultures. This is suggested by the use of the Vinča people made of copper for manufacturing tools, ornaments, etc., and perhaps by the subsequent appearance of actual copper metallurgy among them. However, the most spectacular claim for the Vinča people is that they used writing (Falkenstein 1965; Hood 1967, 1968).

Numerous decorative motifs have been found scratched on Vinča pots. These were regarded skeptically until the discovery of three incised clay tablets at Tartaria in the Transylvanian region of Romania in 1961 (Vlassa 1963) (Figure 6.5). Tartaria is a low mound (250 × 100 m), the lowest levels of which are associated with Vinča occupation. A Vinča pit that was dug into the lowest occupation contained three clay tablets, clay and stone figurines, and a

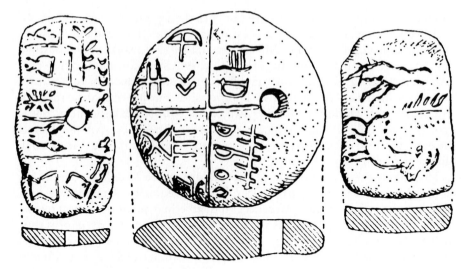

**Figure 6.5.** Tartaria tablets. (From "The Tartaria tablets" by M. S. F. Hood. Copyright © 1968 by Scientific American, Inc. All rights reserved.)

shell bracelet. The possibility exists that the pit is not Vinča, but intrudes into the Vinča level from later levels that are higher up. However, the figurines appear to be of Vinča style.

Two of the Tartaria tablets are rectangular and one is round. They are small: The round one is 6 cm in diameter. One of the rectangular tablets and the round one have holes drilled through them. The various symbols are inscribed only on one face. One of the tablets has only pictographic symbols. Supposedly some of the decorative motifs or incised signs resemble Sumerian writing of the Jemdet Nasr period. The interpretation of marks, motifs, and designs, such as these Tartaria inscriptions, which occasionally turn up on artifacts, should be done with the greatest caution: They may be symbols of some sort such as marks of ownership, but it is unlikely that they are writing. The use of symbols to express ideas may go back to the Lower Paleolithic, but it is extremely difficult to demonstrate archaeologically whether a corpus of symbols constitutes, in a sense, a writing system, such as Linear B or the hieroglyphics.

Usually writing is associated with early state societies or civilizations because such an innovation would be most likely to develop for bookkeeping and administrative purposes in these complex social, political, and economic systems. It would be, however, unusual for the Neolithic tribal or ranked societies in Europe to have had writing. It is unlikely that prestate societies would invent writing independently, since they would not need it. An institutionalized complex administrative system does not exist in the prestate societies. This is not to argue that "savages" or "barbarians" cannot invent anything, but to balance the enthusiastic arguments of some European archaeologists who wish to give Europe priority in relation to the Near East in certain cultural developments such as metallurgy. At present, we can discount Childe's too great reliance on diffusion from the Near East to explain culture change in Europe, but we should not move too far in the opposite direction by crediting the prehistoric Europeans with too many inventions.

## Economic Organization: Subsistence Strategies

No significant differences in the types of plants and animals exploited are observed in comparing the Middle Neolithic farming societies with their Early Neolithic predecessors in most areas of Europe. For example, the data from a Middle Neolithic Rössen culture in central Europe indicate that the same plants were cultivated as during the Early Neolithic (Table 6.2). However, barley appears to have been increasing in importance. Cultivation of barley may have increased in poor soils or those exhausted by long exploitation because it is a hardier cereal than wheat. Also, the cultivation of barley increased reliability of crop yield.

Childe (1957) noted an increase in the hunting of wild animals in central Europe during the Middle Neolithic. On the other hand, other archaeologists have emphasized a decrease in hunting. We should be very cautious about drawing such conclusions. Different methods of faunal analysis or sampling can create illusory differences in subsistence strategies. There is no general trend in the change of subsistence strategies, but there are some differences that can be seen, such as increases in the percentage of wild animals in some areas. Over 50% of the faunal remains at some Middle Neolithic Lengyel sites in Hungary are those of wild animals. Perhaps this may indicate decreasing use of domestic animals for meat and increased utilization of by-products such as cheese and milk. However, the archaeological evidence for this is almost nonexistent at present.

Or again, 60% of the faunal sample is made up of wild animals at some of the sites of the Swiss Cortaillod culture, which is the earliest Neolithic manifestation in the Alpine zone. This culture was contemporary with the Middle Neolithic cultures in central Europe, and its economic organization was discussed in Chapter 5. Ecological variation may account for these differences. For example, the percentage of wild animals from sites in a steppe–forest niche and a pure steppe niche in the same region would be expected to vary; so would the proportions of wild to domesticated animals from sites at different altitudes in a mountainous region. Also, year-to-year fluctuations in crop yields would have made exploitation of wild animals an advantageous strategy for agriculturalists. A few bad years in cereal yields would have encouraged more reliance, for a limited period, on wild animals for subsistence. Also, some hunting and gathering cultures probably adopted farming during the Middle Neolithic, and it is likely that the Cortaillod culture in the Alpine zone

TABLE 6.2  Plant Remains from the Langweiler Site, Rössen Culture[a,b], from Eight Paleobotanical Samples, 59 dm$^3$

| Plant | Number of grains[c] |
|---|---|
| Einkorn wheat (*Triticum monococcum*) | |
| Grain | 75 |
| Spikelet[d] | 100 |
| Glume | 231 |
| Emmer wheat (*Triticum* cf. *dicoccum*) | |
| Grain | 20 |
| Spikelet | 3 |
| Glume | 35 |
| Club wheat (*Triticum compactum*) | |
| Grain | 17 |
| Spikelet | 7 |
| Wheat (*Triticum* div. sp.) | |
| Grain | 43 |
| Six-row barley (*Hordeum hexastichum*) | |
| Grain | 497 |
| Spikelet | 158 |
| Six-row barley (cf. *Hordeum hexastichum*) | |
| Decayed grain | 72 |
| Wheat–barley (*Triticum–Hordeum*) | |
| Grain | 4,595 |
| Rye Brome (*Bromus secalinus*) | 245 |
| Cockspur grass (*Panicum crus-galli*) | 2 |
| Disease ergot (*Claviceps purpurea*) | 4 |
| Hazelnuts (*Corylus avellana*) | 23 |
| Goosefoot (*Chenopodium album*) | 73 |
| Nipplewort (*Lapsana communis*) | 71 |
| Red-veined dock (*Rumex sanguineus*) | 55 |
| Cleavers (*Galium spurium*) | 20 |
| Black bindweed (*Polygonum convolvulus*) | 19 |
| Blue grass (*Poa* sp.) | 11 |
| Hollow tooth (*Galeopsis* cf. *segetum*) | 8 |
| Vetch (*Vicia* cf. *hirsuta*) | 8 |
| Barren brome (*Bromus sterilis*) | 2 |
| Path ranke (*Sisymbrium officinale*) | 1 |
| Forest navel miere (*Moehringia trinervia*) | 1 |

[a] Data are from Knörzer 1971a.
[b] dm=decimeter; 10 dm=1 m.
[c] Complete and broken grains were combined.
[d] Includes spindle parts, ear base, etc.

132

represented such former hunters and gatherers. This would be an example of local hunters and gatherers adopting farming and not a movement of farming populations from other regions. As previously mentioned, at the end of the Middle Neolithic in Europe, the territory available for hunters and gatherers had shrunk considerably.

New techniques for land exploitation were developed during the Middle Neolithic, and they are associated with the expansion of farming societies. The first utilization of the simple ard, or plow, with oxen as draft animals, may have occurred at this time. Plowing turns the earth to a greater depth than does the digging stock, thereby making possible greater crop yields. This innovation facilitated the expansion of cultivation from the zones of easily worked soils cultivated during the Early Neolithic. With the plow, forest soils could be worked, and large tracts of woodlands were cleared during the Middle Neolithic. The clearing of even larger areas of forest was essential prior to the postulated movements of pastoralists into central and western Europe during the Late Neolithic.

The expansion of farming during the Middle Neolithic led to more restrictions on the choice for agricultural land. The Linear culture people could be more particular about what land to cultivate, for large tracts of good farming lands were available. This usually was no longer the case during the Middle Neolithic, for the areas most easily farmed had been occupied by farmers, and new environmental zones had to be exploited by the expanding population.

In our consideration of Middle Neolithic economic organization, I examine primarily the relevant data from the Tripolye, Lengyel, Funnel Beaker, and Michelsberg cultures. For these cultures we have some quantitative data.

## Tripolye

We have considerable information about some of the subsistence activities of the Tripolye people. However, for the domesticated plant remains, there are little quantitative data. We know only that wheat was the most important cereal, and that barley and millet were also cultivated. Various kinds of wheat, such as emmer, club, and bread, were cultivated. From Tsalkin's excellent synthesis (1970) of the faunal remains from various sites, we know that cattle were the most important domestic animals, with pigs and sheep–goats being next in importance. A variety of wild animals were hunted (Table 6.3). The occurrence of projectile points in the Tripolye sites indicates that bows and arrows were used in hunting and perhaps fighting. For further analysis of faunal remains, we may look at 23 Tripolye sites in the Soviet Union that are noted in Tsalkin's work and that have at least 24 animals based on the minimum number of individuals (Table 6.3; Figure 6.6). Five sites were not utilized, since the sample size was very small.

TABLE 6.3   Frequencies of Animals and Estimated Amount of Usable Meat at Twenty-Three Tripolye Culture Sites[a]

| | Kilograms of usable meat | Number of animals | Percentage of total number of animals | Total estimated weight in kilograms | Percentage of estimated weight | Kilograms of usable meat from total estimated weight |
|---|---|---|---|---|---|---|
| Sabatinovka II (E)[b] | | | | | | |
| Cattle (700)[c] | 350 | 22 | 26 | 15,400 | 66 | 7,700 |
| Sheep–goat (25) | 12.5 | 11 | 13 | 275 | 1 | 137.5 |
| Pig (30) | 15 | 10 | 12 | 300 | 1 | 150 |
| Dog (10) | 5 | 1 | 1 | 10 | — | 5 |
| Horse (600) | 300 | 9 | 10 | 5,400 | 23 | 2,700 |
| Red deer (190) | 95 | 8 | 9 | 1,520 | 6.5 | 760 |
| Roe deer (21) | 10.5 | 4 | 5 | 84 | — | 42 |
| Wild pig (107.5) | 53.75 | 3 | 4 | 322.5 | 1 | 161.25 |
| Other wild animals[d] | — | 18 | 20 | — | — | — |
| Total | | 86 | | 23,311.5 | | |
| Luka-Vrublevetskaya (E)[b] | | | | | | |
| Cattle (700)[c] | 350 | 42 | 11 | 29,400 | 58 | 14,700 |
| Sheep–goat (25) | 12.5 | 38 | 10 | 950 | 2 | 475 |
| Pig (30) | 15 | 93 | 24 | 2,700 | 5 | 1,350 |
| Dog (10) | 5 | 12 | 3 | 120 | — | 60 |
| Horse (600) | 300 | 4 | 1 | 2,400 | 5 | 1,200 |
| Red deer (190) | 95 | 57 | 15 | 10,830 | 21 | 5,415 |
| Roe deer (21) | 10.5 | 31 | 8 | 651 | 1 | 325.5 |
| Wild pig (107.5) | 53.75 | 33 | 8 | 3,547.5 | 7 | 1,773.75 |
| Other wild animals[d] | — | 83 | 20 | — | — | — |
| Total | | 393 | | 50,598.5 | | |
| Bernovo-Luka (E)[b] | | | | | | |
| Cattle (700)[c] | 350 | 23 | 20 | 16,100 | 65 | 8,050 |
| Sheep–goat (25) | 12.5 | 9 | 8 | 225 | 1 | 112.5 |
| Pig (30) | 15 | 11 | 9 | 330 | 1 | 165 |
| Dog (10) | 5 | 1 | 1 | 10 | — | 5 |
| Horse (600) | 300 | 2 | 2 | 1,200 | 5 | 600 |
| Red deer (190) | 95 | 25 | 21 | 4,750 | 19 | 2,375 |
| Roe deer (21) | 10.5 | 17 | 14 | 357 | 1.5 | 178.5 |
| Wild pig (107.5) | 53.75 | 17 | 14 | 1,827.5 | 7 | 913.75 |
| Other wild animals[d] | — | 13 | 11 | — | — | — |
| Total | | 118 | | 24,799.5 | | |

(continued)

[a] Data are from Tsalkin 1970.

[b] E = Early Tripolye, M = Middle Tripolye, L = Late Tripolye. Chronological position of sites according to Tsalkin (1970).

[c] Numbers in parentheses represent estimated adult weight in kilograms.

[d] Aurochs, elk, bear, wolf, fox, etc.

**TABLE 6.3** (*Continued*)

| | Kilograms of usable meat | Number of animals | Percentage of total number of animals | Total estimated weight in kilograms | Percentage of estimated weight | Kilograms of usable meat from total estimated weight |
|---|---|---|---|---|---|---|
| Lenkovtsi (E)[b] | | | | | | |
| Cattle (700)[c] | 350 | 30 | 26 | 21,000 | 68 | 10,500 |
| Sheep–goat (25) | 12.5 | 10 | 9 | 250 | 1 | 125 |
| Pig (30) | 15 | 19 | 16 | 570 | 2 | 285 |
| Dog (10) | 5 | 2 | 2 | 20 | — | 10 |
| Horse (600) | 300 | 5 | 4 | 3,000 | 10 | 1,500 |
| Red deer (190) | 95 | 25 | 22 | 4,750 | 15.5 | 2,375 |
| Roe deer (21) | 10.5 | 9 | 8 | 189 | 0.5 | 94.5 |
| Wild pig (107.5) | 53.75 | 9 | 8 | 967.5 | 3 | 483.75 |
| Other wild animals[d] | — | 7 | 6 | — | — | — |
| Total | | 116 | | 30,746.5 | | |
| Soloncheni I (E)[b] | | | | | | |
| Cattle (700)[c] | 350 | 17 | 17 | 11,900 | 59 | 5,950 |
| Sheep–goat (25) | 12.5 | 14 | 14 | 350 | 1.5 | 175 |
| Pig (30) | 15 | 19 | 18 | 570 | 3 | 285 |
| Dog (10) | 5 | 2 | 2 | 20 | — | 10 |
| Horse (600) | 300 | 3 | 3 | 1,800 | 9 | 900 |
| Red deer (190) | 95 | 20 | 19 | 3,800 | 19 | 1,900 |
| Roe deer (21) | 10.5 | 7 | 7 | 147 | 1 | 73.5 |
| Wild pig (107.5) | 53.75 | 15 | 15 | 1,612.5 | 8 | 806.25 |
| Other wild animals[d] | — | 6 | 6 | — | — | — |
| Total | | 103 | | 20,199.5 | | |
| Galerkani (E)[b] | | | | | | |
| Cattle (700)[c] | 350 | 5 | 16 | 3,500 | 48 | 1,750 |
| Sheep–goat (25) | 12.5 | 4 | 13 | 100 | 1 | 50 |
| Pig (30) | 15 | 1 | 3 | 30 | 0.5 | 15 |
| Dog (10) | 5 | — | — | — | — | — |
| Horse (60)) | 300 | 3 | 10 | 1,800 | 25 | 900 |
| Red deer (190) | 95 | 6 | 19 | 1,140 | 16 | 570 |
| Roe deer (21) | 10.5 | 2 | 7 | 42 | 0.5 | 21 |
| Wild pig (107.5) | 53.75 | 6 | 19 | 645 | 9 | 322.5 |
| Other wild animals[d] | — | 4 | 13 | — | — | — |
| Total | | 31 | | 7,257 | | |
| Karbuna (E)[b] | | | | | | |
| Cattle (700)[c] | 350 | 11 | 31 | 7,700 | 69 | 3,850 |
| Sheep–goat (25) | 12.5 | 7 | 20 | 175 | 1.5 | 87.5 |
| Pig (30) | 15 | 6 | 17 | 180 | 1.5 | 90 |
| Dog (10) | 5 | 1 | 3 | 10 | — | 5 |
| Horse (600) | 300 | 4 | 11 | 2,400 | 22 | 1,200 |
| Red deer (190) | 95 | 2 | 6 | 380 | 3.5 | 190 |
| Roe deer (21) | 10.5 | 2 | 6 | 42 | — | 21 |
| Wild pig (107.5) | 53.75 | 2 | 6 | 215 | 2 | 107.5 |
| Other wild animals[d] | — | — | — | — | — | — |
| Total | | 35 | | 11,102 | | |

(*continued*)

TABLE 6.3 (*Continued*)

| | Kilograms of usable meat | Number of animals | Percentage of total number of animals | Total estimated weight in kilograms | Percentage of estimated weight | Kilograms of usable meat from total estimated weight |
|---|---|---|---|---|---|---|
| Sabatinovka I (M)[b] | | | | | | |
| Cattle (700)[c] | 350 | 30 | 26 | 21,000 | 70 | 10,500 |
| Sheep–goat (25) | 12.5 | 14 | 12 | 350 | 1 | 175 |
| Pig (30) | 15 | 14 | 12 | 420 | 1 | 210 |
| Dog (10) | 5 | 14 | 12 | 140 | 0.5 | 70 |
| Horse (600) | 300 | 9 | 8 | 5,400 | 18 | 2,700 |
| Red deer (190) | 95 | 10 | 9 | 1,900 | 6 | 950 |
| Roe deer (21) | 10.5 | 4 | 3 | 84 | — | 42 |
| Wild pig (107.5) | 53.75 | 8 | 7 | 860 | 3 | 430 |
| Other wild animals[d] | — | 14 | 12 | — | — | — |
| Total | | 117 | | 30,154 | | |
| Berezovskaya (M)[b] | | | | | | |
| Cattle (700)[c] | 350 | 12 | 17 | 8,400 | 55 | 4,200 |
| Sheep–goat (25) | 12.5 | 6 | 8 | 150 | 1 | 125 |
| Pig (30) | 15 | 6 | 8 | 180 | 1 | 90 |
| Dog (10) | 5 | 2 | 3 | 20 | — | 10 |
| Horse (600 | 300 | 3 | 4 | 1,800 | 12 | 900 |
| Red deer (190) | 95 | 20 | 28 | 3,800 | 25 | 1,900 |
| Roe deer (21) | 10.5 | 3 | 4 | 63 | 0.5 | 31.5 |
| Wild pig (107.5) | 53.75 | 8 | 11 | 860 | 5.5 | 430 |
| Other wild animals[d] | — | 12 | 17 | — | — | — |
| Total | | 72 | | 15,273 | | |
| Soloncheni II (M)[b] | | | | | | |
| Cattle (700)[c] | 350 | 39 | 25 | 27,300 | 67 | 13,650 |
| Sheep–goat (25) | 12.5 | 14 | 9 | 350 | 1 | 175 |
| Pig (30) | 15 | 26 | 17 | 780 | 2 | 390 |
| Dog (10) | 5 | 7 | 4 | 70 | — | 35 |
| Horse (600) | 300 | 6 | 4 | 3,600 | 9 | 1,800 |
| Red deer (190) | 95 | 34 | 22 | 6,460 | 16 | 3,230 |
| Roe deer (21) | 10.5 | 7 | 4 | 147 | — | 73.5 |
| Wild pig (107.5) | 53.75 | 20 | 13 | 2,150 | 5 | 1,075 |
| Other wild animals[d] | — | 5 | 3 | — | — | — |
| Total | | 158 | | 40,857 | | |
| Khalepie (M)[b] | | | | | | |
| Cattle (700)[c] | 350 | 11 | 24 | 7,700 | 76.5 | 3,850 |
| Sheep–goat (25) | 12.5 | 17 | 37 | 425 | 4 | 212.5 |
| Pig (30) | 15 | 8 | 17 | 240 | 2 | 120 |
| Dog (10) | 5 | 1 | 2 | 10 | — | 5 |
| Horse (600) | 300 | 2 | 4 | 1,200 | 12 | 600 |
| Red deer (190) | 95 | 2 | 4 | 380 | 4 | 190 |
| Roe deer (21) | 10.5 | — | — | — | — | — |
| Wild pig (107.5) | 53.75 | 1 | 2 | 107.5 | 1 | 53.75 |
| Other wild animals[d] | — | 4 | 9 | — | — | — |
| Total | | 46 | | 10,062.5 | | |

(*continued*)

TABLE 6.3 *(Continued)*

| | Kilograms of usable meat | Number of animals | Percentage of total number of animals | Total estimated weight in kilograms | Percentage of estimated weight | Kilograms of usable meat from total estimated weight |
|---|---|---|---|---|---|---|
| **Kolomiishchina II (M)[b]** | | | | | | |
| Cattle (700)[c] | 350 | 8 | 32 | 5,600 | 75 | 2,800 |
| Sheep–goat (25) | 12.5 | 5 | 20 | 125 | 1.5 | 62.5 |
| Pig (30) | 15 | 3 | 12 | 90 | 1 | 45 |
| Dog (10) | 5 | 3 | 12 | 30 | 0.5 | 15 |
| Horse (600) | 300 | 2 | 8 | 1,200 | 16 | 600 |
| Red deer (190) | 95 | 1 | 4 | 190 | 2.5 | 95 |
| Roe deer (21) | 10.5 | — | — | — | — | — |
| Wild pig (107.5) | 53.75 | 2 | 8 | 215 | 3 | 107.5 |
| Other wild animals[d] | — | — | — | — | — | — |
| Total | | 25 | | 7,450 | | |
| **Vladimirovka (M)[b]** | | | | | | |
| Cattle (700)[c] | 350 | 36 | 30 | 25,200 | 79 | 12,600 |
| Sheep–goat (25) | 12.5 | 30 | 25 | 750 | 2 | 375 |
| Pig (30) | 15 | 25 | 21 | 625 | 2 | 312.5 |
| Dog (10) | 5 | 2 | 2 | 20 | — | 10 |
| Horse (600) | 300 | 5 | 4 | 3,000 | 9.5 | 1,500 |
| Red deer (190) | 95 | 11 | 9 | 2,090 | 6.5 | 1,045 |
| Roe deer (21) | 10.5 | 3 | 3 | 63 | — | 31.5 |
| Wild pig (107.5) | 53.75 | 1 | 1 | 107.5 | — | 53.75 |
| Other wild animals[d] | — | 7 | 6 | — | — | — |
| Total | | 120 | | 31,855.5 | | |
| **Polivanov Yar (M)[b]** | | | | | | |
| Cattle (700)[c] | 350 | 33 | 13 | 23,100 | 65.5 | 11,550 |
| Sheep–goat (25) | 12.5 | 39 | 15 | 975 | 3 | 487.5 |
| Pig (30) | 15 | 92 | 36 | 2,760 | 8 | 1,380 |
| Dog (10) | 5 | 9 | 4 | 90 | — | 45 |
| Horse (600) | 300 | 3 | 2 | 1,800 | 5 | 900 |
| Red deer (190) | 95 | 24 | 9 | 4,560 | 13 | 2,280 |
| Roe deer (21) | 10.5 | 14 | 6 | 294 | 1 | 147 |
| Wild pig (107.5) | 53.75 | 16 | 6 | 1,720 | 5 | 860 |
| Other wild animals[d] | — | 23 | 9 | — | — | — |
| Total | | 253 | | 35,299 | | |
| **Podgortsi II (M)[b]** | | | | | | |
| Cattle (700)[c] | 350 | 11 | 26 | 7,700 | 46.5 | 3,850 |
| Sheep–goat (25) | 12.5 | 6 | 14 | 150 | 1 | 75 |
| Pig (30) | 15 | 16 | 38 | 4,800 | 29 | 2,400 |
| Dog (10) | 5 | — | — | — | — | — |
| Horse (600) | 300 | 6 | 14 | 3,600 | 22 | 1,800 |
| Red deer (190) | 95 | 1 | 2 | 190 | 1 | 95 |
| Roe deer (21) | 10.5 | — | — | — | — | — |
| Wild pig (107.5) | 53.75 | 1 | 2 | 107.5 | 1 | 53.75 |
| Other wild animals[d] | — | 1 | 2 | — | — | — |
| Total | | 42 | | 16,547.5 | | |

*(continued)*

TABLE 6.3 (*Continued*)

| | Kilograms of usable meat | Number of animals | Percentage of total number of animals | Total estimated weight in kilograms | Percentage of estimated weight | Kilograms of usable meat from total estimated weight |
|---|---|---|---|---|---|---|
| Sirtsi (L)[b] | | | | | | |
| Cattle (700)[c] | 350 | 5 | 21 | 3,500 | 77.5 | 1,750 |
| Sheep–goat (25) | 12.5 | 12 | 50 | 300 | 6.5 | 150 |
| Pig (30) | 15 | 1 | 4 | 30 | 1 | 15 |
| Dog (10) | 5 | — | — | — | — | — |
| Horse (600) | 300 | 1 | 4 | 600 | 13 | 300 |
| Red deer (190) | 95 | — | — | — | — | — |
| Roe deer (21) | 10.5 | 4 | 13 | 84 | 2 | 42 |
| Wild pig (107.5) | 53.75 | — | — | — | — | — |
| Other wild animals[d] | — | 1 | 4 | — | — | — |
| Total | | 24 | | 4,514 | | |
| Sandraki (L)[b] | | | | | | |
| Cattle (700)[c] | 350 | 4 | 11 | 2,800 | 46.5 | 1,400 |
| Sheep–goat (25) | 12.5 | 5 | 13 | 125 | 2 | 62.5 |
| Pig (30) | 15 | 3 | 8 | 90 | 1.5 | 45 |
| Dog (10) | 5 | 3 | 8 | 30 | 0.5 | 15 |
| Horse (600) | 300 | 3 | 8 | 1,800 | 30 | 900 |
| Red deer (190) | 95 | 3 | 8 | 570 | 9.5 | 285 |
| Roe deer (21) | 10.5 | 3 | 8 | 63 | 1 | 31.5 |
| Wild pig (107.5) | 53.75 | 5 | 13 | 537.5 | 9 | 268.75 |
| Other wild animals[d] | — | 9 | 24 | — | — | — |
| Total | | 38 | | 6,015.5 | | |
| Stena (L)[b] | | | | | | |
| Cattle (700)[c] | 350 | 13 | 17 | 9,100 | 54 | 4,550 |
| Sheep–goat (25) | 12.5 | 9 | 12 | 225 | 1 | 112.5 |
| Pig (30) | 15 | 14 | 18 | 420 | 2.5 | 210 |
| Dog (10) | 5 | 3 | 4 | 30 | — | 15 |
| Horse (600) | 300 | 9 | 12 | 5,400 | 32 | 2,700 |
| Red deer (190) | 95 | 6 | 8 | 1,140 | 6.5 | 570 |
| Roe deer (21) | 10.5 | 4 | 5 | 84 | 0.5 | 42 |
| Wild pig (107.5) | 53.75 | 5 | 7 | 537.5 | 3 | 268.75 |
| Other wild animals[d] | — | 13 | 17 | — | — | — |
| Total | | 76 | | 16,936.5 | | |
| Gorodsk (L)[b] | | | | | | |
| Cattle (700)[c] | 350 | 14 | 20 | 9,800 | 62 | 4,900 |
| Sheep–goat (25) | 12.5 | 8 | 11 | 200 | 1 | 100 |
| Pig (30) | 15 | 14 | 20 | 420 | 2.5 | 210 |
| Dog (10) | 5 | 2 | 3 | 20 | — | 10 |
| Horses (600) | 300 | 7 | 10 | 4,200 | 26.5 | 2,100 |
| Eed deer (190) | 95 | 4 | 6 | 760 | 5 | 380 |
| Roe deer (21) | 10.5 | 6 | 9 | 126 | 1 | 63 |
| Wild pig (107.5) | 53.75 | 3 | 4 | 322.5 | 2 | 161.25 |
| Other wild animals[d] | — | 13 | 18 | — | — | — |
| Total | | 71 | | 15,848.5 | | |

(*continued*)

TABLE 6.3  (*Continued*)

| | Kilograms of usable meat | Number of animals | Percentage of total number of animals | Total estimated weight in kilograms | Percentage of estimated weight | Kilograms of usable meat from total estimated weight |
|---|---|---|---|---|---|---|
| Troyanov (L)[b] | | | | | | |
| Cattle (700)[c] | 350 | 13 | 24 | 9,100 | 66 | 4,550 |
| Sheep–goat (25) | 12.5 | 7 | 13 | 175 | 1 | 87.5 |
| Pig (30) | 15 | 6 | 11 | 180 | 1 | 90 |
| Dog (10) | 5 | 3 | 6 | 30 | — | 15 |
| Horse (600) | 300 | 5 | 9 | 3,000 | 22 | 1,500 |
| Red deer (190) | 95 | 4 | 7 | 760 | 5.5 | 380 |
| Roe deer (21) | 10.5 | 2 | 4 | 42 | — | 21 |
| Wild pig (107.5) | 53.75 | 4 | 7 | 430 | 3 | 215 |
| Other wild animals[d] | — | 10 | 19 | — | — | — |
| Total | | 54 | | 13,717 | | |
| Pavoloch (L)[b] | | | | | | |
| Cattle (700)[c] | 350 | 6 | 21 | 4,200 | 73 | 2,100 |
| Sheep–goat (25) | 12.5 | 6 | 21 | 150 | 2.5 | 75 |
| Pig (30) | 15 | 3 | 10 | 90 | 1.5 | 45 |
| Dog (10) | 5 | 1 | 3 | 10 | — | 5 |
| Horse (600) | 300 | 1 | 3 | 600 | 10.5 | 300 |
| Red deer (190) | 95 | 3 | 10 | 570 | 10 | 285 |
| Roe deer (21) | 10.5 | 1 | 3 | 21 | — | 10.5 |
| Wild pig (107.5) | 53.75 | 1 | 3 | 107.5 | 2 | 53.75 |
| Other wild animals[d] | — | 7 | 24 | — | — | — |
| Total | | 29 | | 5,748.5 | | |
| Kolomiishchina I (L)[b] | | | | | | |
| Cattle (700)[c] | 350 | 12 | 31 | 8,400 | 79 | 4,200 |
| Sheep–goat (25) | 12.5 | 8 | 21 | 200 | 2 | 100 |
| Pig (30) | 15 | 7 | 18 | 210 | 2 | 105 |
| Dog (10) | 5 | — | — | — | — | — |
| Horse (600) | 300 | 3 | 8 | 1,800 | 17 | 900 |
| Red deer (190) | 95 | — | — | — | — | — |
| Roe deer (21) | 10.5 | — | — | — | — | — |
| Wild pig (107.5) | 53.75 | — | — | — | — | — |
| Other wild animals[d] | — | 9 | 23 | — | — | — |
| Total | | 39 | | 10,610 | | |
| Podgortsi I (L)[b] | | | | | | |
| Cattle (700)[c] | 350 | 12 | 36 | 8,400 | 76 | 4,200 |
| Sheep–goat (25) | 12.5 | 2 | 6 | 50 | 0.5 | 25 |
| Pig (30) | 15 | 2 | 6 | 60 | 0.5 | 30 |
| Dog (10) | 5 | 1 | 3 | 10 | — | 5 |
| Horse (600) | 300 | 2 | 6 | 1,200 | 11 | 600 |
| Red deer (190) | 95 | 5 | 15 | 950 | 8.5 | 475 |
| Roe deer (21) | 10.5 | 1 | 3 | 21 | — | 10.5 |
| Wild pig (107.5) | 53.75 | 3 | 9 | 322.5 | 3 | 161.25 |
| Other wild animals[d] | — | 5 | 15 | — | — | — |
| Total | | 33 | | 11,013.5 | | |

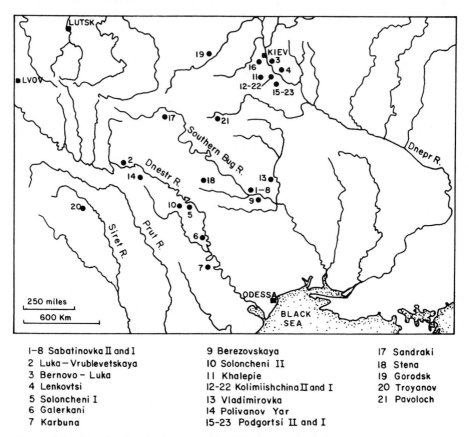

| | | |
|---|---|---|
| 1–8 Sabatinovka II and I | 9 Berezovskaya | 17 Sandraki |
| 2 Luka–Vrublevetskaya | 10 Soloncheni II | 18 Stena |
| 3 Bernovo–Luka | 11 Khalepie | 19 Gorodsk |
| 4 Lenkovtsi | 12–22 Kolimiishchina II and I | 20 Troyanov |
| 5 Soloncheni I | 13 Vladimirovka | 21 Pavoloch |
| 6 Galerkani | 14 Polivanov Yar | |
| 7 Karbuna | 15–23 Podgortsi II and I | |

**Figure 6.6.** Map showing the location of the Tripolyean culture sites.

It has been suggested that a number of changes occurred through time in the roles played by the various domestic and wild animals in the Tripolye economy. For example, it is believed that the importance of pigs decreased through time and that this correlates with the shrinkage of forested areas (Wiślański 1969).

To test these assumptions, I used statistical procedures, such as Kendall's rank correlation test, on the data from the 23 Tripolye sites to check if the postulated changes in proportions of different animal species through time are significant. Chronologically the sites fall into three phases (Table 6.3). To ensure that sample size was not affecting the results, I divided the sites into four groups based on the frequencies of various animals at the different sites. Some of the results can be considered significant (Table 6.4). There is an indication that the increase in the number of horses through time is significant, and it is possible that this reflects the domestication of horses. This is an especially important result in view of the pastoralist incursions into central and western Europe postulated for the Late Neolithic.

Bökönyi (1974) postulated that horses were domesticated in the Ukraine during the Middle Neolithic. This would affect the adaptation of various Neolithic societies, for horses could be utilized for transportation, work force, food, including mare's milk, and warfare. Bökönyi (1974) placed the earliest domesticated horses at the Tripolyean B settlement of Dereivka on the Dnepr River in southern Ukraine. Probably this occurred between 3000 (3610) and 2500 (3110) B.C. It is doubtful, however, that horse bones found on Funnel Beaker sites, such as Ćmielów in Poland, represent domesticated animals (Bökönyi 1974:240). In Greece, the first domesticated horses appeared during the Middle Helladic period, 1900–1550 (2180–1870) B.C., and on Crete in approximately 1600 (1800) B.C.

Some of the statistical results probably reflect only the size of samples and not any changes in subsistence strategy. For example, the increase in the number of pigs correlated positively with the increase of the sample size. The effect on the frequencies of sheep–goat is just the opposite. With the increase of the sample size they decrease. Thus, the size of the samples of different species is influencing the results.

The site of Usatovo, near the Black Sea, was not included in the preceding analysis because it is not a Tripolyean site. The frequencies of the various species recovered at Usatovo reflect the site's situation in a steppe zone: Roughly 45% of the 992 animals found at Usatovo were sheep–goat; 3% were wild ass, an ungulate associated with steppe and parkland environment.

TABLE 6.4   Approximate Significance According to Kendall's S for Twenty-Three Tripolyean Sites

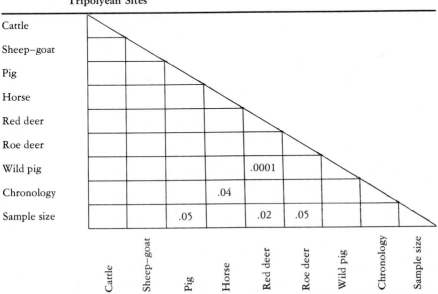

## Lengyel

The subsistence strategy of the Lengyel people in central Europe was similar to that of the Early Neolithic cultures. However, the percentage of wild animals at some Hungarian sites is very high. For example, at Pécsvárad-Aranyhegy and Zengövarkony sites they comprise 57% and 46%, respectively, of the animal total (Table 6.5). Perhaps poor harvests for several years or decreasing soil fertility forced the Lengyel people at those settlements to rely more heavily on hunting. It should be mentioned that some other sites, such as Kraków-Pleszów in Poland, contained very few wild animals (Table 6.5).

## Funnel Beaker

The Middle Neolithic changes in economic organization are well illustrated by evidence from the Funnel Beaker culture.

The Funnel Beaker people had more complex techniques of land exploitation than those used by the Linear people. The occurrence of ard, or plow, marks under Funnel Beaker burial mounds such as at Sarnowo, Poland, and Steneng, Denmark, as well as figurines that may represent oxen, suggests that ard was utilized in central Europe. Similar marks have been found at contemporary sites in the Netherlands and England. Oxen were already being castrated during the Early Neolithic; thus it is possible that they were utilized as draft animals. Oxen can be utilized for work at 3 or 4 years of age (Higham 1968:87). It is unclear whether the Funnel Beaker people had wagons, although clay models of wagons with four wheels were found in a cemetery of Budakalasz in Hungary belonging to the Baden culture, which occurred near the end of the Neolithic. The presence of rare decorative motifs resembling wagons on Funnel Beaker pots may further support the existence of wagons during the Neolithic (Figure 6.2).

Also the existence of trackways in bog areas may suggest the presence of wheeled transport. However, Coles and Hibbert (1968), and Coles (1975) suggest that trackways in England were unsuitable for wheeled transport. For example, at Abbot's Way in England the track was over 1200 m in length, and it was built of split alder trunks. It was only 1–1.5 m wide, and the surface of the track was irregular. However, these trackways indicate that the members of these communities could be mobilized from time to time for communal activities.

The ard would have permitted the exploitation of poorer soils, and this might have affected the shape of fields. Square or rectangular field systems would be more likely to be associated with oxen-pulled ards, since they would be pulling them back and forth. The individual ownership of oxen for working small plots would be expensive, therefore, they may have been owned communally. The use of ard and oxen in working fields also suggests greater perma-

**TABLE 6.5  Frequency of Animals and Estimated Amount of Usable Meat at Lengyel Sites**

| | Kilograms of usable meat | Number of animals | Percentage of total number of animals | Total estimated weight in kilograms | Percentage of estimated weight | Kilograms of usable meat from total estimated weight |
|---|---|---|---|---|---|---|
| Zengövarkony, Hungary[a] | | | | | | |
| Cattle (700)[b] | 350 | 277 | 42 | 193,900 | 58.5 | 96,950 |
| Sheep–goat (25) | 12.5 | 7 | 1.1 | 175 | — | 87.5 |
| Pig (30) | 15 | 66 | 10 | 450 | — | 225 |
| Dog (10) | 5 | 8 | 1.2 | 80 | — | 40 |
| Aurochs (900) | 450 | 122 | 18.5 | 109,800 | 33 | 54,900 |
| Red deer (190) | 95 | 119 | 18 | 22,610 | 7 | 11,305 |
| Roe deer (21) | 10.5 | 25 | 3.8 | 525 | — | 262.5 |
| Wild pig (107.5) | 53.75 | 34 | 5.2 | 3,655 | 1 | 1,827.5 |
| Other wild animals | — | 2 | 0.2 | — | — | — |
| Total | | 660 | | 331,195 | | |
| Pécsvárad-Aranyhegy, Hungary[a] | | | | | | |
| Cattle (700)[b] | 350 | 29 | 30.5 | 20,300 | 46 | 10,150 |
| Sheep–goat (25) | 12.5 | 2 | 2 | 50 | — | 25 |
| Pig (30) | 15 | 8 | 8 | 240 | — | 120 |
| Dog (10) | 5 | 2 | 2 | 20 | — | 10 |
| Aurochs (900) | 450 | 20 | 21 | 18,000 | 41 | 9,000 |
| Red deer (190) | 95 | 25 | 26 | 4,750 | 11 | — |
| Roe deer (21) | 10.5 | 3 | 3 | 63 | — | 31.5 |
| Wild pig (107.5) | 53.75 | 4 | 4 | 430 | 1 | 215 |
| Other wild animals | — | 2 | 2 | — | — | — |
| Total | | 95 | | 43,853 | | |
| Aszód-Papi Földek[a] | | | | | | |
| Cattle (700)[b] | 350 | 125 | 40.5 | 87,500 | 59 | 43,750 |
| Sheep–goat (25) | 12.5 | 5 | 2 | 125 | — | 62.5 |
| Pig (30)P | 15 | 27 | 9 | 810 | 0.5 | 405 |
| Dog (10) | 5 | 6 | 2 | 60 | — | 30 |
| Aurochs (900) | 450 | 53 | 17 | 47,700 | 32 | 23,850 |
| Red deer (190) | 95 | 50 | 16 | 9,500 | 6 | 4,750 |
| Roe deer (21) | 10.5 | 9 | 3 | 189 | — | 94.5 |
| Wild pig (107.5) | 53.75 | 28 | 9 | 3,010 | 2 | 1,505 |
| Other wild animals | — | 6 | 2 | — | — | — |
| Total | | 309 | | 148,894 | | |
| Kraków-Pleszów, Poland[c] | | | | | | |
| Cattle (700)[b] | 350 | 24 | — | 16,800 | — | 8,400 |
| Sheep–goat (25) | 12.5 | 6 | — | 150 | — | 75 |
| Pig (30) | 15 | 10[d] | — | — | — | — |
| Dog (10) | 5 | 2 | — | 20 | — | 10 |
| Aurochs (900) | 450 | — | — | — | — | — |
| Red deer (190) | 95 | 1 | — | 190 | — | 95 |
| Roe deer (21) | 10.5 | 2 | — | 42 | — | 21 |
| Wild pig (107.5) | 53.75 | — | — | — | — | — |
| Other wild animals | — | 45 | — | — | — | — |
| Total | | 80 | | 17,202 | | |

[a] Data are from Bökönyi 1959, 1974.
[b] Numbers in parentheses represent estimated adult weight in kilograms.
[c] Data are from Kulczycka-Leciejewiczowa 1969.
[d] Includes wild pigs.

143

nence of settlements. Marxist archaeologists argue that this reflects a shift to patriarchal society, for men were becoming more important in the economy. Supposedly the simple agriculture of the Early Neolithic societies was performed by women with digging sticks; thus women in Early Neolithic societies had more political power. In this explanation, plowing and especially pastoralism are associated with men, and eventually lead to their preeminence in political and economic life (Neustupný 1967).

From cereal imprints in sherds from Denmark, we know that Funnel Beaker people cultivated emmer, einkorn, club wheat, and barley. From the Lietfeld site in Germany, the remains of cereals were recovered in these proportions: einkorn wheat 63.3%, emmer wheat 33.5%, barley 2.4%, and flax 0.8%. The quantitative data on cereal remains from two Polish sites indicate that emmer wheat was the most important crop (Table 6.6). At Radziejów Kujawski in Poland, dated approximately 2900–2650 (3540–3320) B.C. by the radiocarbon method, one pit contained several kg of wheat with over 157,000 specimens. Forty percent of this sample was analyzed with the result that 99.5% is emmer wheat, .4% is einkorn wheat, and .05% is bread wheat (Klichowska 1970). However, the ratios between different types of wheat simply may reflect that this pit was used for drying emmer wheat.

TABLE 6.6  Quantitative Composition of the Wheat Sample from the Funnel Beaker Culture Sites of Zarebowo and Radziejów Kujawski, Poland[a]

| | Zarębowo | | Radziejów Kujawski | | |
| --- | --- | --- | --- | --- | --- |
| | Percentage of wheat | Number of specimens | Percentage of total number of specimens | Volume in cm³ | Number of specimens |
| Emmer wheat (*Triticum dicoccum* Schr.) | 76.5 | 2,590 | 99.50 | 1,791 | 62,685 |
| Einkorn wheat (*Triticum monococcum* L.) | 23.5 | 800 | 0.44 | 8 | 280 |
| Bread wheat (*Triticum aestivum* L.) | 0.002 | 8 | 0.05 | 1 | 35 |
| Sheep's sorrel (*Rumex acetosa* L.) | | | | | 8 |
| Dock (*Rumex* sp.) | | | | | 3 |
| Black bindweed (*Polygonum convolvulus* L.) | | 6 | | | 2 |
| Charlock (*Sinapis arvensis* L.) | | | | | 2 |
| Rye brome (*Bromus secalinus* L.) | | 2 | | | 2 |

[a] Data are from Klichowska 1970.

In the relative importance of various domestic and wild animals, the Funnel Beaker culture is similar to the Linear culture. Data (Table 6.7) based on the minimum number of individuals represented by bones are available only from three Funnel Beaker sites. There are a number of reports on Funnel Beaker sites with percentages of bones on various animals, but I utilize such reports only when no other method of analysis is available.

### Michelsberg

The settlement system of the Michelsberg culture indicates the presence of a complex subsistence strategy.

Michelsberg sites are found along rivers, on lakes, and on high local elevations. The Michelsberg people may have moved seasonally with their herds between their settlements. Higham (1968:95) speculates that the Michelsberg sites in Switzerland occurring at different elevations indicate the presence of transhumant herding. That is, the animals were kept in the lower villages during the winter and driven to pastures at higher elevations in the summer. The upland sites could represent the summer camps of the herders. Data from the Hetzenberg site in Germany indicate that cattle and sheep–goat predominated among the domesticated animals (Table 6.8).

A variety of domesticated and wild plants was recovered from the Michelsberg sites. For example, at Ehrenstein, a Michelsberg site in Germany, the following domesticated and wild plants were recovered: emmer wheat, einkorn wheat, bread wheat, spelt wheat, six-row barley, beech mast, hazelnuts, crab apples, raspberry, dewberry, strawberry, bullace, and Cornelian cherry (J. Renfrew 1973, Zürn 1968). Here we have one of the earliest indications for the collection of beech mast. Various nuts such as acorns, hazelnuts, and beech mast were probably intensively collected in late summer and early fall. They provide rich sources of fats, proteins, and carbohydrates and can be stored for the winter food supply.

### Beginnings of Metallurgy in Europe

During the Middle Neolithic, the first extensive use of metal artifacts occurred in Europe. We find copper artifacts in Mediterranean, western, southeastern, eastern, and central Europe. This does not mean, however, that copper deposits in all those regions were exploited during the Middle Neolithic. Copper deposits occur in several mountainous regions of Europe, but only some were exploited during the Neolithic. The utilization of copper is associated with the appearance of mines and mining techniques. It should be noted that copper was not the only mineral to be mined and exploited extensively at this time; the first large-scale mining of flint occurred during the Middle Neolithic.

**TABLE 6.7**  Frequency of Animals and Estimated Amount of Usable Meat at Funnel Beaker Sites[a]

| | Kilograms of usable meat | Number of animals | Percentage of total number of animals | Total estimated weight in kilograms | Percentage of estimated weight | Kilograms of usable meat from total estimated weight |
|---|---|---|---|---|---|---|
| **Zimno, USSR** | | | | | | |
| Cattle (700)[b] | 350 | 11 | 25 | 7,700 | 68.9 | 3,850 |
| Sheep–goat (25) | 12.5 | 9 | 20 | 225 | 2 | 112.5 |
| Pig (30) | 15 | 8 | 18 | 240 | 2 | 120 |
| Dog (10) | 5 | 3 | 7 | 30 | — | 15 |
| Horse (600) | 300 | 4 | 9 | 2,400 | 21.5 | 1,200 |
| Elk (355) | 177.5 | 1 | 2 | 355 | 3 | 177.5 |
| Red deer (190) | 95 | 1 | 2 | 190 | 2 | 95 |
| Roe deer (21) | 10.5 | 1 | 2 | 21 | — | 10.5 |
| Aurochs (900) | 450 | — | — | — | — | — |
| Wild pig (107.5) | 53.75 | — | — | — | — | — |
| Other wild animals[c] | — | 6 | 14 | — | — | — |
| Total | | 44 | | 11,161 | | |
| **Fuchsberg-Südensee, Germany** | | | | | | |
| Cattle (700)[b] | 350 | 24 | 41 | 16,800 | 72 | 8,400 |
| Sheep–goat (25) | 12.5 | 5 | 9 | 125 | — | 62.5 |
| Pig (30) | 15 | 6 | 10 | 180 | — | 90 |
| Dog (10) | 5 | 3 | 5 | 30 | — | 15 |
| Horse (600) | 300 | 2 | 3 | 1,200 | 5 | 600 |
| Elk (355) | 177.5 | — | — | — | — | — |
| Red deer (190) | 95 | 5 | 9 | 1,710 | 7 | 855 |
| Roe deer (21) | 10.5 | 2 | 3 | 42 | — | 21 |
| Aurochs (900) | 450 | 3 | 5 | 2,700 | 11.5 | 1,350 |
| Wild pig (107.5) | 53.75 | 6 | 10 | 645 | 3 | 322.5 |
| Other wild animals[c] | — | 2 | 3 | — | — | — |
| Total | | 58 | | 23,432 | | |
| **Nosocice, Poland** | | | | | | |
| Cattle (700)[b] | 350 | 14 | 38 | 9,800 | 85 | 4,900 |
| Sheep–goat (25) | 12.5 | 13 | 35 | 875 | 8 | 437.5 |
| Pig (30) | 15 | 10 | 27 | 810 | 7 | 405 |
| Dog (10) | 5 | ?[d] | | | | |
| Horse (600) | 300 | | | | | |
| Elk (355) | 177.5 | | | | | |
| Red deer (190) | 95 | | | | | |
| Roe deer (21) | 10.5 | | | | | |
| Aurochs (900) | 450 | | | | | |
| Wild pig (107.5) | 53.75 | ?[e] | | | | |
| Other wild animals[c] | — | | | | | |
| Total | | 37 | | 11,485 | | |

[a] Data are from Tsalkin 1970; Murray 1970; Sobociński 1961.
[b] Numbers in parentheses indicate estimated adult weight in kilograms.
[c] In estimating the weight, the category of "other wild animals" was not included.
[d] Six bones.
[e] Forty-four bones.

146

TABLE 6.8  Frequency of Animals and Estimated Amount of Usable Meat at Hetzenberg[a]

| | Kilograms of usable meat | Number of animals | Percentage of total number of animals | Total estimated weight in kilograms | Percentage of estimated weight | Kilograms of usable meat from total estimated weight |
|---|---|---|---|---|---|---|
| Cattle (700)[b] | 350 | 28 | 37.8 | 19,600 | 89 | 9,800 |
| Sheep–goat (25) | 12.5 | 26 | 35.1 | 650 | 3 | 325 |
| Pig (30) | 15 | 10 | 13.5 | 300 | 1 | 150 |
| Dog (10) | 5 | 2 | 2.7 | 20 | — | 10 |
| Aurochs (900) | 450 | 1 | 1.4 | 900 | 4 | 450 |
| Red deer (190) | 95 | 2 | 2.7 | 380 | 2 | 190 |
| Roe deer (21) | 10.5 | 2 | 2.7 | 42 | — | 21 |
| Wild pig (107.5) | 53.75 | 2 | 2.7 | 215 | 1 | 107.5 |
| Beaver (16.25) | 8.125 | 1 | 1.4 | 16.25 | — | 8.125 |
| Total | | 74 | | 22,123.25 | | |

[a] Data are from Beyer 1972.
[b] Numbers in parentheses indicate estimated adult weight in kilograms.

At Krzemionki in Poland, a Funnel Beaker culture flint mine has been found, where the characteristic "banded" flint was mined. The workings extended over an area of 4 km (2.5 miles) in length and 30–120 m in width (Krukowski 1939, Tabaczyński 1970). In this area, approximately 1000 shafts, 4 to 11 m deep, were found. Some of the shafts were interconnected by galleries averaging 63 cm in height (Jażdżewski 1965). Mining tools such as antler picks and stone hammers were found in the mine area. In some galleries, charcoal drawings of people and animals were found. Numerous rough-outs or semifinished pieces of flint for making axes were traded from the Krzemionki area (Figure 6.7). It took no longer than 10 minutes to produce a semifinished piece for making of an ax (Balcer 1975). It is interesting to note that one of the more impressive Funnel Beaker settlements, Ćmielów in Poland, is located only 9 km (5.5 miles) from the flint mines at Krzemionki. However, we should not assume that Funnel Beaker axes in Poland were made only of banded flint. The Świeciechów and Volynian flint was used extensively for that same purpose (Table 6.9).

We know that copper was fashioned into artifacts by the simple technique of hammering the cold metal as early as 6500 B.C. in the Near East. But during the Middle Neolithic, in southeastern and central Europe, we find what looks like actual metallurgy, that is, the technique of melting the metal and casting it. It appears that some of the earliest centers of European metallurgy were in the Carpathian Mountains, whose ranges form an arch extending between Slovakia and Romania.

In the past, archaeologists looked to the Aegean and Anatolia for the origin of European metallurgy. It seems now that the metallurgical developments in

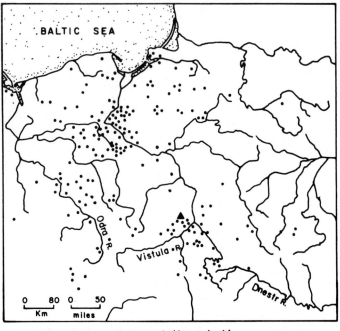

• Axes ▲ Krzemionki

**Figure 6.7.** Distribution of banded flint axes. (After Tabaszyński 1970.)

**TABLE 6.9 Flint Varieties Used in Making of Funnel Beaker Axes[a]**

| Site | Flint type | | |
|---|---|---|---|
| | Świeciechów | Krzemionki (banded) | Volynian |
| Ćmielów | 38% | 62% | |
| Gródek Nadbużny 1C | 39% | 22% | 39% |
| Kamień Łukawski | 60% | 40% | |
| Zawichost | 65% | 27% | 8% |

[a] Data are from Balcer 1975:123.

those areas may be later than those in Europe (C. Renfrew 1969). The Caucasus Mountain area represents another center of early metallurgy, and this is frequently underemphasized or overlooked by European archaeologists in deriving the origins of metallurgy.

European copper artifacts occurred as early as the Starčevo culture, as hammered copper artifacts found at Obre I in Yugoslavia indicate (Gimbutas 1973:166). The Tripolyean A site of Solonchene in the Ukraine yielded copper pins, beads, and fishhooks produced by cold hammering and by annealing, that is, by heating the metal and then hammering it into shape.

It should be noted that copper objects found in Tripolye A sites in the Soviet Union exhibit quite sophisticated techniques of metal working (Ryndina 1971, Greeves 1975). Most of the copper artifacts were made by annealing rather than by cold hammering. Some Tripolyean copper artifacts were welded. This is a complicated process even if it requires only temperatures between 350 and 450°C. It is not clear from what source the Tripolye people in the Soviet Union received copper or copper artifacts, perhaps southeastern Europe. This area of Europe probably had the earliest utilization of copper sources. Artifacts of arsenic bronze occur in the later phases of the Tripolye culture. However, I am not placing this phase into the chapter discussing the Bronze Age. All observations made about the Tripolye culture will be found in the chapters dealing with the Neolithic.

Artifacts made by casting are found later in Europe. For example, as a result of several studies, we now know that the copper axes were cast in an open mold, and the shape of the ax was produced by subsequent hammering of the heated metal (Charles 1969). In making the axes, bivalve molds were not utilized, and the shaft holes present in axes were produced by casting.

Conditions essential for casting copper, such as a temperature of about 1100°C (C. Renfrew 1969) and a reducing atmosphere, supposedly were available at that time in Europe. Frierman's analysis (1969) of Karanovo V–VI graphiteware sherd from the Gumelnitsa culture in Bulgaria, which is contemporary with the Central European Middle Neolithic, indicates that the pot was fired in an oxidizing atmosphere between 1000 and 1105°C. Furthermore, she states that the evenness and interior color show that the vessel was fired under reducing conditions. This would have been necessary to prevent the graphite from burning and to obtain an evenly fired pot. To make pots in such a manner would have required some kind of kiln to produce the period of reduction. We do not have actual evidence for kilns, but ovens are found in houses that are usually associated with breadmaking or drying of grain and that may also have been used for pottery making. However, Kingery and Frierman reexamined the same Karanovo sherd, and it seems that it was originally fired at 700°C. Thus, the ancient firing temperature of this sherd does not support C. Renfrew's claims for the melting and smelting of copper in southeastern Europe at this time (Kingery and Frierman 1974).

The majority of copper artifacts are found in the Carpathian and Balkan mountain region of central and southeastern Europe. The small quantities of copper artifacts that are found far from the centers of production are mostly ornaments. For example, in the Lengyel cemetery at Brześć Kujawski in Poland, most copper finds are beads. At Karbuna, a Tripolyean A or B site near Kishinev in Moldavia, Soviet Union, a hoard of 852 stone, bone, shell, and copper artifacts was found in a beautiful pot decorated in the Phase A style (Sergeev 1963). Of the 444 copper objects in the pot, only 2 were large tools, that is, axes–adzes, whereas 388 were beads. The remaining copper artifacts consisted of bracelets, discs, plaques, and anthropomorphic pendants made of thin copper plates. Among the noncopper objects two stone axes–adzes were found. The majority of the artifacts consisted of bone or shell beads and pendants. Many of the shell pendants were made of *Spondylus,* probably from the Black Sea. It is evident that it was mostly small trinkets that were traded into the non-copper-producing areas, where they were more important as status symbols, or ritual paraphernalia, than as utilitarian tools.

## *Trade*

The evidence for trade is shown by the presence of artifacts made of nonlocal raw materials at the Middle Neolithic sites. We know that copper, stone, flint, obsidian, shells, and pottery were exchanged among the Middle Neolithic communities. Probably certain traded items were only involved with higher-status individuals, since we are postulating the existence of ranked societies or simple chiefdoms during the Middle Neolithic. For example, copper artifacts are not numerous outside the source areas, and perhaps they were exchanged mainly among the tribal elites. Some aspects of the organization of intercommunity exchange can be illustrated by the distribution of Funnel Beaker flint artifacts. The flint tools of this culture, such as scrapers, blades, sickle blades, burins, axes, were made from nonlocal as well as local raw materials. Some of this flint was obtained by mining at such sites as Krzemionki Opatowskie near Opatów and Świeciechów in Poland. At the same time, flint mines are found in other parts of Europe, for example, at the Michelsberg site of Spiennes in Belgium. We find that there was a much more intensive exchange in flint between various communities during the Middle Neolithic than in the Early Neolithic. Thus in central Europe, Jurassic flint from the Kraków area in Poland, flint from the Rügen area in Germany, flint from Volynia in the Soviet Union, banded flint from the Krzemionki area in Poland, Świeciechów flint from the Annopol area in Poland, and "Chocolate" flint from the Radom area in Poland were exchanged between the Funnel Beaker settlements. These varieties of flint are found hundreds of kilometers away from their sources (Figures 6.7 and 6.8). Settlements located near the flint sources, such as Ćmielów, Poland, have much higher frequencies of flint debitage in their lithic assemblages than those farther away. The Polish archaeologist, Balcer (1975) refers to such settlements as "production settlements." However, those sites located farther away from the flint sources tend to have more finished tools than those close to the sources.

A good example of an exchange system between Funnel Beaker communities is available from southeastern Poland (Figure 6.9; Table 6.10). It is evident that each community obtained the greatest amount of flint from the nearest source. However, the availability of good local flint did not eliminate interest in nonlocal or "exotic" flint. Furthermore, there are differences in the usage of imported versus local raw material at some sites. For example, the source of the Volynian flint was approximately 30 km (18.5 miles) from

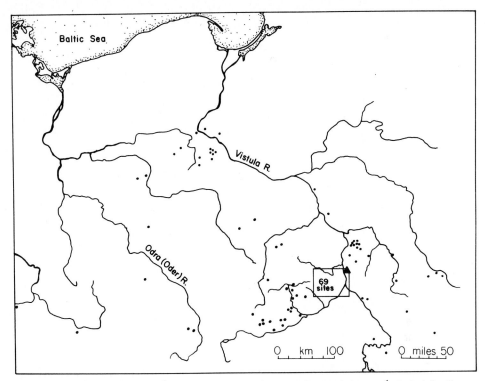

**Figure 6.8.** Distribution of Świeciechów flint artifacts. Black triangle locates Świeciechów flint mines. (After Balcer 1975.)

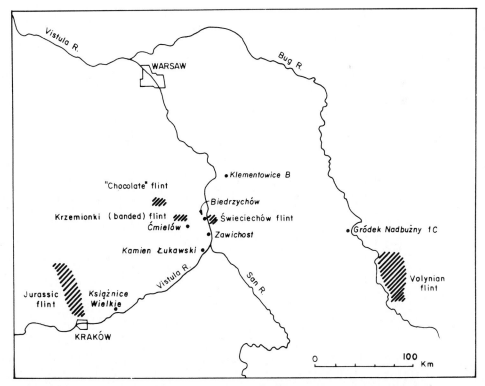

**Figure 6.9.** Flint sources utilized by the Funnel Beaker people in southeastern Poland.

TABLE 6.10  Varieties of Flint at Funnel Beaker Sites in Southeastern Poland[a]

| Site | Sample size | Flint type | | | | | | | | | | | | |
| --- | --- | --- | --- | --- | --- | --- | --- | --- | --- | --- | --- | --- | --- | --- |
| | | Świeciechów | | Krzemionki (banded) | | Volynian | | Jurassic | | "Chocolate" | | Baltic (erratic) | | Other or unidentified | |
| | | N | % | N | % | N | % | N | % | N | % | N | % | N | % |
| Biedrzychów | 768 | 742 | 96.62 | 17 | 2.21 | 2 | 0.26 | — | — | — | — | — | — | 7 | 0.91 |
| Ćmielów | 38,411 | 14,545 | 37.87 | 23,852 | 62.10 | 1 | 0.003 | 6 | 0.02 | 4 | 0.01 | 1 | 0.003 | 2 | 0.006 |
| Gródek Nadbużny 1C | 3,236 | 286 | 8.84 | 48 | 1.48 | 2,542 | 78.55 | 3 | 0.09 | 12 | 0.37 | 15 | 0.46 | — | — |
| Kamień Łukawski | 361 | 284 | 78.67 | 33 | 9.14 | 4 | 1.11 | — | — | 15 | 4.15 | 10 | 2.77 | 14 | 3.88 |
| Klementowice B | 141 | 35 | 24.82 | 54 | 38.30 | 30 | 21.28 | — | — | 6 | 4.25 | 7 | 4.96 | 9 | 6.38 |
| Książnice Wielkie | 190 | 3 | 1.60 | — | — | 4 | 2.14 | 183 | 96.26 | — | — | — | — | — | — |
| Zawichost | 5,672 | 5,449 | 96.07 | 73 | 1.29 | 23 | 0.41 | 3 | 0.05 | 14 | 0.25 | 3 | 0.05 | 107 | 1.88 |

[a] Data are from Balcer 1975.

the Gródek Nadbużny site, but 61% of the axes found there were made of the Świeciechów and banded flint, whose source was roughly 150 and 170 km away (Figure 6.9).

A model called down-the-line-exchange was proposed by C. Renfrew (1972) to describe this type of trade. In this model, the percentage of a particular raw material in a lithic assemblage decreases as the distance from the source of the material increases. In the source area, the decrease is gradual. The source area is called the contact zone, which may be equivalent to a culture region; thus exchange within it can be regarded as internal trade. Consequently, the traded material is very abundant within the contact zone.

> Beyond the edge of this region the percentage (of the raw material) decreases exponentially, if the percentages are plotted on a logarithmic scale, the distribution assumes the shape of a straight line, falling off steadily as the distance from the edge of the contact zone increases [C. Renfrew 1972:465].

The distribution of the Świeciechów flint artifacts fits a down-the-line-exchange model except for the Gródek Nadbużny 1C site (Figure 6.10). For example, Klementowice B fits the down-the-line-exchange model, since it is not close to Świeciechów or Volynian sources. However, the distribution of

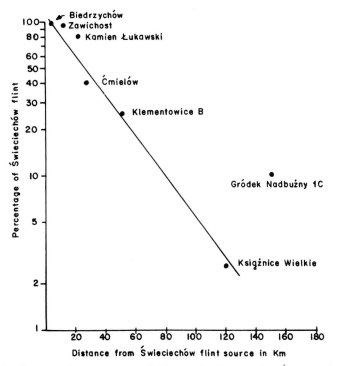

**Figure 6.10.** Down-the-line exchange model for the distribution of the Świeciechów flint from seven Funnel Beaker sites in southeastern Poland.

the banded flint axes does not fit this model at present (Figure 6.7). Furthermore, if the percentages of Świeciechów flint artifacts from seven Funnel Beaker sites in southeastern Poland are plotted, the model does not work so elegantly. There are different varieties of flint exploited in a small geographical area, therefore, the distance is not the primary factor in determining the distribution. For example, at Biedrzychów, Ćmielów, Kamień Łukawski, and Zawichost the amount of Volynian flint is lower than expected due to proximity to the Świeciechów source. We have to consider various social, political, and economic factors in such cases and not only distance. The high proportion of Świeciechów flint at Gródek Nadbużny 1C may reflect the location of a high-status settlement. It should be noted that the Świeciechów flint is not of higher quality than the Volynian flint. However, the percentages of the Volynian flint found to the west of its source area fit C. Renfrew's model for the seven Funnel Beaker sites (Figure 6.11). In this area of the Soviet Union, there

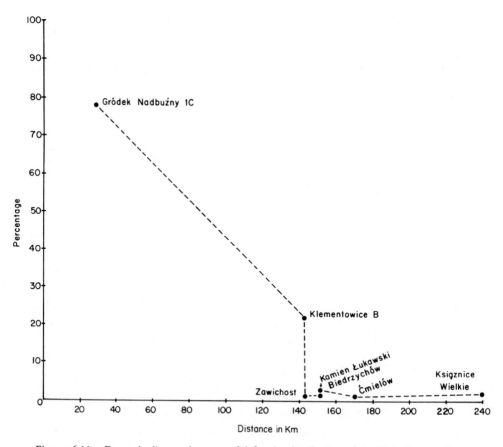

**Figure 6.11.** Down-the-line exchange model for the distribution of the Volynian flint from seven Funnel Beaker sites in southeastern Poland.

is only one source of flint; thus the increase in distance decreases the quantity of the Volynian flint.

In the Carpathian Mountains, south of the Funnel Beaker culture area, the beginnings of copper metallurgy occur during the Middle Neolithic period. The small quantities of copper artifacts that turn up in Funnel Beaker sites indicate that some sort of exchange network linked them to the Carpathian region.

## Settlement Organization

The settlement patterns of the Middle Neolithic cultures are more complex than those of the Early Neolithic. Sites vary in their size and in their location with respect to soil types, elevation, topography, and other environmental factors.

Middle Neolithic settlements appear to have denser population than those of the Early Neolithic, as is shown by the amount of material recovered from their features. For example, the pits found in Linear villages yielded relatively little material. However, the features in Lengyel, Funnel Beaker, or other Middle Neolithic settlements are frequently packed with ceramics, flints, bones, stone, etc.

My discussion of Middle Neolithic settlement organization is based on data from the Funnel Beaker, Lengyel, Michelsberg, Rössen, Aichbühl, and Tripolye cultures.

### Funnel Beaker

The Funnel Beaker culture settlement system is much more complex than that of the Early Neolithic cultures. As in the Linear culture, Funnel Beaker sites are found in the areas of fertile soil in river valleys. However, for the first time, the loess-covered hills and uplands were also occupied, as evidence from Germany and southern Poland shows. Furthermore, greater expansion into nonloess soils took place. The following observations on Funnel Beaker sites are based on surface surveys, such as Kruk's (1973a) work in southern Poland, which has contributed to a clearer understanding of the settlement system. However, excavations are needed to obtain information about organizational differences distinguishing each type of Funnel Beaker culture settlement. The Funnel Beaker culture sites in the southeastern Polish uplands and the Ukraine differ from the ones on the plains of northern Poland, the German Democratic Republic, and Denmark. The location and size of some Funnel Beaker sites in southeastern Poland and the northwestern Ukraine resemble those of the Tripolye sites of the Ukraine.

In southeastern Poland, Funnel Beaker sites vary in size, topographical location, and the nature of the artifacts they contain (Figure 6.12). These

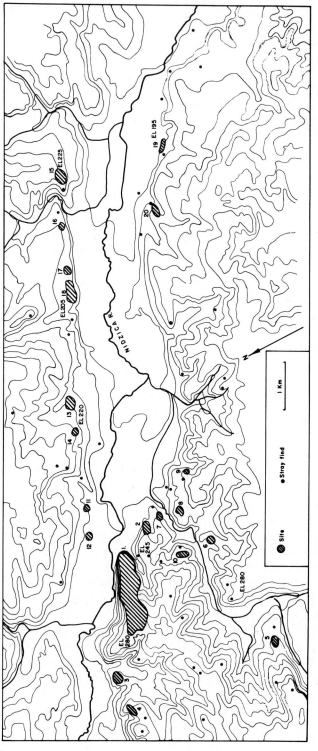

**Figure 6.12.** Funnel Beaker sites in the Middle Nidzica basin, Poland. (Contours are approximate elevations in meters.) (After S. Milisauskas and J. Kruk in press.)

156

differences may reflect functional variation. There are three types of Funnel Beaker sites based on their site area: large, medium, and small. The large sites are located on high elevations and have a great variety of archaeological material on the surface. Some of the large sites occupy an extensive area, e.g., Bronocice in southeastern Poland is over 50 ha in size (site no. 1, Figure 6.12), (Milisauskas and Kruk in press). The medium-sized sites show further variation on the basis of the surface material, and some of them have little pottery on the surface and more stone and flint artifacts. However, in some sites plowing may have destroyed most of the pottery on the surface. These sites are located both in the valleys and in the uplands. The small sites have meager quantities of artifacts and occur at both low and high elevations, but the latter are more common. They may have been the temporary camps of herders. Usually the large sites occur at least several kilometers from one another, and interspersed between them are the smaller sites. The large Funnel Beaker sites may represent the seats of sociopolitical authority of small polities. The ranking lineage or family may have resided in the large sites and dominated the groups residing in dependent settlements. The proportions for the large, the medium, and the small sites are 5:9:30 (1:2:6 ratio), respectively (Kruk 1973a).

Unfortunately, we have little information about the internal organization of the Funnel Beaker sites in central Europe. None of them has been excavated extensively enough to give us an actual settlement layout. At present the Wallendorf site in Germany yields the best information: Here, 9 or 10 houses 8–10 m in length, were uncovered. Inside the large settlements in southeastern Poland we find concentrations of different features and artifacts such as ovens and flint remains which may reflect specific activity areas within a village (Milisauskas and Kruk in press). There is great intersite and interregional variability in Funnel Beaker house styles. In central Europe, both large and small rectangular houses are constructed of a framework of posts, with mud-daubed walls; the largest houses do not exceed 20 m in length. In the Funnel Beaker sites of the southeastern zone there are concentrations of burnt clay with imprints of posts which may be similar in construction the the Tripolye houses. Such concentrations of burnt clay may represent remains of collapsed walls of houses.

However, in Denmark, quite a different kind of Funnel Beaker settlement has been found. At the Barkaer site a large rectangular structure built of stone was found which contained numerous single rooms, 3 × 7 m (21 m²) in area, possibly the dwellings of single nuclear families (Gløb 1949). It should be noted that the Early Neolithic houses such as at Karanovo in southeastern and central Europe were roughly on the average 60m² in area. Such a small floor area of the houses at the Barkaer site may indicate a centralized storage area in some other part of the settlement. No such structures as at Barkaer have been found in central Europe. The Barkaer structures belong to the late phase of the Funnel Beaker culture.

## Lengyel

Most Lengyel culture sites are located in areas of fertile soil. Unlike those of the preceding Linear culture, they are more frequently located at higher elevations; however, the village layouts of the two cultures are similar. Polish and Czechoslovakian Lengyel longhouses had trapezoidal floor plans, in contrast to the rectangular and slightly trapezoidal Linear culture houses (Figure 6.13). Whether this reflects anything more than stylistic variation is not at present known. The exterior wall posts of many Lengyel longhouses were placed in trenches or wall slots. Probably the size and/or population of Lengyel culture villages was similar to those of the Linear culture.

## Rössen

The settlements of Rössen culture probably are of similar size to those of the Lengyel culture. The Rössen settlement on the Taubenberg, near Wahlitz, German Democratic Republic, occupied an area of 2 ha (B. Schmidt 1970). Rössen villages were also made up of trapezoidal longhouses. At the Inden I site in Rhineland, a 35,000 m² area was uncovered containing the remains of 30 houses (Lüning 1975). They varied from 12 to 52 m in length and from 6.20 to 9.0 m in width, at the wider end of the house. The area enclosed by individual houses ranged from 61 to 295 m². Lüning estimates that from 6 to 8 houses existed at any one time.

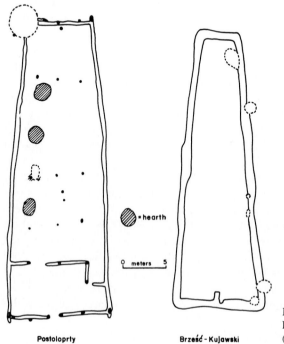

= hearth

0 meters 5

Postoloprty          Brześć - Kujawski

**Figure 6.13.** Lengyel houses at Postoloprty and Brześć-Kujawski. (After Schlette 1958.)

## *Michelsberg*

The Michelsberg culture that some archaeologists consider just an extension of the Funnel Beaker culture occupied Switzerland, southern Germany, northeastern France, and Belgium. We find Michelsberg culture villages such as Ehrenstein on the shores of the Alpine Lakes in Germany and Switzerland. Another type of settlement was located on hilltops; it was sometimes surrounded by ditches, which were crossed at intervals by causeways (Lüning 1968). The areas enclosed by the ditches vary. For example, the enclosed area at the Miel site is 90 × 54 m, that at the Mayen site 360 × 220 m, and that at the Urmitz site 1275 × 840 m. The Urmitz site was surrounded on three sides by ditches having 22 causeways, and on the north side it was protected by the Rhine River (Figure 6.14). Some of the sites had palisades in addition to the ditches. Only a few archaeological features have been found inside these enclosures, giving rise to numerous controversies about their function. In England, similar enclosures are found associated with the contemporary Windmill Hill culture. Since the ditches are not continuous, some archaeologists regard them as kraals or cattle enclosures, although one would not think that palisades would be needed in a kraal. It would be easier to protect the cattle within encampments from a surprise cattle raid or predators.

## *Aichbühl*

Some of the Middle Neolithic settlements in central Europe are not associated with major archaeological cultures (ceramic styles). Aichbühl, located

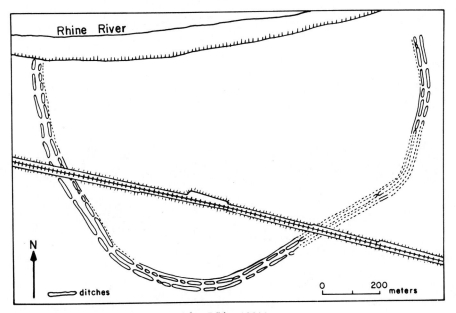

**Figure 6.14.** Plan of Urmitz site. (After Röder 1951.)

on the shore of the Federsee Lake, is an example of such a settlement. Its ceramics belong to the unpainted type of Neolithic ceramics in southern Germany. R. Schmidt (1930) uncovered 25 rectangular houses arranged in an irregular row along the shore of the lake (Figures 6.15 and 6.16). They were built of wooden posts and were divided into two rooms. Hearths and clay ovens were found inside the houses. The houses were divided into three types:

1. Habitations, approximately 20, and the average size 5 × 8 m
2. A central building, approximately 20 × 20 m
3. Storage houses

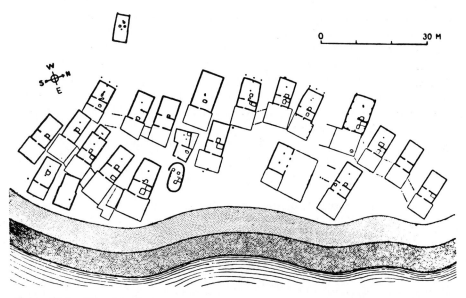

Figure 6.15.   Plan of Aichbühl. (Reprinted from *Prehistoric Europe: The Economic Basis* by J. G. D. Clark with the permission of the publishers, Stanford University Press. Copyright © 1952 by J. G. D. Clark.)

Figure 6.16.   Aichbühl Village reconstructed. (From Müller-Karpe 1968.)

## Tripolye

In terms of location and fortification, there is great variability in Tripolyean settlements. Some of the Tripolye villages are located on high elevations or promontories near rivers, whereas others are located on low-lying river terraces. The location of some Tripolye sites, as well as the occurrence of fortifications, strongly suggests intense competition among various communities. This militaristic interpretation of these features does not appeal to some archaeologists, who would prefer to see the Tripolye people as living a life of pastoral innocence and tranquility. Such scholars interpret the ditches as enclosures for cattle kraals.

Fortifications are found at a number of Tripolye sites. For example, Polivanov Yar in the Ukraine is located on a high promontory: On three sides

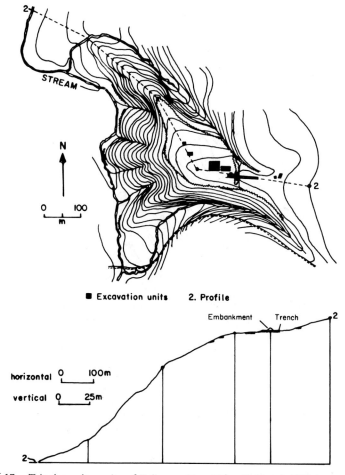

Figure 6.17. Tripolye culture site of Polivanov Yar. (After T. Passek 1961.)

The population of the Tripolye villages appears to have been larger than those of the Early Neolithic settlements in central Europe. If every oven in the houses at Kolomiishchina were used by one family, then the village held 72 families. However, by using the size of the houses to estimate the population, we get a smaller figure. If we calculate 1 family per house having an area less than 60 m² (using Early Neolithic houses in southeastern Europe as an analogy) and 2 families per house with an area of more than 60 m², then the estimated number of families is reduced to 47. Even this lower figure represents at least twice as many families as were found in Linear culture villages. There is a direct correlation between the size of the houses and the quantity of pots found in them, leading to the assumption that the larger Tripolye houses had multiple-family occupation. Thus Passek had divided the houses into three groups based on their area. The small houses had 10 to 15 pots, the medium houses had 20 to 30 pots, and large houses had 35 to 50 pots. There is some evidence for repairs and enlargement of Tripolye houses. Houses may have been enlarged from time to time to accommodate increases in family size.

Our knowledge of Tripolye structures is supplemented by models of houses, made of clay, which have been found at various sites such as Popudnia. From these models, and the excavated floor plans, it is possible to describe Tripolye houses in some detail. The interiors of Tripolye houses were usually divided into two or four rooms (Figure 6.19). In the rooms, dome-shaped ovens up to 60 cm in diameter were located against the wall. Also each room usually contained a low clay platform, on the floor, cruciform or four-lobed in shape, the function of which is unclear. Soviet archaeologists suggest that the platforms were used for ritual purposes. The houses had thick floors of burnt clay, and judging from clay models, they had gabled roofs. However, some Soviet archaeologists speculate that the so-called Tripolye burnt-clay floors are just remains of collapsed walls of houses. The house models give us some information about the house interior, especially the layout of the features and the type of furniture. Ovens, clay benches, the cruciform platforms, grinding stones, and a few large pottery vessels are shown inside these house models. Some models have short legs, which led some archaeologists to suggest that the actual houses were built on stilts. This is highly unlikely in the forest–steppe environment of the Ukraine.

**Figure 6.19.** Interior of a Tripolye house at Kolomiishchina. (From Müller-Karpe 1968.)

The excavated houses contained grinding stones, clay figurines, and bone, antler, flint, and stone artifacts. The pottery consisted of two main types: painted and unpainted. The painted vessels are very well made and represent some of the most beautifully ornamented ceramics of the European Neolithic. The clay figurines usually represent females and only rarely males. Figurines of animals, especially cattle, were also found. A few of these hollow clay figurines have been found packed with wheat, suggesting that they were used in harvest or crop protection rituals. The occurrence of figurines and cruciform pediments inside the houses indicates that some rituals were performed by individual families. The figurines undergo stylistic changes through time. Figurines belonging to the early phase were frequently decorated with closely incised lines, whereas later figurines are undecorated and the female body is represented in somewhat different dimensions.

## Social and Political Organization

### Chiefdoms

As we might suspect, the various archaeologically observable changes during the Middle Neolithic are associated with an increase in social and political complexity. At this time, institutional changes occurred in some tribal societies. Societies with inherited inequality in personal status probably appeared in central Europe during the Middle Neolithic. Such societies are called ranked societies, chiefdoms, or complex-kin-organized societies. Chiefdoms are best exemplified by societies in Polynesia, the southeastern United States, Central Asia, and Africa (Sahlins 1968).

The chiefdoms that have been observed ethnographically reflect a large range of variation in their complexity. For example, Tahiti and Tonga represent highly complex chiefdoms. Here, the chiefs had specialized warrior corps at their disposal that acted as an armed body of executioners. This political and military power gave the chiefs mastery over the lower-status people. We may refer to these societies as *complex chiefdoms.* Other chiefdoms display much less social and political complexity. To reflect this fact, we may refer to them as *simple chiefdoms.* While any chiefdom probably is located at a slightly different point along a range of increasing political complexity, the two different terms help us to discuss the relatively simple chiefdoms of the Middle Neolithic, and to differentiate them from the more complex polities of the Bronze and Iron Ages.

It is evident that chiefdoms have greater sociopolitical complexity than tribal societies. Service (1971:133) has noted that chiefdoms are "particularly distinguished from tribes by the presence of centers which coordinate economic, social and religious activities." Social and political relations in chiefdoms are still based on kinship, but status differentiation becomes more prominent. The status positions may be inherited. High rank in such societies is frequently emphasized by different dress or the wearing of certain ornaments. High-status individuals usually possess more material goods, especially nonlocal ones or those made of exotic materials. High status may be expressed by the possession of more wives. The size, location, or the construction method of the houses also can reflect the higher status of an individual.

A chiefdom may have the attributes listed below, though not all of them need necessarily be present (C. Renfrew 1973a; Sahlins 1968; Service 1971). It should be noted that these attributes specifically apply to complex chiefdoms.

1. Individuals and groups are hierarchically arranged in the social system.
2. The leader or chief holds an official position with built-in privileges and obligations.
3. No true government exists to back up decisions by legalized force, but there is authority and centralized direction.
4. Individuals wield unequal control over and have unequal access to goods and services.
5. High-status persons have distinctive dress or ornament.
6. The high-status individuals inherit their positions.
7. There are permanent central agencies that coordinate social, religious, and economic activities.
8. The society is more integrated, with a greater number of statuses.
9. Public works are organized, such as for irrigation, building temples, temple mounds, pyramids, or megaliths.
10. The economy is more diversified.
11. There is ecological specialization between communities.
12. Religious specialists appear, overseeing ceremonies and rituals.
13. There is more highly developed craft specialization.
14. Chiefdoms have greater population densities than tribes.
15. There is an increase in the total population of the society.
16. Individual residence groups increase in size.
17. There is greater productivity.
18. Territorial boundaries are more clearly defined.
19. There is potential for territorial expansion.
20. There is reduction of internal strife.

Archaeologists usually attempt to demonstrate the presence of chiefdoms with data from cemeteries, individual settlements, or settlement systems. The presence of chiefdoms can best be demonstrated using settlement and mortuary data from the same region.

### Evidence for Chieftainship in Burial Practices

In chiefdoms we may find a greater variety of burial practices. Exotic or luxury goods found in burials may be associated with high-status individuals. If burials of children contain such goods, this may indicate that social status is inherited and not acquired by an individual through his own deeds or character. For the higher-ranking individuals, larger or different types of burial structures, such as mounds, may be constructed. However, we should be careful in assuming that variations in burials, especially in grave goods deposited with the deceased, are signs of status differences. They may be the symbols of offices held in a sodality or voluntary tribal association.

The mortuary evidence for the appearance of simple chiefdoms consists of the differences in burial treatment of some individuals in central Europe around 3000 B.C.; specifically, it is based on the small number and size of the Funnel Beaker culture burial mounds. The huge burial mounds of this culture usually contain one or two individuals. Furthermore, the number of these mounds, as in the Kuyavia and Chełmno regions in Poland, is small, thus we can assume that there was a cultural selection that determined who was buried in such structures (Figure 6.20). Therefore, we may assume that only high-status persons were selected for interment in these mounds.

It should be noted that in the southeastern zone of the Funnel Beaker culture (i.e., southeastern Poland and northwestern Ukraine) no burial

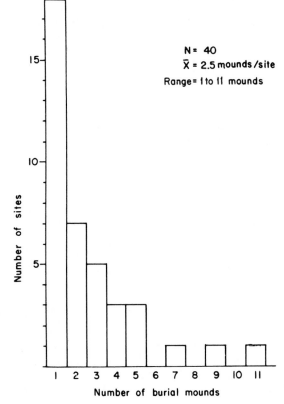

N = 40
$\bar{X}$ = 2.5 mounds/site
Range = 1 to 11 mounds

**Figure 6.20.** Histogram showing the frequency of Funnel Beaker mounds at sites in the Kuyavia and Chełmno regions of Poland. (Six sites containing one burial mound were not included, because originally they probably had more mounds.) (Data are from Chmielewski 1952.)

**Figure 6.21.** Multiple Funnel Beaker burial from Bronocice, Poland. (From J. Kruk and S. Milisauskas excavations; W. Hensel, project director.)

mounds are found. Instead we find single and, on rare occasions, multiple burials in pits within the settlement (Figure 6.21).

While the burial mounds indicate that status differences existed, we cannot assume that simple chiefdoms were prevalent in all parts of central Europe during the Middle Neolithic. The burial data from Lengyel and Tiszapolgár cemeteries only indicate status differences based on sex and age (Figures 6.25 and 6.26). In fairness, it should be mentioned that some archaeologists hypothesize the presence of chiefdoms during the Early Neolithic. C. Renfrew (1973a:554) argues that in Britain chiefdoms were emerging in the Early Neolithic. However, the Early Neolithic in Britain falls within the time segment of Middle Neolithic in central Europe. The British Early Neolithic societies were constructing long earthen mounds or barrows at this time; the causewayed enclosures date also to this period. Renfrew proposes "that each early neolithic region served by a causewayed camp was the home of an emerging chiefdom. Each had on the average 20 long barrows which might suggest a population of between 400 and 2000 persons [1973a: 549]." It is likely that only some individuals were buried in the long barrows: the local chiefs or high-status individuals.

### Evidence for Chieftainship in Settlement Hierarchies

Johnson (1973) uses settlement hierarchy as an indicator variable of the complexity of sociopolitical organization. For example, with the appearance of a chiefdom, we may have a two-level settlement hierarchy reflecting two levels of administrative organization, one at a single-community level and one at a regional level. Societies with one level of specialized leadership are classified as tribal societies. In societies with two levels of administration, some settlements may dominate an entire region because they are a locus of regional sociopolitical authority and their number is smaller than the number of dependent sites.

The greater sociopolitical complexity in Europe during the Middle Neolithic is reflected by a more complex settlement system. Settlement systems with a two-level hierarchy may have appeared at this time. The Funnel Beaker settlement system, for example, appears to have had a two-level hierarchy of sites. This may reflect the emergence of chiefdoms in Europe during the Middle Neolithic (Figure 6.12). The reader is referred to page 155 for the discussion of the Funnel Beaker settlement system.

## Ritual Organization

The Middle Neolithic apparently saw considerable changes in ritual practices, especially those connected with mortuary beliefs, in western, southern, central, and part of northern Europe. In these regions, large stone structures, the famous megalithic monuments, were erected around 3500–3000 B.C. (4190–3610 B.C.) (Figure 6.22). This term usually includes burial structures of stone and earth, as well as large freestanding stones, set up in groups or individually (Daniel 1963). These structures vary in size, construction techniques, form and chronological position, and they cut across various archaeological cultures. Furthermore, some of the stone tombs are composite monuments, meaning that, their construction was accomplished in several phases, over a long period of time. Henshall (1974: 140–141) noted that in Scotland "they were first built as relatively small and simple structures, later added to, altered and embellished." Clearly, different groups of people may have been involved in building and altering the same monument. This complicates the functional interpretation of some monuments, for the first builders may have been of a different culture than the later builders.

The variability of the megalithic structures probably reflects some functional differences. Also, the social criteria for mound interment very likely differed among megalithic building societies. Thus, in some areas the burial mounds or structures may be associated with high-status individuals, and, in turn, this may

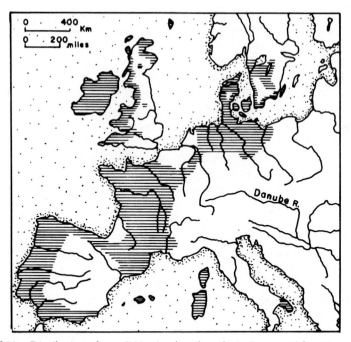

**Figure 6.22.** Distribution of megalithic chambered tombs in Europe. (After Piggott 1965.)

reflect the appearance of ranked or complex-kin-organized societies. On the other hand, in some areas the mounds served as burial structures for entire lineages or clans, as is the case among the present-day Merina people in Malagasy (Bloch 1968).

When dealing with Middle Neolithic mortuary customs we should consider the burial mounds constructed of stone and/or dirt. These so-called unchambered long barrows occur in France, England, Poland, and Germany. In northern Germany and Poland these mounds are associated with the Funnel Beaker culture. For example, in Poland we find the so-called Kuyavian trapezoidal mounds, which range from 25 to 150 m in length (Jażdżewski 1970). They are from 4 to 10 m in width at the broader end, and 3 to 5 m at the narrower end. The wider end is usually 3 to 4 m high and the narrower end is 1 to 1.5 m high. Large stones were placed around the outside edges of these mounds (Figure 6.23). The burials usually occurred at the wider end of the mound in a shallow pit on the ground surface or on a pavement built of stones. No burial chambers of large stones were constructed; only the impressive size of these mounds puts them in the megalithic monument category. Just small quantities of grave goods were buried with the dead: a pot, a flint blade, and, rarely, polished stone tools and flint projectile points. These Funnel Beaker mounds usually contain one or two individuals, although, in exceptional cases, the remains of several individuals have been found (Table 6.12). Such burial mounds are not found with all the Funnel Beaker settlements. Most Kuyavian

**Figure 6.23.** Funnel Beaker burial mound at Wietrzychowice, Poland. (Courtesy of W. Hensel.)

TABLE 6.12 Number of Skeletons Found in
Funnel Beaker Culture Burial Mounds
in Western Poland

| Number of skeletons | Number of mounds |
|---|---|
| 1 | 5 |
| 2 | 6 |
| 3 | 2 |

mounds contain skeletons of adult males (Table 6.13). In a few instances, the skulls show evidence of trephanation (Kapica 1970).

In northern Germany we find long rectangular or trapezoidal mounds built of stones associated with the Funnel Beaker culture. Round, square, or rectangular stone structures are found with late phases of the Funnel Beaker culture in Denmark. These frequently contain multiple burials.

**TABLE 6.13** Proportions of Each Sex by Age Group in Thirteen Funnel Beaker Culture Burial Mounds in Western Poland

| | Young adult 16–30 years | | Adult 31–45 years | | Old 46 years | | Total | |
|---|---|---|---|---|---|---|---|---|
| | N | % | N | % | N | % | N | % |
| Female | 2 | 17 | | | | | 2 | 17 |
| Male | 2 | 17 | 3 | 25 | 5 | 42 | 10 | 84 |
| Age group totals | 4 | 34 | 3 | 25 | 5 | 42 | 12 | 101 |

With regard to ritual practices, the same differences between southeastern and central Europe that were observable in the Early Neolithic can still be seen in the Middle Neolithic. Human figurines are rarely found in north–central Europe, while they are quite numerous in the Tripolye culture area of the Ukraine and Romania. Also, the Vinča culture sites in Yugoslavia have numerous figurines. It should be noted that animal figurines are found in north–central Europe as, for example, in Funnel Beaker sites (Figure 6.24).

## Status Differences Based on Sex and Age

Excellent published reports on Lengyel and Tiszapolgár cemeteries allow inferences to be made about differences based on sex and age in Middle Neolithic society. The analysis by Bognár-Kutzián (1963) of the large Tisza-

**Figure 6.24.** Funnel Beaker figurine of a ram from Jordanów, Poland. (Courtesy of W. Hensel.)

polgár and Bodrogkeresztúr cemetery at Tiszapolgár-Basatanya is especially useful in this respect. We also have interesting reports of the Lengyel cemeteries at Brześć Kujawski in Poland (Jażdżewski 1938; Gabałówna 1966), and Zengövarkony in Hungary (Dombay 1960).

Burial data from Lengyel and Tiszapolgár cemeteries reveal that the sex of the skeleton is associated with the position of burial: Males were interred lying on their right sides, females on their left. Such consistent differences in skeletal position are not found in Early Neolithic burials. If we assume that children of each sex received the same treatment as adults during the Middle Neolithic, then we can infer their sex from the body position.

At the Tiszapolgár-Basatanya cemetery, the burials indicate that fighting, hunting, and trading were male activities, for men were buried with flint tools, weapons, animal bones, and copper tools (Figure 6.25). The control of exchange activities by males is suggested by the association of products made of nonlocal raw material. Males were buried with copper and obsidian. Pottery was probably made by females and used mainly by them in domestic activities. This is reflected by finds of pottery with female remains. Also certain ornaments such as beads are found with females. It should be noted that no domesticated or wild animals are associated with female burials. This would imply that it was the male's task to perform the subsistence activities involving animals.

The burial data from the Lengyel Brześć Kujawski cemetery in Poland are not as diverse as those from Tiszapolgár-Basatanya, but statistical analysis indicates similar behavior patterns (Figure 6.26). For example, that men did the fighting is indicated by the association of antler axes with male burials.

It seems also that animals played important roles in mortuary rituals or feasts. Their remains, especially those of pig, are found in Lengyel and Tiszapolgár burials. Probably pigs were not only important in subsistence, but also as symbols of status or wealth.

## Mortality, Longevity, Sex Ratios, and Population Composition

The cemeteries that have been investigated by archaeologists have small populations; therefore, it is very difficult to establish conclusively various cultural practices such as infanticide. Sex ratios are more unequal in Lengyel and Tiszapolgár cemeteries than in those of the Linear culture. Generally, the Brześć Kujawski, Zengövarkony, and Tiszapolgár-Basatanya cemeteries contain greater numbers of males than females, and it is evident that not all females were buried in these cemeteries.

Sex determination of children's skeletons is very difficult, and many archaeological reports omit this information. However, the context of a child's burial may help in determining the sex.

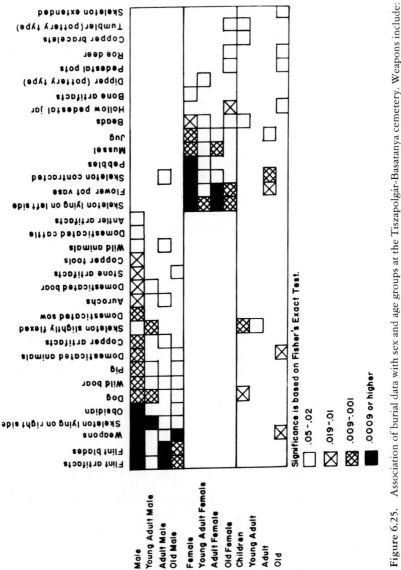

**Figure 6.25.** Association of burial data with sex and age groups at the Tiszapolgár-Basatanya cemetery. Weapons include: macehead, stone hammer axe, antler hammer axe, flint projectile point, copper dagger, obsidian projectile point, antler projectile point. Copper tools include: ingot, awl, dagger blade. (Data are from Bognár-Kutzián 1963.)

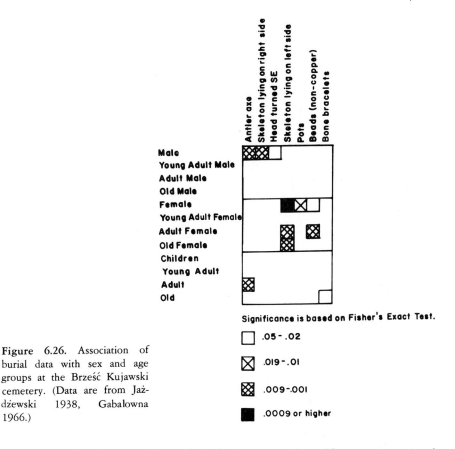

**Figure 6.26.** Association of burial data with sex and age groups at the Brześć Kujawski cemetery. (Data are from Jaźdźewski 1938, Gabalowna 1966.)

For example, if the position of the body or certain artifacts are associated with a particular sex in adult burials, we can hypothesize that at the same site, sex differences among children are similarly reflected. As previously mentioned, at the Tiszapolgár-Basatanya I cemetery males were buried on the right side and females on the left side. Four of the children's burials were lying on the left side and only six on the right side. However, if these individuals are added to the 36 adult males and adult females, the new sex ratio (42:29) is even more unbalanced in favor of males. The greater mortality rate of female children probably reflects differential treatment at birth or subsequently by some societies. At the Tiszapolgár-Basatanya cemetery, the ratios of males to females are unequal for the Tiszapolgár period, but are quite similar for the Bodrogkeresztúr culture (Tables 6.14 and 6.15). Even if we assume that children's skeletons were positioned by sex, that sex ratios for the Tiszapolgár period are still quite unequal: There are more burials for boys than girls (Table 6.16). Bognár-Kutzián (1963) explains the disproportion by suggesting that these people practiced female infanticide. Perhaps this is related to the great decrease of available land for agriculture. Once the agricultural land niche was

TABLE 6.14   Proportions of Each Sex by Age Group at Tiszapolgár-Basatanya I[a]

|  | Young adult 16–30 years | | Adult 31–45 years | | Old 46 years | | Total | |
| --- | --- | --- | --- | --- | --- | --- | --- | --- |
|  | N | % | N | % | N | % | N | % |
| Female | 2 | 5.5 | 2 | 5.5 | 7 | 19 | 11 | 30 |
| Male | 13 | 36 | 5 | 14 | 7 | 19 | 25 | 69 |
| Age group totals | 15 | 41.5 | 7 | 19.5 | 14 | 38 | 36 | 99 |

[a] Data are from Bognár-Kutzián 1963.

TABLE 6.15   Proportions of Each Sex by Age Group at Tiszapolgár-Basatanya II[a]

|  | Young adult 16–30 years | | Adult 31–45 years | | Old 46 years | | Total | |
| --- | --- | --- | --- | --- | --- | --- | --- | --- |
|  | N | % | N | % | N | % | N | % |
| Female | 13 | 18 | 15 | 21 | 6 | 8 | 34 | 47 |
| Male | 12 | 17 | 13 | 18 | 13 | 18 | 38 | 53 |
| Age group totals | 25 | 35 | 28 | 39 | 19 | 26 | 72 | 100 |

[a] Data are from Bognár-Kutzián 1963.

TABLE 6.16   Proportions of Children by Age Group at Tiszapolgár-Basatanya I and II Cemetery[a]

|  | 0–5 years | | 6–10 years | | 11–15 years | |
| --- | --- | --- | --- | --- | --- | --- |
|  | N | % | N | % | N | % |
| Tiszapolgár period | 8 | 42 | 9 | 47 | 2 | 11 |
| Bodrogkeresztúr period | 3 | 37.5 | 4 | 50 | 1 | 12.5 |

[a] Data from Bongnár-Kutzián 1963.

filled, an increase in the population was not advantageous. The previously postulated heavy labor demand of an expanding pioneering population during the Early Neolithic probably came to an end around 3500–3000 B.C. in central Europe. One way to stop the population growth was to decrease the number of females by infanticide. However, as previously mentioned, the data from the Early Neolithic cemeteries in central Europe reflect near balanced sex ratios which may be associated with no shortage of land.

The lengths of the extended skeletons in the Tiszapolgár-Basatanya cemetery were measured. The male skeletons averaged 170 cm in length and the females, 160 cm. Since this represents the stature of the skeleton, the actual height of living individuals was several centimeters greater. Out of the 54 individuals assigned to the Tiszapolgár phase of the cemetery, 10 had an estimated age of 50 years or more; 14 out of the 82 individuals represented by the Bodrogkeresztúr burials had achieved this age. Thus, in the earlier period one had an 18.5% chance of surviving to age 50, while one's chances dropped to 17% in the later period. This indicates very little change. As in the Early Neolithic, few children died between the ages of 11 and 15.

Previously, the practice of female infanticide was postulated for the Tisza-polgár people. However, even if infanticide were practiced in that society to limit the population, many disabled or diseased adults survived only through the help of their fellows. This is shown by the presence of diseases and deformities in the skeletal material. Of course, only diseases that left traces on bones could be analysed. Also because of differential preservation not every skeleton could be analysed for evidence of pathologies (Bognár-Kutzián 1963:392–395). Evidence for the following diseases, pathologies, and injuries was found: paralysis of arms, deformation of skull, plagiocephalism, osteoporosis symmetrica, neurosis of spinal cord (baastrub and arthrosis), fracture of spine, head wounds (bashed skull), brain tumor, stiff pine, scaphocephaly, and arthritis–rheumatism. Fifteen skeletons (8 females, 7 males) from the Bodrogkeresztúr period showed signs of rheumatism. There is evidence that some of the individuals with head wounds survived their injuries. Whoever would idealize the primitive man's way of life in the manner of Rousseau should consider this evidence. Not only was life short, but also various pathological miseries hounded men and women, and there was little possibility of relief. It is doubtful that shamans could cure or relieve the pain of many of these diseases. However, we should note that any dead population will show signs of disease and disease stress.

## Warfare

Site locations, the presence of fortifications, and weapons suggest that there was more warfare occurring in the Middle Neolithic than during the Early Neolithic. The cause of increased warfare might have been increasing competition among various communities over land and other resources. The previous discussion of unbalanced sex ratios may be related to this.

An increase in warfare during the Middle Neolithic period is also reflected by the appearance of a great variety of polished axes–adzes. During the Early Neolithic in central Europe almost all axes–adzes were made of stone. Bored stone axes–adzes and polished flint axes–adzes were rare. Not only are more bored axes–adzes from the Middle Neolithic found, but also a greater variety of raw materials was utilized in making them: flint, stone, antler, and copper. Probably the copper axes were not much more efficient than the ones made of stone. Pure copper is a soft metal, therefore, copper axes were more suitable for cracking skulls than woodworking.

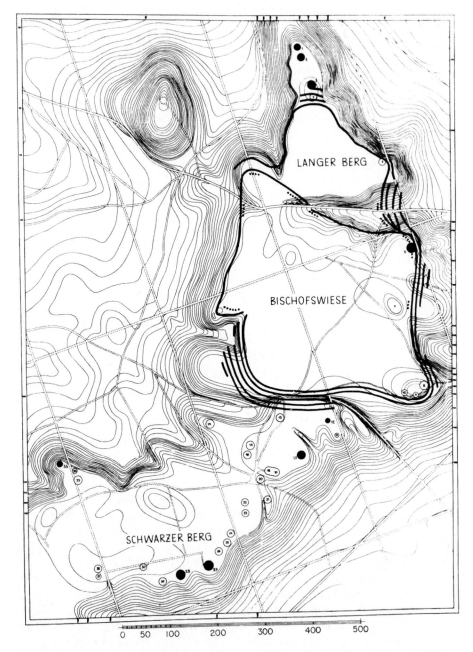

**Figure 6.27.** Funnel Beaker fortified settlement of Dölauer Heide. (From Behrens 1973.)

However, we should not think that axes–adzes were used only for fighting. Aside from their obvious utilitarian function as woodworking tools, certain kinds may have played a role in the social or ideological system of these societies as symbols of rank or as ceremonial artifacts. The fact that axes–adzes made of exotic raw materials were traded extensively supports this suggestion, as does the discovery at certain sites of miniature stone and clay axes, which would have been useless for "practical" purposes. All types of axes–adzes are usually found in male burials; therefore, we may assume that men dominated the social situations in which they were used.

It appears that Funnel Beaker communities were engaged in warfare more intensively than those of the earlier Linear culture. This is suggested by the location of some Funnel Beaker sites on hilltops and by the numerous battle-axes found at some sites. The numerous Funnel Beaker battle-axes also reflect more fighting than during the Early Neolithic. Examples of Funnel Beaker sites are Sarup in Denmark (N. Anderson 1975), Derenburg, Dölauer Heide, and Wallendorf in the German Democratic Republic (Figure 6.27). Fortifications at some of these sites enclosed very large areas: 10 ha at Wallendorf and 25 ha at Dölauer Heide (Behrens 1973). At Derenburg palisaded ditches surrounded the settlements on three sides, the fourth side being naturally protected by a steep slope. The protected area was roughly 190 × 145 m or approximately 2.5 to 3 ha. Inside the settlement the postmolds of one house, 14.3 × 6.5 m, were uncovered (Schlette 1964). However, some archaeologists note that it would be difficult to defend such large fortified areas if the population of a Funnel Beaker village were 100–200 people. Thus, they consider that these "forts" are actually kraals.

As in some other Middle Neolithic cultures, there is evidence suggesting an increase in warfare at Lengyel sites. We find fortified settlements, battle-axes, and projectile points. However, it is possible that the appearance of more projectile points or axes may simply reflect greater settlement stability. Probably hunting equipment would be more frequently found at settlements with longer occupation. An example of a fortified village is the Hluboké Mašůvky site in Czechoslovakia, which is surrounded by a ditch. However, it should be pointed out that at many Lengyel sites no evidence for fortifications has been found.

# Chapter 7

# Late Neolithic

By the beginning of the Late Neolithic most of Europe was occupied by farmers. Only the coniferous and tundra areas of northern Europe remained inhabited by hunters and gatherers. In some areas simple chiefdoms already existed; this type of society persisted and expanded throughout Europe during the Late Neolithic, Bronze Age and Iron Age.

Using archaeological material, it is hard to separate the Late Neolithic from the Middle Neolithic. Perhaps it would make more sense simply to divide the European Neolithic into two major phases: Early and Late (and, therefore, combine Middle and Late Neolithic). The Late Neolithic began at different times in various regions in Europe, for example, in central Europe, around 2600–2500 (3180–3110) B.C. The central European Bronze Age, which succeeded the Late Neolithic, began about 1900–1800 (2180–2140) B.C. However, the Bronze Age in Greece was already under way during the transalpine European Late Neolithic.

As expected, archaeologists have defined the Late Neolithic cultures mainly on the basis of variation in pottery styles. The following are the more important of the archaeological cultures, which fall within the timespan of the Late Neolithic: the southeastern European Vinča-Pločnik, Late Gumelnitsa, Salcutsa, and the Late Tripolye culture of the Ukraine, the central European Corded Ware, Globular Amphora, Bodrogkeresztúr, Baden or Channelled Ware (Figures 7.1 and 7.2), late Funnel Beaker, and Bell Beaker cultures. Some authorities regard some of these cultures as Early Bronze Age, such as the Bell Beaker and Baden cultures, especially in southeastern and western Europe. However, considerable variation among the Late Neolithic cultures in other archaeological manifestations such as burial practices and settlement systems is apparent. The most difficult problem is explaining these observed

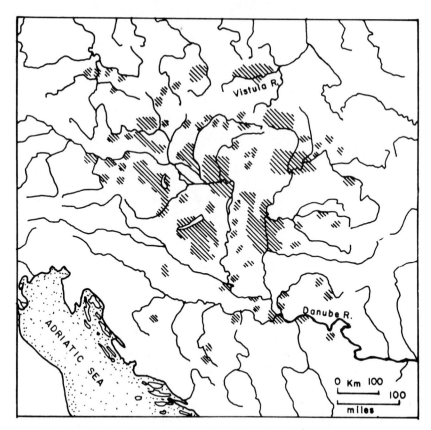

**Figure 7.1.** Distribution of Baden culture sites. (After Sochacki 1970.)

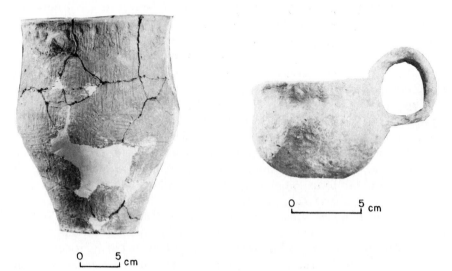

**Figure 7.2.** Baden vessels from Igołomia, Poland. (Courtesy of Z. Liguzińska-Kruk.)

differences in archaeological material during the Late Neolithic. Some archaeologists rely on theories involving the invasion of central, western, and northern Europe by new peoples from eastern Europe to explain these changes.

During the Late Neolithic we also find large ceramic style zones in Europe. The Corded Ware, Globular Amphora, Baden and Bell Beaker cultures may be regarded as such style zones. There is nothing particularly new about style zones in the European Neolithic: The Early Neolithic Linear culture and the Middle Neolithic Funnel Beaker culture also can be regarded as artifact style zones. However, in the Late Neolithic stylistic differences among regions and among individual communities can be seen more frequently. The occupation of specific territories by specific social groups may have become important at this time, and different artifact styles may have been created to identify each group and its territory.

To some archaeologists, the onset of the Late Neolithic coincided with large-scale movements of ethnic groups in Europe. Therefore, when dealing with this period we must discuss the hypothesized migrations of pastoral groups into central, western, and northern Europe. Many scholars, especially Gimbutas (1956, 1965, 1973), have maintained that the Late Neolithic saw not only the influx of pastoralists from the steppe regions of the southern Ukraine but also the appearance of the Indo-European speaking peoples in various parts of Europe. However, to demonstrate a prehistoric migration or even the presence of a pastoral economy is not a simple matter. As we shall see, the migration hypothesis should be treated with caution.

In discussing the problems related to these events during the Late Neolithic, the greatest emphasis will be placed on the Corded Ware, Globular Amphora, and Baden cultures since they are frequently cited as examples for a migrationist interpretation of culture change. The Corded Ware culture is also called Battle-Axe, or Kurgan, culture.

The Corded Ware culture is one of the most widely known of the Late Neolithic. It is defined by particular types of axes, amphorae, and beakers (Figures 7.3 and 7.4). This culture extended from the Rhine River to the Upper Volga River and from Finland to the Alps and Carpathian Mountains. Included under the general name of the Corded Ware culture are many local cultures such as Swiss, Saxon–Thuringian, Single Grave, Swedish Boat–Axe, Finnish, East Baltic, Rzucewo (*Haffküste*), Little Polish, Middle Dnepr, and Fatianovo. The Corded Ware culture occupied mostly the northern part of the deciduous-forest zone.

Since some cultural traits occur in both the Pit–Grave culture of the southern Ukraine and Russian steppes and the Corded Ware culture (e.g., barrows or mounds, cord-ornamented pottery, battle-axes, and red ocher in burials), some archaeologists believe that the Corded Ware peoples were immigrant descendants from the Pit–Grave population to the east. However, there is little evidence to support this. Corded Ware culture finds appear around 2500

Figure 7.3. Corded Ware vessels from Bronocice, Poland. (From J. Kruk and S. Milisauskas excavations; W. Hensel project director.)

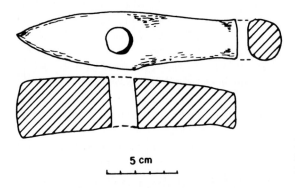

5 cm

Figure 7.4. Corded Ware axe from Koniusza, Poland. (After Kruk 1973b.)

(3110) B.C. in central Europe as shown by the $^{14}$C dates of 2470 ± 55 (3060) B.C. (GrN–1855) from the Anlo site in the Netherlands. Thus, if we accept the migration hypothesis, we must allow that the Pit–Grave culture populations expanded before 2500 (3110) B.C. into central Europe from the steppe region of the southern Ukraine. However, the Corded Ware culture appeared in the forested zone of the southwestern Ukraine only after the end of the Tripolye culture, which was at the end of the Neolithic. Some of the traits associated with the Corded Ware culture are found in other Neolithic cultures in central and eastern Europe; for example, cord-ornamented pottery is found with Funnel Beaker, Globular Amphora, and Comb-and-Pit Ornamented Pottery cultures. Also Funnel Beaker sites often yielded battle-axes.

It is difficult to establish from the available archaeological evidence the routes by which the Pit–Grave populations would have migrated into central Europe before 2500 (3110) B.C. The most likely route would have been from Romania through the Carpathian Mountains into central Europe. There are graves in Romanian Moldavia and southeastern Hungary that are similar to those occurring around the Black Sea. At Baia-Hamangia in Romania, graves containing burials adorned with red ocher have been dated at 2140 ± 160 (2580) B.C. (Berlin 29), and 2110 ± 160 (2560) B.C. (Köln 38) (Quitta and Kohl 1969). Also at Ketegyhaza, Hungary, a burial sprinkled with ocher was found under a mound which is dated 2315 ± 80 (2860) B.C. (Berlin 609) (Quitta and Kohl 1969). These finds may indicate the expansion of steppe cultures from the Ukraine into southeastern and central Europe, although red ocher occurs so frequently in prehistoric ritual contexts that it is very difficult to base any argument of population expansion solely on its presence.

As previously mentioned, we find Bodrogkeresztúr, Funnel Beaker, and other Neolithic cultures in central Europe before 2500(3110) B.C. If we accept Neustupný's (1969) view that the Corded Ware culture had a subsistence strategy based on agriculture, we can probably discount migration to explain its appearance in central Europe. It is possible that different ethnic groups could have exploited the same ecological niche at different periods, but archaeologists cannot usually distinguish ethnic differences on the basis of material remains alone. It would be easier to recognize different ethnic groups if the groups in question had different subsistence strategies. For example, if the Corded Ware culture were based on a pastoral economy, the possibility exists that it represented a new population in central Europe that migrated from the east along the Carpathians. We know that in historic times pastoral groups have moved back and forth through the Carpathians and Balkan ranges.

Another question we should ask is what would have caused the Pit–Grave peoples to migrate into central Europe. We know that in historic times the pressure from one set of pastoralists on another often triggered a chain reaction of migrations that eventually affected Europe. For example, in Asia, group A would press against group B, which, in turn, would press against group C, etc., which eventually would affect the groups living in Europe. It is very difficult to demonstrate that any society in Asia or Europe had such a military advantage over its neighbors during the Late Neolithic that it could have forced them to migrate. Thus even if we postulate a pastoral economy for the Corded Ware culture, it does not mean that it originated in the steppe region.

The Corded Ware, Globular Amphora, and Baden artifact style zones overlapped with one another in some regions during the Late Neolithic. One explanation for this might be that they represent three different peoples with different subsistence strategies occupying the same region. However, as Machnik (1970) has demonstrated, only the Early Phase of the Corded Ware culture overlapped with the Globular Amphora culture. Machnik has also noted that in some areas where a large concentration of the Globular Amphora sites occur, the Corded Ware sites are fewer and vice versa. For example, there is a great concentration of Globular Amphora sites along the Warta, Middle Vistula, and Bug rivers, while the Corded Ware culture finds are rare in those areas (Machnik 1970). In the Upper Dnestr and San rivers, large numbers of the Corded Ware culture finds occur. In some areas, the Late Corded Ware material overlaps in distribution with Bell Beaker and Comb-and-Pit Ornamented Pottery material.

The Bell Beaker culture is found in the Mediterranean, western, and central areas of Europe (Figures 7.5 and 7.6). As with some other Late Neolithic cultures, most of our evidence for the Bell Beaker culture, which continued through the Early Bronze Age, comes from burials. Various hypotheses have been proposed to explain the Bell Beaker distribution, such as that by Childe (1957), who argued that nomadic communities of merchants, warriors, or prospectors for metals were responsible for this manifestation. The historically known example of the Gypsies of Medieval Europe reminds us that it is indeed possible that nonpastoral nomadic groups, practicing some economic or technological specialization, existed in Europe during the Late Neolithic.

**Figure 7.5.** Distribution of Bell Beaker culture sites. (After Kamieńska and Kulczycka-Leciejewiczowa 1970a.)

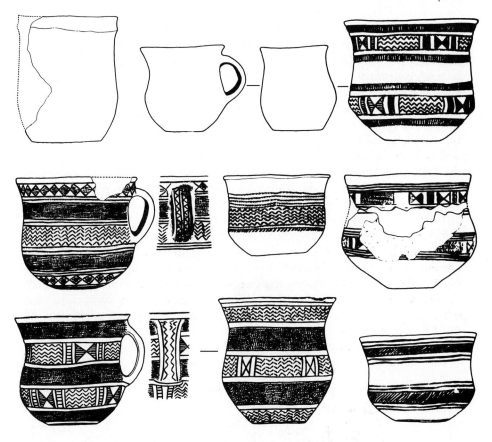

**Figure 7.6.** Bell Beaker ceramics from Germany. (From Behrens 1973.)

However, since archaeologists cannot yet demonstrate ethnic variability from material culture alone, and since only little is known about Bell Beaker subsistence and settlement systems, all our interpretations of such ways of life are just speculation. Lanting and van der Waals (1976) can be consulted for more detailed information about the Bell Beaker culture in various regions of Europe.

The picture is further complicated by the occurrence of the Comb-and-Pit Ornamented Pottery culture in Poland, Finland, Kaliningrad district of RSFSR, Lithuania, Latvia, Estonia, and the northern RSFSR, which overlaps with Corded Ware culture in some areas. Sites of this culture (sometimes called North Eurasian or Proto–Ugro–Finnish culture) are found near lakes, rivers, or on sand dunes, from which pottery, flint, and stone have been recovered. Many archaeologists believe that these people practiced a hunting, fishing, and gathering economy because no bones of domesticated animals are found at the sites. However, sherds of the Comb-and-Pit Ornamented Pottery contain imprints of domesticated grains.

The Globular Amphora culture is another important Late Neolithic manifestation in central Europe and parts of eastern Europe. It is found in the Elbe, Odra (Oder), Vistula, Upper Siret, Upper Prut, and Upper Dnestr basins and it extends up to the Middle Dnepr basin (Figure 7.7). The culture is named after a characteristic type of vessel, the globular amphora. We find both ornamented and nonornamented vessels. The decoration on the former is usually located on the neck and upper part of the vessel body. The motifs can be stamped, cord impressed, or incised. The frequency of vessels ornamented with cord increases through time (Wiślański 1966, 1969, 1970). Since some of the Globular Amphora burials are of the passage grave type, the culture is sometimes considered to be connected with "megalithic cultures," which are cultures that built monuments or structures of large stones.

The traditional assumptions about the Corded Ware and Globular Amphora cultures may be wrong. The different ceramic styles may not represent different ethnic groups at all, but may reflect some other cultural variation. The presence of different cultures in central and eastern Europe during the Late Neolithic is difficult to explain, and one way of making some progress is to try to correlate the artifact styles with ecological niches, human adaptations, and subsistence practices. Much has been written about the pastoral economy of the Corded Ware and Globular Amphora cultures, but such an economy remains only a hypothesis, for no tests have been carried out to substantiate it.

The Neolithic ended at various times across Europe. For example, it oc-

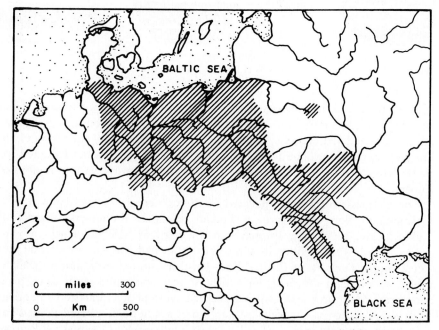

**Figure 7.7.** Distribution of Globular Amphora culture sites. (After Wiślański 1970.)

curred around 1900–1800 (2180–2140) B.C. in central Europe, but it is not so clear in southeastern Europe. Recently C. Renfrew (1969) attempted to modify the accepted cultural sequence in southeastern Europe by moving some cultures such as Baden from the Late Neolithic into the Bronze Age.

## Economic Organization: Subsistence Strategies

As discussed in Chapter 5, it is not easy to interpret the archaeological data about the subsistence strategies of the various Neolithic societies. This is especially true of the Late Neolithic, for we have very little data about its economy. There are some differences in the archaeological data on subsistence strategies among different sites and regions, but the causes of these differences have yet to be explained. To some extent this variability may be associated with ecological zones. For example, the animal remains from Pit–Grave sites in the Soviet Union may reflect adaptation to a steppe environment. Other differences are not so easy to interpret, however.

The data from the Pit–Grave site of Mikhailovska in the U.S.S.R. (Table 7.1) show that cattle and sheep–goat were the two most important animals in the steppe-adapted economy, while the pig played an insignificant role (Tsalkin 1970). The large number of cattle and sheep–goat at Mikhailovska may indicate a pastoral economy. However, it is more likely that this bias simply presents the adaptations of a mixed farming economy to the steppe ecological zone; indeed, cattle and sheep–goat are usually dominant animals on any sites located within the steppes. (Pig requires shade and tends to thrive in a forested habitat.) There are also remains of numerous horses at Mikhailovska. As mentioned earlier, horses are also numerous in the Middle and Late Tripolyean sites; this evidence has prompted some Soviet scholars to argue that the horses were domesticated.

The association between the ecological zone and the type of animals present is also reflected in the Gumelnitsa sites in the steppe zone of the Lower Dnestr and Southern Bug basins in the Soviet Union (Table 7.2). The frequencies of sheep–goat are the same as, or greater than, those of cattle. However, Tsalkin includes the remains of aurochs with those of domesticated cattle. On the other hand, the frequencies of red deer and wild pig, which are forest animals, are relatively low. Again, it should be emphasized that the Gumelnitsa culture spans the Middle and Late Neolithic. Thus, different phases of this culture can be used to illustrate economic and settlement organization for the Middle and/or Late Neolithic.

It has already been noted that some Middle Neolithic domestic plant assemblages showed an increase in the proportion of barley remains. The same is true for some Late Neolithic domestic plant assemblages (Table 7.3). As near as can be established, the cultivation of bread wheat also became more prevalent at this time (Table 7.4).

TABLE 7.1   Frequency of Animals and Estimated Amount of Usable Meat at the Pit-Grave
Culture Site of Mikhailovska in USSR[a]

| | Kilograms of usable meat | Number of animals | Percentage of total number of animals | Total estimated weight in kilograms | Percentage of estimated weight | Kilograms of usable meat from total estimated weight |
|---|---|---|---|---|---|---|
| Cattle (700)[b] | 350 | 1,627 | 41 | 1,138,900 | 70 | 569,450 |
| Sheep–goat (25) | 12.5 | 1,202 | 30.5 | 30,050 | 2 | 15,025 |
| Pig (30) | 15 | 82 | 2 | 2,460 | — | 1,230 |
| Dog (10) | 5 | 112 | 3 | 1,120 | — | 560 |
| Aurochs (900) | 450 | 17 | 0.5 | 15,300 | 1 | 7,650 |
| Wild horse (600) | 300 | 656 | 17 | 393,600 | 24 | 196,800 |
| Red deer (190) | 95 | 33 | 0.1 | 6,270 | — | 3,135 |
| Roe deer (21) | 10.5 | — | — | — | — | — |
| Wild pig (107.5) | 53.75 | 24 | 1 | 2,580 | — | 1,290 |
| Wild ass (350) | 175 | 118 | 3 | 41,300 | 2.5 | 20,650 |
| Other wild animals | — | 75 (including 27 saiga) | 2 | — | — | — |
| Total | | 3,946 | | 1,631,580 | | |

[a] Data are from Tsalkin 1970.
[b] Numbers in parentheses indicate estimated adult weight in kilograms.

Although it is often assumed that the transition to the Late Neolithic is marked by the appearance of pastoral peoples in some regions of Europe, this hypothesis has not yet been tested. Many archaeologists consider nomadic pastoralism and sedentary agriculture to be two mutually exclusive subsistence strategies. We know that pastoralism involves livestock rearing and spatial mobility to some extent, but we do not know enough, yet, about the possible range of variation in subsistence practices that may have existed during the Late Neolithic. Certainly, modern, ethnographically known pastoralists display a considerable range of variation in this respect: Herders may inhabit villages part of the year, the cultivate crops, or hire themselves out to work for members of their own or another ethnic group. They may produce the fodder needed during the winter themselves, or purchase or extract it from the sedentary farmers with whom they come into contact (Dyson-Hudson 1972). Thus, the traditional picture of groups of pure pastoralists displacing groups of pure farmers represents a naive oversimplification.

Even if the practice of pastoralism during the Late Neolithic could be demonstrated, it would be far from any detailed analysis of that subsistence strategy. For example, one would need to know the variety and number of animals herded. This depends not only on the size of the group and availability of pastures, but also on various social and economic needs such as land, fodder, and food, as well as rituals, ceremonies, and prestige arising from interrelationship with local and nonlocal groups. It would be helpful to know the degree of

TABLE 7.2  Frequency of Animals and Estimated Amount of Usable Meat at Gumelnitsa Sites in USSR[a]

| | Kilograms of usable meat | Number of animals | Percentage of total number of animals | Total estimated weight in kilograms | Percentage of estimated weight | Kilograms of usable meat from total estimated weight |
|---|---|---|---|---|---|---|
| **Bolgrad** | | | | | | |
| Cattle and aurochs (800)[bc] | 400 | 47 | 32 | 37,600 | 71 | 18,800 |
| Sheep–goat (25) | 12.5 | 46 | 31 | 1,150 | 2 | 575 |
| Pig (30) | 15 | 20 | 14 | 600 | 1 | 300 |
| Dog (10) | 5 | 5 | 3 | 50 | — | 25 |
| Horse (600) | 300 | 19 | 13 | 11,400 | 22 | 5,700 |
| Red deer (190) | 95 | — | — | — | — | — |
| Roe deer (21) | 10.5 | 2 | 1 | 380 | 1 | 190 |
| Wild pig (107.5) | 53.75 | 1 | 1 | 107.5 | — | 53.75 |
| Wild ass (350) | 175 | 4 | 3 | 1,400 | 3 | 700 |
| Other wild animals | — | 3 | 2 | — | — | — |
| Total | | 147 | | 52,687.5 | | |
| **Ozernoe** | | | | | | |
| Cattle and aurochs (800)[bc] | 400 | 30 | 20 | 24,000 | 67 | 12,000 |
| Sheep–goat (25) | 12.5 | 50 | 33 | 1,250 | 3.5 | 625 |
| Pig (30) | 15 | 26 | 17 | 780 | 2 | 390 |
| Dog (10) | 5 | 13 | 9 | 130 | — | 65 |
| Horse (600) | 300 | 9 | 6 | 5,400 | 15 | 2,700 |
| Red deer (190) | 95 | 7 | 5 | 1,330 | 4 | 665 |
| Roe deer (21) | 10.5 | 3 | 2 | 63 | — | 31.5 |
| Wild pig (107.5) | 53.75 | — | — | — | — | — |
| Wild ass (350) | 175 | 8 | 5 | 2,800 | 8 | 1,400 |
| Other wild animals | — | 6 | 4 | — | — | — |
| Total | | 152 | | 35,753 | | |
| **Vulcaneshti** | | | | | | |
| Cattle and aurochs (800)[bc] | 400 | 17 | 35 | 13,600 | 81 | 6,800 |
| Sheep–goat (25) | 12.5 | 17 | 35 | 425 | 3 | 212.5 |
| Pig (30) | 15 | 7 | 14 | 210 | 1 | 105 |
| Dog (10) | 5 | 1 | 2 | 10 | — | 5 |
| Horse (600) | 300 | 3 | 6 | 1,800 | 11 | 900 |
| Red deer (190) | 95 | 1 | 2 | 190 | 1 | 95 |
| Roe deer (21) | 10.5 | — | — | — | — | — |
| Wild pig (107.5) | 53.75 | 2 | 4 | 215 | 1 | 107.5 |
| Wild ass (350) | 175 | 1 | 2 | 350 | 2 | 175 |
| Other wild animals | — | — | — | — | — | — |
| Total | | 149 | | 16,800 | | |

[a] Data are from Tsalkin 1970.

[b] Numbers in parentheses indicate estimated adult weight in kilograms.

[c] This average is derived from the weight of cattle (700 kg) and aurochs (900 kg).

191

TABLE 7.3 **Domesticated Plant Remains Found at Gumelnitsa Sites in the Maritsa Valley, Bulgaria**[a]

| | Einkorn wheat | Emmer wheat | Club wheat | Hulled six-row barley | Naked six-row barley | Lentils | Vetch | Peas |
|---|---|---|---|---|---|---|---|---|
| Azmak | 1 (5)[b] | 1 (8) | — | 7 (1) | (1) | 3 (1) | 9 (3) | (5) |
| Karanovo VI | 1 (1) | 1 | — | — | — | — | 1 | — |
| Dončova mogila | (2) | (1) | (1) | (1) | 1 (1) | (1) | (1) | — |
| Kapitan Dimitrievo | (2) | 3 (2) | — | (1) | — | 1 (1) | 1 | — |
| Unacité | 1 | — | — | (1) | (1) | — | — | — |
| Yassatepe II | — | — | — | — | — | — | 1 | — |
| Imamava Dubka | — | — | — | — | — | — | — | — |
| Totals | 3 (10) | 5 (11) | (1) | 8 (4) | 1 (3) | 4 (3) | 13 (3) | (5) |

[a] After J. Renfrew, *Palaeoethnobotany: The prehistoric food plants of the Near East and Europe.* London: Methuen & Co. Ltd., 1973.

[b] Numbers indicate the number of samples in which the species formed the chief part; those in parentheses represent the other samples in which the species was found in smaller quantities.

TABLE 7.4 **Plant Remains from Late Neolithic Sites in the Netherlands**[a]

| | Vlaardingen (sample from one pit) | Zandverven (three samples from two pits) |
|---|---|---|
| Emmer wheat (*Triticum dicoccum*) | 21[b] | 95 |
| Bread wheat (*Triticum aestivum* s.l.) | 199 | |
| Wheat (*Triticum* sp.) | 65 | |
| Six-row barley (*Hordeum vulgare*) | 4 | |
| Naked six-row barley (*Hordeum vulgare* var. *nudum*) | | 177 |
| Oat (*Avena* sp.) | 1 | |
| Orache (*Atriplex hastasta/patula*) | | 73 |
| Pale persicaria (*Polygonum lapathifolium*) | | 1 |
| Dewbery (*Rubus ceasius*) | | 2 |
| Holly-leaved Najas (*Najas marina*) | | 1 |
| Hazelnut (*Corylus avellana*) | | Fragment of nut |
| Unidentified | 1 | 3½ |

[a] After van Zeist 1968.

[b] Number of seeds or grains.

dependence on livestock and the alternative possibilities of resource exploitation, such as agriculture, hunting, fishing, or even warfare. At present little can be said about these matters.

Similarly, the hypothesis that Corded Ware people practiced a pastoral economy remains an undemonstrated speculation because there is very little archaeological information about that culture's subsistence practices.

Neustupný (1969) has argued to the contrary that the Corded Ware culture in central Europe depended on farming for subsistence. He cites the following points to support his hypothesis:

1. Plow marks were found under some Corded Ware mounds such as that at Aldrupsgaarde in Denmark (Kjaerum 1954).
2. Sickle blades occur in some Corded Ware burials.
3. The remains of domesticated animals and cereal imprints in pottery are found in some Corded Ware culture sites.
4. The Pit–Grave people in the USSR practiced agriculture in addition to raising stock.

Neustupný's arguments are based on the misconception that any evidence for the presence of agriculture immediately eliminates the possibility of pastoralism. If one were to look only for two such mutually exclusive subsistence strategies during the Late Neolithic, one probably would find neither.

According to Strahm and Malmer, the Corded Ware culture probably practiced agriculture in Switzerland and Scandinavia. Strahm (1971) maintains that the Corded Ware subsistence strategy in Switzerland was based on agriculture, since archaeological material of that culture occurs in villages located on the edge of lakes. Malmer (1962, 1969) argues that the Swedish Corded Ware culture was agricultural. He found 58 settlements and 244 burial mounds of the Corded Ware culture in Sweden; however, it is unclear whether the settlements were permanent villages, occupied year round. It is very interesting that in Scania the heaviest concentration of the Corded Ware culture material occurs in the same areas where most of the Scanian Funnel Beaker burials and settlements are found (Figure 7.8). Therefore, the fact that the Late Neolithic Corded Ware groups occupied terrain and utilized soil similar to that of the agricultural Funnel Beaker culture suggests that they were farmers, too. It also suggests that the Swedish Corded Ware communities were descendants of the local Funnel Beaker communities and not immigrants.

There are very little quantitative data on animal or plant remains from Corded Ware sites; most of our evidence about this culture comes from burials. At the so-called settlements, pits are usually found, but seldom any other features. From such evidence, many prehistorians reason that the Corded Ware people were nomadic pastoralists after all.

Much of our evidence on the Corded Ware economy comes from the studies of cereal imprints found on pottery, and also from bone artifacts found in burials. For example, Matthias and Schultze-Motel (1971) analysed 125 pots for plant remains from the German Democratic Republic and found 46 imprints of barley, 40 imprints of emmer wheat, 18 imprints of einkorn wheat, 24 imprints of wheat, 2 imprints of oats, and 43 unidentifiable imprints.

The evidence for the role played by various animals in the economy of the Corded Ware culture is poor. We have no choice but to use the percentages of bones found at settlements or burials. At the Bottendorf settlement in Ger-

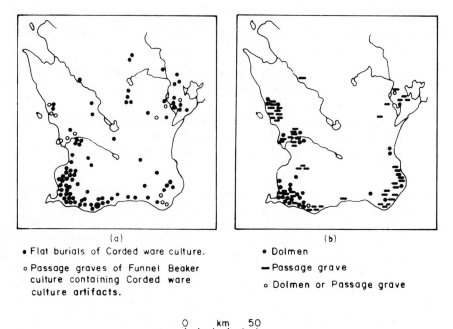

(a)

- • Flat burials of Corded ware culture.
- ○ Passage graves of Funnel Beaker culture containing Corded ware culture artifacts.

(b)

- • Dolmen
- — Passage grave
- ○ Dolmen or Passage grave

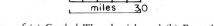

**Figure 7.8.** Distribution of (a) Corded Ware burials and (b) Funnel Beaker burials in Scania, Sweden. (After Malmer 1962.)

many the following quantities of bones were found belonging to various domesticated and wild animals (Clason 1969:183):

| | |
|---|---|
| Cattle | 126 |
| Sheep–goat | 16 |
| Pig | 23 |
| Dog | 4 |
| Wild pig | 1 |
| Red deer | 1 |
| Not identifiable | 150 |

It seems that cattle were dominant in the economy. As in other Neolithic cultures in the forested areas of Europe, the pig probably was the next most important animal.

The Rzucewo or *Haffküste* (bay coast) local group of the Corded Ware culture occurs along the Baltic coast of northeastern Poland, Kaliningrad (in pre-World War II, called Königsberg) district, and Lithuania. These people appear to have subsisted to a great extent on maritime fishing and sea-mammal hunting (Figure 7.9). At Rzucewo itself, the remains of over 100 seals (*Phoca groenlandica neolithica*) were recovered, as well as those of other wild and domesticated animals (Niezabitowski 1933). This implies that perhaps archaeologists should study adaptation of the Corded Ware people in the differ-

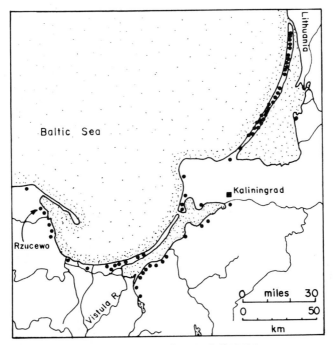

**Figure 7.9.** Distribution of Rzucewo sites. (After Tetzlaff 1970.)

ent ecological zones; it is unrealistic to expect a similar adaptation in the coastal areas of the Baltic Sea and the loess uplands of southeastern Poland and the northwestern Ukraine.

As is the case with most Late Neolithic cultures in central Europe, there is little information available concerning the subsistence of the Globular Amphora culture. Some graves have yielded sickle blades, and the remains of wheat, barley, and pulses (leguminous plants) that have been found in baked clay. Globular Amphora burials often contain the remains of cattle and pig, the latter usually represented by their lower jaw bones. Occasionally, deliberate interments of whole cattle are found. Sheep–goat appear to have been of less importance.

The remains of animals from two Baden sites in Hungary indicate that cattle and sheep–goat predominated (Table 7.5). There are also many remains of wild animals at those sites. Given the present state of our knowledge of the Baden culture, it cannot be said whether similar results would be found in other regions of central Europe.

Finally, the animal remains from one Bell Beaker site, Csepel-Háros in Hungary, should be mentioned. As can be seen from Table 7.6, the horse dominated the faunal remains at this site. Since this the only Bell Beaker faunal assemblage known in central Europe, one should be cautious in drawing conclusions from it concerning the adaptations of the entire Bell Beaker

TABLE 7.5    Frequency of Animals and Estimated Amount of Usable Meat at Baden Culture Sites in Hungary[a]

| | Kilograms of usable meat | Number of animals | Percentage of total number of animals | Total estimated weight in kilograms | Percentage of estimated weight | Kilograms of usable meat from total estimated weight |
|---|---|---|---|---|---|---|
| Fertörákos-Golgota | | | | | | |
| Cattle (700)[b] | 350 | 20 | 53 | 14,000 | 84 | 7,000 |
| Sheep–goat (25) | 12.5 | 9 | 24 | 225 | 1 | 112.5 |
| Pig (30) | 15 | 3 | 8 | 90 | 0.5 | 45 |
| Dog (10) | 5 | 1 | 3 | 10 | — | 5 |
| Aurochs (900) | 450 | 2 | 5 | 1,800 | 11 | 900 |
| Wild horse (600) | 300 | — | — | — | — | — |
| Red deer (190) | 95 | 3 | 8 | 570 | 3 | 285 |
| Roe deer (21) | 10.5 | — | — | — | — | — |
| Wild pig (107.5) | 53.75 | — | — | — | — | — |
| Other wild animals | — | — | — | — | — | — |
| Total | | 38 | | 16,695 | | |
| Tiszaszöllös-Csákányszeg | | | | | | |
| Cattle (700)[b] | 350 | 20 | 22 | 1,400 | 22 | 700 |
| Sheep–goat (25) | 12.5 | 43 | 48 | 1,075 | 17 | 537.5 |
| Pig (30) | 15 | 14 | 15.5 | 420 | 7 | 210 |
| Dog (10) | 5 | 5 | 5.5 | 50 | 1 | 25 |
| Aurochs (900) | 450 | 3 | 3 | 2,700 | 45.5 | 1,350 |
| Wild horse (600) | 300 | — | — | — | — | — |
| Red deer (190) | 95 | 2 | 2 | 380 | 6 | 190 |
| Roe deer (21) | 10.5 | — | — | — | — | — |
| Wild pig (107.5) | 53.75 | 3 | 3 | 322.5 | 5 | 161.25 |
| Other wild animals | — | — | — | — | — | — |
| Total | | 90 | | 6,347.5 | | |

[a] Data are from Bökönyi 1974.
[b] Numbers in parentheses indicate estimated adult weight in kilograms.

culture. However, cattle and sheep–goat dominate the faunal assemblages at contemporary Early Bronze Age sites of other cultures in Hungary. This may indicate significantly different adaptations between the Bell Beaker people and their neighbors.

## Settlement Organization

The settlement data on the Late Neolithic cultures consist of the results of excavations at many sites, but it is impossible to reconstruct the settlement system of any given region. Since some Middle Neolithic cultures such as Tripolye, Gumelnitsa, and Funnel Beaker continue into the Late Neolithic period, it can be assumed that there was continuity in their settlement systems.

Very little evidence exists to indicate that the Corded Ware and Globular

TABLE 7.6  Frequency of Animals and Estimated Amount of Usable Meat at Csepel-Háros Site in Hungary[a]

| | Kilograms of usable meat | Number of animals | Percentage of total number of animals | Total estimated weight in kilograms | Percentage of estimated weight | Kilograms of usable meat from total estimated weight |
|---|---|---|---|---|---|---|
| Cattle (700)[b] | 350 | 31 | 20 | 21,700 | 31.5 | 10,850 |
| Sheep–goat (25) | 12.5 | 16 | 10 | 400 | 0.5 | 200 |
| Pig (30) | 15 | 13 | 8 | 390 | 0.5 | 195 |
| Dog (10) | 5 | 7 | 4.5 | 70 | — | 35 |
| Horse (600) | 300 | 57 | 36.5 | 34,200 | 50 | 17,100 |
| Aurochs (900) | 450 | 10 | 6 | 9,000 | 13 | 4,500 |
| Red deer (190) | 95 | 12 | 8 | 2,280 | 3 | 1,140 |
| Roe deer (21) | 10.5 | — | — | — | — | — |
| Wild pig (107.5) | 53.75 | 8 | 5 | 860 | 1 | 430 |
| Other wild animals | — | 2 | 1 | — | — | — |
| Total | | 156 | | 68,900 | | |

[a] After Bökönyi 1974.
[b] Numbers in parentheses indicate estimated adult weight in kilograms.

Amphora cultures had permanent villages during the Late Neolithic, but other cultures, such as the late phase of the Gumelnitsa in southeastern Europe, have yielded good data for their presence. In the Mediterranean zone of Europe we find impressive fortified settlements built of stone, such as those at Los Millares and Vila Nova de Sao Pedro in Iberia. Since many of these settlements were not excavated systematically, it is difficult to estimate their size. Probably Los Millares enclosed an area of 5 ha (12.5 acres) (Childe 1957). The stone walls at Los Millares were over 2.5 m thick and semicircular bastions were constructed at regular intervals.

In eastern and southeastern Europe we find excellent data on Late Neolithic structures, including the Late Tripolye structures, such as those at Kolimiishchina in the Soviet Union (Figure 6.18). A good example of a Late Neolithic village is Căscioarele in Romania, approximately 60 km (37 miles) south of Bucharest. The Gumelnitsa culture settlement is located on a small island, less than 100 m in diameter, in Lake Catalui (Dumitrescu 1965). During phase B of the Gumelnitsa culture the settlement consisted of 16 scattered houses (Figure 7.10). There is no discernible plan and the orientations of the houses vary. The village was destroyed by fire. The houses were constructed of wooden-post frameworks and the walls were plastered with clay. Most of the houses had one square hearth, usually over 1 m². Inside the houses artifacts such as clay loom weights, clay spindle whorls, querns, flint, and bone tools were found. The smallest house was 4.5 × 4.5 m and the largest 16 × 8.8 m (Figure 7.11). Using Naroll's method, the population of the village consisted of 135 individuals.

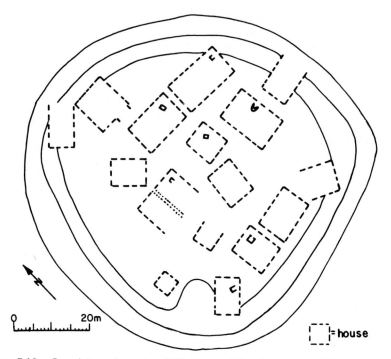

**Figure 7.10.** Gumelnitsa culture site of Căscioarele. (After Dumitrescu 1965.)

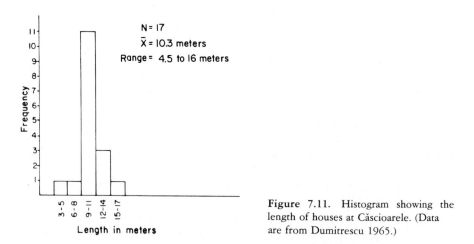

**Figure 7.11.** Histogram showing the length of houses at Căscioarele. (Data are from Dumitrescu 1965.)

Remains of rectangular wooden structures have been found for the Rzucewo "group" of the Corded Ware culture along the east Baltic coast (Figure 7.12), but for other groups we have only very poor evidence for any houses.

In addition to burial mounds and cemeteries, the Corded Ware culture is

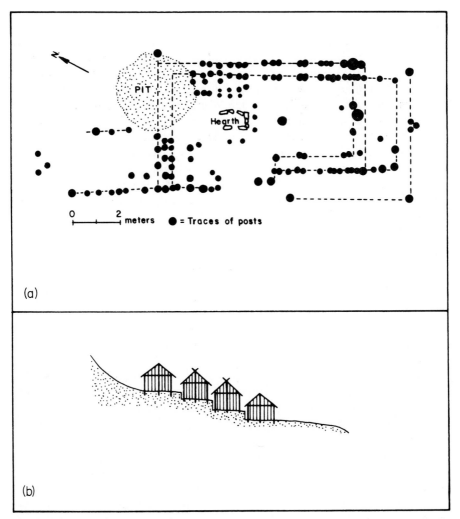

**Figure 7.12.** (a) Rzucewo house at Suchacz, Poland. (After Gimbutas 1965.) (b) Reconstruction of Rzucewo houses. (After Tetzlaff 1970.)

represented by settlements that yield pits but no identifiable structures. In central Europe, intensive archaeological investigations were carried out on the Corded Ware culture, but no permanent villages have been found. We have evidence for the presence of villages consisting of wooden structures during the Early and Middle Neolithic in central Europe, therefore, the absence of such structures in most groups of the Corded Ware culture is very interesting. This absence was interpreted by many European archaeologists to mean that the Corded Ware people were pastoral nomads who did not need to construct permanent houses. However, large cemeteries of the Corded Ware culture, such as Vikletice in Czechoslovakia, may indicate the presence of permanent settlements.

Data on the settlement system of the Globular Amphora culture are sketchy. Permanent villages are believed to have consisted of a few small, square, and trapezoidal houses, rare examples of which were found. The archaeological materials found on sand dunes and sandy hills probably represent seasonal camps. Like the Corded Ware culture, the Globular Amphora culture is frequently considered to have been one of nomadic herders.

We do have good data on excavated Late Neolithic settlements in eastern and southeastern Europe. The data from some areas of central Europe are ambiguous. The arguments pertaining to the settlement system of the Corded Ware or Globular Amphora cultures will continue. Hopefully, more systematic regional studies of settlement systems will give us a clearer picture of these cultures.

## Social and Ritual Organization

We can assume that tribes and simple chiefdoms predominated in Europe during the Late Neolithic. The discussion about chiefdoms in the Middle Neolithic is also applicable to the Late Neolithic. However, archaeological data from central Europe on the Late Neolithic do not present stronger evidence for the presence of chiefdoms.

The impressive megalithic monuments of the Middle Neolithic continued to be constructed in western and north-central Europe. These monuments indicate that a variety of social and ritual practices were carried out.

The following observations on the social and ritual organization of the Late Neolithic cultures will be limited to central and eastern Europe. Traditionally, the social organization of the Corded Ware and Globular Amphora cultures is considered to have been patrilineal. These cultures are believed to have been associated with a pastoral economy, and ethnographic data indicate that most pastoral societies are patrilineal. However, as indicated earlier, the data about the Corded Ware and Globular Amphora economy and settlement system are so poor that any speculations about their social organization are not very informative.

Most of our data about the social and ritual organization come from mounds and cemeteries. The mortuary practices of the Corded Ware culture are reflected by burial mounds and flat graves (that is, without mounds). Originally, some of the flat graves probably had mounds. Many mounds were destroyed by subsequent farming activity, and their fill scattered over the fields. The Corded Ware people were buried in pits dug in the ground (Figure 7.13). Most frequently a grave contains a single skeleton in a contracted position. Pottery, stone axes, and flint artifacts are the most common burial goods.

**Figure 7.13.** Corded Ware burial from Bronocice, Poland. (From J. Kruk and S. Milisauskas excavations; W. Hensel, project director.)

Judging from the Vikletice cemetery in Czechoslovakia there is no significant association of sex and age groups with any type of burial goods (Buchvaldek and Koutecký 1970). Only a small number of skeletons could be identified for sex at Vikletice, thus any analysis is limited by the weakness of the sample.

Most information on the Globular Amphora social and ritual organization also comes from burials. Cist graves constructed of stones are very characteristic of this culture. In Germany, existing megalithic structures were frequently used for burials. Rectangular or trapezoidal passage graves are rare. The number of skeletons in the graves range from 1 to 17; however, usually only 1, 2, or 3 skeletons are found. Only rarely are completely articulated skeletons found. Probably after a person died his body was placed in a tree or a scaffold. After the flesh had been removed, or had decayed, the bones were placed in the grave. The most common types of grave goods are pots, flint axes, and the remains of animals, especially pigs.

The occurrence of animals in burials may indicate that they played some role in rituals, ceremonials, and feasts. We should remember that pigs were probably important not only for their nutritional value, but as symbols of wealth and social prestige, as is the case with modern Melanesian societies. Also, in

Melanesia pigs were usually eaten on ceremonial occasions such as funeral feasts.

It is possible that the occurrence of cattle and sheep–goat burials during the Late Neolithic indicates the presence of nomadic herders. Animal burials are not only associated with the Globular Amphora culture during the Late Neolithic, but with Baden and some other cultures.

There is little information about the social organization of the Globular Amphora culture. If it practiced a pastoral economy, perhaps it was patrilineal. Burial data reflect age and probably sex differences. Out of 122 analysed skeletons, roughly 10% belong to children (Wiślański 1969). Why were only certain children buried? Various explanations can be offered. If we have a simple chiefdom, only children having higher status at birth may be buried. The small number of individuals in the Globular Amphora culture burial structures may point to cultural selection as to who was buried in them. Wiślański (1969) has summarized burial data from 124 Globular Amphora graves in Germany and Poland. The frequency of individuals per grave is as follows:

| Number of persons per grave | Number of graves |
|:---:|:---:|
| 1 | 57 |
| 2 | 33 |
| 3 | 16 |
| 4 | 6 |
| 5 | 4 |
| 6 or more | 7 |
| | Total 123 |

In eight double burials the sex of the individuals was determined. One of the burials had two females and seven burials contained one female and one male each. In double burials the females are usually younger than the males. There is a possibility that some women were put to death at the same time the men died.

The burial data of the Late Tripolye cemetery of Vikhvatintsi, which belongs to the Late Neolithic period or perhaps even the Early Bronze Age, show no association of a particular age or sex group with burial goods, either in regard to kind or quantity of goods. There are only a few positive correlations. One that is statistically significant is that of undecorated pots with adult males. This is contrary to what we expect, for usually we assume that pottery was made by women and, therefore, it is associated with women's activities. However, the making of pots and the disposing of them are two different activities.

The Vikhvatintsi cemetery has a very large number of children's burials, roughly 50% of the entire cemetery (Passek 1961). If we divide the children into three age groups, we find the fewest deaths between the ages of 11 and 15. Here is the distribution of children's age at death:

| Age groupings | Number | Percentage |
|:---:|:---:|:---:|
| 1–5 | 13 | 48% |
| 6–10 | 11 | 41% |
| 11–15 | 3 | 9% |

This distribution still indicates underrepresentation of infants in terms of normal mortality, if the sample is considered representative. Out of 53 skeletons, 9 were classified 50 years or over. Thus, at birth a person had a 17% chance to reach the age of 50. This is essentially unchanged from the Middle Neolithic.

In summary, there is little information about the social and ritual organization of the Late Neolithic cultures in central Europe. However, further analysis of burial data may give us more information about these matters.

## Warfare

The presence of fortified settlements in the Middle Neolithic has indicated the appearance of intergroup warfare in the different regions of Europe. Likewise, the Late Neolithic fortified settlements such as Los Millares in Spain suggest warfare among different societies. Supposedly there was an increase of warfare in central Europe during the Late Neolithic. As previously mentioned, some archaeologists speculate that large parts of central and western Europe were conquered by people from eastern Europe, thus one would expect to find more evidence for conflicts in the late Neolithic than in the Middle Neolithic. The poor quality of settlement data for the Late Neolithic societies in central Europe basically limits the discussion of warfare to the greater number of battle-axes, projectile points (arrowheads), and other artifacts assumed to be weapons. However, there are a few fortified sites, such as Homolka in Bohemia, belonging to the Řivnáč culture (Ehrich and Pleslová-Štiková 1968) and Bronocice (late Funnel Beaker phase) in Poland (Milisauskas and Kruk in press).

As discussed, the hypothesized pastoral economy of some Late Neolithic cultures, such as the Corded Ware in central Europe, and the numerous battle-axes are interpreted as evidence for the increase of warfare or raiding. Sometimes the Corded Ware culture is even called the Battle-Axe culture, which supposedly reflects its militaristic character.

If there were some type of pastoralism practiced, cattle raiding could have occurred on an extensive scale. Herd animals are very mobile resources and it would be relatively easy to steal them and move them away. Few men are needed merely to look after a herd, but more would be necessary to protect it from an attack. Cattle-raiding activities may have caused a warlike value system to develop, in which the military exploits of successful warriers were rewarded with higher social status. However, the actual archaeological data for this type of warfare are nonexistent at the present time.

There is even less evidence for warfare in the Globular Amphora culture than in the Corded Ware culture, notwithstanding Childe's (1957:195) remarkable statement concerning the Globular Amphora people, "swine-breeders who roamed about in small groups far and wide, presumably mainly as hunters and swineherds, but doubtless engaging in casual robbery and trade." Only a few battle-axes have been found in the Globular Amphora sites. This contrasts with the numerous battle-axes found in the Corded Ware culture sites, which supposedly indicated intensive warfare or raiding. The most common type of axe found in Globular Amphora burials is a flat axe made of flint. The Globular Amphora people exploited the Krzemionki banded flint mines in Poland to make axes, as did the Funnel Beaker people.

# Chapter 8

# Bronze Age

The appearance of the first bronze artifacts in Europe marks the beginning of the Bronze Age. As implied by the name, it is the use of this new material to produce tools and ornaments that characterizes this period. The European Bronze Age is a very peculiar period of prehistoric times, for it is associated with spectacular flowering of complex chiefdoms using bronze tools. As in the case with domesticated plants and animals, the earliest known bronze artifacts are found in Greece, where they appeared around 2700–2600 (3340–3180) B.C. The central European Bronze Age began around 1900 (2180) B.C., while that of Scandinavia dates to 1500 (1710) B.C. Since the world's earliest bronze artifacts were made about 3500 (4180) B.C. in the Near East, it may be that the technique of bronze metallurgy diffused from there to Europe. *but see M 206-207*

Like most archaeological periods, the Bronze Age is divided into Early, Middle, and Late phases. Incidentally, a different terminology is used to describe various chronological phases in Greece at the beginning of the Bronze Age (Table 8.1). The Early Bronze Age in central and western Europe dates between 1900–1800 (2180–2140) B.C. and 1450 (1680) B.C. The Middle Bronze Age, or *Tumulus* phase dates between 1450 (1680) and 1250 (1480) B.C. The term *tumulus*, which is Latin for mound, was applied because the diagnostic feature of this period was once thought to be burials under mounds. However, as we have seen, this practice is not limited to the Middle Bronze Age. The Late Bronze Age dates between 1250 (1480) and 750 (840) B.C.; due to the predominance of cremation burials in urns the term *urnfield* was applied to this period. The cremation burials are actually found in the Early Bronze Age, but their incidence gradually increases throughout the Bronze Age.

**TABLE 8.1  Chronological Chart for the Bronze Age**[a]

| Approximate dates | Period | | |
|---|---|---|---|
| | Central and western Europe | | Greece |
| 750 B.C. | | | |
| | | V | Geometric |
| | Late | IV | Protogeometric |
| | Bronze Age | III | Sub-Mycenaean |
| | | II | Late Helladic III C |
| | | I | Late Helladic III B |
| 1250 B.C. | | | |
| | | late | |
| | Middle | middle | Late Helladic III A |
| | Bronze Age | early | |
| 1450 B.C. | | | |
| | | late | Late Helladic II |
| | Early | | Late Helladic I |
| | | middle | |
| | Bronze Age | early | Middle Helladic |
| ca. 1900–1800 B.C. | | | |

[a] After Gimbutas 1965, with modifications.

The archaeological cultures of the European Bronze Age and their chronological relationship to one another may now be defined using such bronze artifacts as axes, daggers, swords, and fibulae (safety pins). For example, in Britain riveted daggers, socked spearheads, and flanged axes are characteristic for the Early Bronze Age; dirks, rapiers, hollow midribbed spearheads, and palstaves for the Middle Bronze Age; and leaf-shaped swords, socketed axes, and pegged, leaf-shaped spearheads for the Late Bronze Age (Burgess 1970). However, traits such as pottery styles and burial practices are still widely used by archaeologists to characterize the various periods.

European metallurgy may precede the Bronze Age by half a millennium or more. Copper metallurgy probably was already practiced in southeast Europe during the Middle Neolithic. Metallurgy advanced when it was discovered that the addition of a small amount of tin to copper produces a harder alloy—bronze, which ideally consists of 90% copper and 10% tin. However, the earliest European "bronze" consisted usually of 95% copper mixed with arsenic, antimony, silver, nickel, or tin. Some archaeologists (Hartmann and Sangmeister 1972) suggest that the first "bronze" (actually copper) alloys were derived from naturally occurring ore deposits, which were located in the area from the eastern Carpathians to the Harz Mountains in Germany, and which contained significant traces of arsenic, bismuth, silver, antimony, and nickel. Artifacts made of this copper resemble light-colored bronzes. This is due to the high proportion, 5% to 10%, of silver or nickel in them: They are neither arsenic nor tin bronzes.

The onset of true bronze metallurgy was accompanied by innovations that made possible the production of more elaborate metal artifacts. The copper artifacts of the Neolithic were cast in an open mold that produced artifacts on which one surface was always flat. Then the two-piece, or bivalve, mold came into use, which made more complex shapes possible. During the Bronze Age the *cire perdue* (lost wax) casting technique was developed: "A wax model is made in the shape of the desired bronze casting, and coated with clay which forms the mould. The wax melts as the molten bronze is poured in to replace it in the mould. The mould itself is broken and removed when the bronze cools [C. Renfrew 1973b:173]."

We may assume that the domestication of bees occurred early in the Bronze Age, not only to supply a sweetener for food and drink, but, primarily, to supply wax for this bronze casting process. We should also consider the use of honey for making the alcoholic beverage, mead.

The range of the metal artifacts produced during the Neolithic is small: axes, pins, beads, and spiral bracelets. But, with the onset of the Bronze Age, an increase both in the quantity and variety of metal goods occurred. In addition to bronze versions of the artifacts just listed, there were neck rings, belt plates, earrings, bracelets, pendants, flanged axes, halberds, riveted daggers, and swords of various types. Near the end of this period, bronze spearheads and sickles appeared. During the Middle Bronze Age there was further proliferation in the types of swords, daggers, and axes made; also, for the first time, wrist guards, razors, arrowheads, and embossed plates were made. The development of bronze technology continued in the Late Bronze Age with the addition of body armor, shields, and large storage vessels (*situlae*) to the assemblages.

The advantages of copper and bronze artifacts over those of stone are readily apparent: The metals can be cast into shapes not possible for stone, wood, or bone. Likewise, there is no inherent size limit on the artifacts produced: The artisan's skill and wants determine this. On the other hand, there are some limitations to the use of these metals. Copper, for one, is softer than stone for utilitarian artifacts. Also these materials are rarer than stone, etc., and the skills to work them are more difficult to acquire. It is significant that most of the articles produced were ornaments or weapons, that is, items made for the elites. Since bronze artifacts had high value, low-status individuals had to content themselves with tools and jewelry of the same stone, wood, and bone that had satisfied their ancestors.

The appearance of bronze artifacts in Europe did not have as great an ecological impact as did the diffusion of agricultural techniques in the Early

Neolithic. Though a new material was being used to make some tools and new processes were developed to work this material, the subsistence base of the various cultures remained essentially the same. Just as there are no sharp breaks between the various subdivisions of the Neolithic, likewise, the beginning of the Bronze Age does not involve a drastic break with the past. The cultural processes that were intensified during the Bronze Age had already made their appearance in the Neolithic: metallurgy, mining, interregional trade, the development of chiefdoms, and warfare. However, during the Bronze Age, we see an increase in the complexity of the technoeconomic organization of society as a result of increases in trade, craft specialization, mining, and war, which in turn favored the development of a more complex sociopolitical organization.

The European Bronze Age witnessed the flowering of complex chiefdoms, some of which, such as Mycenae in the Aegean region, may have attained the status of state societies. To some archaeologists, the Bronze Age represents a "Heroic Age" in Europe, because warriors and warfare played such prominent roles. Homer's epics, *The Iliad* and *The Odyssey,* are generally held to depict Greek society in the Late Bronze Age and Early Iron Age, but may also reflect life in many other societies in Europe: Achilles, Ajax, Pactrolus, Agammemnon, and Odysseus may be pan-European hero figures. The Greek legends present us with a picture of a society dominated by the values of the warrior elite. The heroes pass their time engaging in plundering raids for cattle and spoils, hunting, feasting, and boasting of their prowess. They are sensitive about matters tainting their personal honor and courage, but successful chicanery is admired. The chivalry of the medieval heroes like Lancelot or Beowulf is not a virtue in this earlier society; it developed when the ideology of so-called barbarian Europe fused with Christianity during the Dark Ages.

As might be expected, the earliest European metallurgy occurred in regions possessing the necessary raw materials, particularly copper. In areas of Europe lacking mineral resources, such as Denmark or the Netherlands, the metals or the finished goods had to be imported throughout the Bronze Age. Most bronze artifacts are found close to the sources of ore and along the major trade routes. In other parts of Europe, the term *Early Bronze Age* is almost a courtesy title, since most of the tools were still made of wood, bone, or stone. For example, in southern Poland, the Early Bronze Age cemetery at Iwanowice yielded only a few copper artifacts (A. and J. Machnik 1973). On the other hand, the Vel'ký Grob cemetery in Slovakia, which is closer to the Carpathian Mountains copper sources, contained numerous bronze artifacts: Forty out of the 65 graves (62.5%) had such goods (Chropovský 1960).

The production of bronze artifacts was never on a scale large enough to provide readily available goods to all the people. Only high-ranking individuals could obtain bronze tools, ornaments, and weapons; most people had to continue to use stone, bone, and wooden implements. This also reflected in the continuation of flint mining as, for example, at Polany Kolonie in Poland during the Early Bronze Age (Schild *et al.* 1977). However, now the form or shape of flint celts, sickles, and knives or daggers showed imitation of similar tools made of copper and bronze.

In general, copper and bronze were not used much for utilitarian or subsistence tools at this time, except in regions rich in the ores. The further away a community was from these sources and production centers, the rarer, and, presumably, more highly valued, the bronze artifacts were. The flowering of bronze technology may be related to the increased use of bronze artifacts in the social and idealogical subsystems of these cultures as symbols of rank and status, and as objects in rituals. The more practical need for bronze weapons should not be overlooked: The advantages of metal daggers, axes, and swords in battle provided a strong incentive for communities to acquire them, or the means to make their own.

It is evident that the control and exploitation of the sources of ore needed for metal production became very important during the Bronze Age. These deposits are not evenly distributed throughout Europe, as is the case with stone, bone, or wood. Copper is found in Spain, England, Ireland, Czechoslovakia, and in the Ural Mountains of Russia (Figure 8.1). Tin occurs in Czechoslovakia, Italy, Spain, Brittany, and England. Thus, the two basic ingredients of bronze are found in close proximity only in a few localities. Gold, another mineral which became more important to this period, is found in Ireland, Czechoslovakia, Romania, Yugoslavia, and in the Urals. Because these and other materials have a distribution far beyond their source areas, it is

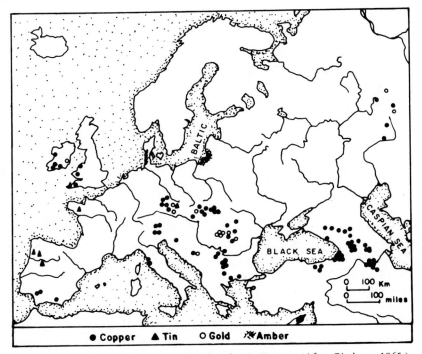

**Figure 8.1.** Sources of copper, tin, gold, and amber in Europe. (After Gimbutas 1965.)

evident that some sort of trade system linked various areas of Europe during the Bronze Age. There has been much extravagant speculation on this subject. To assess the presence and significance of interregional trade, it is necessary first to have a detailed picture of the sources of the items involved. The German scholars Hartmann (1970) and Junghans *et al.* (1960, 1968) have analyzed over 20,000 copper and about 3300 gold objects from various parts of Europe to determine their sources. Trade networks can be inferred from these studies. However, most of the material analyzed comes from western and central Europe. Some regions, such as Poland, Romania, and the German Democratic Republic, are distinctly underrepresented. Metal artifacts exhibiting the same combinations of elements have been classified into *material groups* (*Materiallgruppen*). Such a group "comprises all those objects made of a material whose content of accompanying elements is the same with regard to quality and quantity [Hartmann and Sangmeister 1972:626]." It is assumed that artifacts belonging to the same material group were made from metals from the same geographic region or even the same natural deposit. For example, the distribution of the gold Group A3 indicates the area in which this material has been most frequently used (Figure 8.2). The heaviest concentration of gold Group A3 probably occurs around its source area.

The copper used in southeastern and central Europe during the Neolithic is almost free of impurities. Its source may be in the region of Niš in Yugoslavia or in the Carpathians. In the Bronze Age, more copper sources were exploited in Europe. Each material group of copper has its own area of distribution. For example, Group A has a much more restricted distribution than Group 11B copper.

There are fewer gold than copper deposits in Europe. As with copper, gold material groups based on the impurity content have been established. Group B gold (Early Bronze Age) is tin-free; Group A3 gold contains, on the average, 25% silver (Figure 8.2). This latter group has its sources, probably, in Transylvania (Romania). Gold with a similar percentage of silver has been mined in the Brad area of Romania, so it is possible that A3 gold was obtained from alluvial deposits in this region in prehistoric times. Group N gold (with a relatively high percentage of tin and copper) was widely distributed in Europe during the Late Bronze Age (Figure 8.3).

The multiplication of types and quantities of metal artifacts in the Bronze Age entailed the exploitation of increasing amounts of copper and tin. Initially, surface ores were sufficient, but by 1700 to 1500 B.C. mining on quite an impressive scale was being carried out in the eastern Alpine region. The techniques of mining in the Salzburg region of Austria have been studied in some detail (Pittioni 1951, Clark 1952). For example, at Mitterberg, shafts were driven as far as 100 m into the hillside (Clark 1952). Here a 2-m-wide vein of copper pyrites, which sloped into the mountain at a 20–30° angle, was worked. According to Zschoske and Preuschen (1932), as cited by Pittioni and Clark, the technique of working an ore face was as follows: The exploitation of a mineral source began with the working of a vein where it cropped out on the

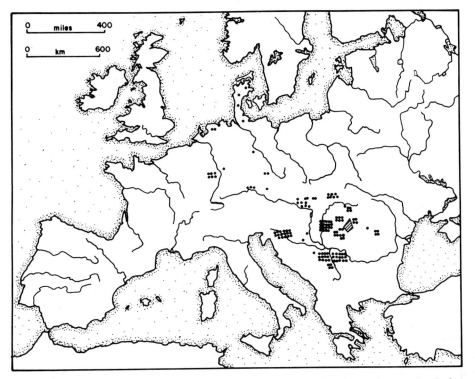

**Figure 8.2.** Distribution of Gold A₃. Natural gold deposits in Transylvania shown as hatched area. (After Hartmann and Sangmeister 1972.)

surface (Figure 8.4). The rock would be loosened by heating it with fire, then rapidly cooling it with water. The rapid alternate expansion and contraction of the rock would split it off the face, and help break it into manageable pieces. Square-socketed bronze picks, up to 28 cm in length, as well as stone and bone tools, were also used to extract the ore. As soon as the face of the pit was driven a little way into the hillside by this means, the fire-and-water technique could be applied to the roof of the tunnel as well. Wooden stagings would then be set up to carry out the rock wastes and also to serve as platforms from which the roof of the gallery could be excavated. Thus, two passages, above and below the staging, were driven into the mountainside to permit free access to workable deposits, and also to allow for the free circulation of air in the mine. Ground water was collected in buckets for disposal by damming up the lower passage to create a sump. As the mine was excavated further into the hill, "blind" passages were dug to prevent the overburden of waste rock from becoming too heavy for the staging. The mining might continue until the gallery was 160 m long and 30 m high at its opening. When the workings reached these proportions they were abandoned.

It is estimated that each of the 32 mines that exploited the Mitterberg lode took about 7 years to exhaust (Pittioni 1951). Pittioni suggests that a

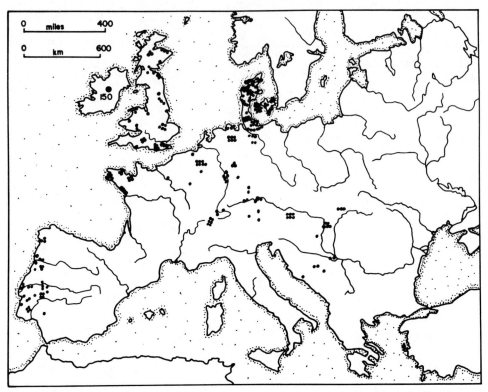

**Figure 8.3.** Distribution of Group N gold. About 150 objects were found in Ireland. (After Hartmann and Sangmeister 1972.)

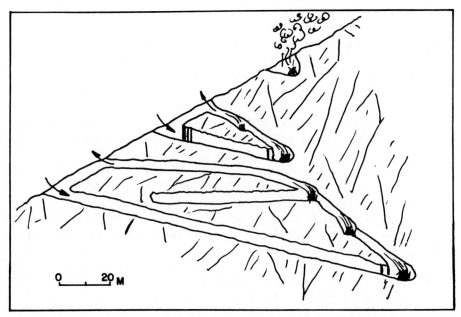

**Figure 8.4.** Supposed method of operating prehistoric copper mines by means of fire-setting. (After Clark 1952.)

maximum of 180 workers would have been needed to operate such an enterprise, though the work force would vary depending on the stage of the mine's operation. He also estimates that only about 40 workers could actually be hacking away at the face of the pit; 60 others would have been needed to cut the timber to make the props and stagings, and to fuel the mining fires; also, there were 20 ore workers, 30 smelters, 10 porters, 10 cowmen (to supply food to the miners), and 10 security and managerial personnel. The estimate for the total quantity of crude copper produced in the Mühlbach-Bischofshofen area, in which the Mitterberg is located, is 20,000 metric tons, of which perhaps two-thirds came from the Mitterberg lode itself (Clark 1952). Pittioni (1951) estimated that the quantity of timber required per day for such an operation was 20 $m^3$.

Many archaeologists have assumed that the production of metal tools was a very complicated process in the Bronze Age, requiring the presence of full-time specialist craftsmen in a community or region. Childe (1930:4) speculated that "the smith's art was so complicated that a prolonged apprenticeship was required. His labour was so exacting that it could not be performed just in odd moments of leisure; it was essentially a full-time job." Childe (1958:168) believed that the agricultural or pastoral communities of the Bronze Age could not have maintained such specialists and that whole ethnic groups specialized as smiths and tinkers, wandering about Europe peddling their skills and wares to the local people, "carrying with them their simple tools, raw materials, and half-finished products." Especially fortunate members of such a group might attach themselves to the court of a petty chief and serve his needs in the way of ornaments and weapons. The Bell Beaker culture is supposed by many archaeologists to represent this tribe of wandering smiths. However, none of these ingenious speculations have been subjected to archaeological testing.

Rowlands (1971) has recently drawn an analogy with ethnographically known metal-using tribes to discuss the possible organization of metallurgical production in Europe during the Bronze Age. He suggests that previous beliefs concerning the organization of Bronze Age metallurgy should be modified. Great variability is observed ethnographically in the organization of metallurgy, but the following generalizations could be made:

1. Full-time specialists are found only where they are supported by full-time administrative specialists, that is, elites.
2. Ordinary smiths are rarely employed as full-time metallurgical craftsmen.
3. The demand for new tools, weapons, etc., is often seasonal.
4. Smiths may specialize among themselves, on the basis of superior technical skills in a particular craft; for example, some may specialize in swords.
5. In some cultures the smith contributes only his skill in producing the tool; his customer supplies the raw material, and, perhaps, labor, or fuel.
6. The status of smiths is variable in different cultures: In some they are feared and despised, while in others they are respected or even revered.

If Rowlands' observations are applicable to Bronze Age tool production, we should not expect to find full-time metallurgical craftsmen, except in the Aegean area.

## Economic Organization: Subsistence Strategies

The cultivation of certain plants became more important during the Bronze Age in some geographical areas of Europe. For example, C. Renfrew (1973b) has stressed the importance of economic changes during the Late Neolithic and Early Bronze Age in the Aegean. He noted that improved cereal varieties such as bread wheat were extensively cultivated. The domestication of the vine and the olive by the Early Bronze Age transformed farming in the Aegean. The evidence from the Sitagroi site in Greece indicates that the domestication of the vine occurred around 2500 B.C. Mediterranean polyculture was established at this time, consisting of wheat, olives, and grapes. Vines and olives grew in areas that were not suitable for wheat and barley cultivation. Thus, new areas of land were opened for agriculture. Also, the harvesting of these new domesticated plants did not overlap seasonally with harvesting of wheat and barley. Furthermore, olives and grapes became high-value exports from the Aegean region. Renfrew associated these economic changes with the appearance of more complex sociopolitical organization during the Bronze Age in the Aegean area. J. Renfrew (1973) also noted that in Thessaly, Greece, there was a transition from a wheat dominated cereal agriculture to one mainly based on cultivation of hulled six-row barley. Furthermore, horsebeans were established as a crop during the Early Bronze Age, as shown by the evidence from Lerna in the Argolid (J. Renfrew 1973). Judging from the use of horsebeans by the Romans, they could have been ground into flour for making bread, porridge, and puree during the Bronze Age (J. Renfrew 1973).

In regions outside the Mediterranean zone, the farmers of the Bronze Age continued to exploit essentially the same plants and animals that their Neolithic predecessors had exploited. Barley and wheat were still the most frequently cultivated types of domestic cereals. However, we find greater variability in the plants, such as spelt wheat and dense-eared, six-row barley. It is difficult to discuss regional differences. For example, the results from Early Bronze Age excavations at Slovakian sites show how sharply contrasting interpretations of subsistence practices can be made from the results of the work of different field seasons (Table 8.2). It is unclear if the remains of goosefoot in Slovakia represent cultivation of that plant. The Slovakian sites indicate that cultivation of rye was not very important.

Plant remains from Hungarian Bronze Age sites show that wheat and barley were the chief cultivated crops (Table 8.3). The same observation can be made for Bulgaria (Table 8.4). However, in Bulgaria the yield per hectare of land may have been lower than during the Neolithic. In Bulgaria, Dennel and Webley (1975:103) observed that "the amount of arable land had decreased

**TABLE 8.2  Plant Remains from Early Bronze Age Sites in Slovakia[a]**

| | Barca | | Male Kosihy | | |
|---|---|---|---|---|---|
| | I (1933) | II (1952–1954) | I (1956) | II (1956) | III (1956) |
| **Wheat (*Triticum*)** | | | | | |
| Eikorn (*monococcum*) | 1.0[b] | | 3.2 | | |
| Emmer (*dicoccum*) | 70.0 | 0.5 | 92.0 | 100.0 | 100.00 |
| Bread (*aestivum*) | 9.0 | 0.6 | 4.S | | |
| Club (*compactum*) | | | | | |
| Unidentified | | 0.9 | | | |
| **Barley (*Hordeum*)** | | | | | |
| Six-row (*vulgare*) | | 28.2 | | | |
| Two-row (*vulgare distichon*) | | | | | |
| ? (*vulgare tetratichon*) | 20.0 | | | | |
| **Mixed** | | | | | |
| Rye (*secale cereale*) | | | | | |
| Field pea (*pisum sativum*) | | 47.0 | | | |
| Lentil (*lens esculenta*) | | 22.7 | | | |
| Goosefoot (*chenopodium album a hybridum*) | | | | | |

| | Nitriansky Hrádok | | | | |
|---|---|---|---|---|---|
| | I (1935) | II (1958) | III (1959) | IV (1959) | V (1959) |
| **Wheat (*Triticum*)** | | | | | |
| Eikorn (*monococcum*) | | | 31.5 | 35.9 | 4.9 |
| Emmer (*dicoccum*) | 25.0 | | 61.9 | 59.2 | 85.7 |
| Bread (*aestivum*) | | 93.2 | 4.6 | 3.9 | |
| Club (*compactum*) | | | | | |
| Unidentified | | | | | |
| **Barley (*Hordeum*)** | | | | | |
| Six-row (*vulgare*) | | 1.3 | 0.2 | | 9.4 |
| Two-row (*vulgare distichon*) | | | | | |
| ? (*vulgare tetratichon*) | 75.0 | | | | |
| **Mixed** | | | | | |
| Rye (*secale cereale*) | | 5.1 | | | |
| Field pea (*pisum sativum*) | | | | | |
| Lentil (*lens esculenta*) | | 0.4 | | | |
| Goosefoot (*chenopodium album a hybridum*) | | | | | |

*(continued)*

[a] After Hajnalová 1973.
[b] Percentages of total plant remains at each site (if not 100%, then some weeds were present).

**TABLE 8.2** *(Continued)*

| | Nitriansky Hrádok | | | |
| --- | --- | --- | --- | --- |
| | VI (1961) | VII (1958) | VIII (1958) | IX (1958) |
| Wheat (*Triticum*) | | | | |
|   Eikorn (*monococcum*) | | 1.4 | | |
|   Emmer (*dicoccum*) | 0.4 | 83.3 | | |
|   Bread (*aestivum*) | | | 1.2 | |
|   Club (*compactum*) | | | | |
|   Unidentified | | | | |
| Barley (*Hordeum*) | | | | |
|   Six-row (*vulgare*) | | | 9.8 | |
|   Two-row (*vulgare distichon*) | | 1.4 | 89.0 | |
|   ? (*vulgare tetratichon*) | | | | |
| Mixed | | | | |
|   Rye (*secale cereale*) | | | | |
|   Field pea (*pisum sativum*) | 99.6 | | | |
|   Lentil (*lens esculenta*) | | | | |
|   Goosefoot (*chenopodium album a hybridum*) | | | | 100.0 |

| | Veselé | | Spišský Štvrtok | |
| --- | --- | --- | --- | --- |
| | 1935 | 1954 | 1969 | Starý Tekov |
| Wheat (*Triticum*) | | | | |
|   Eikorn (*monococcum*) | | | | |
|   Emmer (*dicoccum*) | | | 55.9 | 97.2 |
|   Bread (*aestivum*) | | | 26.4 | |
|   Club (*compactum*) | | | | 0.07 |
|   Unidentified | | | | 2.1 |
| Barley (*Hordeum*) | | | | |
|   Six-row (*vulgare*) | | 100.0 | | |
|   Two-row (*vulgare distichon*) | | | | |
|   ? (*vulgare tetratichon*) | 100.0 | | 3.0 | |
| Mixed | | | | |
|   Rye (*secale cereale*) | | | 14.7 | |
|   Field pea (*pisum sativum*) | | | | |
|   Lentil (*lens esculenta*) | | | | |
|   Goosefoot (*chenopodium album a hybridum*) | | | | |

TABLE 8.3 Plant Remains from Bronze Age Sites in Hungary[a]

| | Nagyárpás | Dunapentele-Kosziderpadlás Excavation unit a | Dunapentele-Kosziderpadlás Excavation unit I | Dunapentele-Kosziderpadlás Excavation unit A/20 | Toszeg | Sütto |
|---|---|---|---|---|---|---|
| Emmer wheat (*Triticum dicoccum* Schrk) | 82[b] | 5 | 2 | 2 | 240 | |
| Einkorn wheat (*Triticum monococcum* L.) | 239 | | 80 | | 1 | 141 |
| Bread wheat (*Triticum aestivum* L. rsp.) | | | | | | 15 |
| Hulled six-row barley (*Hordeum vulgare* L.) | | 134 | | 97 | | |
| Hulled two-row barley (*Hordeum distichon* L.) | | | | | 4 | |
| Barley (*Hordeum* sp.) | | | 2 | 2 | | 1 |
| Rye brome (*Bromus secalinus* L.) | 8 | 1 | | 2 | | |
| Barren brome (*Barren brome*) | 1 | | | | | |
| Goosefoot (*Chenopodium album* L.) | 2 | | 5 | | | |
| Goosefoot (*Chenopodium murale* L.) | 1 | | | | | |
| Bitter vetch (*Vicia ervilia* L. Willd.) | | | | 212 | | |
| Black bindweed (*Polygonum convolvulus*) | 1 | | | | | |
| Corn cockle (*Agrostema githago* L.) | 21 | 2 | | | | |
| Thistle (*Cirsium* sp.) | | 1 | 1 | | | |
| Shepherd's purse (*Capsella bursa pastoris* L. Medik) | | | 1 | | | |
| Poppy (*Papaver* sp.) | | | | | | |
| Grasses (*Graminae* sp. div.) | 2 | 3 | | 2 | | |
| Weeds | | | | | 6 | |
| Cruciferae | | | | | | |
| Wild carrot (*Daucus* sp.) | | 1 | 1 | | | |

[a] After Tempir 1964.
[b] Number of grains.

TABLE 8.4  Plant Remains from Early Bronze Age Deposits at Ezero, Bulgaria[a]

| | Einkorn wheat | Emmer wheat | Bread wheat | Barley | (Cereals) | Legumes | Fruit | Others | Total number of seeds in sample |
|---|---|---|---|---|---|---|---|---|---|
| | | | | | Percentage of total sample | | | | |
| **F Deposits** | | | | | | | | | |
| Level XII | [27.0][b] | [36.2] | — | [5.6] | [(68.8)] | [13.3] | — | [17.9] | [39] |
| Level XI | 3.9 | 45.8 | 4.9 | 29.6 | (84.2) | 12.4 | — | 3.4 | 205 |
| **B Deposits** | | | | | | | | | |
| Level X | — | — | — | 100.0 | (100.0) | — | — | — | 2000 |
| Level IX | 0.5 | 98.7 | 0.2 | 0.4 | (99.8) | 0.2 | — | — | 755 |
| | 20.8 | 31.1 | 3.5 | 22.8 | (78.2) | 19.4 | 0.6 | 1.8 | 151 |
| | 5.3 | 9.3 | 0.8 | 2.8 | (18.2) | 77.5 | — | 4.3 | 251 |
| | 13.0 | 31.5 | 2.5 | 15.0 | (62.0) | 13.0 | — | 18.0 | 200 |

[a] After R. W. Dennell, The interpretation of plant remains: Bulgaria. In *Papers in economic prehistory*, edited by E. S. Higgs. New York: Cambridge University Press, 1972.
[b] Sample of less than 100 shown in square brackets.

and the number of sites increased, thus forcing settlement of the more marginal areas with poor drainage and less workable soils." Remains of bread wheat occurred in small quantities. Small quantities of wild plants also were found. Some of these plants, such as pale persicaria and goosefoot, may have been more extensively exploited by man. In Britain, we have an increase in the importance of barley, whereas some cereals such as millets never seem to have been cultivated (J. Renfrew 1973). The data from the Netherlands and Germany indicate that barley and wheat predominated during the Late Bronze Age (Knörzer 1972, van Zeist 1968) (Tables 8.5 and 8.6). While paleobotanical data from sites in Hungary and the Netherlands (Table 8.6) indicate that wild plants were not very important in the subsistence strategy, data from the Rhineland area of Germany show the exploitation of numerous wild varieties (Knörzer 1972) (Table 8.5).

Among faunal resources cattle continued to play the most important role in the economy (Table 8.7). Sheep–goats or pigs ranked second. The hunting of wild animals such as aurochs, red deer, roe deer, and wild pigs was still practiced quite extensively in the temperate areas of Europe. However, Bökönyi (1974) maintains that the number of wild fauna decreased during the Bronze Age because of the increased human population. He also notes that a cooler and more humid climate may have contributed to this decrease. The remains of horses usually belonged to domesticated animals during the Bronze Age. As previously mentioned, the domestication of the horse was very important for economy and to warfare.

## *Trade*

Bronze Age trade has always received an extensive treatment from archaeologists. An increase in the variety of goods and materials traded in different parts of Europe is evident. Different regions began to specialize in producing certain raw materials and finished products for exchange. It is clear from the distribution of nonlocal goods in various parts of Europe that copper, bronze, gold, amber, faience beads, and sea shells were exchanged, but the mechanisms and reasons for this trade remain obscure. Traditionally, archaeologists emphasized the role of the Minoan–Mycenaean civilization in the establishment of the complex trade networks tying central, western, and northern Europe with the Mediterranean world. According to Childe (1958:163), "The commercial system thus disclosed had been called into being to supply the Aegean market; it was the accumulated resources of the Minoan–Mycenaean civilization that guaranteed to the distributors a livelihood, indeed, an adequate recompense, for the hazards and hardships of their travels." It is clear that the Aegean states had direct trade contracts with the societies located on the periphery of their zones of political control. It may be that the Minoan and Mycenaean states maintained full-time specialist traders to handle this foreign-exchange system.

**TABLE 8.5**  Plant Remains from Langweiler 3 and 6 Sites (Late Bronze Age), Germany[a]

|  | Number |
|---|---|
| Dense-eared six-row barley (*Hordeum hexastichon*) | |
| Grain | 1402 |
| Spikelet | 27 |
| Barley–wheat (*Hordeum/Triticum*) | |
| broken grain | 646 |
| Spelt or emmer wheat (*Triticum spelta/dicoccum*) | |
| grain | 225 |
| Spelt wheat (*Triticum spelta*) | |
| spikelet | 13 |
| Emmer wheat (*Triticum* cf. *dicoccum*) | |
| spikelet | 27 |
| Spelt or emmer wheat (*Triticum spelta/dicoccum*) | |
| glume | 33 |
| Oat (*Avena* sp.) | |
| grain | 129 |
| Cultivated oat (*Avena sativa*) | |
| spikelet | 13 |
| Wild oat (*Avena fatua*) | |
| spikelet | 43 |
| Rye brome (*Bromus secalinus*) | 6 |
| Bristle grass (*Setaria* cf. *italica*) | 4 |
| Pink weed, Persicaria (*Polygonum persicaria*) | 96 |
| Goosefoot (*Chenopodium album*) | 45 |
| Horsebean (*Vicia* cf. *hirsuta*) | 14 |
| Clover (*Trifolium* sp.; Klee) | 11 |
| Black bindweed (*Polygonum convolvulus*) | 8 |
| Sorrel (*Rumex tenuifolius*) | 7 |
| Pale persicaria (*Polygonum lapathifolium*) | 6 |
| Knotgrass (*Polygonum aviculare*) | 4 |
| Grasses (*Graminae*) | 2 |
| Water pepper (*Polygonum* cf. *cydropiper*) | 1 |
| Annual Knawel (*Scleranthus annuus*) | 1 |
| Corn spurrey (*Spergula arvensis*) | 1 |

[a] After Knörzer 1972.

**TABLE 8.6**  Plant Remains from Elp Site (Late Bronze Age), Netherlands[a]

|  | Number |
|---|---|
| Emmer wheat (*Triticum dicoccum*) | 3650 |
| Naked six-row barley (*Hordeum vulgare* var. nudum) | 1350 |
| Hulled six-row barley (*Hordeum vulgare* L.) | 174 |
| Six-row barley (*Hordeum vulgare*) | 92 |
| Wild oat (*Avena fatua*) | 8 |
| Millet (*Panicum miliaceum*) | 2 |
| Pink weed (*Polygonum persicaria*) | 2 |
| Black bindweed (*Polygonum convolvulus*) | 1 |
| Hazelnut (*Corylus avellana*) | 2 |

[a] After van Zeist 1968.

**TABLE 8.7** Frequency of Animals and Estimated Amount of Usable Meat at Early Bronze Age Sites in Hungary[a]

| | Kilograms of usable meat | Number of animals | Percentage of total number of animals | Total estimated weight in kilograms | Percentage of estimated weight | Kilograms of usable meat from total estimated weight |
|---|---|---|---|---|---|---|
| **Békés-Városerdö** | | | | | | |
| Cattle (700)[b] | 350 | 190 | 25 | 133,000 | 61 | 66,500 |
| Sheep–goat (25) | 12.5 | 107 | 14 | 2,675 | 1 | 1,337.5 |
| Pig (30) | 15 | 177 | 23 | 5,310 | 2 | 2,655 |
| Dog (10) | 5 | 31 | 4 | 310 | — | 155 |
| Horse (600) | 300 | 36 | 5 | 21,600 | 10 | 10,800 |
| Aurochs (900) | 450 | 37 | 5 | 33,300 | 15 | 16,650 |
| Red deer (190) | 95 | 69 | 9 | 252 | 6 | 6,555 |
| Roe deer (21) | 10.5 | 12 | 2 | 7,202.5 | — | 126 |
| Wild pig (107.5) | 53.75 | 67 | 9 | — | 3 | 3,601.25 |
| Bison (575) | 287.5 | — | — | — | — | — |
| Other wild animals | — | 34 | 4 | — | — | — |
| Total | | 760 | | 216,759.5 | | |
| **Dunapentele-Kosziderpadlás** | | | | | | |
| Cattle (700)[b] | 350 | 232 | 37 | 162,400 | 67 | 81,200 |
| Sheep–goat (25) | 12.5 | 150 | 24 | 3,750 | 2 | 1,875 |
| Pig (30) | 15 | 77 | 12 | 2,310 | 1 | 1,155 |
| Dog (10) | 5 | 29 | 5 | 290 | — | 145 |
| Horse (600) | 300 | 95 | 15 | 57,000 | 24 | 28,500 |
| Aurochs (900) | 450 | 11 | 2 | 9,900 | 4 | 4,950 |
| Red deer (190) | 95 | 25 | 4 | 4,750 | 2 | 2,375 |
| Roe deer (21) | 10.5 | 4 | 1 | 84 | — | 42 |
| Wild pig (107.5) | 53.75 | 6 | 1 | 645 | — | 322.5 |
| Bison (575) | 287.5 | — | — | — | --- | — |
| Other wild animals | — | 4 | — | — | — | — |
| Total | | 633 | | 241,129 | | |
| **Polgár-Basatanya** | | | | | | |
| Cattle (700)[b] | 350 | 45 | 42 | 31,500 | 73 | 15,750 |
| Sheep–goat (25) | 12.5 | 17 | 16 | 425 | 1 | 212.5 |
| Pig (30) | 15 | 27 | 25 | 810 | 2 | 405 |
| Dog (10) | 5 | 1 | 1 | 10 | — | 5 |
| Horse (600) | 300 | 9 | 8 | 5,400 | 12 | 2,700 |
| Aurochs (900) | 450 | 5 | 5 | 4,500 | 10 | 2,250 |
| Red deer (190) | 95 | 3 | 3 | 570 | 1 | 285 |
| Roe deer (21) | 10.5 | 1 | 1 | 21 | — | 10.5 |
| Wild pig (107.5) | 53.75 | — | — | — | — | — |
| Bison (575) | 287.5 | — | — | — | — | — |
| Other wild animals | — | — | — | — | — | — |
| Total | | 108 | | 43,236 | | |

(*continued*)

[a] Data are from Bökönyi 1959, 1974.
[b] Numbers in parentheses represent estimated adult weight in kilograms.

TABLE 8.7 (Continued)

| | Kilograms of usable meat | Number of animals | Percentage of total number of animals | Total estimated weight in kilograms | Percentage of estimated weight | Kilograms of usable meat from total estimated weight |
|---|---|---|---|---|---|---|
| Tapiószele-Tüzköves | | | | | | |
| Cattle (700)[b] | 350 | 101 | 31 | 70,700 | 67 | 35,350 |
| Sheep–goat (25) | 12.5 | 85 | 26 | 2,125 | 2 | 1,062.5 |
| Pig (30) | 15 | 45 | 14 | 1,350 | 1 | 675 |
| Dog (10) | 5 | 3 | 1 | 10 | — | 5 |
| Horse (600) | 300 | 26 | 8 | 15,600 | 15 | 7,800 |
| Aurochs (900) | 450 | 9 | 3 | 8,100 | 8 | 4,050 |
| Red deer (190) | 95 | 32 | 10 | 6,080 | 6 | 3,040 |
| Roe deer (21) | 10.5 | 6 | 2 | 126 | — | 63 |
| Wild pig (107.5) | 53.75 | 13 | 4 | 1,397.5 | 1 | 698.75 |
| Bison (575) | 287.5 | — | — | — | — | — |
| Other wild animals | — | 3 | 1 | — | — | — |
| Total | | 323 | | 105,488.5 | | |
| Toszeg-Laposhalom | | | | | | |
| Cattle (700)[b] | 350 | 82 | 31 | 57,400 | 59 | 28,700 |
| Sheep–goat (25) | 12.5 | 38 | 14 | 950 | 1 | 475 |
| Pig (30) | 15 | 29 | 11 | 870 | 1 | 435 |
| Dog (10) | 5 | 16 | 6 | 160 | — | 800 |
| Horse (600) | 300 | 37 | 14 | 22,200 | 23 | 11,100 |
| Aurochs (900) | 450 | 7 | 3 | 6,300 | 6 | 3,150 |
| Red deer (190) | 95 | 30 | 11 | 5,700 | 6 | 2,850 |
| Roe deer (21) | 10.5 | 14 | 5 | 294 | — | 147 |
| Wild pig (107.5) | 53.75 | 5 | 2 | 537.5 | — | 268.75 |
| Bison (575) | 287.5 | 5 | 2 | 2,875 | 3 | 1,437.5 |
| Other wild animals | — | 2 | 1 | — | — | — |
| Total | | 265 | | 97,286.5 | | |
| Congrád-Petőfi Tsz Homokgrödre | | | | | | |
| Cattle (700)[b] | 350 | 38 | 44 | 26,600 | 89 | 13,300 |
| Sheep–goat (25) | 12.5 | 22 | 25.5 | 550 | 2 | 275 |
| Pig (30) | 15 | 18 | 21 | 540 | 2 | 270 |
| Dog (10) | 5 | 3 | 3.5 | 30 | — | 15 |
| Horse (600) | 300 | — | — | — | — | — |
| Aurochs (900) | 450 | 2 | 2 | 1,800 | 6 | 900 |
| Red deer (190) | 95 | 1 | 1 | 190 | 1 | 95 |
| Roe deer (21) | 10.5 | — | — | — | — | — |
| Wild pig (107.5) | 53.75 | 2 | 2 | 115 | — | 57.5 |
| Bison (575) | 287.5 | — | — | — | — | — |
| Other wild animals | — | — | — | — | — | — |
| Total | | 86 | | 29,825 | | |
| Tiszaluc-Dankadomb | | | | | | |
| Cattle (700)[b] | 350 | 238 | 29 | 166,600 | 68.5 | 83,300 |
| Sheep–goat (25) | 12.5 | 183 | 22.5 | 4,575 | 2 | 2,287.5 |
| Pig (30) | 15 | 165 | 20 | 4,950 | 2 | 2,475 |
| Dog (10) | 5 | 20 | 2.5 | 200 | — | 100 |
| Horse (600) | 300 | 38 | 5 | 22,800 | 9 | 11,400 |
| Aurochs (900) | 450 | 27 | 3 | 24,300 | 10 | 12,150 |
| Red deer (190) | 95 | 88 | 11 | 16,720 | 7 | 8,360 |
| Roe deer (21) | 10.5 | 15 | 2 | 315 | — | 157.5 |
| Wild pig (107.5) | 53.75 | 28 | 3.5 | 3,010 | 1 | 1,505 |
| Bison (575) | 287.5 | — | — | — | — | — |
| Other wild animals | — | 12 | 1.5 | — | — | — |
| Total | | 814 | | 243,470 | | |

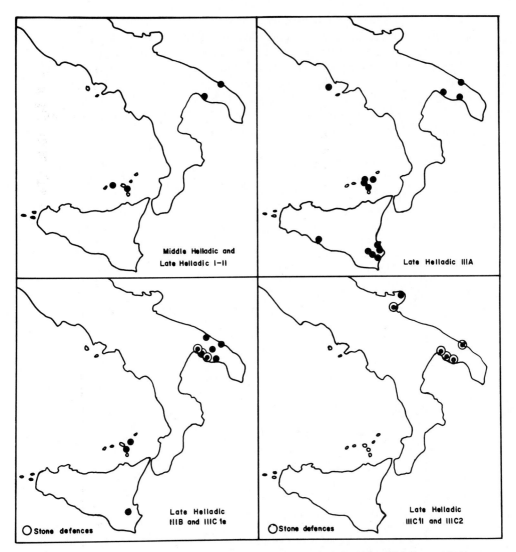

**Figure 8.5.** The distribution of Mycenaean pottery in southern Italy. (After Whitehouse 1973.)

The concentration of Mycenaean ceramics at Scoglio del Tonno, Torre Guaceto, and other coastal sites in southern Italy indicates that an interregional exchange system existed between the Aegean and Adriatic areas (Figure 8.5). In view of the small amount of Mycenaean ceramics, it is unlikely that there were Mycenaean colonies or trading posts there. Rather, it is more probable that the local communities were the middlemen in the trade between Greece and northern Italy. Through this network flowed goods from western, central, and northern Europe during the fourteenth to twelfth centuries B.C. (Whitehouse 1973). These southern Italian settlements were small, less than 1 ha in area, but some of them were surrounded by stone defenses (Figure 8.6). Probably minerals such as copper and tin moved to southern Italy from northern regions. The existence of such an exchange is indicated by the presence of Terramara and Peschiera bronzes in southern Italy. These are nonlocal products in southern Italy, which lacks mineral resources. With the collapse of the Mycenaean state societies, between 1200–1100 (1400–1300) B.C., the trade between the Aegean and Adriatic areas declined until the expansion of the Greeks to the western Mediterranean in the eighth century B.C. The small Mycenaean states have received too much credit for the increase of trade and establishment of long distance trade routes in Europe. C. Renfrew (1972) estimated the population for Crete and the Messenia area of the Peloponnesus peninsula in mainland Greece, one of the centers of the Mycenaean civilization, as follows:

|  | Early Bronze Age | Middle Bronze Age | Late Bronze Age |
|---|---|---|---|
| Crete (Minoan) | 75,000 | 214,000 | 256,000 |
| Messenia (Mycenaean) | 23,000 | 118,000 | 178,000 |

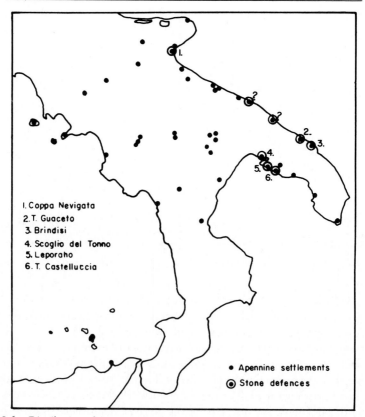

1. Coppa Nevigata
2. T. Guaceto
3. Brindisi
4. Scoglio del Tonno
5. Leporaho
6. T. Castelluccia

• Apennine settlements
◉ Stone defences

**Figure 8.6.** Distribution of Apennine settlements in southern Italy. (After Whitehouse 1973.)

It is hardly possible that the entire European continent supplied such a small market given the many types of trade goods known archaeologically. Greece and Crete are poor in mineral resources, and we know that Mycenaean and Minoan traders obtained in other Mediterranean lands the raw materials needed to produce metal and luxury goods. The volume of this trade is suggested by finds in the Aegean areas of bars and ingots of copper and bronze. However, we should not underestimate the developments in temperate Europe during the Bronze Age. The cultures here also produced spectacular luxury goods and the demand for the raw materials and luxury goods was not limited only to the Aegean area.

We know from the spectacular Únětice burials in Germany and Poland that a variety of luxury goods made of bronze, copper, and gold were deposited in the graves of high-ranking individuals. Such burials appeared by 1700–1600 (2060–1800) B.C. and their contents indicate a substantial indigenous demand for luxury artifacts. Therefore, the attraction of the "accumulated surplus" of the Aegean market need not be invoked as the main reason for Bronze Age trade.

The increase in complexity of trade networks during the Bronze Age is reflected by the presence of *hoards* of tools and ornaments buried in the earth. Such a hoard may consist of several daggers, or spearheads, or bronze drinking vessels, the whole collection of which may be buried inside a clay pot. The European Bronze Age trade routes have been reconstructed by archaeologists using the distribution of these hoards and assuming that they were buried for security by traders along the routes. However, Rowlands (1971) has suggested that hoards containing broken metal artifacts may represent the exchange between a customer and smith for new artifacts. Furthermore, he has suggested that big hoards containing great numbers of similar artifacts may indicate a system of large-scale production, limited however to only a brief period during the year.

Most of our evidence for Bronze Age exchange networks comes from nonperishable materials such as copper, bronze, gold, amber, or faience beads. Trade in foodstuffs, furs, or salt rarely left evidence at archaeological sites, and must be inferred from the distribution of the preserved artifacts. Trade in perishable goods usually occurred in a limited area because it was a trade involving neighboring communities. The exchange in nonperishable goods may have involved local and long-distance trading. In the latter case, goods may have moved great distances, through many intermediaries. The value of the objects traded may have varied in different areas and this may have depended on weight, place of origin, availability, or status of previous owner, etc.

When considering trade during the Bronze Age, we should put it in its proper sociopolitical context. Trade and economic exchange are institutionalized quite differently in state societies than in politically less centralized societies. We are dealing with chiefdoms and tribal societies in Europe outside the Aegean area during the Bronze Age. The trade networks involved hundreds of small independent sociopolitical units. As previously stated, intervillage, intertribal, and interregional exchanges probably occurred in the Bronze Age. Goods moved vertically and horizontally. The exchange of low-value goods, such as foodstuffs, may have involved all members of a society, whereas high-value objects may only have been exchanged among the high-ranking individuals of different tribes or chiefdoms.

No evidence exists for the presence of specialized traders or markets among the Bronze Age tribes and chiefdoms in Europe. To explain the movement of goods we have to rely on models from contemporary tribal and chiefdom societies. As Rowlands (1973:596) states,

> The present evidence supports the hypothesis that during the Bronze Age Europe was connected by a number of inter-locking regional exchange networks, in which goods moved internally by such mechanisms as gift or redistribution and in the peripheral areas and between networks by barter and trade.

Such an explanation is more consistent with the available archaeological evidence than the older theories invoking itinerant traders, prospectors, missionaries, and bandits roaming around Europe to distribute or obtain the needed goods and raw materials. In this discussion we have not dealt with the role of warfare, which can also be considered as an exchange system of negative reciprocity type.

Trade among the various communities in Europe depended upon certain raw materials, craft products, or artifacts symbolizing prestige. Much of the trade in so-called luxury goods like gold or amber probably only involved the elites of various sociopolitical groups. Most of the population was not directly involved in such a trade.

Much emphasis has been placed on trade goods appearing at the extreme ends of the European exchange networks, such as Baltic amber in Mycenaean Greece. This amber trade has received great emphasis in archaeological publications showing how barbarian Europe was supposedly tied with the Aegean state societies (Figure 8.7).

Amber is found in Portugal, Sicily, southern Italy, France, Romania, West Jutland (Denmark), and the Baltic coasts of Lithuania, Kaliningrad area, and northeastern Poland. Amber artifacts, mostly beads, are found in Poland, Germany, Soviet Union, Czechoslovakia, Austria, Hungary, Italy, and Greece. The discovery of the amber artifacts in most of these countries did not cause undue excitement among archaeologists, except for the occurrence of amber in the Mycenaean tombs. Such finds are dated as early as 1600 (1800) B.C. Studies made of this amber indicate that it came from the Baltic area. Amber from the Baltic coast has a relatively high content of succinic acid (3–8%), and this supposedly distinguishes it from southern European amber. Studies did in fact show that the Mycenaean amber had a succinic acid content similar to that of Baltic amber. However, further studies indicated that amber from Portugal, France, Italy, and Romania had comparable levels of succinic acid (Beck *et al.*

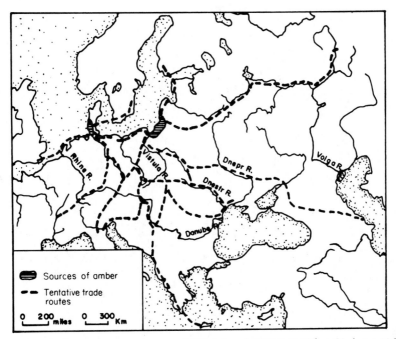

**Figure 8.7.** Amber trade routes between 1600 B.C. and 1100 B.C. (After Gimbutas 1965.)

1971). Subsequently, infrared spectroscopy was carried out on the amber found in Greece that indicated that it did indeed come from the Baltic area (Beck *et al.* 1971).

It is impossible to estimate the amount of Baltic amber that reached Greece, although it was not a large amount, even when taking into account the large number of beads found at some sites.

The fact that flattened spherical beads are the most common archaeological finds suggests that most of the amber was traded as finished products. In Greece, amber occurs in the burials, suggesting that it was highly valued. Goods symbolizing high wealth, value, or prestige are seldom available in large quantities. If they were easily available to all members of society, their value would drop. By being placed in burials they were eliminated from circulation (G. Wright 1974). Thus, amber never became too common in Greece, while at the same time a demand was maintained.

It seems that mostly nonutilitarian goods moved from the Mediterranean region to other areas of Europe. For example, we find faience beads and shells, such as *Cardium Columbella rustica* and *Dentalium,* from the Mediterranean region in central Europe (Vladár 1973a). Other goods could have been exchanged, such as textiles. However, they are perishable and seldom leave any evidence for their presence in archaeological sites. The faience beads probably originated in the eastern Mediterranean, possibly Egypt (Figure 8.8). This source of origin has been questioned by some archaeologists (Newton and

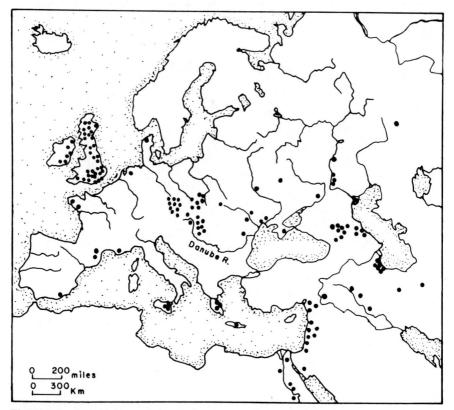

**Figure 8.8.** Distribution of faience beads. (After Gimbutas 1965.)

Renfrew 1970), but McKerrell's (1972) analysis of faience beads in England still points to an eastern origin. The interregional exchange system between the eastern Mediterranean and central Europe is reflected by decorative motifs appearing around 1600–1500 (1800–1710) B.C. We find metal and bone objects decorated with concentric circles in central Europe and such motifs are considered to be of Mycenaean influence (Gimbutas 1965, Vladár 1973a).

## Settlement Organization

For the Bronze Age and Iron Age it will not be possible to describe the details of the settlement system of any one region in western or central Europe because of a lack of published data. Unfortunately, the emphasis by archaeologists on excavating Bronze Age and Iron Age mounds and cemeteries does not help our attempts to reconstruct settlement systems.

The settlement organization and architecture of the central European Bronze Age reflects an increasingly complex sociopolitical organization and an intensification of warfare. These trends can be seen in Vladár's (1973a) study of the Otomani and Madarovce cultures in Slovakia. It suggests that a two-level hierarchical settlement existed, which would be appropriate to a well developed chiefdom. Probably the system consisted of villages at the lower level and fortified settlements at the upper level. However, Vladár does not give the ratio of villages to fortified sites, so the two-level model is still tentative (Figure 8.9). According to Vladár, the elite and the craftsmen of the chiefdoms lived in fortified settlements. It is unclear if craftsmen involved in the production of metal tools and precious objects were full-time specialists. Rowland's (1973) study of smiths during the Bronze Age in Britain suggests that most of them were not full-time specialists. Specialists were needed only for the production of more elaborate bronze and gold objects. Probably most of the craftsmen were engaged in agriculture, production of artifacts, and various other activities.

The architecture of some of the Madarovce and Otomani settlements is very impressive. A good example of a fortified settlement is Spišský Štvrtok, an Otomani site in Slovakia. This settlement was strategically located to control the trade route running through a mountain pass across the Carpathians along the Hornád River (Figure 8.9). The fortifications at Spišský Štvrtok enclosed an oval area of roughly 6600 m$^2$ (.66 ha), and consisted of a ditch (6 m wide by 2 m deep), and a rampart with a stone core. Vladár (1973a) estimated that the whole wall measured 4.8 m wide at base, and 4 m wide at the top (Figure 8.10). The whole structure, including a wooden palisade, may have been as high as 6 m. Furthermore, there are differentiated areas within the fortified settlement. One part of the settlement, called the *acropolis*, had an area of 660 m$^2$. Houses were found in various areas of the fortified settlement, but the structures in the acropolis area differed in construction techniques from the other houses: The lower parts or foundations of these were constructed of stones. During the 1968–1972 field seasons, 26 rectangular houses were uncovered at the Spišský Štvrtok site. The houses were laid out in rows, and usually had two rooms. It is evident from the nonrandom distribution of luxury goods in the settlement that there were economic and presumably social distinctions among the inhabitants. A hoard of 36 gold artifacts and numerous bronze items was found in the acropolis. It is unclear if this gold was from Slovakian sources, such as the Slovakian Ore Mountains, or other regions of central or southeastern Europe.

Another impressive fortified settlement in Slovakia is Barca (Figure 8.11). The houses excavated within the settlement indicate little socioeconomic differentiation among the inhabitants. Twenty-three rectangular houses were uncovered in the excavated part of the site. They were arranged in rows with 40–60-cm intervals separating one house from another. Most of the houses had three rooms, but there were also one- or two-room houses. The three-room houses usually contained two hearths.

Many Bronze Age settlements are no more impressive than Neolithic ones.

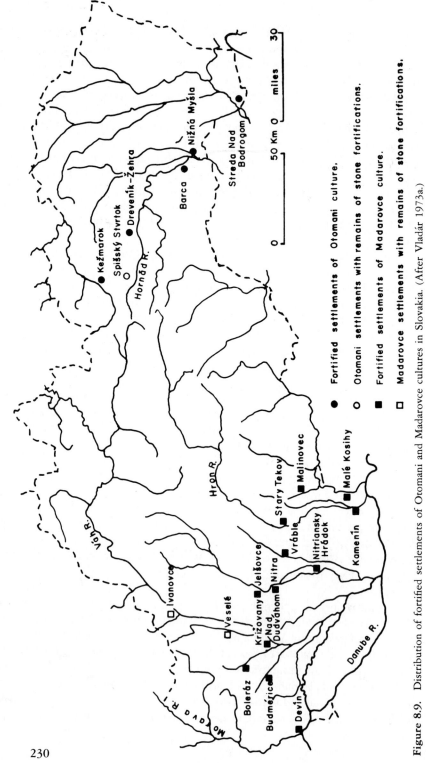

**Figure 8.9.** Distribution of fortified settlements of Otomani and Madarovce cultures in Slovakia. (After Vladár 1973a.)

- ● Fortified settlements of Otomani culture.
- ○ Otomani settlements with remains of stone fortifications.
- ■ Fortified settlements of Madarovce culture.
- □ Madarovce settlements with remains of stone fortifications.

230

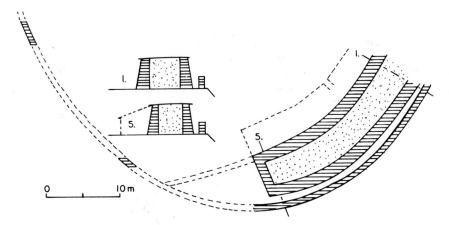

**Figure 8.10.** Reconstruction of fortifications at Spišský Štvrtok. (After Vladár 1973a.)

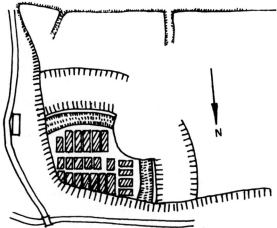

**Figure 8.11.** Plan of the Otomani settlement at Barca, Slovakia. (After Gimbutas 1965.)

For example, the Late Bronze Age settlement of Buchau (Wasserburg) is located on an island in the Federsee moor, southern Germany (Reinerth 1936). This settlement had two occupations and it was surrounded by a multiple palisade of wooden posts (Figure 8.12). The first settlement had 38 roughly rectangular wooden houses. Thirty-seven of them were about 4 × 5 m in size. The larger house had two rooms and may have been occupied by a village leader. The second occupation at Buchau consisted of nine house complexes. Each house had three or more rooms, and there were also buildings that could have served as barns. The largest of the houses had six rooms, and four hearths. It is unclear why there was a change in village organization between the first and second occupations.

In the German Democratic Republic, the Late Bronze Age village of Perleberg consisted of 16 houses, averaging approximately 10 m in length

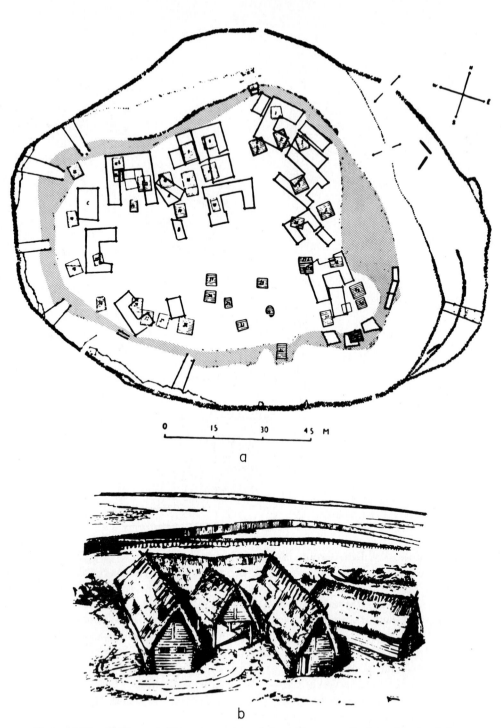

0    15    30    45 M

a

b

**Figure 8.12.** (a) Plan and (b) reconstruction of the settlement at Buchau. (Reprinted from *Prehistoric Europe: The Economic Basis* by J. G. D. Clark with the permission of the publishers, Stanford University Press. Copyright © 1952 by J. G. D. Clark.)

(Schubart 1958). Five of them had hearths inside the houses, and 11 did not. Near the center of the settlement there was an oven that may have been used by the entire community for baking. It seems that Perleberg was not protected by fortifications.

It is evident that we find fortified and unfortified settlements during the Bronze Age. However, little can be said about their ratios or their relationship until more data are available.

## Fortifications

In this section I will discuss briefly the variability in Bronze Age fortifications in central Europe. This discussion will be based mainly on the work of Herrmann (1969) and Coblenz (1963, 1971) (Niesiołowska-Wędzka 1974), and it will deal with fortifications of the Lusatian culture in Czechoslovakia, the German Democratic Republic, and Poland. The Lusatian culture appeared around 1400 (1640) B.C. and it ended in the fifth century B.C. (Figures 8.13, 8.14, and 8.15). Thus, it spans most of the Bronze Age and Early Iron Age in central Europe. It is evident that the observations made about the Lusatian Bronze Age fortifications are also applicable to the Early Iron Age.

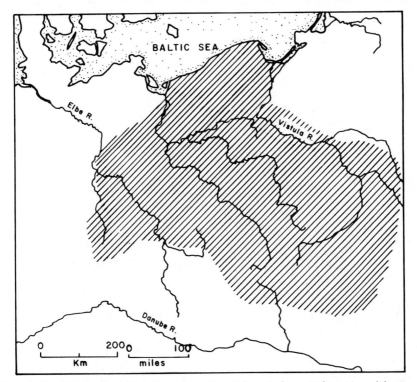

**Figure 8.13.** Distribution of Lusatian culture sites. (After Gimbutas 1965, with modifications.)

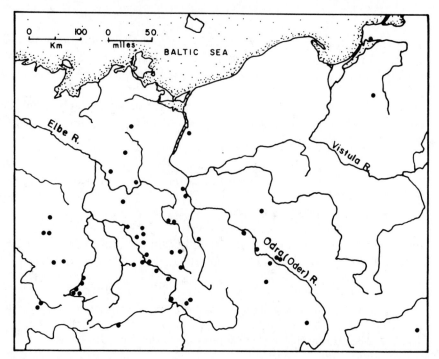

**Figure 8.14.** Fortified settlements during the Late Bronze Age. (After Herrmann 1969.)

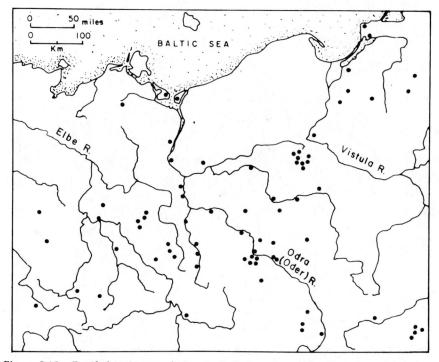

**Figure 8.15.** Fortified settlements during the Early Iron Age. (After Herrmann 1969.)

Herrmann (1969) discussed extensively the fortifications in the German Democratic Republic during the Late Bronze Age and the Early Iron Age (Figure 8.16). He noted three types of locations.

1. On the summits of end moraines, for example, in the Mecklenburg area *stress defense* Size: 0.7 to 18 ha.
2. On the summits of the mountains. Size: 0.8 to 35 ha.
3. In the lowlands and valleys. Size: 0.7 to 1.8 ha.

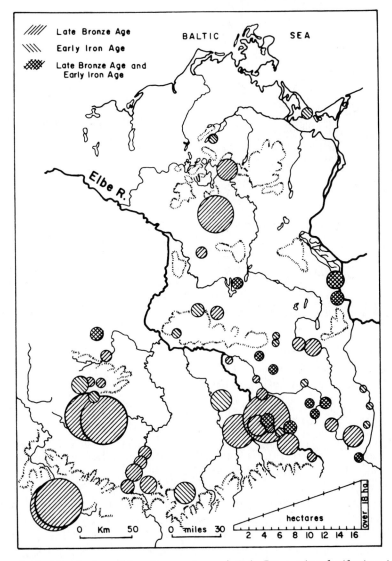

**Figure 8.16.** Distribution of Late Bronze Age and Early Bronze Age fortifications in the German Democratic Republic. (After Herrmann 1969.)

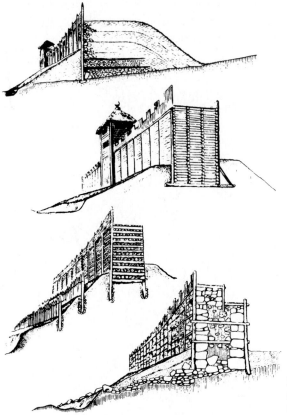

**Figure 8.17.** Reconstruction of different types of Lusatian fortifications. (From Coblenz 1971.)

He also discussed the differences in construction and use of raw materials:

1. Plank and palisade type (wood)
2. Dry wall construction (stone construction)
3. Grid form in construction (wood)
4. Box construction of wood (timber box)

Hamilton (1971) has emphasized that the construction of different types of fortifications is closely related to the presence of raw materials in the area. For example, the North European plain was well wooded, so wood was used extensively in construction. However, we should not overemphasize this geographic determination in describing the different types of fortifications (Figure 8.17).

Interestingly, through time the size of the fortifications decreased (Figure 8.18). The Bronze and Iron Age fortifications occupy much larger areas than the Medieval ones. It is possible that the fortifications of the Bronze Age and Iron Age served the entire population of the area. Thus, at the chiefdom level, all people including domestic animals assembled in the local fortified settle-

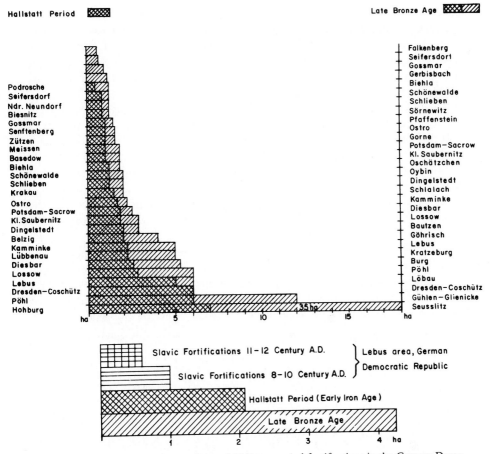

**Figure 8.18.** Size of Late Bronze Age and Hallstatt period fortifications in the German Democratic Republic. (After Herrmann 1969.)

ment during an attack. Probably the medieval fortifications mainly served the elite and their armies. However, the size of the fortified area increased in the late medieval times as entire towns or cities were surrounded by defensive walls. The Bronze Age and Iron Age fortifications were located in strategic places, such as near mountain passes.

## Social Differentiation

Differences in the social status of members of a community were already apparent in the Neolithic, but during the Bronze Age, social differentiation intensified. However, there is no evidence that the scheme of social ranking had crystallized into a class system, as it occurs in state societies. With the exception of the Aegean area, one cannot postulate the existence of any state societies at this time in Europe. In some areas of central and western Europe, however, we had complex chiefdoms. Frequently the high-status individuals of different chiefdoms have more in common among themselves than with their own lower-status kinsmen. Thus, kinship ties play less and less of a role in the complex chiefdoms.

The best evidence for social differentiation comes from areas near important raw material sources and major trade routes. Differences in burial structures and their contents are the data most frequently used to indicate the degree of social differentiation in Bronze Age societies. Between 1700 (2060) and 1500 (1710) B.C. (based on radiocarbon dates) we find spectacular burials at Leubingen and Helmsdorf in Thuringia, German Democratic Republic, and Łęki Małe in western Poland (Figure 8.19). These burials belong to the Únětice culture. In England we also find burial mounds containing luxury objects in the Wessex area.

For the high-status individuals of the Únětice culture in Germany and Poland, a special wooden structure was constructed at ground level or in a pit. The corpse was put in the structure with a variety of luxury goods, which were often made of gold and bronze, and then a mound of earth was raised over the structure. At Leubingen an impressive triangular structure of wood and stone

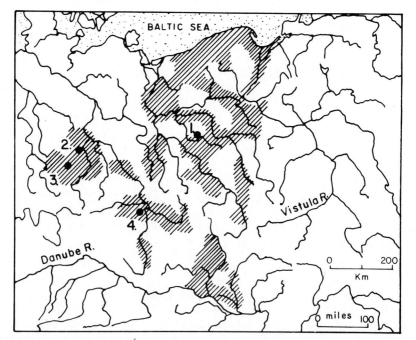

**Figure 8.19.** Distribution of Únětice culture sites. 1, Łęki Małe; 2, Helmsdorf; 3, Leubingen; 4, Únětice. (After Sarnowska 1969.)

was erected for the burial of an adult male and a young female (Figure 8.20). For the central burial at Łęki Małe, a pit was dug, and lined with wood and stones. However, this does not mean that all individuals buried in the mound or mounds at Łęki Małe had a similar quantity and quality of burial goods (Table 8.8; Figure 8.21). Some had very few luxury goods. In a chiefdom, or an individual-stratified society, a person's own status may be reflected by his burial goods.

The ordinary members of a society were buried in pits, usually with pots as the only grave goods. At Wrocław-Oporów, an Únětice cemetery in Silesia, Poland, only 1 burial out of 100 examined had gold, and it only had one such artifact (Table 8.9) (Sarnowska 1969). Only 8 out of 100 burials had bronze artifacts. The excavation here was a salvage job, but the data still give a good indication of social differences. It is apparent that among the lower-status members of a chiefdom, bronze and gold artifacts were very rare. However, if the burials were close to the sources of the metal, the number of metal objects increased. For example, Únětice burials in Bohemia usually contain substantially more bronze and gold objects than those in Silesia.

Shennan (1975) has investigated social differentiation at Branč cemetery in southwest Slovakia. The Branč excavations were conducted by Vladár and the results were presented in a monograph (Vladár 1973b). This cemetery belongs to the so-called Nitra group of the Early Bronze Age in Slovakia. There were 308 inhumation burials at Branč, most of which belonged to the Nitra group. Shennan studied the correlation of various kinds of grave goods and details of interment with age and/or sex of the dead individuals. Certain artifacts were found mostly with males: boars' tusks, willowleaf knives, daggers, bone amulets, arrowheads, metal sheets, amphorae, and chipped stone artifacts, except obsidian. Willowleaf rings, bone beads, and bone spacer plates usually were found with females.

In studying stratification at Branč, Shennan considered the variety of goods in burials and the quantity of particular artifact types, and assigned a number of points on a scale for units of wealth. The number of points per individual was determined a priori on the basis of distance and difficulty in obtaining raw materials and estimated time taken to produce the object. For example, metal rings had higher value than bone awls. Ten or more points classified the burial as rich. Shennan found one cluster of rich burials in the cemetery, and the very elaborate necklaces, bone bead garters, profiled bone pins, spiral rings, and *noppenrings* were almost exclusively associated with the rich burials. Furthermore, Shennan assumed that these artifacts were worn as status symbols by the rich. Interestingly, there was a greater number of rich females than males (Figure 8.22). Most of the richest females were in the juvenile–adult age group or older (Figure 8.23). It is possible that women achieved their wealth through marriage. For males, the wealth was probably hereditary, since some children's and infants' burials were rich.

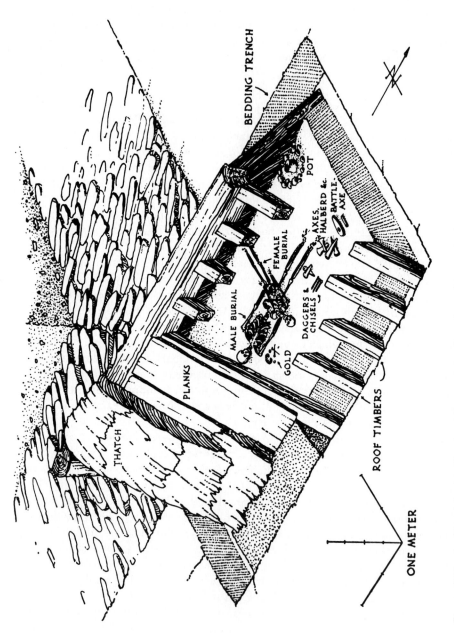

**Figure 8.20.** Leubingen burial. (Reprinted by permission from Stuart Piggott, *Ancient Europe* [Chicago: Aldine Publishing Company; Edinburgh: Edinburgh University Press], copyright © 1965 by Stuart Piggott.)

240

**TABLE 8.8** Contents of the Únĕtice Mounds at Łęki Małe, Leubingen, and Helmsdorf[a]

| | Łęki Małe (Mound I) | | | | Łęki Małe (Mound II) | Łęki Małe (Mound III) | | Leubingen | Helmsdorf |
|---|---|---|---|---|---|---|---|---|---|
| | Burial A | Burial B | Burial C | Burial D | | Burial A | Burial B | | |
| Pottery vessels | 6 | 2 | 1 | 5 | 3 | 4 | 2 | 1 | 1 |
| Stone axe | | | | | | | | 1 | 1 |
| Whetstone | | | | | | | | 1 | |
| Amber beads | | | | 2 | | | | | |
| Bronze hanged axe | 1 | | | 1 | | | | 2 | 1 |
| Bronze halberd | 1 | | | | | | | | |
| Bronze dagger | 1 | | | 1 | | | 1 | 3 | |
| Bronze pins | 1 | | | 2 | | | 2 | | |
| Bronze chisels | | | | 1 | | | | 3 | 1 |
| Bronze armlets | 2 | | | | | | | | |
| Copper dagger | | | | | | | | 1 | |
| Gold pins | | | | | | | | 2 | 2 |
| Gold spirals | 1 | | | 3 | | | 2 | 1 | 1 |
| Gold earrings | | | | | | | | | 2 |
| Gold bracelet | | | | | | | | | 1 |
| Gold armring | | | | | | | | 1 | |
| Gold hair-rings (spirals) | | | | | | | | 2 | |

[a] After Kowiańska-Piaszykowa and Kurnatowski 1953, Kowiańska-Piaszykowa 1957, Sarnowska 1969, Höfer 1906, Grössler 1907.

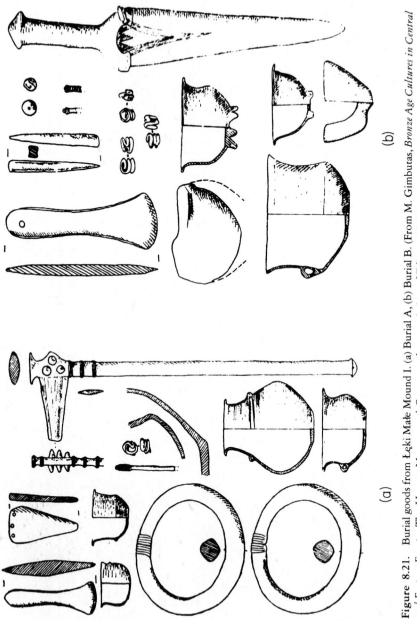

**Figure 8.21.** Burial goods from Łęki Małe Mound I. (a) Burial A, (b) Burial B. (From M. Gimbutas, *Bronze Age Cultures in Central and Eastern Europe*, The Hague: Mouton and Company, by permission of Edicom N. V.)

(a)

(b)

TABLE 8.9  Contents of the Únětice Cemetery at Wrocław-Oporów, Poland[a][b]

| Burial Number | Contents | Burial Number | Contents | Burial Number | Contents | Burial Number | Contents |
|---|---|---|---|---|---|---|---|
| 1 | 2 p | 26 | 3 p | 51 | 2 p | 76 | 1 s |
| 2 | 2 p | 27 | 2 p | 52 | 2 p | 77 | 3 p |
| 3 | 7 p | 28 | 2 p | 53 | 4 p | 78 | 4 p |
| 4 | 2 p | 29 | 2 p | 54 | 1 p | 79 | 1 f |
| 5 | 2 p | 30 | 3 p | 55 | 3 p  1 b | 80 | 4 p |
| 6 | 3 p | 31 |  | 56 | 3 p  2 b | 81 |  |
| 7 | 1 p | 32 | 2 p | 57 | 6 p  1 g | 82 | 2 p |
| 8 | 2 p | 33 | 3 p | 58 | 3 p | 83 | 1 p |
| 9 | 2 p | 34 | 2 p | 59 | 2 p | 84 | 2 p |
| 10 | 2 p | 35 | 4 p  2 b | 60 | 2 p | 85 |  |
| 11 |  | 36 | 1 p | 61 | 3 p 24 f 1 s | 86 |  |
| 12 | 2 p | 37 | 1 p | 62 | 1 s  1 f | 87 | 1 p |
| 13 | 1 p | 38 | 1 p | 63 |  | 88 | 1 p 2 f 1 s |
| 14 | 2 p | 39 | 1 p | 64 |  | 89 | 4 p |
| 15 | 1 p | 40 | 1 p | 65 | 4 p | 90 | 3 p 2 b |
| 16 | 1 p | 41 | 3 p | 66 | 1 p | 91 | 1 p |
| 17 | 2 p | 42 | 2 p | 67 | 2 p  3 f | 92 | 1 p |
| 18 | 2 p | 43 | 6 p | 68 | 1 p  2 b | 93 |  |
| 19 |  | 44 | 2 p | 69 | 1 f  1 s | 94 |  |
| 20 | 2 p | 45 | 1 p | 70 | 2 p  2 f 1 b | 95 |  |
| 21 | 1 p | 46 | Sherds | 71 | 1 p | 96 | 1 p |
| 22 | 1 p | 47 | 2 p | 72 | 3 p  1 b | 97 | 2 p |
| 23 | 1 p  2 b | 48 | 2 p | 73 |  | 98 | 3 p |
| 24 | 4 p | 49 | 2 p | 74 | 1 p | 99 | 1 p |
| 25 | 3 p | 50 | 1 p | 75 | 1 p | 100 | 2 p |

[a] After Sarnowska 1969.
[b] Letter code as follows:  p = clay pot
f = flint artifacts
b = bronze artifacts
g = gold artifacts
s = stone artifacts

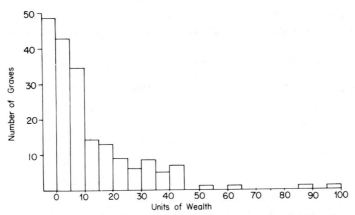

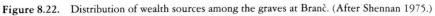

Figure 8.22.  Distribution of wealth sources among the graves at Branč. (After Shennan 1975.)

243

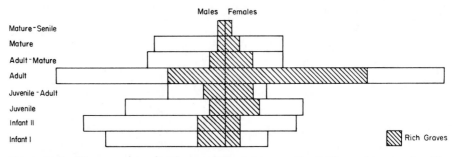

**Figure 8.23.** The age and sex distribution of the skeletons at Brańc. Those with more than 10 units of wealth are distinguished as rich. (After Shennan 1975.)

In some areas of central Europe, no evidence has yet been found for an increase in social differentiation. For example, data from the Early Bronze Age settlement and cemetery of Iwanowice near Kraków, Poland, suggest quite an egalitarian community. Most of the differences observed in the archaeological material found in the Iwanowice cemetery reflect only status differences based on sex. In general, only small quantities of burial goods were found at Iwanowice (A. and J. Machnik 1973). The most commonly found burial goods were bone or mussel shell beads. Pendants made of boars' tusks were found only in male burials. The males were buried on their right sides with their heads oriented toward the west, while the females were lying on the left side with heads pointing east. At the Vel'ký Grob cemetery in Slovakia, mostly female burials show correlation with metal ornaments (Table 8.10) (Chropovský 1960).

In Scandinavia, the social differentiation among members of Bronze Age society was also demonstrated by Randsborg (1973). Randsborg studied the contents of hundreds of burial mounds belonging to the Early Bronze Age 1500–800 (1710–900) B.C. in Denmark. These structures usually contained a single person who was buried with weapons and jewelry. In his study, Randsborg assumed that the different quantities of bronze and gold artifacts, based on weight, reflected status and sex differences. All gold and bronze

TABLE 8.10   Association of Burial Data with Sex Groups at the Vel'ký Grob Cemetery[a][b]

| | Male | Female |
|---|---|---|
| Skeleton lying on the right side | .008 | |
| Skeleton lying on the left side | | .000007 |
| Pottery | | .015 |
| Earrings | | .014 |
| C rings | | .006 |
| Neck rings | | .03 |

[a] Data are from Chropovský 1960.
[b] Significance is based on Fisher's Exact Test.

artifacts can be considered luxury goods in Denmark since no mineral deposits occur there. Randsborg's analysis indicates that graves containing gold were usually also richer in bronze, and, furthermore, burials of men had more bronze and gold than burials of women. Certain gold objects were found only with males, such as twisted arm-rings. In graves of females, bronze arm-rings were deposited. It seems that gold had the greatest ceremonial and prestige value. As was the case during the Neolithic, more of the Danish Early Bronze Age burials were of males than of females: 582 male graves to 236 female ones. This is a very substantial difference and it probably cannot be explained solely by female infanticide as a population-regulatory mechanism.

The best evidence for social differences during the Middle and Late Bronze Ages is again available from cemeteries. By the Late Bronze Age, the so-called Urnfield period, we find spectacular burial mounds in some areas of central Europe, which reflect increasing social differences among the members of Bronze Age chiefdoms. A good example of a mound containing the remains of a high-status individual is found at Očkov in western Slovakia (Paulik 1962) (Figure 8.24). It seems that after the death of the high-ranking person, his corpse was cremated on the ground surface. The remains of the funeral pyre at Očkov consist of ashes, charcoal, burnt bones, and molten bronze objects. After cremation, a rectangular pit 4.25 × 3.65 m and 3.1 m deep was dug in the ground. This pit also contained some of the remains of the funeral pyre. Furthermore, at the bottom of this pit, a smaller pit 2 m deep was dug. The smaller pit contained cremated bones of the high-status individual, probably originally deposited in a pot. Other remains found with this individual were ceramics, a horse bridle, gold ornaments, and bronze objects. Thus the high-status individual was cremated with his belongings. During the funeral ceremonies, numerous pots and some bronze vessels were deposited on the

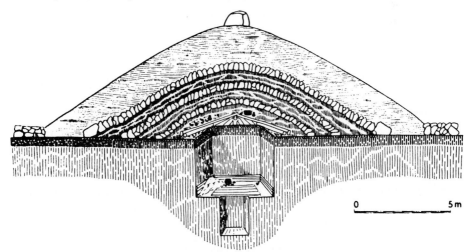

**Figure 8.24.** Burial mound at Očkov. (From Paulik 1962.)

ground surface. Over the funeral pyre and the pits, a mound of earth with three alternating layers of stone was constructed. A tombstone was placed on top of the mound and a low stone wall, 1.5–2 m wide, was constructed around it. The height of the mound was approximately 6 m and the diameter of the stone wall was 25 m.

Paulik (1962) pointed out the possible similarities between the funeral ceremonies of Patroclos and Hector in Homer's *Iliad* and the burial at Očkov. In *The Iliad*, Homer mentions that huge quantities of wood were collected for Patroclos's and Hector's funerals. Probably large amounts of wood were needed for the funeral pyre of the high-status individual at Očkov. In *The Iliad*, Achilles placed offerings near Patroclos's body consisting of pots filled with oil and honey. Originally, the numerous pots of Očkov may have been filled with offerings. Homer mentions that humans and animals were sacrificed for the fallen heroes. For example, 12 Trojan youths were sacrificed by Achilles in honor of Patroclos. Some burnt human bones found on the surface at Očkov may represent remains of such a sacrifice. After the cremation of Patroclos, his remaining bones were collected by Achilles in a vessel and then Achilles asked his companions to build a mound over the remains of his fallen friend. A similar mound covered the human remains at Očkov.

## State Societies in the Aegean Area

During the Bronze Age, the earliest European state societies probably developed in the eastern Mediterranean region, the Aegean area. C. Renfrew (1972) has discussed the development of these societies. Around 1800–1700 (2140–2060) B.C. small Minoan states such as Knossos appeared in Crete and around 1600–1550 B.C. the Mycenaean states such as Mycenae were established on the Greek mainland (Figure 8.25). Homer's *Iliad* describes a Mycenaean attack on Troy during the thirteenth century B.C. The Mycenaean states collapsed around 1200–1100 (1400–1270) B.C. and the Minoan ones around 1400 (1640) B.C. These Aegean societies are classified under various terms: civilizations, urban societies, and state societies. I feel that a brief discussion is necessary to clarify the meaning of these terms.

Civilization is quite an ambiguous term and probably should be used only very carefully or completely dropped by archaeologists in Europe. Definitions of *civilization* are usually not very informative. For example, C. Renfrew (1972:13) defined civilization as a "complex artificial environment of man; it is the insulation created by man, an artefact which mediates between himself and the world of nature." He went on to clarify that definition:

> It may thus be entirely satisfactory to say "civilisation is a constantly recurring assemblage of artefacts including two out of three of the following: written records, ceremonial centres, cities of at least 5000 inhabitants," but this is only an operation-

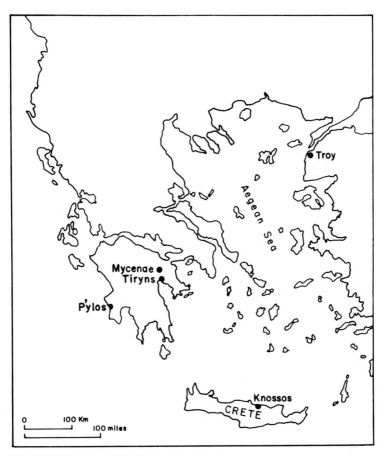

**Figure 8.25.** Aegean state societies.

ally effective way of saying "a civilisation is a constantly recurring assemblage of artefacts documenting a human environment effectively insulating the individual from the world of nature" [C. Renfrew 1972:13].[1]

Some European archaeologists use the term *civilization* loosely; we find archaeologists talking about Neolithic, Bronze Age, and Iron Age civilizations north of the Alps in Europe. Since the word *civilization* can symbolize so many levels of sociopolitical development in Europe, I will not use it. It is quite a meaningless term in European archaeology.

Some archaeologists, like Childe (1951) and Adams (1971), concentrate on the earliest appearance of urbanism. Adams (1971:10) has summarized the traits of Childe's urban society, which, in reality, also coincide with traditional markers of civilization:

[1] This and subsequent quotes cited to C. Renfrew 1972 are from C. Renfrew, *The emergence of civilisation: The Cyclades and the Aegean in the Third Millennium B.C.* London: Methuen & Co. Ltd., 1972.

1. Increase in settlement size
2. Centralized accumulation of capital resulting from the imposition of tribute or taxation
3. Monumental public works
4. The invention of writing
5. Advances toward exact and predictive sciences
6. The appearance and growth of long-distance trade in luxuries
7. The emergence of a class-stratified society
8. The freeing of a part of the population from subsistence tasks for full-time craft specialization
9. The substitution of a politically organized society based on territorial principles—the state—for one based on kin ties
10. The appearance of naturalistic, or rather, representational, art

It should be noted that Adams does keep separate the terms *civilization, urbanism,* and *state society.* He states:

> At least as a form of settlement, however, urbanism seems to have been much less important to the emergence of the state, and even to the development of civilization in the broadest sense, than social stratification and the institutionalization of political authority [Adams 1971:9–10].

Clearly any attempt to list traits defining an urban or a civilized society will lead to arguments about whether a particular society can be so defined even if it does not meet every criterion enumerated. For example, it can be argued that lack of writing among the Incas in the Andean area eliminates them from the category of a civilization.

I will use the term *state society* to denote the level of development succeeding the complex chiefdoms in European archaeology, and ignore the terms *civilization and urbanism.* First, I will discuss what is meant by the term *state society.* Archaeologists should define state societies in such a manner that they can demonstrate the existence of state societies with archaeological data (material culture). Wright and Johnson (1975) have examined the problem of definition and have come up with a very workable definition of a state society:

> Many definitions of states focus on particular features usually associated with state organization, such as private landholding, formal law, or governmental monopoly of force. We believe it is more reasonable to focus on the total organization of decision-making activities rather than on any list of features. A state is defined as a society with specialized administrative activities. By "administrative" we mean "control," thus including what is commonly termed "politics" under administration. In states as defined for purposes of this study, decision-making activities are differentiated or specialized in two ways. First, there is a hierarchy of control in which the highest level involves making decisions about other, lower-order decisions rather than about any particular condition or movement of material goods or people. Any society with three or more levels of decision-making hierarchy must necessarily involve such specialization because the lowest or first-order decision-making will be

directly involved in productive and transfer activities and second-order decision-making will be coordinating these and correcting their material errors. However, third-order decision-making will be concerned with coordinating and correcting these corrections. Second, the effectiveness of such a hierarchy of control is facilitated by the complementary specialization of information processing activities into observing, summarizing, message-carrying, data-storing, and actual decision-making. This both enables the efficient handling of the masses of information and decisions moving through a control hierarchy with three or more levels, and undercuts the independence of subordinates.[2]

Following this definition, I maintain that state societies in Europe should have at least three hierarchical levels of administration. For example, a king, ruler, or oligarchy at the top, then regional governors or administrators, and then village heads at the bottom. (As noted previously, societies with two levels of administration were classified as chiefdoms and with one level as tribes.) One way of approaching this problem is to study the settlement system. A state society should have at least a three-level hierarchical settlement system: major center (capital), provincial centers (smaller settlements), and villages.

There are various theories for the origin of the state societies. Wright (1970:2–5) summarized these theories into four groups:

1.  Management theories, that is, those which stress the presence of human activities, such as irrigation and trade, whose complexity requires certain kinds of management. Wright cites Wittfogel's work *Oriental Despotism* (1957) in which hydraulic or irrigation developments were emphasized.

2.  Internal conflict theories: These theories "involve the existence of differential access to wealth, conflict or threat of conflict, and the subsequent emergence of the state as a mediating and dominating institution [H. Wright 1970:3]." The reference to conflict in this instance refers to class conflict. Examples of the proponents of these theories are Engels (1884) and Diakonov (1969).

3.  External conflict theories: According to these theories, conditions arise "which enable and require one society to dominate and control the means of production in another society [H. Wright 1970:3]." Carneiro (1970) is one proponent of this theory. Furthermore, population growth is emphasized as a key factor in the development of state societies in this theory.

4.  Synthetic theories: These involve the interrelated operation of several processes at once, as discussed by Adams (1971), or by Flannery (1972).

[2] Reproduced by permission of the American Anthropological Association from H. T. Wright and G. A. Johnson, Population, exchange, and early state formation in southwestern Iran. *American Anthropologist* 77 (No. 2): 267, 1975.

As noted, state societies probably appeared in the Aegean area during the Bronze Age. C. Renfrew (1972) has argued that this development can be viewed as the result of the interaction of local processes in the technology, economy, and social arrangements of these societies. He assigns an important role to population growth in his model of the rise of the Aegean states.

I will not deal in any great detail with the various causes that led to the development of state societies in the Aegean as this has been done by C. Renfrew (1972). It is evident that a hierarchical administrative system developed in Greece and Crete during the Bronze Age. Probably the administrative system was operating at three levels: major center, minor centers, and villages. However, the presence of a three-level hierarchical settlement system has not yet been demonstrated archaeologically for Greece or Crete.

The largest and most impressive settlements in Greece and Crete are classified as *palace centers*. The area and population of these settlements were small. For example, the maximum estimate for Knossos in Crete is 5 ha (12 acres) in area, with a population of 5000. Also, according to the estimate, Knossos controlled the surrounding area with a population of 50,000. The settlements on the Greek mainland were even smaller: Pylos 1.25 ha (3 acres; 12,600 m²), Tiryns 2.2 ha (5 acres), and Mycenae 3.85 ha (9.5 acres; 38,500 m²). The minimum population estimate for Pylos is 3000 (Chadwick 1972). In these settlements we find public buildings and craft workshops. However, only the mainland sites have evidence for impressive fortifications. The archaeological data indicate that these palace centers were surrounded by smaller communities (McDonald and Simpson 1972).

In some sites, such as Pylos and Knossos, we find the earliest evidence of writing in Europe. The earliest script, the so-called Linear A, has not yet been deciphered and scholars are not sure about the language of the users. Linear A script was followed by Linear B, which was demonstrated to be an archaic form of Greek by Ventris (Ventris and Chadwick 1956). The evidence for the use of this writing is preserved on clay tablets.

The Linear B tablets do not tell us much about the lives of rulers, their wars, love affairs, or palace intrigues. The tablets

> fall, almost without exception, into three categories: records of receipts of goods, of disbursements of goods, and inventories (including tallies of livestock, landholdings and lists of personnel). The out-payments include rations for personnel and "ritual offerings." The in-payments include carefully calculated tribute assessments, together with a record of any deficit in the actual payment [C. Renfrew 1972:296].

It is clear that palaces were major centers for the redistribution of goods and services.

Furthermore, the tablets give us valuable information on how great a division of labor existed in Crete and Greece. The tablets mention carpenters, masons, potters, smiths, shepherds, messengers, servants, scribes, etc. This is well illustrated by the Pylos tablets. The Linear B tablets found at Pylos occurred in a single area called the *archive room*. They apparently constituted the administrative records of the palace center, and contained information about agricultural production, livestock, bronze-smiths, etc. and some inventories of the storerooms in the palace center (Chadwick 1972). Among the 1200 tablets found at Pylos, 17 of them belong to the so-called Ma series. The Ma tablets list the assessments and contributions of 17 settlements in six products. Most of the products referred to in the tablets cannot be identified, since they are listed in abbreviations. However, the products appear to be agricultural, including some kinds of textiles and hides. Some of the products were counted and some were weighed. One of the tributary settlements in the Ma group called *a-pu ₂-we* had nine smiths, two of whom received no allocation of bronze. Also, the Pylos tablets indicate that men, women, and children received allocations of wheat in the ratio 5:2:1. The tablets from Knossos in Crete show that a census of resources was taken, from which we learn that Knossos controlled about 100,000 sheep. It seems that the entire society of one Mycenaean or Minoan state was run by a palace center that controlled political and economic organization within its territory.

*[handwritten margin note: 2 sheep per person?]*

The small size of the Mycenaean and Minoan states and the absence of large elaborate temples or public buildings led C. Renfrew (1972:369) to question if they were states. "The small territorial size, absence of a clearly defined class structure and the suggestive lack of monumental religious or public buildings could indeed lead us to deny these principalities the status of state." The absence of class structure can be questioned. C. Renfrew (1972:369) concluded that they were "Something more than chiefdoms, something less than states."

However, we are following Johnson and Wright's approach in attempting to demonstrate the presence of a state society. Since we can observe specialized administrative activities at different levels in the Mycenaean and Minoan societies, we can call them states, perhaps more properly "petty" states. Furthermore, it is evident that state societies can appear without a sharp increase in regional population or without large aggregates of population forming cities.

Most archaeologists have ignored the problem of the appearance of the earliest state societies north of the Alps in Europe during the Bronze or the Iron Age. Since European societies outside the Mediterranean world lacked writing, elaborate temples, palaces, etc., they were automatically excluded from consideration as states. Thus, little research has been done on the problem of whether state societies evolved here before the expansion of Roman control into barbarian Europe. We should not exclude the possibility of appearance of state societies during the Late Iron Age in barbarian Europe. Incidentally, I freely use the term barbarian Europe, but one should not get the impression that it has a derogatory connotation. There is no suitable term to define Europe outside the Greek, Etruscan, and Roman states in the Mediterranean area.

Also, I would like to stress that our traditional conception of a "civilized" man or woman has little relevance here. The so-called civilized man or woman may have the proper manners in his or her own culture, but an evaluation of the presence of state societies should not be based on such a criterion. I am interested in a particular level of sociopolitical development. For example, the Late Iron Age Celtic societies in Europe were described by Posidonius in the second and first centuries B.C. as headhunters, but this does not influence my judgment of whether some Celts were at the state level of sociopolitical development.

# Chapter 9

# Iron Age

The beginning of the Iron Age is defined by the appearance of iron technology and tools. Since iron technology was also utilized in historic times in Europe, the term *Iron Age* is conventionally limited to the pre-Roman period in Europe. The expansion of the Roman Empire into central and western Europe marked the end of the Iron Age and, at the same time, initiated the beginning of the so-called Roman period. The traditional date for the end of the Iron Age north of the Alps is about 1 A.D.

The earliest known practice of iron metallurgy dates to the second half of the third millennium B.C. in Anatolia (Turkey). For several centuries the Hittite Empire had a monopoly on iron-working techniques in that region. The break up of the Hittite Empire around 1200 (1400) B.C. led to the rapid spread of iron technology to the Near East and Europe.

The earliest iron tools in Europe appeared around 1100 (1270) B.C. in Greece. As with agriculture and bronze technology, there was a gradual spread of iron technology to various parts of Europe. In the tenth century B.C. the first iron tools appeared in Italy. Between 1000 (1140) and 750 (840) B.C., iron technology was established in most regions of temperate Europe except Scandinavia and the northern areas of the Soviet Union. In the eastern Baltic area, iron technology first appeared in about 500 B.C. The spread of iron technology across Europe was faster than that of agriculture or bronze working.

The appearance of iron technology does not imply that bronze working disappeared in Europe. The craftsmen of Iron Age societies continued to make bronze artifacts, particularly ornaments and vessels. Because iron is harder than copper or bronze, most cutting and manufacturing tools such as knives and swords were made of iron (Rowlett 1968).

The introduction of iron technology affected some regions, such as Scandinavia, more drastically. As previously mentioned, Denmark lacks tin and copper; therefore, the raw materials for making bronze tools had to be continuously imported. However, this lack of native raw materials did not prevent the development of a very skillful bronze industry; Danish bronze products were even exported to other parts of Europe. The introduction of iron technology upset this industry and led to the collapse of the northern Bronze Age.

Iron ore is more widely distributed in Europe than copper or tin. This availability made it possible for people of all ranks of society to acquire iron tools. Also, in iron tool production, unlike bronze making, alloying is not needed. However, iron technology is not simple. Clark (1952:203) has observed that

> in early times all iron artifacts had to be wrought directly from blooms or lumps of malleable iron reduced immediately from the ore, a process for which a temperature of no more than 800–900 degrees C. was needed. Production was achieved by heating the ore sufficiently to cause its siliceous content to separate and combine with ferrous oxide so as to form a fusible silicate, or slag.

However, as Clark (1952:199) also notes, "until a technique had been devised for toughening the forged metal by repeated hammering of the bloom at red heat in contact with charcoal, so introducing the carbon needed for carburization, it was too soft to be of practical use."

The chronological control of the archaeological data in most areas of Europe improves during the Iron Age. In the Mediterranean area there are written records which help us to establish quite precisely the chronological position of various periods and sites. Even in areas north of the Alps archaeologists have better chronological control of archaeological data, for they do not have to rely only on the radiocarbon method for absolute dates. The presence of Greek and Etruscan artifacts in western, central, and eastern Europe permits approximate absolute dates to be obtained by cross-dating.

The Iron Age in central and western Europe is subdivided into two periods: Hallstatt and La Tène. The Hallstatt period is named after a salt-mining center and a cemetery near Salzburg, Austria, while La Tène is a site on Lake Neuchâtel in Switzerland. Archaeologists have subdivided Hallstatt and La Tène into various different phases A, B, C, D, or I, II, III, and sometimes IV. Table 9.1 gives some of the subdivisions for the Iron Age used by various archaeologists. The Hallstatt A and B phases north of the Alps fall into the Late Bronze Age period. For our purposes, the Hallstatt period will be dated from 750 to 450 B.C. and the La Tène period from 450 B.C. to A.D. 1 The Hallstatt and La Tène *periods* should not be confused with the archaeological *cultures* of the same names: The period names are applied to all of trans-Alpine Europe; the cultures, especially the Hallstatt culture, have a more limited distribution in central and western Europe (Figures 9.1 and 9.2).

# TABLE 9.1 Chronological Chart for the Iron Age[a,b]

Müller-Karpe (1959)
Reinecke[c] (1904–1911)
(For southwestern central Europe)

| Date | Phase |
|---|---|
| 1000–900 B.C. | Ha[c] A |
| 900–800 B.C. | Ha B |
| 800–700 B.C. | |
| 700–600 B.C. | Ha C |
| 600–450 B.C. | Ha D |
| 450–400 B.C. | LT[c] A |
| 400–250 B.C. | LT B |
| 250–100 B.C. | LT C |
| 100–0 B.C. | LT D |

Hodson (1964)
Rowlett (1968)
Viollier (1911)
(For France and adjacent areas)

| Date | Phase |
|---|---|
| 730–600 B.C. | Ha I |
| 600–530 B.C. | Ha IIa |
| 530–480 B.C. | Ha IIb |
| 480–400 B.C. | LT Ia |
| 400–320 B.C. | LT Ib |
| 320–250 B.C. | LT Ic |
| 250–100 B.C. | LT II |
| 100–50 B.C. | LT III |

Godłowski and Woźniak[d]
Kostrzewski (1965)
(For Poland)

| Date | Phase |
|---|---|
| 650–500 B.C. | Early Ha |
| 500–400 B.C. | Late Ha |
| 400–200 B.C. | Early LT |
| 200–0 B.C. | Late LT |

Okulicz (1973)
(For east Baltic area)

| Date | Phase |
|---|---|
| 550–400 B.C. | Early Iron Age |
| 400–250 B.C. | Middle Iron Age |
| 250–0 B.C. | Late Iron Age |

[a] This chronological chart is presented on the basis of recent modifications.

[b] Ha = Hallstatt; LT = La Tène.

[c] The Hallstatt A and B phases of Reinecke's chronology fall into the Late Bronze Age in areas north of the Alps. This chronology is not applicable to north–central and northern Europe.

[d] Personal communication.

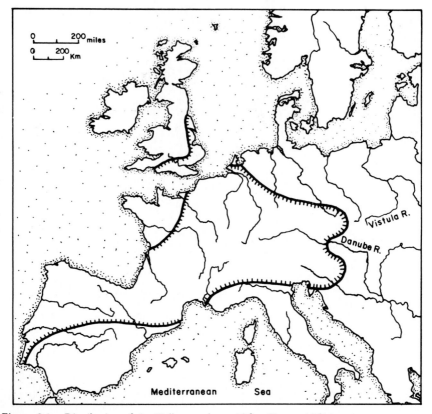

**Figure 9.1.** Distribution of the Hallstatt culture. (After Piggott 1965.)

There are differences in ceramics, tools, vehicles, and other objects that help us to differentiate the two periods. For example, the Hallstatt period is associated with four-wheeled wagon burials and the La Tène period with chariot burials. The wagon burial sites occur from Bohemia through southern Germany, and from northern Switzerland to Burgundy. With the exception of those in Bohemia and the Rhineland, the distribution of Hallstatt wagon burials and that of the Early La Tène chariot burials are largely mutually exclusive.

The Iron Age period in western and central Europe was contemporary with the early historical period of the Mediterranean state societies. Some of our information about Iron Age peoples in eastern, western, and central Europe comes from Greek and, later, Roman writers. Furthermore, oral traditions can be used to recreate some aspects of Iron Age societies. Also, the beginnings of Classical Greek civilization occurred during the Iron Age; for example, the first Olympiad is dated about 776 B.C. The Greek colonization of Sicily and southern Italy began in the second half of the eighth century B.C. Around 700 B.C. the Etruscan states developed in Italy. In present day Tunisia (North

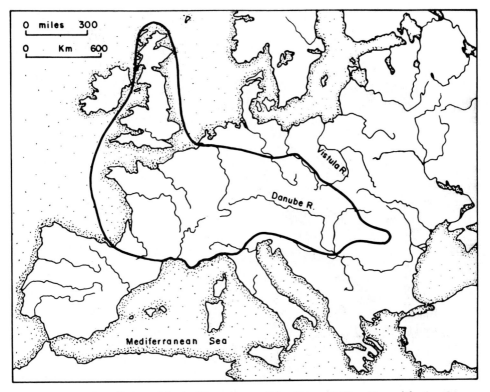

**Figure 9.2.** Distribution of the La Tène culture. (After Piggott 1965, with modifications.)

Africa) the Carthaginian state was established in the ninth century B.C. In the sixth and fifth centuries B.C. the Carthaginians, Greeks, and Etruscans competed for the domination of the western Mediterranean (Figure 9.3). Frequently Etruscans and Carthaginians were allies in their attempts to limit Greek expansion in the western Mediterranean. After 400 B.C. these three competing groups were gradually incorporated into the rising Roman state. These conflicts also affected other European peoples living in the vicinity of these societies. For example, Hannibal led the Carthaginian army from Spain through southern France to Italy in 218 B.C. Furthermore, merchants and probably various adventurers were penetrating into barbarian Europe from the Mediterranean state societies at this time. In a manner similar to that of Europeans in the eighteenth and nineteenth centuries in Africa and America, these people attempted to outwit the so-called barbarians. Fortunes probably could have been made beyond the pale of the Mediterranean state societies.

Archaeologists associate the Hallstatt period and frequently the La Tène period with various historic, linguistic, and ethnic groups in Europe. For example, most archaeologists assume that Celts (Keltoi, Galli) occupied large

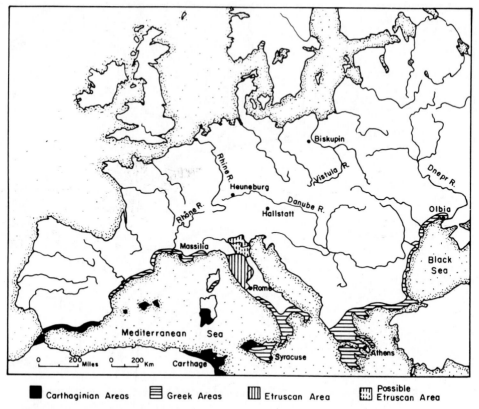

**Figure 9.3.** Europe around 500 B.C.

areas of western and central Europe during the Iron Age. They place Germanic people in Scandinavia whereas the Slavs are put in east–central and eastern Europe. In the eastern Baltic area were located the Balts (ancient Prussians, Lithuanians, and Latvians) and, further north, Finno–Ugric-speaking peoples.

Of all the so-called barbarians of the Iron Age, we have the greatest quantity of information about the Celtic-speaking people. This information comes from archaeology, Greek and Roman writers, and oral traditions, such as the Ulster Cycle, telling of the deeds of Cu Chulainn and other Gaelic heroes, that survived for a long time in Ireland and was later written down during the Middle Ages. For example, Posidonius traveled in Gaul (France) in the late second century B.C. and later wrote about the ways of life of the Celtic people. In the first century B.C. Caesar conquered France (Gaul) for Rome, and wrote his memoirs, *The Gallic War,* about his campaigns against Celts and other peoples. Later Tacitus, a Roman writer, wrote *Germania* about the Germanic people. The writings of Roman and Greek writers were usually slanted against the so-called barbarians. Strange customs of foreign people have always been hard to understand; for example, the wearing of trousers by people north of the Alps did not appear natural to inhabitants of the toga-wearing Mediterranean world. Furthermore, there was probably a political purpose behind the writings of Posidonius, Caesar, and others. The objective was to show how dreadfully savage the barbarians were, and how Mediterranean states such as Rome had a "moral" duty to bring them the benefits of a "civilized" life.

The Greeks also left some written information about the societies of eastern Europe. The steppes of eastern Europe, from the Don River to the Danube and from the Black Sea to Zhitomir–Kiev–Kharkov, were occupied by the Scythians in the seventh century B.C. We have information about these pastoral people from Greek writings, particularly *The Histories* of Herodotus (484–425 B.C.). At the end of the third century B.C. the Scythians were defeated by a new wave of pastoralists from the east called Sarmatians, who drove them into Crimea.

The Scythians were warlike and even raided central Europe. The distribution of Scythian projectile points, usually made of bronze, possibly reflects the extent of their raids. We also know from Herodotus that the Persian emperor Darius led a military campaign against the Scythians in 514–513 B.C. However, he failed to defeat them.

From Roman and Greek records we have the first concrete evidence of migrations or folk movements during the Iron Age in Europe. When we mention folk movements in Europe, we usually think of the Post-Roman Migration period. Frequently archaeologists have speculated on the occurrence of migrations during the Neolithic and Bronze Age periods and have offered this phenomenon as an explanation for culture change. However, it is very difficult to demonstrate the occurrence of migration with archaeological data alone. For the Iron Age, we also have written evidence of migrations by Celtic, Germanic, Sarmatian, and other groups. For example, we know that Celts expanded into northern Italy and sacked Rome in 390 B.C. In the second century B.C. Germanic groups such as the Cimbri, Teutones, and Ambrones migrated from northern Europe into France and Switzerland.

Several stylistic zones and phases in the graphic and plastic arts are recognized in western, central, and eastern Europe during the Iron Age. Megaw (1970) has discussed the artistic traditions in Europe during this period. These art styles are characterized by nonrepresentation of human form. In eastern Europe, the Scythian art objects are distinguished by fluid and abstract treatment of animals. Perhaps it is the Scythian influence that subsequently is seen in La Tène art, which also emphasized curvilinear motifs, palmettes, and leaf forms. Most of our knowledge of La Tène art comes from metal objects, since these are preserved most often in archaeological sites.

The iron technology in barbarian Europe was at the same level of development as that of the Mediterranean world during the Hallstatt and La Tène periods. The iron tools and weapons of Celtic and other peoples equalled those of the Greeks, Etruscans, or Romans. We know from remains of four- and two-wheeled vehicles that Hallstatt and La Tène carpenters, blacksmiths, and wheelwrights produced wagons and chariots with great skill. The decorations found on metal objects, such as swords and pots, show the great skill of their blacksmiths. Even pottery was made on the wheel in many areas north of the Alps during the Iron Age. The defeat of Celtic, Germanic, and other peoples by the rising Roman state should not be attributed to the superior technology of the latter, but to its superior political and military organization. By the end of the Iron Age, large parts of Europe had been incorporated into the Roman Empire (Figure 9.4).

## Economic Organization: Subsistence Strategies

We have written records about the Iron Age economy in Mediterranean Europe from observations made by Greek and Roman writers, who also wrote about some other areas of Europe. For example, Herodotus wrote about the Scythians in the steppes of the Ukraine. Nevertheless, most of our information outside the Mediterranean and Black Sea areas still comes from archaeological excavations.

It is not possible to write a summary of Iron Age economy because there was such a great diversity in sociopolitical organization and local economic adaptations. Frequently we do not know what the recovered faunal and floral remains reflect. For example, such sites as Manching in Germany were probably differentiated internally in terms of occupations and social rank. It is not to be expected that the diets of low-status individuals were the same as those of the elites of the complex chiefdoms. Furthermore, it is likely that the inhabitants of the large fortified centers of such polities had different diets from those of the farmers in villages and hamlets. In the steppes of eastern Europe some Iron Age societies had a pastoral adaptation, but as mentioned in the Neolithic section, archaeologists always discuss this type of adaptation in simplistic terms.

In the Danish peat bogs, human remains were found of the Grauballe and Tollund men. They were so well preserved that even stomach contents were intact; however, we should not consider the diet of these people as characteristic of the average person's diet (Helbaek 1958). These finds, which date to the second or third centuries A.D., represent the remains of men killed in sacrificial rituals or, perhaps, executed for some crime or moral transgression. J. Renfrew (1973:17) states that "Grauballe man's last meal had consisted of some sort of gruel composed of seeds of sixty-six species of plants, only five of which were cultivated." While this gives us information about the great variety of wild plants that were eaten during the second and third centuries A.D. in Scandinavia, we should not expect that a person about to be killed would be presented a tasty roast of pig or deer for his last meal.

The ecological differences that influenced adaptations at the beginning of the Neolithic period continued throughout the Iron Age. For example,

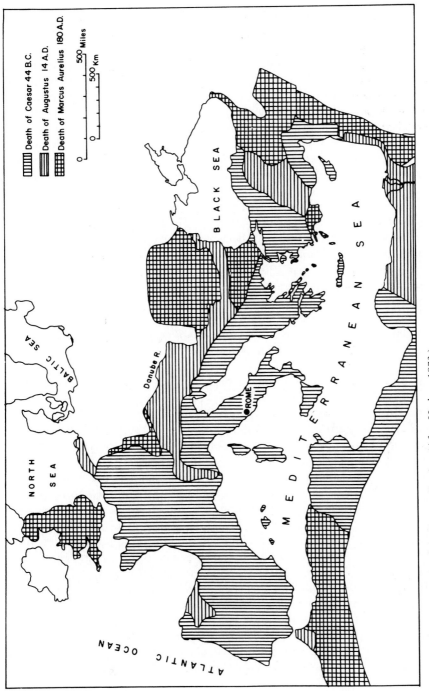

**Figure 9.4.** The growth of the Roman Empire. (After Hackett 1973.)

societies inhabiting the coastal areas of the Baltic Sea exploited the sea resources extensively. There probably was an increase in sophistication of agricultural techniques. The rotation of fields for planting different crops during successive years must have become common. In Italy, viticulture was established (J. Renfrew 1973). J. Renfrew mentions that in the north of Europe rye became more popular during the Iron Age (1973:206). However, looking at the cereal remains from the Lusatian sites, the cultivation of rye appears still to have been insignificant (Table 9.2). Judging from the paleobotanical remains from Lusatian sites in Poland, different varieties of wheat still predominated (Table 9.2). Barley was second, but the cultivation of broomcorn millet was also very important. It is interesting to note that leguminous plants, such as peas and beans, were extensively grown. Perhaps this indicates a decrease of protein in the diet from the meat of wild animals. Einkorn wheat was predominant in the Rhineland, Germany (Table 9.3). In Holland, at the Ermello site, dated around 510 B.C. emmer wheat was the dominant cereal and barley ranked second. The remaining domesticated and wild plants appeared in very small quantities (van Zeist 1968).

As during the Neolithic and Bronze Age periods, cattle predominated in temperate Europe. The faunal remains from the Lusatian sites in Poland indicate that sheep–goat and pig were in second place (Table 9.4). Naturally the domesticated horse was more prevalent. The percentage of wild animal bones range from 23.4 at Biskupin to zero at the Niemcza or Szczecin sites (Ostoja-Zagórski 1974).

As previously mentioned, only a small proportion of the Manching settlement was excavated. In terms of numbers of various species recovered during 1955–1961, domesticated animals greatly predominated, while the proportion of wild species was insignificant (Table 9.5). It is, however, doubtful that similar ratios would have been obtained from an Iron Age village or a hamlet. Cattle, sheep–goat, and pigs yielded about the same numbers, but taking into account the weights of edible meat, cattle clearly predominated. The ratio between cattle and horse is 10:1. Also, the remains of domesticated fowl, such as chickens, were recovered at Manching.

The variety of resources mined during the Iron Age increased. There was extensive salt mining and probably iron mining in some areas. In the Hallstatt area of Austria, extensive salt exploitation began in the eighth century B.C. Around the Hallstatt area, salt is found at 900–1,200 m a.s.l.

In summary, during the Iron Age, barbarian Europe was economically at the same level of advancement in agricultural techniques and mineral exploitation as the Roman Empire of the third and second centuries B.C. The economic value of barbarian Europe to the Roman Empire as it expanded from peninsular Italy should not be underestimated; the mineral wealth and productive agriculture of provinces such as Gaul supplied the increasing economic needs of the Empire.

TABLE 9.2  Domesticated Plant Remains Found at Sites in Northwestern Poland Near the End of the Late Bronze Age and Hallstatt Periods[a]

| Site | Chron-ology | Type of settlement | Cereals | | | | | Leguminous plants | | |
|---|---|---|---|---|---|---|---|---|---|---|
| | | | Wheat[b] (Triticum) | Barley (Hordeum) | Millet (Panicum Miliaceum) | Oat (Avena) | Rye (Secale cereale) | Peas (Pisum sativum) | Celtic bean (Vicia Faba) | Lentils (Lens culinaris) |
| Szczecin-Wał | Ha D | Fortified | 4 | 4 | — | — | 5 | — | 17 | 4 |
| Wolin-Młynówska | BA-V/Ha C–D | Unfortified | — | 7 | — | 2 | 1 | — | — | — |
| Wolin-Wzgórze Wisielców | Ha C–D | Unfortified | 3 | 831 | 3 | — | 1 | 1,743 | 539 | — |
| Biskupin, Żnin district | Ha D | Fortified | 6,865 | 733 | 514 | — | — | 234 | 83 | 209 |
| Kodin, Jarocin district | Ha C | Unfortified | 1 | 30 | 1 | — | — | — | — | — |
| Słupca | Ha D | Fortified | 43 | 18 | — | — | 10 | 57 | — | — |
| Słupca | Ha D | Unfortified | 1 | 1 | — | — | — | 131 | 1 | — |
| Smuszewo, Wągro-wiec district | Ha D | Fortified | 101,616 | 28,025 | 76,460 | 71 | — | 8,885 | 13,762 | 9,648 |
| Sobiejuchy, Żnin district | Ha C | Fortified | 3 | 31 | — | — | — | — | 1 | — |
| Kamieniec, Toruń district | Ha D | Fortified | 140 | 15 | 10 | — | — | 25 | 20 | 1 |
| Wrocław-Osobowice | BA-V/ Ha C | Fortified | 1 | 8 | 3 | 40 | 1 | — | — | — |

[a] From Ostaja-Zagórski 1974.
[b] Includes different varieties of wheat: emmer, spelt, bread wheat, fine grain wheat.

263

TABLE 9.3  Plant Remains from Iron Age Sites in Rheinland, Germany

| | Aldenhoven, Jülich district — Hallstatt B/C | Glehn, Grevenbroich district — Hallstatt D | Langweiler, Jülich district — Hallstatt B/C | Meckenheim, Bonn district — Iron Age | Nettesheim/Butzheim, Grevenbroich district — Hallstatt C/D | Rheydt — Hallstatt | Rommerskirchen, Grevenbroich district — Hallstatt C/D | Wickrath, Grevenbroich district — Iron Age | Total number of grains or seeds |
|---|---|---|---|---|---|---|---|---|---|
| Number of grains or seeds | 97 | 26 | 88 | 38 | 626 | 370 | 153 | 147 | 1,545 |
| Number of plant types found at each site | 10 | 11 | 12 | 12 | 29 | 9 | 26 | 10 | 119 |
| Einkorn wheat (*Triticum monococcum*) | | | | | | | | | |
| Grain | — | — | — | — | — | 17 | — | — | 17 |
| Spikelet | 1 | — | — | — | 2 | — | — | — | 3 |
| Glume | 2 | — | 1 | 1 | 7 | 10 | 1 | — | 22 |
| Emmer wheat (*Triticum dioccum*) | | | | | | | | | |
| Grain | — | 1 | 1 | 2 | — | — | — | — | 4 |
| Spikelet | — | — | 1 | 1 | — | — | — | 4 | 6 |
| Glume | — | 2 | 2 | — | — | — | — | — | 4 |
| Spelt wheat (*Triticum spelta*) | | | | | | | | | |
| Grain | 1 | — | 1 | 1 | 1 | — | 2 | 2 | 8 |
| Spikelet | 1 | — | 1 | — | 1 | — | — | 4 | 7 |
| Glume | 5 | — | — | — | 1 | — | 6 | — | 12 |

| | 1 | 2 | 3 | 4 | 5 | 6 | 7 | 8 | 9 |
|---|---|---|---|---|---|---|---|---|---|
| **Wheat** (*Triticum* sp.) | | | | | | | | | |
| Grain | 1 | 1 | — | 2 | 7 | 11 | 1 | 6 | 29 |
| Spikelet | — | 1 | 1 | — | 5 | 5 | 1 | — | 13 |
| Glume | — | 2 | 1 | — | 4 | 6 | — | — | 13 |
| **Naked dense-eared six-row barley** (*Hordeum hexast. nudum*) | | | | | | | | | |
| Grain | 2 | 1 | 8 | 3 | — | — | — | — | 14 |
| **Naked six-row barley** (*Hordeum tetrast. nudum*) | | | | | | | | | |
| Grain | — | — | — | — | 55 | — | — | — | 55 |
| Glume and grain | — | — | 4 | — | — | 15 | — | — | 19 |
| **Barley** (*Hordeum* sp.) | | | | | | | | | |
| Spikelet | — | 1 | — | — | — | 2 | — | — | 3 |
| **Broomcorn millet** (*Panicum miliaceum*) | | | | | | | | | |
| Grain | 11 | 2 | 55 | 1 | 26 | 58 | — | 106 | 259 |
| **Italian millet** (*Setarica italica*) | | | | | | | | | |
| Grain | — | — | — | — | 267 | — | 1 | — | 268 |
| **Rye** (cf. *Secale cereale*) | | | | | | | | | |
| Grain | — | — | — | 2 | — | — | 1 | 2 | 3 |
| **Cereals** | | | | | | | | | |
| Broken pieces of grain | 5 | 4 | — | 9 | 125 | 32 | 15 | 5 | 195 |
| **Flax** (*Linum usitatissimum*) | — | 3 | — | — | — | — | — | — | 3 |
| **Peas** (*Pisum* sp.) | — | — | — | — | 3 | — | — | — | 3 |
| **Common wild oat** (*Avena* cf. *fatua*) | | | | | | | | | |
| Grain | — | 1 | — | 4 | 3 | — | — | 3 | 11 |
| Awn pieces | — | — | — | — | 4 | — | 1 | — | 5 |

*(continued)*

ᵃ From Knörzer 1971b.

**TABLE 9.3** (*Continued*)

| | Aldenhoven, Jülich district Hallstatt B/C | Glehn, Grevenbroich district Hallstatt D | Langweiler, Jülich district Hallstatt B/C | Meckenheim, Bonn district Iron Age | Nettesheim/Butzheim, Grevenbroich district Hallstatt C/D | Rheydt Hallstatt | Rommerskirchen, Grevenbroich district Hallstatt C/D | Wickrath, Grevenbroich district Iron Age | Total number of grains or seeds |
|---|---|---|---|---|---|---|---|---|---|
| Rye brome (*Bromus secalinus*) Grain | 36 | 5 | — | 6 | 3 | 2 | 3 | 3 | 58 |
| Hazelnut (*Corylus avellana*) | — | 1 | — | — | 4 | — | — | 1 | 6 |
| Opium poppy (*Papaver somniferum*) | — | — | 1 | — | — | — | — | 1 | 2 |
| Poppy (cf. *Papaver argemone*) | — | — | — | — | 2 | — | 1 | — | 3 |
| Cockspur grass (*Panicum crus-galli*) | — | — | — | — | 2 | 223 | 9 | — | 234 |
| Millet (*Panicum ischaemum*) | — | — | — | — | — | 5 | 7 | — | 12 |
| Millet (*Panicum sanguinde*) | — | — | — | — | 3 | — | 2 | — | 5 |
| Horsebean (*Vicia* cf. *hirsuta*) | — | — | — | 1 | 2 | 1 | 10 | — | 14 |

| Species | | | | | | | | | |
|---|---|---|---|---|---|---|---|---|---|
| Narrow-leaved vetch (*Vicia angustifolia*) | — | — | — | — | 4 | — | 2 | — | 6 |
| Moench (*Vicia tetrasperma*) | — | — | — | — | 6 | — | — | — | 6 |
| Gold of pleasure (*Camelina sativa*) | — | — | — | — | 14 | — | — | — | 14 |
| Elderberry (*Sambucus racemosa*) | — | — | — | — | 4 | — | — | — | 4 |
| Goosefoot (*Chenopodium album*) | 11 | — | 1 | 5 | 50 | 5 | 10 | 4 | 96 |
| Pink weed or persicaria (*Polygonum persicaria*) | 1 | 1 | 6 | — | 11 | — | 1 | — | 20 |
| Pale persicaria (*Polygonum lapathifolium*) | 1 | 2 | — | — | 11 | 1 | 2 | — | 17 |
| Black bindweed (*Polygonum convolvulus*) | — | — | 9 | 1 | 3 | — | 4 | — | 17 |
| Sorrel (*Rumex tenuifolius*) | 1 | 3 | — | — | 9 | — | 2 | — | 15 |
| Clover (*Trifolium* sp.) | — | — | — | — | 1 | — | 41 | — | 42 |
| Timothy grass (*Phleum* sp.) | 27 | — | — | — | — | — | — | 4 | 31 |
| Annual Knawel (*Scleranthus annuus*) | — | — | — | — | 2 | — | 6 | — | 8 |
| Knotgrass (*Polygonum aviculare*) | — | — | — | 2 | 3 | — | — | — | 5 |
| Corn spurrey (*Spergula arvensis*) | 1 | 1 | — | — | 1 | — | — | — | 2 |
| Cleavers (*Galium* sp.) | — | — | — | 1 | 1 | — | — | — | 2 |
| Scarlett pimpernel (*Anagallis arvensis*) | — | — | — | — | — | — | 20 | — | 20 |
| Red fescue (cf. *Festuca rubra*) | — | — | — | — | — | — | 5 | — | 5 |

(*continued*)

**TABLE 9.3** (*Continued*)

| | Aldenhoven, Jülich district Hallstatt B/C | Glehn, Grevenbroich district Hallstatt D | Langweiler, Jülich district Hallstatt B/C | Meckenheim, Bonn district Iron Age | Nettesheim/Butzheim, Grevenbroich district Hallstatt C/D | Rheydt Hallstatt | Rommerskirchen, Grevenbroich district Hallstatt C/D | Wickrath, Grevenbroich district Iron Age | Total number of grains or seeds |
|---|---|---|---|---|---|---|---|---|---|
| Fan weed (*Thlaspi arvense*) | — | — | — | — | — | — | 3 | — | 3 |
| Thyme-leaved speedwell (*Veronica serpyllifolia*) | — | — | — | — | 2 | — | — | — | 2 |
| Common orache (*Atriplex* sp.) | — | — | — | — | — | — | 2 | — | 2 |
| Broad-leaved plantain (*Plantago major*) | — | — | — | — | 1 | — | — | — | 1 |
| Eyebright or euphrasy (*Euphrasia* sp.) | — | — | — | — | — | — | 1 | — | 1 |
| Black nightshade (*Solanum nigrum*) | — | — | — | — | — | — | 1 | — | 1 |
| Water pepper (*Polygonum hydropiper*) | — | — | 1 | — | — | — | — | — | 1 |
| Small knotgrass (*Polygonum minus*) | — | — | 1 | — | — | — | — | — | 1 |
| Rush (*Eleocharis* cf. *palustris*) | — | — | — | — | — | — | 1 | — | 1 |

TABLE 9.4 Percentages of Animal Bones Found at Sites in Northwestern Poland Near the End of the Late Bronze Age and Hallstatt Periods[a]

| Site | Chronology | Type of settlement | Percentages of bones | | | | | Percentages of domestic animals |
|---|---|---|---|---|---|---|---|---|
| | | | Cattle | Pig | Sheep–goat | Horse | Dog | |
| Szczecin | Ha | Unfortified | 32 | 40 | 22.4 | 6.6 | +[b] | 94.7 |
| Szczecin-Castle | Ha | Unfortified | 31.9 | 49.4 | 18.7 | — | + | 100.0 |
| Tolkmicko, Elbląg district | Ha | Fortified | 47.0 | 26.5 | 26.5 | — | — | 100.0 |
| Jeziorko, Giżycko district | Ha | Fortified | 17.3 | 12.8 | 30.3 | 39.3 | + | 88.3 |
| Biskupin, Żnin district | Ha D | Fortified | 54.8 | 23.4 | 21.4 | + | + | 76.6 |
| Jankowo, Inowrocław district | Ha C/D | Fortified | 63.2 | 16.3 | 9.4 | 8.2 | + | 91.9 |
| Kotlin, Jarocin district | Ha D | Unfortified | 52.3 | 24.1 | 8.3 | 6.6 | + | 91.4 |
| Smuszewo, Wągrowiec district | Ha D | Fortified | 41.7 | 34.8 | 8.3 | 8.3 | + | 95.6 |
| Słupca | Ha D | Fortified | 65.8 | 14.3 | 20.4 | + | + | 92.6 |
| Sobiejuchy, Żnin district | Ha C | Fortified | 49.9 | 14.8 | 24.6 | 5.8 | + | 98.0 |
| Gzin, Chełmno district | HaD/La | Fortified | 56.4 | 1.3 | 25.5 | 14.4 | + | 99.2 |
| Niemcza, Dzierżoniów district | Ha | Fortified | 45.0 | 22.0 | 21.0 | 12.0 | — | 100.0 |
| Wrocław-Osobowice | Ba-V/ Ha C | Fortified | 57.0 | 17.0 | 15.0 | 10.0 | + | 98.0 |

[a] From Ostoja-Zargórski 1974.
[b] Plus sign indicates presence.

TABLE 9.5  Frequency of Animals and Estimated Amount of Usable Meat at Manching Site (1955–1961 Excavation)[a]

| | Kilograms of usable meat | Number of animals | Percentage of total number of animals | Total estimated weight in kilograms | Percentage of estimated weight | Kilograms of usable meat from total estimated weight |
|---|---|---|---|---|---|---|
| Cattle (700)[b] | 350 | 2,315 | 29 | 1,620,500 | 85 | 810,250 |
| Sheep–goat (25) | 12.5 | 2,600 | 33 | 65,000 | 3.5 | 32,500 |
| Pig (30) | 15 | 2,400 | 30 | 72,000 | 4 | 36,000 |
| Dog (10) | 5 | 318 | 4 | 3,180 | — | 1,590 |
| Horse (600) | 300 | 230 | 3 | 138,000 | 7 | 69,000 |
| Domesticated chicken (1) | .5 | 32 | — | 32 | — | 16 |
| Aurochs (900) | 450 | 2 | — | 1,800 | — | 900 |
| Red deer (190) | 95 | 14 | — | 2,660 | — | 1,330 |
| Roe deer (21) | 10.5 | 6 | — | 126 | — | 63 |
| Wild pig (107.5) | 53.75 | 5 | — | 537.5 | — | 268.75 |
| Elk (355) | 177.5 | 1 | — | 355 | — | 177.5 |
| Other wild animals[c] | — | 20 | — | — | — | — |
| Total | | 7,943 | | 1,904,190.5 | | |

[a] From J. Boessneck, A. von den Driesch, U. Meyer-Lemppenau, and E. Wechsler-von Ohlen 1971.

[b] Numbers in parentheses represent estimated adult weight in kilograms.

[c] Bear 2, badger 1, ermine 1, wolf 1, fox 3, wild or domesticated cat 1, hare 5, beaver 5, hamster 1. In addition, the following birds and fish were found at Manching: wild or domesticated goose 6, wild or domesticated duck 3, heron 1, eagle 1, sea eagle 2, owl 1, curlew 1, swallow 1, common raven 5, crow 4, unidentified birds 3, pike 2, catfish 3, carp 3, chub 1, unidentified fish 1.

## Trade

The Iron Age trade system in Europe is very complex because there were tribes, chiefdoms, and state societies. Tribes and chiefdoms existed north of the Alps while large areas of Mediterranean Europe were occupied by state societies, such as those of the Greeks, Etruscans, and Carthaginians. These societies probably had a market system of economic organization. Greek colonies also were established in the Black Sea region. The Greek and Etruscan settlements located near barbarian Europe engaged extensively in trade with tribes and chiefdoms. Greek settlements along the western Mediterranean and Black Sea coasts served as ports of trade with local societies. For example, around 600 B.C. Greeks established the Massilia settlement (modern Marseilles) near the mouth of the Rhône. It seems that these Greek colonies did not control much of the territory outside the settlement.

From 600 to 500 B.C. the western Greek colonies engaged in extensive trade with the Hallstatt people. It seems that this trade was directed mainly toward two areas: the Rhine and Austria–Bohemia. Figure 9.5 shows that goods such as Greek–Massiliote amphorae filled with wine moved from Massilia via the Rhône River corridor to Burgundy, the Middle Rhine, and the Upper Danube region. Some of the goods reached the famous settlement of Heuneberg in Germany. In addition to wine, the Greeks probably traded finished products, glass, and corals to the Hallstatt people. In return, the Greeks received copper, tin, amber, gold, slaves, and perhaps iron and salt. There were many intermediaries in this trade, for example, amber came from the Baltic coast. It is unclear if salt was extensively traded to the Mediterranean region because most finds connected with the salt trade occur north of the Hallstatt region in Austria. Around 500 B.C., that is, near the end of the Hallstatt period, we can surmise that Greeks stopped dominating the trade north of the Alps, because most nonlocal Mediterranean luxury finds occurring in the Hallstatt area tend to be of Etruscan origin. For example, the archaeological evidence from the Vix oppidum (fortified settlement) in France shows trade with Greeks, probably from Massilia, between 600 and 500 B.C. However, by 500 B.C. Etruscan goods replaced Greek ones at Vix. This trade moved via north Italian and eastern Alpine routes.

During the Early La Tène period we have two regions containing numerous Etruscan imports: the Rhine and Upper Austria–Bohemia. Evidence for the Etruscan trade in bronze vessels is found in these two regions (Figure 9.6).

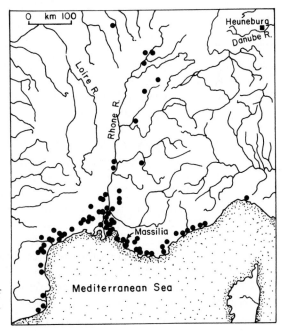

**Figure 9.5.** Distribution of Greek–Massiliote amphorae. (After Kimmig and Gersbach 1971.)

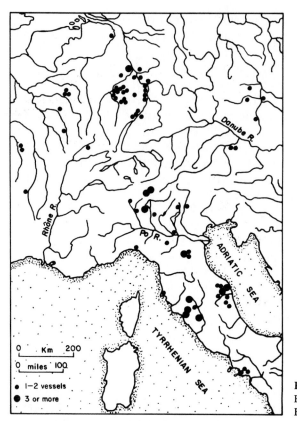

Figure 9.6. Distribution of the Etruscan bronze vessels. (After Frey 1966.)

Pauli (1974) has suggested that the main reason behind the Etruscan trade with Upper Austria–Bohemia was the gold sources of Bohemia. Perhaps societies in Upper Austria acted as middlemen. Also, the salt trade probably was inter-connected with this exchange. There are no salt sources in Bohemia; there-fore, it probably received salt from the Salzburg area in Austria. The Etruscan trade with the La Tène people ended around 400 B.C. when the Celtic invasions of northern Italy greatly diminished Etruscan political power. There is little evidence for extensive trade between the Mediterranean region and the La Tène people after 400 B.C. The main evidence for exchange consists of Greek coins found in the La Tène region.

In the Black Sea area, Greeks established colonies around 600 B.C. such as Olbia at the Southern Bug River, Soviet Union. These colonies were involved in trade with the Scythians and other peoples. Black Sea Greeks shipped grain, especially wheat, to Greece. After Alexander the Great conquered Egypt in the latter part of the fourth century B.C., Greece began to receive grain from the Near East. This led to a decrease of trade with the Black Sea colonies, which caused an economic crisis there. Also, the attacks by Scythians, Sarma-tians, and other peoples contributed to the decline of Greek colonies in the Black Sea area.

**TABLE 9.6**  Source Localities of Selected Materials Found in Fifty-Six Burial Mounds at Dürrnberg, Austria[a]

| Material | Source locality |
|----------|-----------------|
| Jet[b] | Bohemia |
| Tin | Bohemia, German Democratic Republic |
| Copper | Bohemia, Salzburg area of Austria |
| Silver | Bohemia, Slovakia, Dinaric Alps in Yugoslavia |
| Gold | Bohemia, Slovakia, Transylvanian Alps (Romania), Dinaric Alps |
| Amber | Denmark, Poland, Lithuania, Kaliningrad district of RSFSR |
| Coral | Mediterranean coast |
| Glass | Manufactured in the Mediterranean region |

[a] After Penninger 1972.
[b] A type of coal.

It is unclear how trade was organized between the state societies and the Hallstatt and Scythian people. It is possible that Greeks or Etruscans traded with local chiefs and then passed on the products further north. There is also a possibility that some Greek and Etruscan merchants penetrated into the interior of Europe. In the Black Sea colonies, Greek craftsmen manufactured goods that exhibited Scythian styles and motifs for trading to local Scythian communities.

Archaeological evidence from settlements and cemeteries in western and central Europe indicates extensive exchange among regions. Trade linking some tribal societies and chiefdoms in central Europe with the Greeks and Etruscans should not be overemphasized. For example, Iron Age cemeteries around Salzburg, Austria, such as Hallstatt and Dürrnberg, show the presence of a variety of nonlocal materials, but only a small proportion of them are from the Mediterranean area. The greatest number of artifacts are made of bronze and iron, which probably were produced locally. It is evident from the Hallstatt and Dürrnberg sites that these Iron Age societies had extensive trade contacts with several other regions of Europe (Table 9.6). It is difficult to establish precisely the source of many products, since many of the nonlocal materials have several possible sources of origin. If the sources of the different materials were established, it would be possible to determine the trade contacts. In comparison to the Bronze Age, a greater variety of nonlocal materials are present. This probably is related to a more complex sociopolitical organization.

## Settlement Organization

It is not possible to describe the variability and relationships of Iron Age settlement systems in any area of Europe because such studies have not yet been done. The best information probably comes from the Lusatian settlements in north–central Europe. However, there have been numerous excavations of individual Iron Age settlements in other parts of Europe. Four of these—Heuneburg, Manching, Senftenberg, and Biskupin—will be described briefly. Also, the Lusatian settlement system will be sketched in broad terms. Since Iron Age settlement patterns and sites in Greece and Italy are more familiar to the reader, they will not be discussed here.

During the Iron Age, especially in the La Tène period, some settlements grew to be very large. For example, Stradonice in central Bohemia occupied 80 ha, Hradiště in Czechoslovakia 170 ha (Břeň 1972), Manching in Germany 380 ha, and Kelheim in Germany 600 ha. Usually archaeologists associate these sites in southern central Europe with the Celtic speaking people. In *The Gallic War,* Caesar refers to such settlements as *urbs* (city) or *oppida* (tribal capitals) during the first century B.C. in France (Gaul). Probably they were the administrative centers of complex chiefdoms.

## *Heuneburg*

One of the most impressive Iron Age settlements was Heuneburg, southern Germany. It was located on a terrace promontory above the small stream of the Upper Danube River. In the vicinity of the settlement there are large burial mounds that probably contain the remains of some of the occupants of the settlement.

During the sixth and fifth centuries B.C., Heuneburg was a heavily fortified settlement (Figure 9.7), enclosing an area of 300 by 150 m or 4.5 ha (11 acres). The settlement walls were destroyed and rebuilt about 12 times, while the buildings within the settlement were rebuilt even more frequently. Interestingly, before each new building phase within the settlement, the area was intentionally levelled (Kimmig 1975).

The Heuneburg fortifications consisted of timber framed walls, constructed using the *Holzkasten* or timber box technique. Two or three rows of wooden posts were driven into the ground. The horizontal joists, joined with wooden pegs, were placed on a stone footing, and the intervening space filled with dirt and stone rubble (Figure 9.8). Up to five layers of beams and filling were constructed on this foundation and the outer and inner walls were faced with roughly shaped stones (Hawkes 1974:65). During one of the occupational phases, a wall of sun-dried clay bricks was built on top of a 3-m-wide foundation of limestone blocks (Figure 9.9). The brick wall had at least nine towers and probably two gates. This type of fortification was characteristic of the Mediterranean area, but rather unsuitable for rainy central Europe. It may have been built by a local chief who sought to impress others with his knowledge of the Classical or the Mediterranean world, but who apparently was unaware of the unsuitability of this type of military architecture for central Europe. When the brick wall was destroyed, it was replaced by a wall built of wood and stone.

Since there was frequent rebuilding within the settlement, each occupation phase had a different appearance. The houses were built of wooden posts, and were apparently rectangular in shape. During the brick wall settlement phase

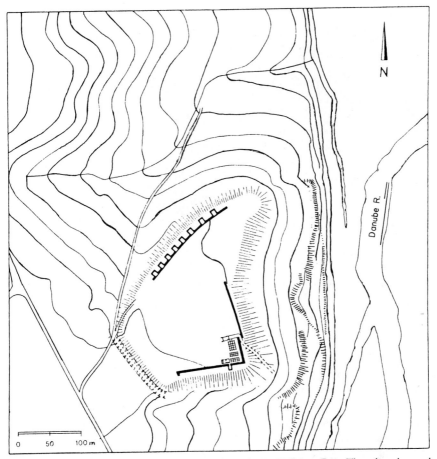

**Figure 9.7.** The Heuneburg in the sixth century B.C. (Hallstatt D1). The plan shows the clay-brick wall and the structure of Period IV ᵃ/₂ in the southeast corner of the citadel. (From W. Kimmig, Early Celts on the upper Danube: The excavations at the Heuneburg. In *Recent archaeological excavations in Europe,* edited by R. Bruce-Mitford. London: Routledge & Kegan Paul Ltd., 1975.)

the site contained a workshop area, located in the southeast corner of the citadel and dwelling areas. The workshop quarter consisted of buildings located along narrow lanes, and possessing special technical features such as smoke outlets and smelting furnaces. Also the buildings contained thousands of tiny globules of bronze. This suggests that bronze objects were made in these workshops. In addition, numerous fragments of casting-molds, and pieces of crucibles of fireclay and slag from bronze and iron processing were found within the workshop area.

As previously mentioned, four mounds were situated approximately 400 m from the fortified settlement at Heuneburg. They contained burials of rich, high-status individuals. The dead were interred in a chamber made of wooden

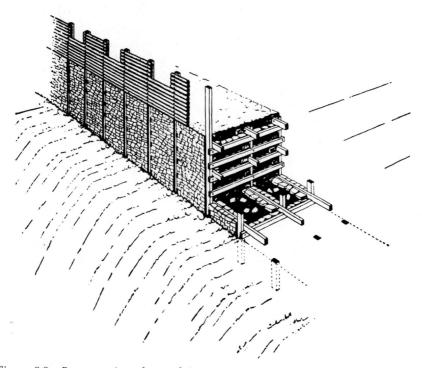

**Figure 9.8.** Reconstruction of one of the many citadel walls made of wood and stone at Heuneburg. (From W. Kimmig, Early Celts on the upper Danube: The excavations at the Heuneburg. In *Recent archaeological excavations in Europe*, edited by R. Bruce-Mitford. London: Routledge & Kegan Paul Ltd., 1975.)

planks, over which the mound had been raised. A four-wheeled wagon and other elaborate grave goods were buried with the deceased (Figures 9.10 and 9.11). Gersbach (1969) has suggested that an unfortified settlement existed in the area of the mounds.

### Manching

Manching, located on a terrace of the Danube near Ingolstadt, southern Germany, was built on an impressively grand scale, for it enclosed an area of 380 ha or 912 acres. The walls surrounding the settlement extended for 7 km (4.2 miles) (Figure 9.12).

There were several excavations at Manching. During the 1955–1960 excavation seasons, an area of about 16,500 m² (1.65 ha) was uncovered. The results of this campaign are being published in several volumes, usually one volume is devoted to particular archaeological finds such as pottery or bones (Boessneck *et al.* 1971, Jacobi 1974, Kappel 1969, Krämer and Schubert 1970, Maier 1970, Pingel 1971). Schubert (1972) continued the excavations at Manching and by the end of 1967 field season he uncovered 30,209 m² (approximately 3 ha or 7.2 acres). From the beginning of the excavations at

**Figure 9.9.** Model of the clay-brick wall superimposed on a photograph of Heuneburg. (Courtesy of W. Kimmig.)

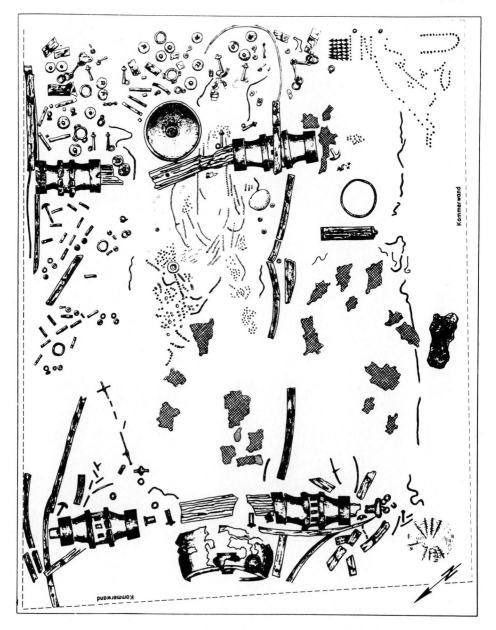

Kammerwand

Kammerwand

**Figure 9.10.** Plan of Wagon-Grave VI in a burial mound near the Heuneburg settlement. (Courtesy of W. Kimmig.)

**Figure 9.11.** Reconstruction of Wagon-Grave VI in a burial mound near the Heuneburg settlement. (Courtesy of W. Kimmig.)

Manching to the end of 1967 field work, an area of over 54,000 m² (5.4 ha or 13 acres) was uncovered (Schubert 1972). This represents approximately 1.5% of the settlement.

The houses uncovered in some areas at Manching were large and rectangular, with one structure, built of posts, measuring 6 × 35 m. Other houses were as long as 41 m, and had trenches or slots dug into the ground to receive the uprights of the outside walls (Schubert 1972).

A great variety of artifacts was found at Manching: horse trappings; razors and shears for shaving and cutting hair; sickles, scythes, and plow shares for agricultural work; ingots for iron production, vessels of metal and wood; jewelry; fire dogs and irons for hearths; spindle whorls and needles for textile working; weapons; metal-working tools. It is clear that the inhabitants practiced a large number of different activities, some of them, perhaps, as occupational specializations.

It is possible that this site was the political center of a highly developed chiefdom, or even a primitive or archaic state. The agricultural land around Manching is poor, but the area has rich iron-ore deposits. Likewise, the east–west route along the Danube, and the route to the south along the Paar River, pass by the site. Thus, control of vital raw materials, plus a central location in the transport and communications network of the region, could have formed the basis of the settlement's political power.

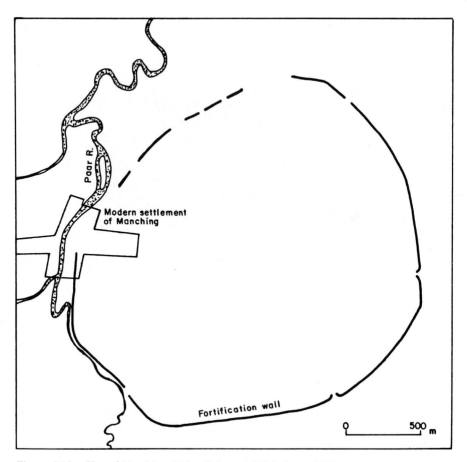

**Figure 9.12.** Plan of Manching. (After Krämer and Schubert 1970.)

## Lusatian

We know more about the Lusatian settlement system during the Hallstatt period than we do about any other archaeological culture north of Alps. As previously mentioned, Lusatian settlements are found in northern Bohemia, the German Democratic Republic, and Poland at this time. The famous fortified Lusatian settlements such as Senftenberg and Biskupin have always attracted the attention of archaeologists.

There appear to be two kinds of settlements: fortified ones and unfortified or open settlements. Much information has been recovered about the former, but the size, function, house types, and so forth, of the latter, remain unclear. In part, this is because of the excessive attention given by archaeologists to Lusatian cemeteries (of which there are 2830 in Poland alone) (T. Malinowski 1961) to the exclusion of Lusatian settlements.

The open sites are known mostly by material collected from their surfaces, mainly pottery (Bukowski 1967). Most excavations have revealed only pits, but at a few sites, notably Konin, Poland (Bronze Age V, EB, or approximately 900–700 B.C.), the remains of houses were found. There were eight houses, of which two were square, with an area of 16 m², and containing one hearth each (Pieczyński 1965). Such houses probably contained one nuclear family, and the overall population of such settlements was small: They could be termed small hamlets. There appears to have been from 10 to 20 such sites for every Lusatian fortified site (Ostoja-Zagórski 1974).

However, as is suggested by the sites found in the Jankowo region, the Lusatian settlement system was probably more complicated than this. Here there are fortified and open sites, but also cemeteries, hoards, and stray finds (Figure 9.13). If they represent settlements at all, these last may be the remains of herding camps, occupied only for a very short time.

The locations of the fortified Lusatian settlements vary in different regions. In the German and Polish lowlands, they are frequently located near lakes,

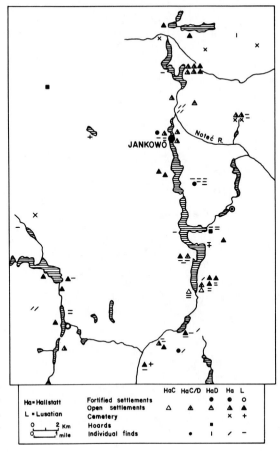

**Figure** 9.13. Lusatian settlements of the Hallstatt period in the Jankowo region, Inowrocław district, Poland. (After Ostoja-Zagórski 1974.)

| | | HaC | HaC/D | HaD | Ha | L |
|---|---|---|---|---|---|---|
| Ha = Hallstatt | Fortified settlements | | • | • | • | ○ |
| L = Lusatian | Open settlements | △ | ▲ | ▲ | ▲ | ▲ |
| | Cemetery | | | | × | + |
| 0 ___ 2 Km | Hoards | | | ■ | | |
| 0 ___ 1 mile | Individual finds | | | • | I | / — |

rivers, or on local elevations. In the mountainous regions of southern Poland, Germany, and Czechoslovakia, they are located on top of the mountains, at 700–800-m elevations a.s.l.

The average distance between fortified settlements is 20–25 km; their sizes range from less than 1 ha to 9 ha or more, though most are no larger than 2.5 ha. Such sites vary in shape: oval, round, square, and trapezoidal plans are known.

Figure 9.14 clearly illustrates this variability of the Lusatian fortified sites in one small area of north–central Poland. The same observation is also seen in Niesiołowska-Wędzka's (1974) data:

| Name of the site | Chronology | Size | Shape of the settlement |
|---|---|---|---|
| Biskupin | Ha D | 2.0 ha | Oval |
| Izdebno | Ha D | 1.7 ha | Oval |
| Jankowo | Ha D | 1.5 ha | Round |
| Sobiejuchy | Ha C | 6.0 ha | Irregular square (quandrangle) |

Most of the walls of Lusatian forts were built using the so-called box construction method, which involved constructing a series of large wooden boxes, which were then filled with earth.

The internal organization of many Lusatian settlements is not the same as that of Biskupin or Senftenberg, where wooden houses are usually rectangular

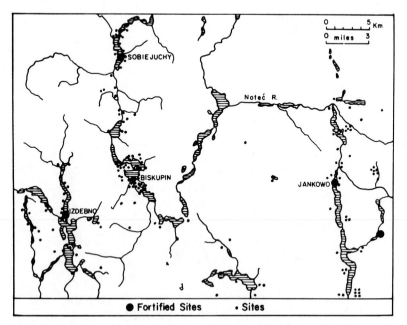

**Figure 9.14.** Distribution of Lusatian sites in Inowrocław area, Poland. (After Ostoja-Zagórski 1974.)

in shape. Usually more than one occupation is found in the fortified sites. That is, the settlements were frequently rebuilt after being destroyed, perhaps in local wars, or perhaps as a result of Scythian raids from eastern Europe.

## Senftenberg

Senftenberg is located in the Elster River Valley in the German Democratic Republic. It is dated to Hallstatt C/D period and belongs to the local or Billendorf phase of the Lusatian culture. There are two phases of occupation at Senftenberg and I will discuss the first one. The fortifications enclose an area of approximately 1 ha, and consist of three wooden palisades, the spaces between which were filled with earth (Herrmann 1969) (Figures 9.15 and 9.16). Approximately 25 rectangular buildings were found in the settlement. They varied in size and were built of wooden posts. It should be noted that the distributions of postmolds at Senftenberg do not always indicate clearly the outlines of square or rectangular houses of a particular size. In fact, in some

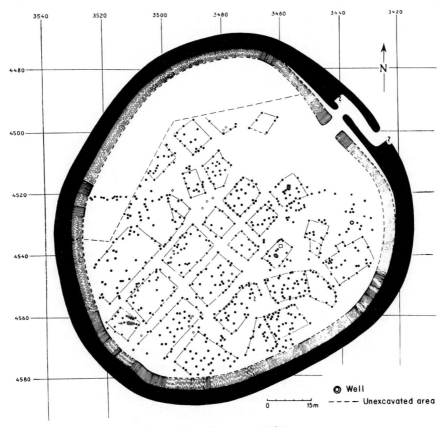

**Figure 9.15.** Plan of Senftenberg. (From Herrmann 1969.)

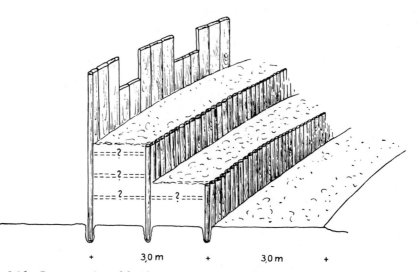

+        3,0 m        +        3,0 m        +

**Figure 9.16.** Reconstruction of fortifications at Senftenberg. (From Herrmann 1969.)

instances, the analyst can reconstruct whatever sort of structure he wishes from the postmold patterns. A street that was 3 m wide ran along the fortification walls inside the settlement. The site had a gate 3–4 m wide, with a square or open space near it inside the site. Within this area was found a well, which was probably used by the entire community.

## Biskupin

Biskupin is one of the most famous Iron Age settlements in Europe. It was located on an island in Biskupin Lake, in north–central Poland. The artifactual remains are very well preserved, and the excavators uncovered large areas of the site, so that Biskupin presents us with an excellent picture of an Iron Age fortified site of the Hallstatt D period in north–central Europe.

The settlement occupied the entire island, an area of approximately 2 ha (5 acres), and was surrounded by a palisade 3 m wide and 6 m high (Figure 9.17). In addition, a breakwater consisting of several rows of oak logs was constructed in the lake near the settlement to protect the shores of the island and the foundations of the palisade from erosion due to wave action, and also to create a further obstacle to attack on the settlement. A bridge, 120 m long, led from the gate in the palisade to the mainland. The gate itself was 3 m wide and was flanked by a tower. The palisade was built of logs in the form of boxes that were filled with earth (Figure 9.18). As in the case of many fortified settlements, Biskupin was destroyed more than once and later rebuilt again.

Inside the settlement, a circular street, 3 m wide, ran for 417 m along the palisade. During one occupational phase, the settlement consisted of 104–106 wooden houses, each roughly 8 × 9 m in area (Figure 9.19) (Rajewski 1965,

**Figure 9.17.** Reconstruction of the settlement at Biskupin. (Courtesy of W. Hensel.)

**Figure 9.18.** Excavation of the palisade at Biskupin. (Courtesy of W. Hensel.)

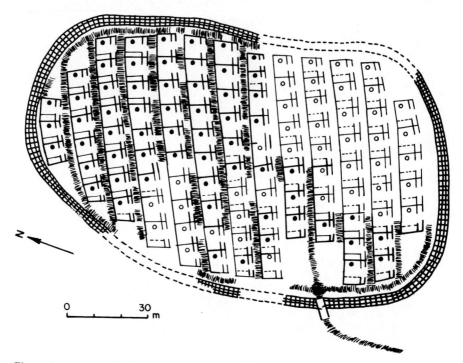

**Figure 9.19.** Plan of Biskupin. (After Rajewski 1970.)

1970). The great similarity of houses at Biskupin has probably been overemphasized. Niesiołowska-Wędzka (1974) mentions that they varied in area from 71.7 to 89.5 m². There were 13 rows of houses and they were separated by 11 streets, 2.6–2.8 m wide. The streets were paved with wooden posts and the longest street was 131 m long. A small square, 358 m², was situated between the seventh and ninth streets.

All the houses of roughly similar size had an entrance hall and a living room. Inside each house, there was a stone hearth and a bed for the whole family, located to the left of the entrance, which was always in the southern wall (Figure 9.20). The floors were made of wood and the roof was thatched. A ladder made of a single tree trunk was used to get to the loft. Altogether the houses covered approximately 8300 m² or 42% of the entire settlement. Over 8000 m³ of wood, mostly oak, pine, alder, and birch as well as 10,000 m³ of dirt and clay were used in building the settlement.

Inside the settlement, numerous stone, wood, bronze, and iron artifacts were found including wooden plows, carts, dugouts, looms, ladders, bone and antler tools, projectile points, pottery, and iron and bronze sickles.

Biskupin's population has probably been overestimated. Rajewski (1970) estimated the population at about 1250, assuming an average 10 to 12 persons per house. If we assume that each house was occupied at the same time and

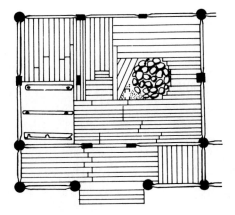

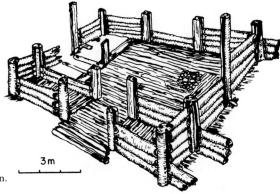

**Figure 9.20.** House of Biskupin.
(After Rajewski 1970.)

had the same function, the population would decrease to 700–750 people using Naroll's (1962) method (assuming the average house size to have been 8 × 9 m or 72 m²).

It should be noted that large amounts of food would have been needed to support such a large population at Biskupin. The surrounding countryside outside the island settlement must have been used for cultivating cereals and leguminous plants. It is unclear where the inhabitants kept the domestic animals during the winter, since there is little free space for such a purpose within the settlement.

In the fifth century B.C., Biskupin was destroyed for the last time. Around that time many other Lusatian fortified sites were destroyed. Some archaeologists blame the Scythian incursions into central Europe for this destruction. As mentioned, the distribution of Scythian projectile points may reflect these raids, as might such rare finds as the gold objects found at Witaszkowo in the Gubin region, Poland (Figure 9.21) (Hensel 1969).

**Figure 9.21.** Scythian gold objects from Witaszkowo, Poland. (Courtesy of W. Hensel.)

## Political Organization

During the Iron Age, there were such state societies as Greek, Etruscan, Roman, and Carthaginian in the Mediterranean and the Black Sea regions. Also, historians speak of Scythian kings in the steppes of the Ukraine; however, such terms might only be appropriate for some Scythian leaders in the Near East. During their military incursions, Scythian leaders sometimes usurped the political authority of local states as they did at Urartu in Azerbaidzhan in the seventh century B.C. (Rice 1957).

As much as I would like to demonstrate the appearance of state societies in barbarian Europe during the Iron Age, the present evidence for this is inconclusive. In the territories adjacent to the Roman Empire, small local states probably developed in the second and first centuries B.C. The Greek city-states could have played the same role to local societies in the Black Sea region.

Crumley (1974) studied the social structure of the Celtic societies during the La Tène II (250–120 B.C.) and La Tène III (120–50 B.C.) periods in France (Gaul) from archaeological and literary sources. Crumley noted that Celtic society was changing very rapidly immediately before the Roman conquest. The initial motivation for that change came as a result of Etruscan, Greek, and Roman economic interest in the natural resources of Gaul and areas to the north, which brought considerable amounts of new wealth into the Celtic economy (Crumley 1974:viii).

Most of the Celtic societies were still only at the chiefdom level of development. However, some Celtic societies in southern France seem to have been small states even if Crumley (1974) considers them only to have been moving toward statehood. For example, Crumley states (1974:70):

> Huge sites like Bibracte and Alesia were the flower of Celtic urban life and give us invaluable information on the increasingly sophisticated class and status differentiations within a society moving rapidly toward statehood. The contemporaneous existence of quarters for the rich, the well-to-do (who may have been merchants and petty officials), the poor and the destitute (as at Bibracte) speaks for the existence of at least three and perhaps four classes: the governing aristocracy, a middle class of merchants, civil employees, and guild members of the skilled trades, followed by agriculturalists, and finally a group of refugees and the destitute who may have worked as jobbers in agriculture and industry. Status distinctions are reflected by the relative wealth of the homes of some members of the trades as compared to others practicing the same occupation.

Literary evidence by classical writers such as Posidonius (ca. 200–118 B.C.) suggests that Celtic society consisted of two status groups: the aristocracy and the commoners. The so-called aristocracy probably was comprised of the elite of the different chiefdoms. Crumley (1974) emphasized that a patron–client relationship was the basis of Celtic political organization and this already had been observed by Polybius in his work *Historia*. We can assume that the elite expected certain obligations such as military and economic services from the lower-status individuals and, vice versa, for the chiefs had to look after the interests of their followers. Crumley offers Wolf's (1966) analysis of patron–client relationship in complex or state societies to explain such an interaction: "the patron offers economic assistance and the protection from legal and illegal authority, while the client offers demonstrations of esteem, information on the machinations of others, and the promise of political support [Crumley 1974:19]."

As discussed, there is no direct archaeological evidence available for the presence of state societies north of the Alps. There are large spectacular sites such as Heuneburg and Manching, and spectacular burials, but this evidence is insufficient to demonstrate the appearance of state societies. Neither the settlement data nor literary information of classical writers can clarify this problem. When sites such as Manching are more extensively excavated and the entire regional settlement system is studied, then we may have the answer for the earliest appearance of state societies north of the Alps. It should be reiterated that I am not emphasizing the traditional markers of a state society, such as the presence of writing.

Probably chiefdoms at different levels of development predominated in western, central, and eastern Europe during the Iron Age. This can be illustrated by the so-called burials of "princes," (*Fürstengräber*) in central and western Europe. I will not call them burials of princes but of the elite individuals of complex chiefdoms. These burials are differentiated from less spectacular or common burials by the presence of nonlocal goods from the Mediterranean area such as gold objects and sometimes chariots (Schaaff 1969). During

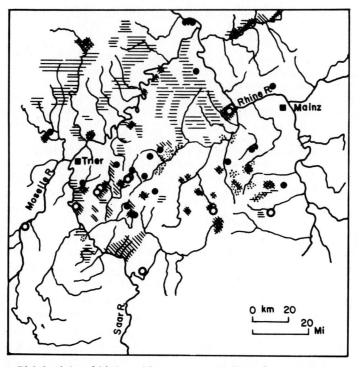

O Rich burials of high ranking persons   ＼Spar iron deposits
● Burials of high ranking persons   ⊏Brown iron deposits
✹ Red iron deposits   ⁖Copper deposits

**Figure 9.22.** Distribution of burials of high-status individuals and sources of iron ore in the Moselle, Rhine, and Saar area. (After Driehaus 1965.)

the La Tène period, the following regional groups of elite burials were found:

1. Upper Palatinate (Oberpfalz) in Germany, Western Austria, Bohemia
2. Marne area of France
3. Central France
4. Rhine–Saar–Moselle area, Germany
5. Upper Rhine area

The accumulation of wealth by the elites of the complex chiefdoms might be related to their control of trade, local mineral resources, etc. For example, Driehaus (1965) noted that there is a correlation between iron sources and rich burials in the Middle Rhine, Moselle, and Saar area during the La Tène period (Figure 9.22). During the Iron Age the elite usually were not cremated and there was a general trend toward inhumation burials. The contents of these rich burials included gold objects and bronze vessels from the Mediterranean area, probably Italy (Figure 9.23) (Driehaus 1966). The rich burials are usually associated with males. However, the very rich burial at Vix, France, belonged to a 35-year-old female. She was buried under a mound 42 m in

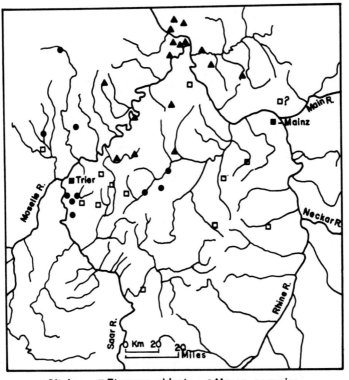

**▲Situlae  □Etruscan objects  ●Marne ceramics**

**Figure 9.23.** Distribution of situlae, Etruscan vessels (except beaked vessels), and Marne ceramics. (After Driehaus 1966.)

diameter and 6 m high. Her grave goods included a wagon, a golden diadem on her head, bracelets, amber beads, brooches, and a bronze vessel (krater) 164 cm high and weighing 208.6 kg (Filip 1962).

It is possible that the exploitation of iron sources in the Middle Rhine, Moselle, and Saar area made it possible for the local elite to accumulate nonlocal luxury goods. Driehaus mentions that Schindler had found evidence for iron exploitation in this area during the Late La Tène period. Also, we should note that the large cemetery near the Hallstatt salt mine probably contained around 2000 burials (Kromer 1959). The burials exhibited a variability in grave goods. Some of the richest burials are of the so-called warriors, who are so named because their graves contain weapons. Probably these burials can be attributed to the elite individuals at Hallstatt.

In summary, presently no conclusive evidence exists for state societies north of the Alps. However, analysis of Iron Age settlement systems such as that of the Manching region may reveal the three-level hierarchy which would suggest the presence of states. Also we should not assume that chiefdoms were found in all areas of the barbarian Europe. In the northern areas of Scandinavia and the Soviet Union, tribal and band societies persisted.

*Chapter 10*
_____

# Conclusion

I have traced cultural evolution, as it is reflected in European prehistory, from its beginnings in hunter–gatherer societies to the origins of states and empires. More than 1 million years of cultural behavior are fossilized in the archaeological remains found in Europe, and these remains are rich, varied, and explored to a greater extent than in other continents. Because of the wide spectrum of information available, the topics of this book had to be selected carefully. I chose to focus on those aspects of culture that are most directly expressed in archaeological data—economy and land use, settlement patterns, trade or exchange, material culture and technology—and I interpreted this evidence in terms of the social behavior that one would expect to have produced such evidence. However, it is quite clear that frequently the archaeological work concentrated on a single site is no longer adequate for the questions I asked or raised about these topics. More emphasis must be placed on archaeological investigations on a regional scale, especially for the Bronze and Iron ages.

The anthropological focus allowed me to compare and contrast the prehistoric societies of Europe with the range of societies that ethnographers have observed during the past 100 years. It brought into clearer view the similarities and differences between societies that are reflected in the ethnographic record and those that have preceded them, and it highlighted the intrinsic characteristics of prehistoric Europe.

Europe has always been a rich cultural mosaic, with strong differences in culture and history compressed into a relatively small part of the world's surface. Consequently, the picture of European cultural evolution that this book has presented is necessarily simplified: Trends of culture change were stressed instead of cultural stability and stagnation, and pattern and regularity were overemphasized at the cost of the range of variation. As archaeological research in Europe progresses, we will gain a better understanding of these cultural differences and of the processes that link European societies to one another and to their past. Thus, I look forward to seeing this account of European prehistory amended, rounded out, corrected, and redrawn. Such action would serve to strengthen a basic assumption that underlies this book, namely, that European prehistory is a dynamic field of research that has made, and will continue to make, important contributions in evaluating our knowledge about the cultural processes of the past.

# References

Adams, R. M.
1971 *The evolution of urban society.* Chicago: Aldine-Atherton.

Allen, W. L., and J. B. Richardson III
1971 The reconstruction of kinship from archaeological data: The Concepts, the methods, and the feasibility. *American Antiquity* 36(No. 1):41–53.

Ammerman, A. J., and L. L. Cavalli-Sforza
1972 Measuring the rate of spread of early farming in Europe. *Man* 6:674–688.

Andersen, K.
1951 Hytter fra Maglemosetid, Danmarks aeldste boliger. *Fra Nationalmuseets Arbejdsmark.* Copenhagen: National Museet. Pp. 69–76.

Andersen, N. A.
1975 Die neolithische Befestingungsanlage in Sarup auf Fünen (Dänemark). *Archäologisches Korrespondenzblatt* 5(No. 1):11–14.

Angel, J. L.
1973 Early Neolithic people of Nea Nikomedeia. In *Die Anfänge des Neolithikums vom Orient bis Nordeuropa,* edited by H. Schwabedissen. Teil VIIIa, Anthropologie, Cologne: Böhlau. Pp. 103–112.

Bakker, J. A., J. C. Vogel, and T. Wiślański
1969 TRB and other C14 dates from Poland (Part B). *Helinium* 9(3):209–238.

Balcer, B.
1971 "O stanie i potrzebach w zakresie badań krzemieniarstwa neolitu i wczesnej epoki brązu." *Wiadomości Archeologiczne,* 36:51–70.
1975 *Krzemień świeciechowski w kulturze pucharów lejkowatych: eksploatacja, obróbka i rozprzestrzenienie.* Wrocław-Warszawa-Kraków, Gdansk: Ossolineum.

Banner, J.
1956 *Die Pecéler Kultur.* Budapest: Archaeologia Hungarica.

Barth, F.
1958 Ecologic relationships of ethnic groups in Swat, north Pakistan. *American Anthropologist* 58:107–189.

Beck, C. W., A. B. Adams, G. C. Southard, and C. Fellows
1971 Determination of the origin of Greek amber artifacts by computer-classification of

infrared spectra. In *Science and archaeology*, edited by R. H. Brill. Cambridge: The MIT Press. Pp. 235–240.

Becker, C. J.
  1945   "En 8000-aarig Stenalderboplads i Holmegaards Mose." *Fra Nationalmuseets Arbejdsmark*. Copenhagen: National Museet. Pp. 61–72.

Behrens, H.
  1973   *Die Jungsteinzeit im Mittelelbe-Saale-Gebiet*. Berlin: VEB Verlag der Wissenschaften.

Beyer, A. I.
  1972   *Das Erdwerk der Michelsberger Kultur auf dem Hetzenberg bei Heilbronn-Neckargartach, Teil II, Die Tierknochenfunde*. Stuttgart: Forschungen und Berichte Vor-und Frühgeschichte in Baden-Württemberg, Vol. 3/II.

Binford, L. R.
  1968   Post-Pleistocene adaptations. In *New perspectives in archeology*, edited by S. R. Binford and L. R. Binford. Chicago: Aldine. Pp. 313–341.
  1973   Interassemblage variability—the Mousterian and the "Functional" argument. In *The explanation of culture change: Models in prehistory*, edited by C. Renfrew. Pittsburgh, Pennsylvania: University of Pittsburgh Press. Pp. 227–254.
  1976   Forty-seven trips: A case study in the character of some formation processes of the archaeological record. In *Contributions to anthropology: The interior peoples of northern Alaska*, edited by E. S. Hall, Jr. Ottawa, Canada: National Museum of Man. Pp. 299–381.

Binford, L. R., and S. R. Binford
  1966   A preliminary analysis of functional variability in the Mousterian of Levallois Facies. *American Anthropologist* (special edition) 68(No. 2, Part 2):238–295.

Bintliff, J.
  1976   The plain of Western Macedonia and the Neolithic site of Nea Nikomedeia. *Proceedings of the Prehistoric Society* 42:241–262.

Bloch, M. E. F.
  1968   Tombs and conservatism among the Merina of Madagascar. *Man* 3:94–104.

Boessneck, A., A. von der Driesch, U. Meyer-Lemppenau, and E. Wechsler-von Ohlen
  1971   *Die Tierknochenfunde aus dem Oppidum von Manching*. Wiesbaden: Franz Steiner.

Bognár-Kutzián, I.
  1963   *The Copper age cemetery of Tiszapolgár-Basatanya* Budapest: Hungarian Academy of Sciences.

Bökönyi, S.
  1959   Die Frühalluviale Wirbeltierfauna Ungarns (Vom Neolithikum bis zur La Tène Zeit). *Acta Archaeologica* 11:39–102.
  1970   Animal remains from Lepenski Vir. *Science* 167:1702–1704.
  1974   *History of domestic mammals in central and eastern Europe*. Budapest: Akadémiai Kiadó.

Bordes, F.
  1953   Essai de classification des industries "moustériennes." *Bulletin de la Société Préhistorique Française*, 50:457–466.
  1961a  *Mousterian cultures in France. Science* 134(No. 3482):803–810.
  1961b  *Typologie du Paléolithique ancien et moyen*, Institut de Préhistoire de l'Université de Bordeaux, Memoire, No. 1.
  1972   *A tale of two caves*. New York: Harper and Row.
  1973   On the chronology and contemporaneity of different Palaeolithic cultures in France. In *The explanation of culture change: Models in prehistory*, edited by C. Renfrew. Pittsburgh, Pennsylvania: University of Pittsburgh Press. Pp. 217–226.

Boriskovskij, P. I.
  1958   Izuchenie paleoliticheskikh zhilishch v Sovetskom Soyuze. *Sovetskaya Arkheologiya* 1:3–19.

Brandtner, F.
1949   Das Niedermoor von Sappl, Kärnten. *Archaeologia Austriaca* 4:72–86.
Břeň, J.
1972   The present state of research into the problems of Celtic oppida in central Europe. *Bulletin of the Institute of Archaeology* 10:13–22.
Bricker, H. M.
1976   Upper Palaeolithic archaeology. In *Annual review of anthropology*, Vol. 5, edited by B. J. Siegel, A. R. Beals, and S. A. Tyler. Palo Alto, California: Annual Reviews Inc. Pp. 133–148.
Buchvaldek, M., and D. Koutecký
1970   *Vikletice, ein Schnurkeramisches Gräberfeld.* Prague: Universita Karlova.
Bukowski, Z.
1967   Uwagi o problematyce badań osadnictwa kultury łużyckiej. In *Studia z Dziejów Osadnictwa*, edited by A. Rutkowska-Płachcińska, Vol. 5. Wrocław-Warszawa-Kraków: Ossolineum. Pp. 54–125.
Burgess, C.
1970   The Bronze Age. *Current Archaeology* 2(No. 8):208–215.
Burkitt, M.
1933   *The Old Stone age.* Cambridge: Cambridge University Press.
Buttler, W., and W. Haberey
1936   *Die bandkeramische Ansiedlung bei Köln-Lindenthal.* Berlin: Walter de Gruyter and Company.
Butzer, K.
1971   *Environment and archaeology: An introduction to Pleistocene geography* (second edition). Chicago: Aldine-Atherton.
1977   Environment, culture, and human evolution. *American Scientist* 65(No. 5):572–584.
Butzer, K. W., and G. L. Isaac, eds.
1975   *After the Australopithecines: Stratigraphy, ecology, and culture change in the Middle Pleistocene.* The Hague: Mouton.
Campbell, J. M.
1968   Territoriality among ancient hunters: Interpretations from ethnography and nature. In *Anthropological archeology in the Americas*, edited by B. J. Meggers. Washington, D.C.: The Anthropological Society of Washington. Pp. 1–21.
Carneiro, R.
1970   A Theory of the origin of the state. *Science* 169:733–738.
Case, H.
1976   Acculturation and the Earlier Neolithic in Western Europe. In *Dissertation Archaeologicae Gandenses*, edited by S. J. De Laet. Brugge. Pp. 45–58.
Chadwick, J.
1972   The Mycenaean documents. In *The Minnesota Messenia expedition: Reconstructing a Bronze Age regional environment*, edited by W. A. McDonald and G. R. Rapp Jr. Minneapolis: The University of Minnesota Press. Pp. 100–116.
Charles, J. A.
1969   A metallurgical examination of south-east European copper axes (Appendix I). In "The autonomy of the south-east European Copper age," by C. Renfrew. *Proceedings of the Prehistoric Society* (New Series) 35:40–42.
Chernysh, A. P.
1953   *Volodymyrivs'ka paleolitychna stoyanka.* Kiev: Akademiya Nauk.
1961   *Paleolitychna stoyanka Molodove 5.* Kiev: Akademiya Nauk.
Childe, V. G.
1929   *The Danube in prehistory.* Oxford: Oxford University Press.
1930   *The Bronze Age.* Cambridge: Cambridge University Press.

1950 *Prehistoric migrations in Europe.* Oslo: Instituttet for Sammelignende Kulturforskning.
1951 *Man makes himself.* New York: The New American Library.
1957 *The dawn of European civilisation.* London: Routledge and Kegan Paul Ltd.
1958 *The prehistory of European society.* Baltimore, Maryland: Penguin Books.
Chmielewska, M.
1954 Grób kultury tardenoaskiej w Janisławicach, pow. Skierniewice. *Wiadomości Archeologiczne* 20(No. 1):23–48.
Chmielewski, W.
1952 *Zagadnienie grobowców kujawskich w świetle ostatnich badań,* Łódź: Wydawnictwo Muzeum Archeologicznego w Łodzi.
1975 Paleolit środkowy i górny. In *Prahistoria Ziem Polskich, Vol. 1, Paleolit i Mezolit,* edited by W. Chmielewski and W. Hensel. Wrocław-Warszawa-Kraków-Gdańsk: Ossolineum. Pp. 9–158.
Chropovský, B.
1960 Gräberfeld aus der älteren Bronzezeit in Vel'ký Grob. In *Gräberfeld aus der älteren Bronzezeit in der Slowakei I,* edited by A. Točik. Bratislava: Verlag der Slowakischen Akademie der Wissenschaften. Pp. 13–89.
Clark, J. G. D.
1936 *The Mesolithic settlement of northern Europe.* Cambridge: Cambridge University Press.
1952 Prehistoric Europe: The economic basis. Stanford: Stanford University Press. (Reissued 1952 edition).
1954 *Excavations at Star Carr.* Cambridge: Cambridge University Press.
1972 *Star Carr: A case study in bioarchaeology.* Reading, Massachusetts: Addison-Wesley Modular Publications, No. 10.
1975 *The earlier Stone Age settlement of Scandinavia.* Cambridge: Cambridge University Press.
Clason, A. T.
1967 The animal bones found at the Bandkeramik settlement by Bylany. *Archeologické rozhledy,* 19(No. 1):(90–96.
1969 Einige Bemerkungen über Viehzucht, Jagd und Knochenbearbeitung bei der mitteldeutschen Schnurkeramik. In *Die neolitischen Becherkulturen im Gebiet der DDR und ihre europäischen Beziehungen,* edited by H. Behrens and F. Schlette, Veröffentlichungen des Landesmuseums für Vorgeschichte in Halle, Vol. 24. Pp. 173–195.
1973 Some aspects of stock-breeding and hunting in the period after the Bandceramic culture north of the Alps. In *Domestikationsforschung und Geschichte der Haustiere,* edited by J. Matolcsi. Budapest: Akadémiei Kiadó. Pp. 205–212.
Coblenz, W.
1963 Bemerkungen zur Funktion der lausitzer Burgen Sachsens. In *Munera Archaeologica Iosepho Kostrzewski,* edited by K. Jażdżewski, W. Hensel, and J. W. Kočka. Poznań: Poznańskie Towarzystwo Przyjaciół Nauk. Pp. 193–200.
1971 Zur Frage der befestigten Siedlungen der Lausitzer Kultur. In *Actes du VII^e Congrès International des Sciences Préhistoriques et Protohistoriques,* Vol. I, edited by J. Filip. Prague: Institut d'Archéologie de l'Academie Tchécoslovaque des Sciences. Pp. 715–719.
Coles, J.
1975 Ancient trackways of the Somerset levels: *Archaeology* 28(3):148–156.
Coles, J. M., and F. A. Hibbert
1968 Prehistoric roads and tracks in Somerset England: 1. Neolithic. *Proceedings of the Prehistoric Society* 34:238–258.
Coles, J. M., and E. S. Higgs
1969 *The archaeology of early man,* New York: Frederick A. Praeger.

Collins, D.
1970 Stone artifact analysis and the recognition of culture traditions. *World Archaeology* 2(No. 1):27–27.

Combier, J., ed.
1976 *L'Évolution de l'Acheuléen en Europe*, Nice: Union Internationale Des Sciences Préhistoriques et Protohistoriques.

Cook, S. F.
1972 *Prehistoric demography*. Reading, Massachusetts: Addison-Wesley Modular Publications, No. 16.

Crumley, C.
1974 *Celtic social structure: The generation of archaeologically testable hypotheses from literary evidence*. Anthropological Papers, Museum of Anthropology No. 54. Ann Arbor: University of Michigan.

Czarnetzki, A., and H.
1971 Gebisse aus dem bandkeramischen Gräberfeld bei Niedermerz. *Bonner Jahrbücher* 171:652–660.

Daniel, G.
1963 *The megalithic builders of western Europe*, Baltimore, Maryland: Penguin.

Darling, F.
1969 *A herd of red deer*. Oxford: Oxford University Press.

David, A. I., and V. I. Markevich
1967 Fauna mlekopitayushchikh poselenya Noviye Ruseshti I. *Izvestia Adademii Nauk Moldavskoi SSR* 4:3–26.

Deetz, J.
1965 *The dynamics of stylistic change in Arikara ceramics*. Urbana: University of Illinois Press.
1968 The inference of residence and descent rules from archeological data. In *New Perspectives in Archeology*, edited by S. R. Binford and L. R. Binford. Chicago: Aldine. Pp. 41–48.

de Lumley, H.
1969 A Paleolithic camp at Nice. *Scientific American* 220(No. 5):42–50.
1975 Cultural evolution in France in its paleoecological setting during the Middle Pleistocene. In *After the Australopithecines: Stratigraphy, ecology, and culture change in the Middle Pleistocene*, edited by K. W. Butzer and G. L. Isaac. The Hague: Mouton. Pp. 745–808.

Dennel, R. W.
1972 The interpretation of plant remains: Bulgaria. In *Papers in economic prehistory*, edited by E. S. Higgs. Cambridge: Cambridge University Press. Pp. 149–159.
1974 Neolithic flax in Bulgaria. *Antiquity* 48(No. 191):220–222.

Dennel, R. W., and D. Webley
1975 Prehistoric settlement and land use in southern Bulgaria. In *Palaeoeconomy*, edited by E. S. Higgs. Cambridge: Cambridge University Press. Pp. 97–109.

Diakonov, I. M.
1969 The rise of the despotic state in ancient Mesopotamia. In *Ancient Mesopotamia, socioeconomic history*, edited by I. M. Diakonov. Moscow: Nauka Publishing House. Pp. 173–203.

Divale, W.
1974 Migration, external warfare and matrilocal residence. *Behavior Science Research* 9(No. 2):75–133.

Dombay, J.
1960 *Die Siedlung und das Gräberfeld in Zengövárkony: Beiträge zur Kultur des Aeneolithikums in Ungarn*. Budapest: Ungarischen Akademie der Wissenschaften.

Driehaus, J.
1965 "Fürstengräber" und Eisenerze zwischen Mittelrhein, Mosel und Saar. *Germania* 43:32–49.

1966   Zur Verbreitung der eisenzeitlichen situlen im mittelrheinischen Gebirgsland. *Bonner Jahrbücher* **166**:26–47.

Dumitrescu, V.
1965   Căsciorele. *Archaeology* **18**(No. 1):34–40.

Dyson-Hudson, N.
1972   The study of nomads. In *Perspectives on nomadism*, edited by W. Irons and N. Dyson-Hudson. Leiden: E. J. Brill.

Efimenko, P. P.
1953   *Pervobytnoe obshchestvo*. Kiev: Akademiya Nauk Ukrainskoi SSR.
1958   *Kosten'ki, I.* Moscow–Leningrad: Akademiya Nauk.

Ehrich, R. W., ed.
1965   *Chronologies in Old World Archaeology*. Chicago: University of Chicago Press.

Ehrich, R. W., and E. Pleslova-Štiková
1968   *Homolka: An eneolithic site in Bohemia*. Prague: Czechoslovakian Academy of Sciences.

Ember, M.
1973   An archaeological indicator of matrilocal versus patrilocal residence. *American Antiquity* **38**(No. 2):177–182.

Engels, K. F.
1884   *The origin of the family, private property, and the state* (1910 edition). Chicago: C. H. Kerr.

Falkenstein, A.
1965   Zu den Tontafeln aus Tartaria. *Germania* **43**:269–273.

Filip, J.
1962   *Celtic civilization and its heritage*. Prague: Czechoslovakian Academy of Sciences and Artia.

Flannery, K.
1969   Origins and ecological effects of early domestication in Iran and the Near East. In *The domestication and exploitation of plants and animals*, edited by P. J. Ucko and G. W. Dimbleby. Chicago: Aldine. Pp. 73–100.
1972   The cultural evolution of civilizations. *Annual Review of Ecology and Systematics* **3**:399–426.

Florescu, A.
1966   Sistemul de Fortificare al Aşezărilor Cucuteniene din Moldova. *Arheologia Moldovei* **4**:23–37.

Fourastié, J.
1960   *The causes of wealth*. Glencoe: The Free Press.

Frey, O.-H.
1966   Der Ostalpenraum und die antike Welt in der frühen Eisenzeit. *Germania* **44**:48–66.

Freeman, L. G.
1973   The significance of mammalian faunas from Paleolithic occupations in Cantabrian Spain. *American Antiquity* **38**(1):3–44.
1976   (ed.) *Les structures d'habitat au Paléolithique moyen*. Nice: Union Internationale des Sciences Préhistoriques et Protohistoriques.

Frierman, J.
1969   The Balkan graphite ware (Appendix II). In "The autonomy of the South-East European Copper Age," by C. Renfrew. *Proceedings of the Prehistoric Society* (New Series), **35**:42–44.

Gabałówna, L.
1966   *Ze studiów nad grupą brzesko-kujawską kultury lendzielskiej*. Łódź: Acta Archaeologica Lodziensia.

Gallay, G., and R. Schweitzer
1971   Das Bandkeramische Gräberfeld von Rixheim (Dep. Haut-Rhin). *Archäologisches Korrespondenzblatt* **1**(No. 1):15–22.

Garrod, D. A.
1926   *The Upper Palaeolithic age in Britain.* London.
Gerasimov, I. P., ed.
1969   *Priroda i razvitye pervobitnovo obshchestva na teritorii evropeiskoi chasti SSSR,* INQUA Vol. VII. Moscow: Nauka.
Gersbach, E.
1969   Heuneburg-Aussensiedlung-jüngere Adelsnekropole. In *Marburgen Beiträge zur Archäologie der Kelten,* edited by O.-H. Frey. Bonn: Rudolf Habelt, Pp. 29–34.
Gimbutas, M.
1956   *The prehistory of eastern Europe.* American School of Prehistoric Research, Peabody Museum. Cambridge: Harvard University.
1965   *Bronze Age cultures in central and eastern Europe.* The Hague: Mouton and Company.
1970   Obre, Yugoslavia: Two Neolithic sites. *Archaeology* 23(No. 4):287–297.
1972   Excavation at Anza, Macedonia: Further insight into the civilization of old Europe, 7000–4000 B.C. *Archaeology* 25(No. 2):112–123.
1973   The beginning of the Bronze Age in Europe and the Indo–Europeans: 3500–2500 B.C. *The Journal of Indo-European Studies.* 3(No. 2):163–214.
1974   Anza, ca. 6500–5000 B.C.: A cultural yardstick for the study of Neolithic southeast Europe. *Journal of Field Archaeology* 1(No. 1/2):27–66.
Gløb, P. V.
1949   Barkaer Danmarks aeldste landsby. *Fra Natiolnalmuseets Arbejdsmark.* Copenhagen: National Museet. Pp. 5–16.
Greeves, T. A.
1975   The use of copper in the Cucuteni-Tripolye culture of south-east Europe. *Proceedings of the Prehistoric Society* 41:153–166.
Grössler, H.
1907   Das Fürstengrab im grossen Galgenhügel am Paulsschachte bei Helmsdorf. *Jahresschrift fur Vorgeschichte der sächsisch-thüringischen Länder* 6:1–87.
Grüss, J.
1933   Über Milchreste aus der Hallstattzeit und andere Funde. *Forschungen und Fortschritte* 9:105–106.
Guyan, W. U.
1954   Das jungsteinzeitliche Moordorf von Thayngen-Weier. In *Das Pfahlbauproblem,* edited by W. U. Guyan. Schaffhausen: Schweizerische Gesellschaft für Urgeschicte. Pp. 223–272.
Hackett, N. J.
1973   Roman civilization. In *The world of Europe.* Saint Charles, Missouri: Forum Press. Pp. 37–49.
Hajnalová, E.
1973   Prispevok k štúdiu, analýze a interpretácii nálezov kultúrnych rastlin na Slovensku. *Slovenská Archeológica* 21(No. 1):211–218.
Hamilton, J.
1971   The origin and development of Iron Age forts in western Britain. *Actes du VIIᵉ Congrès International des Sciences Préhistoriques et Protohistoriques,* Vol. II, edited by J. Filip. Prague: Institut d'Archéologie de l'Academie Tchécoslovaque de Sciences. Pp. 846–849.
Harris, D.
1972   Swidden systems and settlement. In *Man, settlement, and urbanism,* edited by P. J. Ucko, R. Tringham, and G. W. Dimbleby. London: Duckworth. Pp. 245–262.
Hartmann, A.
1970   *Prähistorische Goldfunde aus Europe: Studien zu den Anfängen der Metallurgie,* Vol. 3. Berlin: Mann.

Hartmann, A., and E. Sangmeister
  1972 The study of prehistoric metallurgy. *Angewandte Chemie* 11(No. 7):620–629.
Häusler, A.
  1966 Zum Verhältnis von Männern, Frauen und Kindern in Gräbern der Steinzeit. *Arbeits und Forschungsberichte zur Sächsischen Bodendenkmalpfege* 14–15:25–73.
Hawkes, J.
  1974 *Atlas of ancient archaeology.* New York: McGraw-Hill.
Helbaek, H.
  1958 Grauballemandens Sidste Måltid. *Kuml.* 83–116.
Henshall, A. S.
  1974 Scottish chambered tombs and long mounds. In *British prehistory: A new outline,* edited by C. Renfrew. London: Duckworth. Pp. 137–164.
Hensel, W.
  1969 *Ziemie Polskie w Pradziejach.* Warsaw: Interpress.
Herrmann, J.
  1969 Burgen und befestigte Siedlungen der jüngeren Bronze und frühen Eisenzeit in Mitteleuropa. In *Siedlung Burg und Stadt: Studien zu ihren Anfängen,* edited by K.-H. Otto and J. Herrmann Berlin: Deutsche Akademie der Wissenschaften zu Berlin Schriften der Sektion für Vor- und Frühgeschichte, Vol. 25. Pp. 56–94.
Higgs, E. S., and M. R. Jarman
  1972 The origins of animal and plant husbandry. In *Papers in Economic Prehistory,* edited by E. S. Higgs. Cambridge: Cambridge University Press. Pp. 3–13.
Higham, C. F. W.
  1968 Stock rearing as a cultural factor in prehistoric Europe. *Proceedings of the Prehistoric Society* 33:84–106.
Hill, J. N.
  1970 Broken K pueblo: Prehistoric social organization in the American southwest. *Anthropological Papers of the University of Arizona,* No. 18. Tucson: The University of Arizona Press.
Hodson, F. R.
  1964 La Tène chronology, continental and British. *Bulletin of the Institute of Archaeology* 4:123–141.
Höfer, P.
  1906 Der Leubinger Hügel. *Jahresschrift für die Vorgeschichte der sächsisch-thüringischen Länder* 5:1–99.
Hood, M. S. F.
  1967 The Tartaria Tablets. *Antiquity* 41:99–113.
  1968 The Tartaria Tablets. *Scientific American,* 218(5):30–37.
Hopf, M.
  1971a Vorgeschichtliche Pflanzenreste aus Ostspanien. *Madrider Mitteilungen* 12:101–114.
  1971b Weizen im Neolithikum Spaniens und Beziehungen zum Ostmediterranean Raum. In *Actes du VIII Congrès International des Sciences Préhistoriques et Protohistoriques,* Vol. II, edited by J. Filip. Prague: Institut d'Archéologie de l'Academie Tchéchoslovaque de Sciences. Pp. 1324–1325.
  1975 Frühe Kulturpflanzen aus Bulgarien. *Jahrbuch des Römisch-Germanischen Zentralmuseums Mainz* 20(1973):1–55.
Howell, F. C.
  1966 Observations on the earlier phases of the European Lower Paleolithic, *American Anthropologist* (special edition) 68(No. 2, Part 2):88–201.
Jacobi, G.
  1974 *Werkzeug und Gerät aus dem Oppidum von Manching,* Vol. V. Wiesbaden: Franz Steiner.

Jarman, H. N.
1972    The origins of wheat and barley cultivation. In *Papers in economic prehistory*, edited by E. S. Higgs. Cambridge: Cambridge University Press. Pp. 15–26.

Jażdżewski, K.
1936    *Kultura Puharów Lejkowatych w Polsce Zachodniej i Srodkowej.* Poznań: Nakładem Polskiego Towarzystwa Prehistorycznego.
1938    Cmentarzyska kultury ceramiki wstęgowej i związane z nimi ślady osadnictwa w Brześciu Kujawskim. *Wiadomości Archeologiczne* 15:1–105.
1965    *Poland.* New York: Frederick A. Praeger.
1970    Związki grobowców kujawskich w Polsce z grobami megalitycznymi w Niemczech pólnocnych, w Danii i w krajach zachodnioeuropeijskich. *Prace i Materiały Muzeum Archeologicznego i Etnograficznego w Łodzi* 17:15–36.

Jelinek, A.
1977    The Lower Paleolithic: Current evidence and interpretations. In *Annual Review of Anthropology* Vol. 6, edited by B. J. Siegel, A. R. Beals, and S. A. Tyler, Palo Alto, California: Annual Reviews Inc. Pp. 11–32.

Jochim, M. A.
1976    *Hunter-gatherer subsistence and settlement.* New York: Academic Press.

Johnson, G.
1973    *Local exchange and early state development in southwestern Iran.* Anthropological Papers, Museum of Anthropology, No. 46. Ann Arbor: University of Michigan.

Jovanović, B.
1971    Early copper metallurgy of the central Balkans. *Actes du VIIIᵉ Congrès International des Sciences Préhistoriques et Protohistoriques* I:131–140.
1973    Chronological frames of the Iron Gate group of Early Neolithic period. *Archaeologia Iugoslavica* 10:23–38.

Junghans, S., E. Sangmeister, and M. Schröder
1960    *Metallanalysen kupferzeitlicher und frühbronzezeitlicher Bodenfunde aus Europa: Studien zu den Anfängen der Metallurgie,* Vol. 1. Berlin: Mann.
1968    *Kupfer und Bronze in der frühen Metallzeit Europas: Studien zu den Anfängen der Metallurgie,* Vol. 2. Berlin: Mann.

Kahlke, D.
1954    *Die Bestattungssitten des Donauländischen Kulturkreises der jüngeren Steinzeit,* Vol. I. Berlin: Linienhandkeramik, Rütten and Loening.

Kamieńska, J., and J. K. Kozłowski
1970    The Lengyel and Tisza cultures. In *The Neolithic in Poland,* edited by T. Wiślański. Wrocław-Warszawa-Kraków: Ossolineum. Pp. 76–143.

Kamieńska, J., and A. Kulczycka-Leciejewiczowa
1970a   The Bell Beaker culture. In *The Neolithic in Poland,* edited by T. Wiślański. Wrocław-Warszawa-Kraków: Ossolineum. Pp. 366–382.
1970b   The Neolithic and Early Bronze Age settlement at Samborzec in the Sandomierz district. *Archaeologica Polona* XII:223–246.

Kapica, Z.
1970    Pochówki neolityczne z grobowców kujawskich w Wietrzychowicach, pow, Koło, w świetle badań antropologicznych. *Prace i Materiały Muzeum Archeologicznego i Etnograficznego w Łodzi* 17:145–155.

Kappel, I.
1969    *Die Graphittonkeramik von Manching.* Wiesbaden: Franz Steiner.

Kimmig, W.
1975    Early Celts on the upper Danube: The excavations at the Heuneburg. In *Recent archaeological excavations in Europe,* edited by R. Bruce-Mitford. London: Routledge and Kegan Paul Ltd. Pp. 32–64.

Kimmig, W., and E. Gersbach
1971  Die Grabungen auf der Heuneburg 1966-1969. *Germania* 49:21-91.
Kingery, W. D., and J. D. Frierman
1974  The firing temperature of a Karanova sherd and inferences about south-east European Chalcolithic refractory technology. *Proceedings of the Prehistoric Society* 40:204-205.
Kjaerum, P.
1954  Striber pa Kryds og tvaers. *Kulm* 4:18-29.
Klein, R. G.
1966  Chellean and Acheulean on the territory of the Soviet Union: A critical review of the evidence as presented in the literature. *American Anthropologist* (special publication) 68(No. 2, Part 2):1-45.
1969  *Man and culture in the Late Pleistocene: A case study.* San Francisco: Chandler Publishing Co.
1973  *Ice-age hunters of the Ukraine.* Chicago, Illinois: University of Chicago Press.
Klichowska, M.
1959  Odciski ziarn zbóż i innych gatunków traw na ułamakach naczyń z neolitycznego stanowiska kultury ceramiki wstęgowej w Strzelcach w pow. mogileńskim. *Fontes Archaeologici Posnanienses* 10:101-103.
1970  Neolityzne szczątki roślinne z Radziejowa Kujawskiego. *Prace i Materiały Muzeum Archeologicznego i Etnograficznego w Łodzi* 17:165-177.
Klima, B.
1962  The first ground-plan of an Upper Paleolithic loess settlement in Middle Europe and its meaning. In *Courses toward urban life,* edited by R. J. Braidwood and G. R. Willey. Chicago, Illinois: Aldine. Pp. 193-210.
1976  (ed.) *Périgordien et Gravettien en Europe.* Nice: Union Internationale des Sciences Préhistoriques et Protohistoriques.
Knörzer, K.-H.
1971a  Pflanzliche Grossreste aus der rössenerzeitlichen Siedlung bei Langweiler, Kreis Jülich. *Bonner Jahrbücher* 171:9-33.
1971b  Eisenzeitliche Pflanzenfunde im Rheinland. *Bonner Jahrbücher* 171:40-58.
1972  Subfossile Pflanzenreste aus der bandkeramischen Siedlung Langweiler 3 und 6, Kreis Jülich, und ein urnenfelderzeitlicher Getreidefund innerhalb dieser Siedlung. *Bonner Jahrbücher* 172:395-403.
1973  Pflanzliche Grossreste. In *Der bandkeramische Siedlungsplatz Langweiler 2,* edited by J. P. Farruggia, R. Kuper, J. Lüning, and P. Stehli. Bonn: Rudolf Habelt. Pp. 139-152.
Kostrzewski, J.
1965  Epoka Żelaza. In *Pradzieje Polski,* edited by W. Chmielewski, K. Jażdżewski, and J. Kostrzewski. Wrocław-Warszawa-Kraków: Ossolineum. Pp. 191-255.
Košturik, P.
1972  *Die Lengyel-Kultur in Mähren,* Prague: Studie Archeologického Ústavu Československé Akademie Věd V Brne.
Kowalczyk, J.
1970  The Funnel Beaker culture. In *The Neolithic in Poland,* edited by T. Wiślański. Wrocław-Warszawa-Kraków: Ossolineum. Pp. 144-177.
Kowiańska-Piaszykowa, M.
1957  Wyniki badań archeologicznych kurhanu III kultury unietyckiej w Łękach Małych w pow. kościańskim. *Fontes Archaeologici Posnanienses* 7:116-138.
Kowiańska-Piaszykowa, M., and S. Kurnatowski
1953  Kurhan kultury unietyckiej w Łękach Małych, pow. Kościan. *Fontes Archaeologici Posnanienses* 4:1-34.
Kozłowski, J. K., ed.
1976  *L'Aurignacien en Europe.* Nice: Union Internationale des Sciences Préhistoriques et Protohistoriques.

Kozłowski, J. K., and A. Kulczycka
1961    Materiały kultury starszej ceramiki wstęgowej z Olszanicy, pow. Kraków. *Materiały Archeologiczne* 3:29–43.
Kozłowski, S. K.
1972    *Pradzieje ziem Polskich od IX do V tysiąclecia p.n.e.* Warsaw: Państwowe Wydanictwo Naukowe.
1973    *The Mesolithic in Europe.* Warsaw: University Press.
1976    (ed.) *Les civilisations du 8ᵉ Au 5ᵉ millénaire avant notre ére en Europe: Paléoenvironnment, structures, d'habitat, outillages, économie.* Nice: Union Internationale des Sciences Préhistoriques et Protohistoriques.
Krämer, W., and F. Schubert
1970    *Die Ausgrabungen in Manching 1955–1961 Einführung und Fundstellenübersicht.* Vol. I. Wiesbaden: Franz Steiner.
Kratochvil, A.
1972    Knochenüberreste von der neolithischen Siedlung Jeleni Louka bei Mikulov. *Přehled Vyzkumů, 1971:* 24–27.
Krauss, B. S.
1959    Occurrence of the Carabelli trait in southwest ethnic groups. *American Journal of Physical Anthropology* 17:117–123.
Kromer, K.
1959    *Das Gräberfeld von Hallstatt.* Florence, Italy: Sansoni.
Kruk, J.
1973a   *Studia osadnicze nad neolitem wyżyn lessowych,* Polska Akademia Nauk. Wrocław-Warszawa-Kraków-Gdańsk: Ossolineum.
1973b   Grób kultury ceramiki sznurowej z Koniuszy, pow. Proszowice. *Sprawozdania Archeologiczne* 25:61–69.
Krukowski, S.
1939    *Krzemionki Opatowskie.* Warsaw.
Kulczycka-Leciejewiczowa, A.
1968    Ze studiów nad kulturą ceramiki wstęgowej w Polsce. *Archaeologia Polski* **XII**(No. 1):56–124.
1969    Nowa Huta—Pleszów osada neolityczna kultury ceramiki wstęgowej rytej i lendzielskiej. *Materiały Archeologiczne Nowej Huty* 2:7–124.
1970a   The Linear and Stroked Pottery cultures. In *The Neolithic in Poland,* edited by T. Wiślański. Wrocław-Warszawa-Kraków: Ossolineum. Pp. 14–75.
1970b   Kultura ceramiki wstęgowej rytej w Polsce (zarys problematyki). In *Z badań nad kulturą ceramiki wstęgowej rytej,* edited by J. K. Kozłowski. Kraków: Polskie Towarzystwo Archeologiczne Oddział w Nowej Hucie.
Lanting, J. N., and J. D. van der Waals
1976    *Glockenbecker Symposium, Oberried 1974.* Bussem/Haarlem: Fibula-van Dishoeck.
Leroi-Gourhan, A., ed.
1976    *Les structures d'habitat au Paléolithique superieur.* Nice: Union Internationale des Sciences Préhistoriques et Protohistoriques.
Lewis, H. S.
1968    Typology and Process in Political Evolution. In *Essays on the problem of tribe,* edited by J. Helm. Seattle: University of Washington Press. Pp. 101–110.
Lichardus, J.
1974    *Studien zur Bükker Kultur.* Bonn: Rudolf Habelt.
Lichardus, J., and J. Pavúk
1963    Bemerkungen zum präkeramischen Neolithikum in der Argissa Magula und zu seiner Existenz in Europa. *Slovenská Archeológia* 11(No. 2):459–476.
Longacre, W. A.
1970    Archaeology as anthropology: A case study. *Anthropological Papers of the Univeristy of Arizona,* No. 17. Tucson: The University of Arizona Press.

Newell, R. R.
    1970    The flint industry of the Dutch Linearbandkeramik. In *Linearbandkeramik aus Elsloo und Stein,* edited by P. J. R. Modderman. Leiden: Analecta Praehistorica Leidensia III. Pp. 144–183.
Newton, R. G., and C. Renfrew
    1970    British faience beads reconsidered. *Antiquity* 64(No. 175):199–206.
Niesiołowska-Wędzka, A.
    1974    *Początki i rozwój grodów kultury łużyckiej.* Wrocław-Warszawa-Kraków-Gdańsk: Ossolineum.
Niezabitowski, E. L.
    1933    Szczątki zwierzęce z osady neolitycznej w Rzucewie na polskiem wybrzeżu Bałtyku. *Przegląd Archeologiczny* 4:64–81.
Okulicz, J.
    1973    *Pradzieje ziem pruskich od późnego paleolitu do VII w.n.e.* Wrocław-Warszawa-Krakow-Gdańsk: Ossolineum.
Olsen, S. J.
    1971    *Zooarchaeology: Animal bones in archaeology and their interpretation.* No. 2. Reading, Massachusetts: Addison-Wesley Modular Publications.
Osterhaus, U.
    1975    Jungsteinzeitliche Gräberfelder am Donantal Gewinne und Verluste. *Ausgrabungsnotizen aus Bayern* 2:1–6.
Osterhaus, U., and R. Pleyer
    1973    Ein bandkeramisches Gräberfeld bei Sengkofen, Ldkr. Regensburg. *Archäologisches Korrespondenzblatt* 3(No. 4):399–402.
Ostoja-Zagórski, J.
    1974    From studies on the economic structure at the decline of the Bronze Age and the Hallstatt Period in the north and west zone of the Odra and Vistula basins. *Przegląd Archeologiczny* 22:123–150.
Passek, T. S.
    1949    Periodizatsya tripolskikh poselenii. *Materialy i Issledovaniya po Arkheologii SSSR,* Vol. 10. Moscow-Leningrad: Akademiya Nauk SSSR.
    1961    Rannezemledelcheskie (tripolske) plemena Podnestrovya, *Materialy i Issledovaniya po Arkheologii SSSR,* Vol. 84. Moscow-Leningrad: Akademiya Nauk SSSR.
Passek, T. S., and E. K. Chernysh
    1963    *Pamyatniki kultury lineyno-lentochnoy keramiki na territorii SSSR,* Moscow: Akademiya Nauk SSSR.
Pauli, L.
    1974    Der goldene Steig. *Studien zur Vor-und Frühgeschichtlichen Archäologie* 1:115–139.
Paulik, J.
    1962    Das Velatice-Baierdorfer Hügelgrab in Očkov. *Slovenská Archeológia* 10(No. 1):6–96.
Pavúk, J.
    1972    Neolithisches Gräberfeld in Nitra. *Slovenská Archeológia* 20(No. 1):5–105.
Pavúk, J., and S. Šiška
    1971    Neolitické a eneolitické osidlenie Slovenska. *Slovenská Archeológia* 19(No. 2):319–364.
Penninger, E.
    1972    *Der Dürrnberg bei Hallein: Katalog der Grabfunde aus der Hallstatt und Latènezeit.* Munich: C. H. Beck.
Petersen, E. B.
    1973    A Survey of the Late Palaeolithic and the Mesolithic of Denmark. In *The Mesolithic in Europe,* edited by S. K. Kozłowski. Warsaw: University Press. Pp. 77–121.
Peyrony, D.
    1949    *Le Périgord prehistorique.* Périgueux: Publication de la Société Historique et Archéologique du Périgord.

Pidoplichko, I. G.
1969  *Pozdnepaleolitichneskie zhilishcha iz kostej mamonta na Ukraine.* Kiev: Naukowa Dumka.
1976  *Mezhiricheskiye zhilishcha iz kostej mamonta na Ukraine.* Kiev: Naukowa Dumka.

Pieczyński, Z.
1965  Osada kultury łużyckiej z V okresu epoki brązu z Konina. *Fontes Archaeologici Posnanienses* 16:1–9.

Piggott, S.
1965  *Ancient Europe: From the beginnings of agriculture to Classical Antiquity.* Chicago: Aldine.
1972  Conclusion. In *Man, settlement and urbanism,* edited by P. J. Ucko, R. Tringham, and G. W. Dimbleby. London: Duckworth. Pp. 947–953.

Pilbeam, D.
1972  *The ascent of man: An introduction to human evolution.* New York: Macmillan Co.

Pingel, V.
1971  *Die glatte Drehscheiben Keramik von Manching.* Wiesbaden: Franz Steiner.

Pittioni, R.
1951  Prehistoric copper-mining in Austria: Problems and facts. In *Institute of Archaeology, Seventh Annual Report.* London: University of London. Pp. 16–43.

Price, T. D., R. Whallon, Jr., and S. Chappell
1974  Mesolithic sites near Havelte, province of Drenthe (Netherlands): A preliminary report of the Havelte project. *Palaeohistorica* 16:7–61.

Quitta, H.
1967  The C¹⁴ chronology of the central and se European Neolithic. *Antiquity* 41:263–270.

Quitta, H., and G. Kohl
1969  Neue Radiocarbondaten zum Neolithikum und zur frühen Bronzezeit Südosteuropas und der Sowjetunion. *Zeitschrift für Archäologie* 3:223–254.

Rajewski, Z.
1965  *10000 lat Biskupina i jego okolic.* Warsaw: Państwowe Zakłady Wydawnictw Szkolnych.
1970  *Biskupin: osiedle obronne wspólnot pierwotnych sprzed 2500 lat.* Warsaw: Arkady.

Ralph, E. K., H. N. Michael, and M. C. Han
1973  Radiocarbon dates and reality. *MASCA Newsletter* 9(No. 1):1–20.

Randsborg, K.
1973  Wealth and social structure as reflected in Bronze Age burials—a quantitative approach. In *The explanation of culture change: Models in prehistory,* edited by C. Renfrew. London: Duckworth, Pp. 565–570.

Rappaport, R. A.
1967  *Pigs for the ancestors,* New Haven: Yale University Press.

Reinecke, P.
1904–1911  Attertümer unserer heidnischen Vorzeit (1904–1911), Band V, Römisch-Germanisches Zentralmuseum zu Mainz.

Reinerth, H.
1936  *Das Federseemoor als Siedlungsland des Vorzeitmenschen.* Leipzig: Führer Zur Urgeschichte Bd. 9, Neuauflage.

Renfrew, C.
1969  The autonomy of the south-east European Copper Age. *Proceedings of the Prehistoric Society* 35:12–47.
1972  *The emergence of civilization: The Cyclades and the Aegean in the third millennium B.C.* London: Methuen and Co.
1973a Monuments, mobilization and social organization in Neolithic Wessex. In *The explanation of culture change: Models in prehistory,* edited by C. Renfrew. London: Duckworth. Pp. 539–558.
1973b *Before Civilization: The radiocarbon revolution and prehistoric Europe.* London: Jonathan Cape.
1974  *British Prehistory.* London: Duckworth.

Renfrew, J. M.
 1969   The archaeological evidence for the domestication of plants: Methods and problems. In *The domestication and exploitation of plants and animals,* edited by P. J. Ucko and G. W. Dimbleby. Chicago: Aldine-Atherton. Pp. 149–172.
 1973   *Palaeoethnobotany: The prehistoric food plants of the Near East and Europe.* London: Methuen and Company.
Rice, T.
 1957   *The Scythians.* New York: Frederick A. Praeger.
Rodden, R. J.
 1962   Excavations at the Early Neolithic site at Nea Nikomedeia, Greek Macedonia (1961 season). *Proceedings of the Prehistoric Society* 28:267–288.
 1965   An Early Neolithic village in Greece. *Scientific American* 212(No 4):83–92.
Röder, J.
 1951   Erdwerk Urmitz. Gesamtplan und Periodenteilung. *Germania* 29:187–190.
Roe, D. A.
 1968   British Lower and Middle Paleolithic handaxe groups. *Proceedings of the Prehistoric Society* 35:1–82.
Rogachev, A. N.
 1970   Paleoliticheskie zhilishcha i poseleniya. In *Kamennyj vek territorii SSSR,* edited by A. A. Formozov. Moscow: Akademiya Nauk SSSR. Pp. 64–77.
Rowlands, M. J.
 1971   The archaeological interpretation of prehistoric metalworking. *World Archaeology* 3(No. 2):210–224.
 1973   Modes of exchange and the incentives for trade, with reference to later European prehistory. In *The explanation of culture change: Models in prehistory,* edited by C. Renfrew. London: Duckworth. Pp. 589–600.
Rowlett, R.
 1968   The Iron Age north of the Alps. *Science* 161(No. 3837):123–134.
Rust, A.
 1937   *Das eiszeitliche Rentierlager Meiendorf.* Neumünster: Karl Wachhotz Verlag.
 1943   *Die alt-und mittelsteinzeitlichen Funde von Stellmoor.* Neumünster: Karl Wachholtz Verlag.
Ryndina, N. V.
 1971   *Drevneyshie Metalloobrabatyvayushchie Proizvodstvo Vostochnoy Evropi.* Moscow.
Sackett, J. R.
 1966   Quantitative analysis of the Upper Paleolithic stone tools. *American Anthropologist* (special edition) 68(No. 2, Part 2):356–394.
Sahlins, M.
 1963   Poor man, rich man, big-man, chief: Political types in Melanesia and Polynesia. *Comparative studies in society and history.* 5(No. 3):285–303.
 1968   *Tribesmen.* Englewood Cliffs: Prentice-Hall.
 1972   *Stone Age economics.* Chicago: Aldine-Atherton.
Sangmeister, E.
 1951   Zum Charakter der bandkeramischen Siedlung. *33 Bericht der Römisch-Germanischen Kommission 1943–1950.* Pp. 89–109.
Sarnowska, W.
 1969   *Kultura Unietycka w Polsce,* Vol. I. Wrocław-Warszawa-Kraków: Ossolineum.
Saxe, A. A.
 1971   Social Dimensions of mortuary practices in a Mesolithic population from Wadi Halfa, Sudan. In *Approaches to the social dimensions of mortuary practices,* edited by J. A. Brown. *Memoirs of the Society for American Archaeology,* No. 25, Pp. 39–57.
Schaaff, U.
 1969   Versuch einer regionalen Gliederung frühlatènezeitlicher Fürstengräber. In *Marburgen Beiträge zur Archäeologie der Kelten,* edited by O.-H. Frey. Bonn: Rudolf Habelt. Pp. 187–202.

Schietzel, K.
1965   *Müddersheim: eine Ansiedlung der jüngeren Bandkeramik im Rheinland*. Cologne: Böhlau.
Schild, R.
1975   Paózny Paleolit. In *Prahistoria Ziem Polskich, Vol. 1: Paleolit i Mezolit*, edited by W. Chmielewski and W. Hensel. Wrocław-Warszawa-Kraków-Gdańsk: Ossolineum. Pp. 159–338.
1976   The final Paleolithic settlements of the European plain. *Scientific American* 234(No. 2):88–99.
Schild, R., H. Królik, and J. Mościbrodzka
1977   *Koplnia Krzemienia Czekoladowego z Przełomu Neolitu i Epoki Brązu W. Polanach Koloniach*. Wrocław-Warszawa-Kraków-Gdańsk: Ossolineum.
Schlette, F.
1958   *Die ältesten Haus-und Siedlungsformen des Menschen*, Vol. 5. Ethnographisch-Archäologische Forshungen Berlin: VEB Deutscher Verlag der Wissenschaften.
1964   Grabungen auf dem Steinkuhlenberg, Kr. Wernigerode—Ein Beitrag zum Seidlungswesen der Trichterbecherkultur. In *Varia Archaeologica*, edited by P. Grimm. Berlin: Deutsch Akademie der Wissenchaften zu Berlin, Schriften der sektion für Vor- und Frühgeschichte Band 16. Pp. 48–61.
Schmidt, B.
1970   Die Landschaft östlich von Magdeburg im Neolithikum. *Jahresschrift für Mitteldeutsche Vorgeschichte* 54:83–136.
Schmidt, R. R.
1930   *Jungsteinzeit-Siedlungen im Federseemoor*, Augsburg.
Schubart, H.
1958   Nordische Bronzezeit in der DDR. *Ausgrabungen und Funde* 3:210–221.
Schubert, F.
1972   Manching IV: Vorbericht über die Ausgrabungen in den Jahren 1965 bis 1967. *Germania* 50:110–121.
Schultze-Motel, J.
1969   Kulturpflanzenfunde der Becherkulturen. In *Die neolitischen Becherkulturen im Gebiet der DDR und ihre europäischen Beziehungen*, edited by H. Behrens and F. Schlette. Veröffentlichungen des Landesmuseums für Vorgeschichte in Halle, Vol. 24. Pp. 169–172.
Schweingruber F.
1973   Holzarten. In *Der bandkeramische Siedlungsplatz Langweiler 2,* edited by J.-P. Farruggia, R. Kuper, J. Lüning, and P. Stehli. Bonn: Rudolf Habelt. Pp. 152–156.
Sergeev, G. P.
1963   Rannetripolskii klad u s. Karbuna. *Sovetskaya Arkheologiya* 1:135–151.
Service, E.
1962   *Primitive social organization: An evolutionary perspective*. New York: Random House.
1971   *Primitive social organization: An evolutionary perspective* (second edition). New York: Random House.
Shackleton, M. R.
1965   *Europe: A regional geography* (seventh edition). New York: Frederick A. Praeger.
Shackleton, N., and C. Renfrew
1970   Neolithic trade routes re-aligned by oxygen isotope analyses. *Nature* 228(No. 5276):1062–1065.
Shennan, S.
1975   The social organization at Branć. *Antiquity* **XLIX**(No. 196):279–288.
Sherratt, A. G.
1973   The interpretation of change in European prehistory. In *The explanation of culture change: Models in prehistory*, edited by C. Renfrew. London: Duckworth. Pp. 419–428.
Sielmann, B.
1971   Der Einfluss der Umwelt auf die neolithische Besiedlung Südwestdeutschlands unter

besonderer Berücksichtigung der Verhältnisse am nördlichen Oberrhein. *Acta Praehistorica et Archaeologica* 2:65–197.

1972 Die frühneolithische Besiedlung Mitteleuropas. In *Die Anfänge des Neolithikums vom Orient bis Nordeuropa* Part Va, edited by H. Schwabedissen. Cologne: Böhlau. Pp. 1–65.

Sobociński, M.
1961 Zwierzęta udomowione i łowne z mlodszej epoki kamienia w Nosocicach, w pow. Głogowskim. *Przegląd Archeologiczny* 13:122–136.

Sochacki, Z.
1970 The Radial-Decorated Pottery culture. In *The Neolithic in Poland*, edited by T. Wiślański. Wrocław-Warszawa-Kraków: Ossolineum. Pp. 296–332.

Soudský, B.
1962 The Neolithic site of Bylany. *Antiquity* 36: (No. 143):190–200.
1964 Sozialökonomische Geschichte des alteren Neolithikums in Mitteleuropa. *Aus der Ur-und Frühgeschichte II*. Pp. 62–81.
1966 *Bylany osada nejstaršich zemědělců z mladši doby kammené*. Prague: Československa akademie věd.

Soudský, B., and I. Pavlů
1972 The Linear pottery culture settlement patterns in central Europe. In *Man, settlement and urbanism*, edited by P. J. Ucko, R. Tringham, and G. W. Dimbleby. London: Duckworth. Pp. 317–328.

Srejović, D.
1967 *Lepenski Vir*. Belgrade: Narodni Muzej.
1972 *Europe's first monumental sculpture: New discoveries at Lepenski Vir*. New York: Stein and Day.

Stampfli, H. R.
1965 Tierreste der Grabung Müddersheim, Kr. Düren. In *Müddersheim, eine Ansiedlung der jüngeren Bandkeramik in Rheinland*, edited by K. Schietzel. Cologne: Böhlau. Pp. 115–123.

Steward, J. H.
1969 Postscript to bands: On taxonomy, processes, and causes. In *Contributions to anthropology: Band societies*, edited by D. Damas. National Museums of Canada Bulletin 228. Pp. 228–295.

Strahm, C.
1971 *Die Gliederung der schnurkeramischen Kultur in der Schweiz* Acta Bernesia VI. Bern: Stampfli.

Tabaczyński, S.
1970 *Neolit Środkowo Europejski: Podstawy Gospodarcze*. Wrocław-Warszawa-Kraków: Ossolineum.

Tempir, Z.
1964 Beiträge zu ältesten Geschichte des Pflanzenbaus in Ungarn. *Acta Archaeologica* 16:65–98.
1971 Einige Ergebnisse der archäoagrobotanischen Untersuchungen des Anbaus von Kulturpflazen auf dem Gebiet der ČSSR. *Actes due VIII Congrès International des Sciences Préhistoriques et Protohistoriques*, Vol. II. Prague: Institut d'Archéologie de l'Academie Tchécoslavaque des Sciences. Pp. 1326–1329.

Tetzlaff, W.
1970 The Rzucewo culture. In *The Neolithic in Poland*, edited by T. Wiślański, Wrocław-Warszawa-Kraków: Ossolineum. Pp. 356–365.

Thomas, H. L.
1967 *Near Eastern, Mediterranean, and European chronology*. Lund: Studies in Mediterranean Archaeology, Vol. 17, No. 1 and 2.

Tobias, P. V.
1973 New developments in hominid paleontology in south and east Africa. In *Annual Review*

*of Anthropology* Vol. 2, edited by B. H. Siegel, A. R. Beals, and S. A. Tyler. Pp. 311–334.

Tobias, P. V., and Y. Coppens, eds.
1976 *Les plus anciens hominidés*. Nice: Union Internationale des Sciences Préhistoriques et Protohistoriques.

Tringham, R.
1971 *Hunters, fishers and farmers of eastern Europe: 6000–3000 B.C.* London: Hutchinson.
1973 The Mesolithic of Southeastern Europe. In *The Mesolithic in Europe,* edited by S. K. Kozłowski. Warsaw: University Press. Pp. 551–565.

Tsalkin, V. I.
1970 *Drevneyshie domashnie zhivotnie vostochnoy evropi.* Moscow: Akademiya Nauk SSSR.

Tschumi, O.
1949 *Urgeschichte der Schweiz.* Fraeunfeld.

Ucko, P. J., and A. Rosenfeld
1967 *Palaeolithic cave art.* New York: McGraw-Hill.

Valoch, K.
1968 Evolution of the Palaeolithic in central and eastern Europe. *Current Anthropology* 9(5):351–368.
1976 (ed.) *Les premières industries de l'Europe.* Nice: Union Internationale des Sciences Préhistoriques et Protohistoriques.

van Zeist, W.
1968 Prehistoric and early historic food plants in the Netherlands. *Palaeohistoria* 14:41–173.

Ventris, M., and J. Chadwick
1956 *Documents in Mycenaean Greek.* Cambridge: Cambridge University Press.

Villaret-von Rochow, M.
1969 Fruit size variability of Swiss prehistoric Malus sylvestris. In *The domestication and exploitation of plants and animals,* edited by P. J. Ucko and G. W. Dimbleby. Chicago: Aldine-Atherton. Pp. 201–206.

Viollier, D.
1911 Une nouvelle subdivision de l'époque de La Tène. In *Comptes-rendus du Congrès de l'Association française pour l'avancement des Sciences,* Session de Dijon. Pp. 636–642.

Vladár, J.
1973a Osteuropäische und Mediterrane Einflüsse im Gebiet der Slowakei während der Bronzezeit. *Slovenská Archeológia* 21(No. 2):253–357.
1973b *Pohrebiská zo Staršej Doby Bronzovej v Brančí.* Bratislava: Slovenska Akademie Vied.

Vlassa, N.
1963 Chronology of the Neolithic in Transylvania in the light of the Tartaria settlement. *Dacia* 7:1–94.

Vogt, E.
1954 Pfahlbaustudien. In *Das Pfahlbauproblem,* edited by W. U. Guyan. Schaffhausen: Schweizerische Gesellschaft für Urgeschichte. Pp. 119–219.

Weiss, M. L., and A. E. Mann
1975 *Human biology and behavior: An anthropological perspective,* Boston: Little, Brown.

Whallon, R., Jr.
1973 Spatial analysis of Paleolithic occupation areas: The present problem and the "functional argument." In *The explanation of culture change: Models in prehistory,* edited by C. Renfrew. Pittsburgh, Pennsylvania: University of Pittsburgh Press. Pp. 115–130.

Whitehouse, R. D.
1973 The earliest towns in peninsular Italy. In *The explanation of culture change: Models in prehistory,* edited by C. Renfrew. Pittsburgh, Pennsylvania: University of Pittsburgh Press. Pp. 617–614.

Więckowska, H.
1975   Społeczności łowiecko-rybackie wczesnego holocenu. In *Prehistoria Ziem Polskich, Vol. 1: Paleolit i Mezolit*, edited by W. Chmielewski and W. Hensel. Wrocław-Warszawa-Kraków-Gdańsk: Ossolineum. Pp. 339–438.

Wilmsen, E. N.
1972   Introduction: The study of exchange as social interaction. In *Social exchange and interaction,* edited by E. N. Wilmsen. Anthropological Papers, Museum of Anthropology No. 46. Ann Arbor: University of Michigan. Pp. 1–4.

Wiślański, T.
1966   *Kultura amfor kulistych w Polsce pólnocno-zachodniej.* Institut Historii Kultury Materialnej Polskiej Akademii Nauk, Polskie Badania Archaeologiczne, Vol. 13. Wrocław-Warszawa-Kraków: Ossolineum.
1969   *Podstawy gospodarcze plemion neolitycznych w Polsce pólnocno-zachodniej.* Wrocław-Warszawa-Kraków: Ossolineum.
1970   The Globular Amphora culture. In *The Neolithic in Poland*, edited by T. Wiślański. Wrocław-Warszawa-Kraków: Ossolineum. Pp. 178–231.

Wittfogel, K.
1957   *Oriental despotism.* New Haven: Yale University Press.

Wobst, H. M.
1974   Boundary conditions for Paleolithic social systems: A simulation approach. *American Antiquity* 39(No. 2, Part 1):147–178.
1976   Locational relationships in Paleolithic society. *Journal of Human Evolution* 5:49–58.
1977   Stylistic behavior and information exchange. In *For the Director: Research essays in honor of James B. Griffin,* edited by C. E. Cleland. Anthropological Papers, Museum of Anthropology No. 61. Ann Arbor: University of Michigan. Pp. 317–342.

Wolf, E.
1966   Kinship, friendship, and patron-client relations in complex societies. In *Social anthropology of complex societies,* edited by M. Banton. New York: Frederick A. Praeger. Pp. 1–22.

Wright, G. A.
1974   *Archaeology and trade.* Reading, Massachusetts: Addison-Wesley.

Wright, H. T.
1970   Toward an explanation of the origin of the state. Paper delivered in 1970 at the School of American Research Symposium entitled "The Explanation of Prehistoric Organization Change," J. N. Hill, Chairman.

Wright, H. T. and G. A. Johnson
1975   Population, exchange, and early state formation in southwestern Iran. *American Anthropologist* 77(No. 2):267–289.

Wyss, R.
1969   Wirtschaft und Technik. In *Ur-und Frühgeschichtliche Archäologie der Schweiz,* Vol. II, *Die Jüngere Steinzeit,* edited by W. Drack. Basel: Schweizerische Gesellschaft für Ur-und Frühgeschichte. Pp. 117–138.

Yellen, J. E.
1977   *Archaeological approaches to the present: Models for reconstructing the past.* New York: Academic Press.

Yengoyan, A. A.
1972   Ritual and exchange in aboriginal Australia: An adaptive interpretation of male initiation rites. In *Social exchange and interaction,* edited by E. N. Wilmsen. Anthropological Papers, Museum of Anthropology No. 46. Ann Arbor: University of Michigan. Pp. 5–9.

Zeuner, F. E.
1963   *A history of domesticated animals.* London: Hutchinson

Zohary, D., and P. Spiegel-Roy
1975   Beginnings of fruit growing in the Old World. *Science* 187:319–327.

Zschocke, K., and E. Preuschen
    1932    *Das urzeitliche Bergbaugebiet von Mühlbach-Bischofshofen.* Vienna: Materialen zur Urge-
            schichte Österreichs, HeftVI.
Zürn, H.
    1968    *Das jungsteinzeitliche Dorf Ehrenstein.* Stuttgart.

# Index

# STUDIES IN ARCHEOLOGY

## Consulting Editor: Stuart Struever

Department of Anthropology
Northwestern University
Evanston, Illinois